THE YALE EDITION OF THE

WORKS OF SAMUEL JOHNSON

VOLUME XVII

A Commentary on Mr. Pope's

Principles of Morality,

Or Essay on Man

PREVIOUSLY PUBLISHED

VOLUME I, *Diaries, Prayers, and Annals*
Edited by E. L. McAdam, Jr., with Donald and Mary Hyde

VOLUME II, *The Idler and the Adventurer*
Edited by W. J. Bate, John M. Bullitt, and L. F. Powell

VOLUMES III, IV, and V, *The Rambler*
Edited by W. J. Bate and Albrecht B. Strauss

VOLUME VI, *Poems*
Edited by E. L. McAdam, Jr., with George Milne

VOLUMES VII and VIII, *Johnson on Shakespeare*
Edited by Arthur Sherbo, Introduction by Bertrand H. Bronson

VOLUME IX, *A Journey to the Western Islands of Scotland*
Edited by Mary Lascelles

VOLUME X, *Political Writings*
Edited by Donald J. Greene

VOLUME XIV, *Sermons*
Edited by Jean H. Hagstrum and James Gray

VOLUME XV, *A Voyage to Abyssinia*
Edited by Joel J. Gold

VOLUME XVI, *Rasselas and Other Tales*
Edited by Gwin J. Kolb

SAMUEL JOHNSON

A Commentary on Mr. Pope's Principles of Morality, Or Essay on Man

(A Translation from the French)

EDITED BY O M BRACK, JR.

NEW HAVEN AND LONDON: YALE UNIVERSITY PRESS

2004

Copyright © 2004 by Yale University.
All rights reserved.
This book may not be reproduced, in whole
or in part, including illustrations, in
any form (beyond that copying permitted by
Sections 107 and 108 of the U.S. Copyright
Law and except by reviewers for the
public press), without written
permission from the publishers.

Set in Baskerville type by
Tseng Information Systems, Inc.
Printed in the United States of America by
Vail Ballou Press.

Library of Congress Cataloging-in-Publication Data

Crousaz, Jean-Pierre de, 1663–1750.
[Commentaire sur la traduction en vers de M. l'abbé
du Resnel, de l'Essai de M. Pope sur l'homme. English]
A commentary on Mr. Pope's principles of morality,
or Essay on man : a translation from the French /
Samuel Johnson.
p. cm. — (The Yale edition of the works of
Samuel Johnson ; v. 17)
Includes bibliographical references.
ISBN 0-300-09270-9 (alk. paper)

1. Pope, Alexander, 1688–1744. Essay on man.
2. Du Resnel, Jean-François, 1692–1761.
I. Johnson, Samuel, 1709–1784. II. Title.
PR3627.C813   2004
821'.5—dc21   2003050057

A catalogue record for this book is available
from the British Library.

The paper in this book meets the guidelines for
permanence and durability of the Committee on
Production Guidelines for Book Longevity of the
Council on Library Resources

10 9 8 7 6 5 4 3 2 1

EDITORIAL COMMITTEE

John H. Middendorf, *Chairman*
John H. Middendorf, *General Editor*
Albrecht B. Strauss, *Secretary*

O M Brack, Jr.	Benjamin B. Hoover
Bertram H. Davis	Thomas Kaminski
Robert DeMaria, Jr.	Gwin J. Kolb
Mary Hyde Eccles	Bruce Redford
James Engell	Loren R. Rothschild
Stephen E. Fix	Howard D. Weinbrot
James Gray	Richard Wendorf

IN AFFECTIONATE MEMORY OF
David Fleeman
FRIEND, JOHNSONIAN, BIBLIOGRAPHER

PREFACE

Samuel Johnson's translation of Jean Pierre de Crousaz's *Commentaire sur la traduction en vers de M. Abbé Du Resnel, de l'Essai de M. Pope sur l'homme*, first published in 1739, appears for the first time in a scholarly edition. Included are notes comparing Johnson's translation with the French original to show his method of translation, and historical annotations. Of particular interest to scholars are several lengthy footnotes, added by Johnson to his translation, that contain ideas to which he would return in later writings. His attack on the dominance of the passion of love on the stage, for example, would be reiterated in briefer form in the *Preface to Shakespeare* and the "Life of Dryden." More important are the footnotes relating to the problem of evil, particularly the ruling passion and the necessity of free will. From these scattered observations it is clear that Johnson comes down firmly on the side of orthodoxy, believing that God created man for happiness but that both physical and moral evil entered the world because of Original Sin and, hence, that many of the miseries of life are the responsibility of man.

Johnson's review of Soame Jenyns' *A Free Inquiry into the Nature and Origin of Evil*, included in this volume, also addresses the problem of evil but focuses on the issues raised by Pope's *Essay on Man* in a more systematic way. The review continues Johnson's critique of Pope's poem which began with his footnotes to the *Commentary*, and concludes in the "Life of Pope."

No edition can be completed without incurring many debts to both individuals and institutions.

Fellowships from the American Council of Learned Societies, the Henry E. Huntington Library, the Newberry Library, and from Arizona State University have provided financial support for this edition. Funding from the National Endowment for the Humanities awarded to the Yale Edition of the Works of Samuel Johnson provided a research assistant for a semester.

Much of the work was done at the British Library, and I am grateful to the staff for their assistance, particularly Ian Willison and Michael Crump. At the Bodleian Library, Oxford, my friend of thirty-five years, Julian Roberts, gave generously of his advice and expertise. My work in the Beinecke Library, Yale University, was assisted greatly by Marjorie Wynne and Stephen Parks and at the Houghton Library, Harvard University, by Richard Wendorf, Hugh Amory, and Roger Stoddard. At Arizona State University, Hayden Library, Chuck Brownson and Marilyn Wurtzburger have facilitated my research in numerous ways. The Huntington Library has always served as my local, my home away from home, and my debts are numerous: James Thorpe, Dan Woodward, Virginia Renner, the late Mary Wright, the late Carey Bliss, Martin Ridge, Alan Jutzi, Tom Lange, Kent and Carol Clark, and Paul Zall have all given encouragement and assistance along the way. Ron Crown of the Pius XII Memorial Library, University of St. Louis, and Bruce Whiteman of the William Andrews Clark Memorial Library answered some late queries.

In the early stages of the project I received advice on the French from two late friends, Robert Tate and Mildred Greene. Nick Salerno, chair of the Department of English in the early stages of this project, found funding that was important in getting the project off to a good start.

Several people have read and commented on various portions of the introductions and notes and have made it a better book: the late W. J. Bate, Bertram H. Davis, Robert De Maria, Jr., Donald D. Eddy, the late Jean H. Hagstrum, Thomas Kaminski, the late Donald F. McKenzie, Loren Rothschild, Albrecht B. Strauss, Howard D. Weinbrot, and Richard Wendorf.

Donald Greene and I developed a plan in the mid-1970s for editing Johnson's shorter prose writings and publishing them in chronological order. Our editing had reached as far as the book reviews in 1756 when, for a variety of reasons beyond our control, the project languished. The first volume was to have included only Johnson's major notes to Crousaz, with enough text to make them intelligible, and the other two pieces in this volume. Much of our research went into Greene's *Samuel Johnson* in the Oxford Authors series and, where appropriate, is used again here.

The late Dan Brink introduced me to the mysteries of the computer almost twenty years ago and his patience and good humor have been sorely missed. In the past year I am grateful to Tiffany C. J. Chen for her computer wizardry, for her advice and assistance, and for seeing that this project got back on track. Kerrie Savage has kindly assisted me in completing the necessary final details before sending the manuscript to Yale University Press.

Over the years I have been assisted on this project by several graduate students and friends. Leslie Chilton has helped with all phases of the project, from entering the text into the computer to collating and reading proof. Mary Jane Early served as a research assistant in the early days of the project. Gary Lane Hatch entered the review of Soame Jenyns' *An Inquiry* into the computer and assisted with reading proof. Barbara Rasnick also helped with the reading of proof.

Don Eddy's enthusiasm for Johnson and eighteenth-century bibliography is boundless, and I am grateful for his encouragement and his unselfishness in sharing his knowledge.

Tim Erwin cheerfully read through the entire manuscript in its final stages and made helpful suggestions for improvement.

To Gwin Kolb I am grateful for thirty-five years of friendship, and to Gwin and Ruth I am thankful for their kindness and encouragement during dark days.

Mary Hyde Eccles has been generous in supplying materials from the Hyde Collection, answering queries, and sharing her wisdom about the eighteenth century.

I met the late Herman W. Liebert, beloved Fritz, in the summer of 1967, and he turned me into a Johnsonian. He first suggested that I undertake this project and assisted in a variety of ways until the end of his life.

Over many years John Middendorf has always been at the end of the telephone line to listen and give advice from the storehouse of information he has gained as both general editor and chairman of the Editorial Committee of the Yale Johnson. I have fond memories of lunches on occasional visits to New York where we talked extensively of Johnson.

Cynthia A. Burns assisted with the final proofs, providing encouragement and much more.

The greatest measure of gratitude and credit for completion of this volume must be given to my friend James Gray, who served as general editor for the Crousaz portion. Jim read numerous drafts, writing extensive comments on all matters, but especially on the annotations and the French. His letters urging me on to completion have been successful.

Most of the scholarly world will remember J. D. Fleeman as the man who accomplished the incredible feat of producing a comprehensive, descriptive bibliography of Johnson's writings. But to those who had the privilege of calling him friend, he was much more. No one knew better than David how to keep a friendship in repair. He was the master of the scholarly letter. A one-line query to David, in good time, would bring a typewritten letter, opening with an apology for the delay in answering, followed by two or three pages of erudite, clear, cogent prose, giving a larger answer to the query than anyone would have thought possible in this world or the next, interspersed with news and humorous asides. Because everyone remotely interested in Johnson had a large file of these letters, it is hard to believe that he did anything besides correspond. David, of course, thought that he learned something from these exchanges, but we were always in his debt. A story goes that when he arrived in Oxford for post-graduate study, he had to decide which author he should pick. Only William Shakespeare and Samuel Johnson were truly major English literary figures, he thought, and since Shakespeare already had numerous advocates, he chose Johnson. We are glad he did. David has made many friends for Johnson; his friends dedicate this volume to David's memory with great affection.

OMB

ILLUSTRATIONS

The title page of the 1739 edition of *A Commentary*   xvi

The title page of the 1742 edition of *A Commentary*   xxxvi

A
COMMENTARY
ON
Mr *POPE*'s
PRINCIPLES of MORALITY,
Or ESSAY on MAN.

By *Monſ.* CROUSAZ,
Member of the Royal Academies of Sciences at PARIS
and BOURDEAUX, and Profeſſor of Philoſophy and
Mathematics at LAUSANNE;

In ANSWER to a LETTER of
REMARKS on his EXAMEN, &c.

CONTAINING ALSO
I. The LETTER of REMARKS to Monſ. CROUSAZ.
II. The Abbe DU RESNEL's Tranſlation of the ESSAY into FRENCH Verſe.
III. An Interlineary *Engliſh* Verſion of the ſame.
IV. A PRELIMINARY DISCOURSE, by DU RESNEL, on *French* and *Engliſh* Poetry: And
V. Some curſory Annotations by the Tranſlator.

LONDON:
Printed for A. DODD without *Temple-Bar.*
M.DCC.XXXIX.

INTRODUCTION

On 2 March 1737 Samuel Johnson left Lichfield for London, accompanied by David Garrick. On the same day Gilbert Walmsley wrote a letter to the Reverend John Colson: "Mr. Johnson [is] to try his fate with a tragedy, and to see to get himself employed in some translation, either from the Latin or the French. Johnson is a very good scholar and poet, and I have great hopes will turn out a fine tragedy-writer."[1] Johnson, already twenty-seven, had accomplished little since leaving Pembroke College, Oxford, in December 1729 after a residency of only thirteen months. A series of unsuccessful attempts to secure or hold teaching positions ended with the establishment of his own school at Edial, only to have it close a year later in February 1737. During this same period he had written a few poems; contributed an unknown number of essays to Thomas Warren's *Birmingham Journal;* translated Joachim Le Grand's *Relation historique d'Abissinie*, a French translation of an unpublished manuscript by Portuguese Jesuit Jerónimo Lobo, as *A Voyage to Abyssinia;* written proposals for an edition of the poems of Angelo Poliziano,[2] and composed some portion of his tragedy, *Irene.*

Little is known about how Johnson spent his early months in London. But the well-known story of Johnson and Garrick borrowing five pounds from the bookseller John Wilcox suggests that Johnson needed to find work as a translator or writer, although no trans-

---

1. *Life*, I.102. This account of SJ's early career is particularly indebted to Thomas Kaminski, *The Early Career of Samuel Johnson* (1987), pp. 1–82.

2. Both Boswell and Hawkins saw the proposals for printing by subscription *Angeli Politiani Poemata Latina*, but no copy is now known. The work never appeared. See *Life*, I.90 and Sir John Hawkins, *The Life of Samuel Johnson, LL.D.*, 2d ed. (1787), pp. 26–27. Robert DeMaria, Jr. observes that "if he had done it well, Johnson would have moved into the circle of European scholar-poets that he most admired." See *The Life of Samuel Johnson, A Critical Biography* (1993), p. 32.

lations or other writings have been discovered for this period.³ By summer, certainly, Johnson felt the need to earn some money, for on 12 July 1737 he writes from Greenwich to Edward Cave proposing that he translate Paolo Sarpi's *Istoria del concilio Tridentino* from the Italian together with the notes from Pierre François Le Courayer's recent French translation.⁴ Nothing came of this proposal, and Johnson returned to Lichfield to clear up unfinished business and complete his tragedy. By the end of the year he again traveled to London, this time with his wife, to take up a lifelong residency.

On his return to London he seems to have spent some time in an unsuccessful attempt to have *Irene* brought on stage, but soon he visited St. John's Gate, the home of the *Gentleman's Magazine*.⁵ His first contribution to the *Gentleman's Magazine* is a Latin poem, "Ad Urbanum," in March 1738, addressed to the editor, Edward Cave. At about the same time he began corresponding with Cave to negotiate the publication of *London*, published 12 or 13 May 1738.⁶

By June 1738 Johnson had taken an editorial position with the *Gentleman's Magazine*⁷ and had written at least part of the introduction to the "Debates in the Senate of Magna Lilliputia" published in the June issue.⁸ Johnson provides a glimpse of the kind of editorial duties he performed in a letter to Cave, probably written in August 1738: he is revising the debates written by William Guthrie, composing verses on Lady Firebrace, selecting "Chinese Stories" for the magazine to puff Cave's publication of a *Description of China*,⁹

---

3. Sir John Hawkins calls the story of borrowing money from Wilcox "a fact concerning them both, that I had from a person now living, who was a witness to it, and of whose veracity the least doubt cannot be entertained." See Hawkins, *Life*, p. 43.

4. *Letters*, I.12–13.

5. *Life*, I.111.

6. *Letters*, I.14–18.

7. See *The Correspondence and other Papers of James Boswell Relating to the Making of the LIFE OF JOHNSON*, ed. Marshall Waingrow (1969), p. 234.

8. See Kaminski, pp. 42–43.

9. *Description géographique, historique, chronologique, politique, et physique de l'empire de la Chine et de la Tartarie chinoise*, compiled by Jean Baptiste Du Halde largely from accounts of China by Jesuit missionaries, was published in four folio volumes in Paris in 1735. The first fascicles of Cave's edition, *Description of China*, translated by John Green and William Guthrie, began appearing in March 1737. It was November 1738 before the *Gentleman's Magazine* announced the first bound volume was ready and the bound two-volume work was not announced until May 1742. SJ contributed at least six paragraphs on Chinese manners in a letter signed "Eubulus" to the July issue of

INTRODUCTION   xix

and procrastinating about awarding the prize in the poetry contest.[1] In addition he proposes "An Answer to another Query," probably like the letter on condolence signed "Pamphilus" he contributed to the July issue.[2] His letter to Cave concludes with an apology: "As to Father Paul, I have not yet been just to my proposal, but have met with impediments which I hope, are now at an end, and if you find the Progress hereafter not such as You have a right to expect, You can easily stimulate a negligent Translator." Johnson began receiving payments for the translation on 2 August.[3]

Johnson's contributions to the *Gentleman's Magazine* in the autumn of 1738 would not have provided a hired writer enough income to live on—some slight editorial work, a few epigrams, and only one short but significant essay, a second "Pamphilus" letter on the impropriety of John Gay's epitaph.[4] As Thomas Kaminski has persuasively argued, at this time "Johnson's primary obligation to Cave was not to edit but translate."[5] Earlier, when Johnson needed money he had translated Lobo from the French, and when he joined Cave's staff, he again turned to translation from the French for a livelihood.

His first major project was Sarpi's *History of the Council of Trent*, for which he received £49 7s. from 2 August 1738 to 21 April 1739, but abandoned after some 400 to 800 pages had been translated.[6] Of this project all that remains is his translation and epitome, the "Life of Father Paul Sarpi," reduced to about one-eighth the size of the French original in order to fit the pages of the November 1738 issue of the *Gentleman's Magazine*.[7] At the same time Johnson was working on his monumental translation of Sarpi he turned to an-

---

the *Gentleman's Magazine*, no doubt to interest readers in Cave's publication. It has been published with an introduction in *Political Writings*, ed. Donald Greene (Vol. X, Yale Edition of the Works of Samuel Johnson, 1977), pp. 14–18. See Kaminski, pp. 46–47.

1. *Letters*, I.18–20.
2. *Political Writings*, pp. 3–13.
3. The proposals for printing *The History of the Council of Trent* were published in October 1738. See J. A. V. Chapple, "Samuel Johnson's *Proposals for Printing The History of the Council of Trent* [1738]," *John Rylands Library Bulletin*, XLV (1963), 340–69.
4. The letter appeared in the October issue.
5. Kaminski, p. 67.
6. *Life*, I.135–36; Kaminski, pp. 67–76.
7. VIII. 581–83; John L. Abbott, "Dr. Johnson and the Making of 'The Life of Father Paul Sarpi,'" *Bulletin of the John Rylands Library*, XLVIII (1966), 255–67.

other translation and epitome, this time from Latin, for his second biography: a "Life of Dr. Herman Boerhaave" from the eulogy of Albert Schultens, shaped for the first four issues of the 1739 *Gentleman's Magazine*.[8] To this already heavy burden of translation Johnson added in late 1738 and early 1739 the work on his translation of Crousaz's *Commentaire*.

I

Thanks in part to Alexander Pope's shrewdness in publishing his ambitious *Essay on Man* anonymously, so that his enemies were beguiled into praising the poem on its merits, there was a "chorus of approbation" for some years after its appearance in 1733–34.[9] As Johnson observed in his "Life of Pope,"

> philosophy and poetry have not often the same readers, and the *Essay* abounded in splendid amplifications and sparkling sentences, which were read and admired with no great attention to their ultimate purpose: its flowers caught the eye which did not see what the gay foliage concealed, and for a time flourished in the sunshine of universal approbation.[1]

On the Continent, however, after the publication in 1736 of a French prose translation of the *Essay on Man* by Etienne de Silhouette,[2] the poem aroused the suspicion of Jean Pierre de Crousaz (1663–1750), professor at Lausanne, mathematician, logician, and Protestant theologian. Recalling the ensuing controversy years later in his "Life of Pope," Johnson praised Crousaz as "no mean antagonist":

> He was accustomed to argument and disquisition, and perhaps was grown too desirous of detecting faults; but his inten-

---

8. IX.37–38, 72–73, 114–16, 172–76; Richard R. Reynolds, "Johnson's *Life of Boerhaave* in Perspective," *Yearbook of English Studies*, V (1975), 115–29.

9. The history of the reception of the *Essay on Man* is concisely told by Maynard Mack in his Twickenham Edition (1950), pp. xv–xxvi. The four epistles were published successively on 20 February, 29 March, 8 May 1733, and 24 January 1734.

1. *Lives*, III.164.

2. *Essai sur l'homme. Par M. Pope. Traduit de l'Anglois en François, par M. D. S.*****. N.p. M.DCC.XXXVI. The first edition is no. 14 in E. Audra, *Les traductions Françaises de Pope (1717–1824)* (1931).

tions were always right, his opinions were solid, and his religion pure.

His incessant vigilance for the promotion of piety disposed him to look with distrust upon all metaphysical systems of Theology, and all schemes of virtue and happiness purely rational, and therefore it was not long before he was persuaded that the positions of Pope, as they terminated for the most part in natural religion, were intended to draw mankind away from revelation, and to represent the whole course of things as a necessary concatenation of indissoluble fatality.[3]

That Pope was a Roman Catholic may have had something to do with Crousaz's hostility, but his first attack on the *Essay on Man*, *Examen de l'essai de monsieur Pope sur l'homme* (1737), is chiefly directed at what Crousaz believed to be its Leibnitzian content. Being told that Silhouette misrepresented Pope, Crousaz, who knew no English, then turned to a new translation—more accurately translation-imitation—by the Abbé Jean-François du Bellay du Resnel (1737). For his poem Du Resnel rearranged the *Essay on Man*, omitting some sections but adding others to extend Pope's 1,300 lines to 2,000 in French Alexandrines.[4] Crousaz reprinted the entire poem with remarks interspersed in his *Commentaire sur la traduction en vers de M. l'Abbé Du Resnel, de l'Essai de M. Pope sur l'homme* (1738).[5]

---

3. *Lives*, III.165. SJ recommends Crousaz's logic in his Preface to *The Preceptor* (1748), 1825 *Works*, V. 242.

4. *Les principes de la morale et du goût, en deux poëmes, traduits de l'Anglois de M. Pope, par M. Du Resnel, Abbé de Sept-Fontaines, de l'Académie des Inscriptions et Belles Lettres*. A Paris, chez Briasson Libraire, rue Saint-Jacques, à la Science. M.DCC.XXXVII. The first edition is no. 22 in Audra. Du Resnel explains how and why he changed Pope's *Essay on Man* in his Preface, included by SJ in his translation of the *Commentaire*. In the same preface Du Resnel identifies the faults of Silhouette's French prose translation: "those who are in the same degree masters of the English and French say, in plain terms, that there is nothing of Mr Pope to be found in them [*Essai sur l'homme* and *Essai sur la critique*], and that if they sometimes discover the philosopher, the poet is always lost" (p. 372). Crousaz responded in the *Commentary*: "I do not understand *English*, and how loudly soever I might declare my approbation of the judicious comparison of the poetry of the two nations made by Mr. du Resnel, my suffrage ought to be made no account of, being given on a subject I do not understand" (p. 36). SJ mentions Du Resnel in the "Life of Garth" (*Lives*, II.63–64).

5. The full title is *Commentaire sur la traduction en vers, de M. l'Abbé Du Resnel, de L'Essai de M. Pope sur l'homme, par M. de Crousaz, Conseiller des Ambassades de S. M. le Roi de Suede & Landgrave de Hesse, ci-devant Gouverneur de S. A. S. le Prince Frederic de Hesse,*

Considerable confusion has surrounded Samuel Johnson's role in the translations from the French of Crousaz's two attacks on Pope's *Essay on Man*. *An Examination of Mr Pope's Essay on Man* and *A Commentary on Mr Pope's Principles of Morality, or Essay on Man*, were easily confused: both translators are anonymous, both are projects of Edward Cave, publisher of the *Gentleman's Magazine*, and both are dated "M.DCC.XXXIX." and "Printed for A. DODD" (Anne Dodd, a mercury used by Cave as a trade publisher).[6] Once it was known that it was Elizabeth Carter who translated the *Examen* and Johnson who translated the *Commentaire*, Johnsonians ignored the *Examination*. But Johnson was involved in the publication of both the *Examination* and the *Commentary* and it is necessary to straighten out their tangled history.

II

Identifying Johnson's contribution to the translation and publication of Crousaz's two attacks on Pope's *Essay on Man* has been difficult. James Boswell reports in *The Journal of a Tour to the Hebrides* (1786) that on 19 August 1773 when visiting St. Andrews, Johnson, in speaking of how quickly he could compose, mentioned that he had "written six sheets in a day of translation from the French."[7] Later, on 3 June 1781, Boswell records in his journal that Johnson "Told us at night he had once written six sheets in one day: forty-eight quarto pages of a translation of Crousaz on Pope, published by itself in 1740 or 1741."[8] If this is exactly what Johnson said, the confusion about the role Johnson may have had in a translation of

---

& membre des Académies Royales des Sciences de Paris & de Bourdeaux. A Geneve, Chez Pellisari & Comp. MDCCXXXVIII.

6. See Michael Treadwell, "London Trade Publishers 1675–1750," *Library*, 6th ser., IV (1982), 123–24. To be accurate, the imprint on the title page of the 1739 issue of the *Commentary* has "M.DCC.XXiX." See J. D. Fleeman, *A Bibliography of the Works of Samuel Johnson*, 2 vols. (2000), I.43–47 (39.10CP).

7. *Life*, V.67. L. F. Powell suggests that since this sentence does not appear in the manuscript of the *Tour* Boswell may have taken it from his journal of 3 June 1781. In perusing this journal Boswell may have been reminded that SJ had first mentioned the six sheets of French translation while in St. Andrews.

8. James Boswell, *Laird of Auchinleck 1778–1782*, ed. Joseph W. Reed and Frederick A. Pottle (1977), p. 375.

INTRODUCTION   xxiii

Crousaz was introduced for Boswell by his source. One problem is the publication date for the translation: all copies of the *Commentary* are dated either 1739 or 1742, although the latter were issued in late 1741. The second problem is the format: the *Commentary* is not a quarto but a duodecimo. A third problem, although less obvious, is the amount of translation Johnson performed in one day. The text of the volume fills fourteen and a half sheets. Translating six sheets, 144 duodecimo pages of prose and verse, or about forty-two percent of the total work, would seem to be beyond the reach of even Johnson. Perhaps two sheets or forty-eight duodecimo pages is closer to the truth.[9]

By the time Boswell came to write the *Life of Samuel Johnson, LL.D.* (1791) he was convinced that the *Examination* had been translated by Elizabeth Carter but apparently was unaware of the *Commentary*. In spite of the confused account Boswell received from Johnson, he gathers three pieces of evidence in the *Life* to prove Johnson did not translate Crousaz and leaves the impression that the issue has been settled. After reprinting Johnson's letter to Cave of 21 or 22 Novem-

---

9. A. D. Barker suggests that translating two sheets or forty-eight duodecimo pages, about fourteen percent of the work, in one day would be "quite a feat" and "is probably right" ("Edward Cave, Samuel Johnson, and the *Gentleman's Magazine*," D.Phil thesis, Oxford University, 1981, p. 316). Perhaps SJ thought he remembered translating forty-eight pages. If he also remembered that the book was in quarto, a little arithmetic, of which he was very fond, would have given him six sheets to make forty-eight pages, instead of two to make the same number in duodecimo. I am assuming that "sheets" refer to *printed* sheets. SJ, as a professional writer, who was also "bred a Bookseller," certainly knew that translators were paid by the printed sheet (*Letters*, III.159). He may, of course, have been talking loosely or he may have been misunderstood by his auditors. David L. Vander Meulen has suggested that SJ may be remembering the amount of paper on which he wrote the translation. The Sallust translation, for example, is written on sheets folded into a quarto format. Each Sallust manuscript page contains about 140 words and each Crousaz printed page about 300 words, if completely in prose (although many pages have varying amounts of poetry). At this ratio forty-eight manuscript pages would fill a little over twenty-two printed pages, or slightly less than one printed sheet. Poetry would make SJ's task easier as a manuscript page would fill faster. If, in fact, SJ is referring to *printed* sheets, which seems most likely, perhaps the number of sheets grew with the years. One of his harmless vanities was his pride in the speed with which he could compose, and reports of his Herculean labors should be viewed with skepticism. See, for example, William Cooke, *The Life of Samuel Johnson, LL.D.* (1785) in *The Early Biographies of Samuel Johnson*, ed. O M Brack, Jr. and Robert E. Kelley (1974), pp. 131–32, and Hawkins, *Life*, pp. 381–82 n.

ber 1738 suggesting that "the Examen should be pushed forward with the utmost expedition," Boswell comments, "But although he corresponded with Mr. Cave concerning a translation of Crousaz's Examen of Pope's Essay on Man, and gave advice for its success, I was long ago convinced by a perusal of the Preface, that this translation was erroneously ascribed to him."[1] As early as 12 March 1786 Boswell had written to Edmond Malone that Dr. Richard Palmer "shewed me the translation of Crousaz which has been ascribed to Dr. Johnson; But which is certainly not his. I agree with you that the translation itself is not a test. But the Preface is."[2]

Boswell's statement in the *Life*, it should be noted, is a hit at Sir John Hawkins who, in his *Life of Samuel Johnson, LL.D.* (1787), attributes the *Examination* to Johnson, citing the letter of 21 or 22 November as evidence.[3] As will be seen below, Boswell's attempt to keep as much distance as possible between his own life and that of Hawkins prevented him from using valuable information that Hawkins offered. In any case, Boswell's first piece of evidence, based on a recognition of Johnson's style, is also faulty as the preface is only a translation from Crousaz; Johnson's translation of the *Commentaire* would undoubtedly be rejected on the same stylistic grounds.

With his second and third pieces of evidence, Boswell is on safe ground. He first cites a manuscript in the British Museum:

ELISAE CARTERAE. S.P.D. THOMAS BIRCH.
Versionem tuam Examinis Crousaziani jam perlegi. Summam styli et elegantiam, et in re difficillimâ proprietatem, admiratus. Dabam Novemb. 27° 1738.[4]

---

1. *Life*, I.137–38; *Letters*, I.20–21. James L. Clifford suggests that this letter might be dated 21 or 22 November 1738 (*Young Sam Johnson* [1955], p. 346, n. 19). Since the letter is in response to Edmund Curll's announcement in the *Daily Advertiser* for 21 November of the publication of a translation of the *Commentaire*, and the advertisement for the *Examen* suggested by SJ appears in the *Daily Advertiser* for 23 November, Clifford is surely right in his dating of the letter. See p. xxxi below.

2. *The Correspondence of James Boswell with David Garrick, Edmund Burke, and Edmond Malone*, ed. George M. Kahrl, Rachel McClellan, Thomas W. Copeland, James M. Osborn, and Peter S. Baker (1987), p. 299.

3. Hawkins, *Life*, pp. 66–67.

4. *Life*, I.138. "I have now perused your translation of Crousaz's Examination; and admire the great propriety and elegance of the style in a subject attended with so

Then he says, "Indeed Mrs. Carter has lately acknowledged to Mr. Seward, that she was the translator of the 'Examen.'"[5] Boswell, apparently unaware of the *Commentary,* but aware that the *Examination* had been translated by Elizabeth Carter, was at a stand. When he arrived at 3 June 1781 in the *Life* he revised his journal account to read: "He told us, that he had in one day written six sheets of a translation from the French," bringing it into accord with his earlier published account in the *Tour,* in which he also omits any reference to Crousaz.[6]

Boswell, Hawkins, and other early biographers had received no help from Johnson on his role as translator of Crousaz. In the "Life of Pope" there is no indication that Johnson has any connection with a work by Crousaz: "It was first turned into French prose, and afterwards by Resnel into verse. Both translations fell into the hands of Crousaz, who first, when he had the version in prose, wrote a general censure, and afterwards reprinted Resnel's version with particular remarks upon every paragraph."[7] Nevertheless the *Commentary* was attributed to Johnson shortly after his death, in plenty of time to allow Hawkins and Boswell to avoid omitting the attribution.

The earliest attribution in print of a translation of Crousaz to Johnson seems to be that in "An Account of the Writings of Dr. Samuel Johnson, Including Some Incidents of His Life" in the *European Magazine* for January 1785: "In November [1738], he is believed to have published a translation of An Examination of Mr. Pope's Essay on Man, by M. Crousaz, Professor of Philosophy and

---

much difficulty." (Translation from Montagu Pennington, *Memoirs of the Life of Mrs. Elizabeth Carter,* 2d ed. [1808], I.45.) For discussion of Thomas Birch's relationship with Elizabeth Carter at this time see Edward Ruhe, "Birch, Johnson, and Elizabeth Carter: An Episode 1738–39," *PMLA,* LXXIII (1958), 491–500.

5. *Life,* I.138. William Seward, man of letters, and friend of SJ, the Thrales, and other members of the circle.

6. *Life,* IV.127.

7. *Lives,* III.164 (par. 181). See Hawkins's indebtedness to this passage in the quotation from his *Life* given below. Whitwell Elwin, who splices together SJ's discussions of the *Essay on Man* from the "Life of Pope" in his introduction to the poem, adds a footnote to this passage: "The first treatise of Crousaz was translated by Miss Carter, and published in 1738 [1739], under the title of An Examination of Mr. Pope's Essay on Man. The second treatise was translated by Johnson himself, and published in 1742, with the title, A Commentary on Mr. Pope's Principles of Morality." See *The Works of Alexander Pope,* Vol. II, ed. Whitwell Elwin (1871), p. 264, n. 2.

Mathematics at Lausanne, 12mo. whose Commentary on Pope's Principles of Morality, or Essay on Man, we can ascribe to him with confidence."[8] For some reason Boswell appears not to have consulted this work, or at least not this portion of it, even though it may have been written by Isaac Reed or George Steevens, or both.[9] In his haste to condemn Hawkins for attributing the *Examination* to Johnson, Boswell fails to note that Hawkins follows Johnson's account in the "Life of Pope" by mentioning a second work by Crousaz:

> Cave engaged him to undertake a translation of an Examen of Pope's Essay on Man, written by Mr. Crousaz. . . . The reputation of the Essay on Man soon after its publication invited a translation of it into French, which was undertaken and completed by the Abbé Resnel, and falling into the hands of Crousaz, drew from him first a general censure of the principles maintained in the poem, and afterwards, a commentary thereon containing particular remarks on every paragraph. The former of these [*Examination*] it was that Johnson translated, as appears in the following letter of his to Cave, which is rendered somewhat remarkable by his stiling himself *Impransus*.[1]

Further clues in Johnson's own writings suggested the existence of not one but two attacks by Crousaz on Pope's *Essay on Man*. The most important hint is Johnson's letter of 21 or 22 November to Cave. The letter begins: "I am pretty much of your Opinion, that the Commentary cannot be prosecuted with any appearance of success," and after suggesting to Cave an advertisement for the *Examen* to forestall a rival, Johnson adds: "It will above all be necessary to take notice that it is a thing distinct from the Commentary." Hawkins, even though he misses the full significance of the sentence, recognizes that there are two works, whereas Boswell apparently does not. Had Boswell, for example, looked carefully at the *Examination* when he read the Preface, he would have noticed on the

---

8. *Early Biographies*, p. 46.
9. *Early Biographies*, pp. 301–2. Dr. Richard Brocklesby, in a letter to Boswell of 13 December 1784, reports hearing that Steevens had taken away the Catalogue of SJ's works, which seems to have served as the basis of this "Account." See Waingrow, pp. 26 and n. 6, 146, n. 1.
1. Hawkins, *Life*, pp. 65–67.

INTRODUCTION   xxvii

verso of the last leaf a full-page advertisement for the forthcoming *Commentary*. Had he actually read carefully the two-part essay in the *Gentleman's Magazine* for March and November 1743 that he attributed to Johnson on the basis of internal evidence, which he named "Considerations on the Dispute between Crousaz and Warburton, on Pope's Essay on Man," and then asserted that "while he defends Crousaz, he shews an admirable metaphysical acuteness and temperance in controversy," Boswell would have discovered that the English translation of the *Commentaire* is mentioned explicitly, and nearly half of the essay consists of quotations from it. In fact, the second installment has as its title: "*Specimens of M. Crousaz's Sentiments from the English Translation of his Commentary on Mr Pope's Essay on Man, continued from p. 152.*" The running head reads "*Sentiments from M. Crousaz's Commentary*, &c." and the entry in the index reads "*Crousaz* M. Specimens of his Sentiments 587."[2]

Had Hawkins, who first attributed the essay to Johnson, been taken more seriously by Boswell, he would have alerted Boswell to the real nature of the essay, although not to Johnson's role in the *Commentary*. Johnson, Hawkins suggests, decided to become a moderator between Crousaz's attacks on the *Essay on Man* in his *Examination* and *Commentary* on one side and William Warburton's defense in his *Vindication*, as it has come to be known, on the other, "but proceeded no farther than to state the sentiments of Mr. Crousaz respecting the poem, from a seeming conviction that he was discussing an uninteresting question."[3] Another clue, one which admittedly would have been difficult for the biographers to locate, is a quotation from Johnson's *Commentary* in his *Dictionary* under "Consoler."[4]

John Wilson Croker and other editors of Boswell's *Life* made often ingenious attempts to explain the 21 or 22 November 1738 letter, but it was not until L. F. Powell undertook his massive revision of G. B. Hill's edition of the *Life* that the attribution to Johnson of the *Commentary* was finally resolved. True, Whitwell Elwin in his 1871 introduction to the *Essay on Man* in *The Works of Alexander Pope* quoted a sentence from Johnson's long footnote on the ruling pas-

---

2. The essay is reprinted below with commentary, pp. 379–86.

3. Hawkins, *Life*, pp. 70, 351. Boswell could also have found the essay in the *Works* (1787), IX.364–68.

4. See p. 190 below.

sion: "'Every Observer,' says Johnson, 'has remark'd, that in many men the love of pleasure is the *ruling passion* of their youth, and the love of money that of their advanced years'" (p. 145). Elwin's footnote reads: "Crousaz's Commentary on Pope's Essay, translated by Johnson, p. 109."[5] But this reference, and an earlier footnote identifying Johnson as the translator, were overlooked by Johnsonians. Also overlooked was a statement in William John Courthope's 1889 *The Life of Alexander Pope,* included as part of the same edition of *The Works of Alexander Pope,* that "Johnson was himself engaged with Crousaz' Commentary on the Abbé du Resnel's translation of the 'Essay on Man,' but he temporarily abandoned it in deference to the opinion of his publisher, Cave."[6]

Powell, then, unaware of the earlier attributions of the *Commentary* to Johnson by Pope scholars, made an independent attribution in 1934.[7] Powell had seen only the 1742 issue of the *Commentary* and gave a quasi-facsimile description of the title page. Allen T. Hazen, while preparing an exhibition of Johnson books and manuscripts, which opened at Yale University on 8 November 1935, identified what to date is the unique copy of the 1739 issue. The discovery was reported initially by Hazen in the *Times Literary Supplement* for 2 November 1935 with a fuller account and a reproduction of the title page the following January in an essay co-authored with E. L. McAdam, Jr., in the *Yale University Library Gazette.*[8]

III

With the various components of the controversy surrounding Johnson's role in the translation of the *Commentaire* identified, it is

---

5. *Works of Pope,* II.307. See p. xxv, n. 7 above. Elwin cites Johnson's *Commentary* (page references in parentheses) in the following footnotes to the *Essay on Man:* pp. 358, n. 4; 360, n. 1; 361, n. 6; 381, n. 6; and 433, n. 3.

6. *The Works of Alexander Pope,* Vol. V (1889). Courthope draws on SJ's letter of 21 or 22 November, although he misdates it September 1738, citing Croker's edition of the *Life* as his source. The index to the *Works* appears in Vol. V and under "Johnson, Dr.," under the subheading *"An Essay on Man,"* is an entry: "translated a treatise of Crousaz on."

7. *Life,* IV.494–96.

8. *Times Literary Supplement,* p. 704. "First Editions of Samuel Johnson, An Important Exhibition and a Discovery," *Yale University Library Gazette,* X (1936), 45–51.

INTRODUCTION   xxix

next necessary to sort out the chronological and textual relationships of the various translations of Crousaz. Confusion surrounds the dates of publication of both the *Examination* and the *Commentary*. As Johnson points out in his letter of 21 or 22 November 1738, in a controversy such as that surrounding Pope's *Essay on Man* "the names of the Authours concerned are of more weight in the performance than its own intrinsick merit"; thus, "the Publick will be soon satisfied with it." To profit from the controversy it was necessary for Cave to publish the two works in a timely fashion and forestall any rivals, neither of which he managed to do.

It is not known when Cave and Johnson decided to publish translations of Crousaz's two attacks on the *Essay on Man,* but we can assume that Elizabeth Carter began work on the translation of the *Examen* by late summer 1738, as it is difficult to imagine Cave making a preliminary announcement of its publication without some copy in hand. The translation of the *Examen* was announced in the *Daily Advertiser* for 9 September 1738 and in the *London Evening Post* for 7–9 September as in the press; a similar advertisement appeared at the end of the "Register of Books" in the *Gentleman's Magazine* for September 1738 (VIII.496):

> In the Press, and speedily will be publish'd by *A. Dodd,* An Examination of Mr. *Pope*'s Essay on Man. Translated from the *French* of Monsi. *de Crousaz,* Member of the Royal Academies of Sciences at *Paris* and *Bourdeaux.* With Remarks by the Translator.[9]

Perhaps a preliminary announcement was deemed necessary because a rumor of a rival publication had reached St. John's Gate, but a search of the newspapers and magazines has not uncovered an announcement for any publication Cave might have felt the need to preempt.

What occurred during the next ten weeks is something of a mystery. In a letter of 26 September 1738 to his daughter, Elizabeth,

---

9. The announcement in the *Daily Advertiser* for 9 September reads: "*In the Press, and speedily will be publish'd, Printed for* A. DODD, AN Examination.... Translated from the French of Monsieur DE CRUSAR.... With Remarks by the Translator." Except for the *Daily Advertiser* in the Beinecke Library, Yale University, I have used the Burney Collection of Eighteenth-Century Newspapers available on microfilm.

Nicholas Carter suggests one explanation. He expresses satisfaction with Johnson's praise of her translation but frustration with Cave's lack of progress in printing the work: "That will, I suppose, please Cave; but is not sufficient it seems, to make him hasten the Press. . . . Dilatoriness is an inseparable Part of his Constitution."[1] This letter suggests that Elizabeth Carter had completed her share of the work on the translation before 26 September and was only awaiting its appearance in print.

But before Cave could publish Carter's translation, Edmund Curll advertised on 21 November a translation by Charles Forman of Crousaz's *Commentaire:*

> This Day is publish'd, (Price 1 s. 6 d.)
> Translated by CHARLES FORMAN, Esq;
> A Commentary upon Mr. POPE's Four Ethic Epistles, entitled *An Essay on Man.* Wherein his System is fully examin'd. By Monsieur DE CROUSAZ, Counsellor of the Embassies of Sweden, &c. formerly Governor to the Prince of Hesse, and Member of the Royal Academies of Sciences of Paris and Bourdeaux.
> This Commentary is a critical Satire upon the Essay on Man. "We have endeavour'd to be impartially just in our Translation of it; and had we not been persuaded that Mr. Pope will think his Honour engaged to make some Reply to the heavy Charge brought against him by Monsieur Crousaz, we would have enlarged the Remarks we have made on Abbe Du Resnel, the Translator of The Essay on Man into French Verse."
> Printed only for E. Curll, at Pope's Head in Rose-Street, Covent-Garden. And sold by Mess. Jackson, Jolliffe, and Dods-

---

1. Quoted in Barker, p. 274, citing the introduction to Gwen Hampshire, "Elizabeth Carter's Unpublished Correspondence," B. Litt. thesis, Oxford University, 1971, p. xii. There would be a similar delay in publishing Carter's translation of Francesco Algarotti's *Il Newtonianisimo per le Dame.* On 13 December 1738 in the *Daily Advertiser* Cave announced it as "In the Press," and announced its publication as 10 May 1739. As in the case of the *Examination,* the announced date may not have been the actual date of publication. Thomas Birch's copy with his signature has an inscription dated 31 May 1739, and probably represents a more accurate date of publication as Birch, patron of the translation from the beginning and one of its reviewers, must have received an early copy. See Ruhe, p. 496. As Kaminski observes, Cave frequently had difficulty publishing a work in a timely fashion. See, for example, his discussion of Cave's edition of Jean Baptiste Du Halde's *Description of China* (pp. 66–67).

ley, at St. James's; Brindley and Shropshire, in Bond-Street; Winbush and Amy, at Charing-Cross; Gilliver, in Fleet-Street; Dodd, without Temple-Bar; and Cooke and Nutt, at the Royal Exchange.[2]

The news of Curll's publication caused a flurry at St. John's Gate. Cave apparently wrote to Johnson seeking his advice, and the letter of 21 or 22 November is his response:

> I am pretty much of your Opinion, that the Commentary cannot be prosecuted with any appearance of success. . . . And I think the Examen should be push'd forward with the utmost expedition. Thus, This day, etc. An Examen of Mr. Pope's Essay etc. containing a succinct account of the Philosophy of Mr. Leibnitz on the System of the Fatalists, with a confutation of their Opinions, and an Illustration of the doctrine of Free-wil; [with what else you think proper.]
>
> It will above all be necessary to take notice that it is a thing distinct from the Commentary.

Cave followed Johnson's advice, and on 23 November in the *Daily Advertiser* appeared the following advertisement, perhaps written by Johnson:

> *This Day is publish'd.*
> An Examination of Mr. POPE's Essay on Man: Containing a succinct View of the System of the Fatalists, and a Confutation of their Opinions; with an Illustration of the Doctrine of Free Will; and an Enquiry what View Mr. Pope might have touching upon the Leibnitzian Philosophy.
> *By Mons. CROUSAZ*
> *Professor of Philosophy and Mathematics at Lausanne &c.*
> Printed for A. Dodd, without Temple-Bar; and sold by the

---

2. This announcement in the *Daily Advertiser* was repeated on 22 and 23 November. Forman's name does not appear on the title page or elsewhere in the work. The "Monthly Catalogue" in the November 1738 issue of the *London Magazine* has the following entry: "21. A Commentary upon Mr. *Pope*'s Essay on Man. Part I. By M. *de Crousaz*. Translated by *Ch. Forman*, Esq.; Printed for *E. Curll*, price 1*s*. 6*d*." The item immediately above reads: "20. An Examination of Mr. *Pope*'s Essay on Man. By M. *Crousaz*. Printed for *A. Dodd*, price 1*s*. 6*d*." (VII.582).

Booksellers. *Where may speedily be had, having been some Weeks in the Press, translated likewise from the French of Mr. Crousaz,*

A COMMENTARY on MR. POPE's *Principles of Morality:* or, *Essay on Man;* being a more minute Enquiry into the Tendency of the said Principles, occasion'd by a Letter written to Mr. Crousaz concerning his *Examination,* &c. To which are added, The Abbe *Du Resnel*'s Preliminary Discourse on English and French Poetry, and some cursory Observations by the Translator.

N.B. As the Commentary is built upon the Abbe *Du Resnel*'s Translation of the Essay into French Verse, the entire Translation is inserted, with an interlineary English Version, exactly correspondent to the French, for the Use of those who do not understand that Language, or are newly engaged in the Study of it.[3]

Because Johnson's letter of 21 or 22 November suggests that Cave's *Commentary* had little chance of appearing soon, the announcement of 23 November in the *Daily Advertiser* seems an attempt to ward off the competition by arguing a prior claim, at least for the *Commentary:* "*Where may speedily be had, having been some Weeks in the Press.*" Johnson himself used a similar ploy of arguing a prior claim a month earlier for the *History of the Council of Trent* when he wrote on 20 October 1738 to the *Daily Advertiser,* "It is generally agreed, that when any person has inform'd the world by advertisements, that he is engag'd in a design of this kind, to snatch the hint and supplant the first undertaker, is mean and disingenuous."[4]

---

3. Publication of the *Examination* was also announced in the *General Evening Post* for 21–23 November, *London Evening Post* for 23–25 and 25–28 November, and the *Daily Gazetteer* for 28 November, where we are told it is "Translated from the French of M. CROUSNER." It appears prominently displayed as the first item in the "Register of Books for November, 1738" in the *Gentleman's Magazine* with a large numeral "1" and an initial "A" five lines high: "AN EXAMINATION of Mr POPE's ESSAY on MAN. By Mons. *Crousaz,* Professor of Philosophy and Mathematicks at *Lausanne.* Printed for *A. Dodd.* Price 2 *s.*" (VIII.608). At the bottom of the right-hand column at the end of the "Register of Books for December, 1738" appears an additional advertisement. Beginning "*This Month* was publish'd," it repeats the announcement as it appears in the *Daily Advertiser* for 23 November but only for the *Examination* (VIII.664).

4. The letter appeared in the 21 October 1738 issue of the *Daily Advertiser* above Cave's signature, but it is certainly by SJ.

When Cave reprinted the advertisement of 23 November for the *Examination* and *Commentary* in the 24 November *Daily Advertiser*, he inserted as the second line the description "*Beautifully printed, Price Two Shillings sew'd*," and tried to ward off the threat from Curll by noting: "N.B. The Commentary of Mr. Pope's four Epistles publish'd by Mr. Curll, price 1 s. 6 d. goes not further than the first Epistle."[5] Curll countered in the *Daily Advertiser* of 25 November by revising the opening of the advertisement and adding a note of his own: "*This Day is publish'd, (With* The Essay on Man *inserted) Price but* 1 s. 6 d. MR. FORMAN's Translation of A COMMENTARY.... N.B. We shall pursue M. Crousaz in his Attacks upon Mr. Pope regularly, but not precipitately, without regarding whatever comes from Mrs. Dodd, who is only a Screen for anonymous Persons and Performances. *E. Curll.*" Mrs. Dodd, it is curious to note, is among the booksellers and publishers listed in Curll's advertisement of 21 November.[6] In the *Daily Advertiser* for 27 November, Cave's advertisement appears as the second and Curll's as the third item from the top of a left-hand column, allowing the reader to compare conveniently the two offerings.

It is unlikely that Cave was able to ready the *Examination* for publication on 23 November, two days after Curll announced his publication of the *Commentary* on 21 November. Thomas Birch, because of his close relationship with Carter at the time, must have received one of the first complete copies of the *Examination,* and likely wrote his Latin note of praise to her immediately. Therefore, Monday, 27 November, the date of Birch's note, would very probably be the first day the book was available.[7]

The *Examination* was now published, but what was the status of

5. The announcement in the *London Evening Post* of 23–25 November has the note in a slightly different form: "N.B. The Commentary advertis'd by Mr. Curll, price Sixpence, takes in no more than the first Epistle of the Essay on Man." It is repeated 25–28 November.

6. In this 25 November version of the advertisement, Curll has omitted all of the booksellers and publishers but himself.

7. Ruhe, p. 495. To keep the *Examination* before the public Cave advertised it on 23, 24, 27 November and later in the *Daily Advertiser;* thus the announcements are not a reliable record of the actual publication date. The publication of the *Examination* is discussed in greater detail in Brack, "Samuel Johnson and the Translations of Jean Pierre de Crousaz's *Examen* and *Commentaire*," *Studies in Bibliography*, XLVIII (1995), 60–84.

Johnson's *Commentary?* There is no evidence that Cave thought of abandoning the *Commentary;* instead he continued to spar with Curll. The advertisement for the *Commentary* on the verso of the last leaf of the *Examination,* taken from the announcement in the *Daily Advertiser* of 23 November—"*In the Press, Translated likewise from the* French *of Mr* Crousaz. A COMMENTARY. . . . French, for the Use of those who do not understand that Language, or are newly engaged in it"—argues for the superiority of Cave's publication. Cave needed to establish both that he was the first to have the idea of publishing Crousaz's two attacks on the *Essay on Man* and that only he was making available not only the *Examination* but also the complete *Commentary.*

Curll's initial announcement in the *Daily Advertiser* and his general threat to continue to pursue Crousaz were serious enough, but on acquiring a copy of Curll's publication Cave and Johnson discovered from the end of his Preface that Curll was proceeding with his translation: "The COMMENTARY of Monsieur DE CROUSAZ upon Mr POPE's *Second* EPISTLE is in the Press; and in the *Conclusion* of this *Work* will be subjoined the *various Readings* of its *several Editions,* with REMARKS thereon" (p. x). This volume never appeared and Forman died 28 April 1739.[8] In fact, unknown apparently to Cave and Johnson, Forman's translation of the first epistle was not selling well; it was reissued by Curll, without the title page and Preface, in *Miscellanies In Prose and Verse, By the Honourable Lady Margaret Pennyman* in December 1740.[9]

Johnson, in spite of threats from Curll, continued to press on with his translation of Crousaz's *Commentaire,* even though, for all Cave and Johnson knew, Curll and Forman were hard at work preparing the second epistle of their *Commentary* for publication. It must have been in late November or early December 1738 that Johnson made his heroic effort to complete the *Commentary* and translated "six" sheets, or at least a substantial amount, in one day. Exactly when he completed his translation is unknown. He presumably finished it in

---

8. *Gentleman's Magazine,* IX (May 1739), 272. For an account of Forman's career, see George A. Bonnard, "Note on the English Translations of Crousaz' Two Books on Pope's 'Essay on Man,'" in *Recueil de Travaux à l'occasion du quatrième centenaire de la fondation de l'Université* (1937), pp. 178–81.

9. J. V. Guerinot, *Pamphlet Attacks on Alexander Pope, 1711–1744* (1969), pp. 274–75.

the winter of 1738–39, but certainly in time to have it printed with 1739 on the title page.

No announcement of its publication has been discovered, suggesting that it was never published. It appears to have been withdrawn in order to privilege Elizabeth Carter's *Examination,* and the only known copy of the *Commentary* with "Printed for A. DODD" and "M.DCC.XXXix" in the imprint once belonged to Carter.[1] Cave, for reasons now obscure, stored the work for three years. Then in November 1741, the 1739 title page was cancelled and replaced by a bifolium containing the 1742 title page with Cave's name in the imprint and an Errata listing four errors discovered by Johnson.[2] The work was advertised in the November 1741 issue of the *Gentleman's Magazine* (XI.614) and in the *Scots Magazine* of the same month (III.524).

Johnson's prediction in his letter of 21 or 22 November 1738 that "the Publick will be soon satisfied" proved correct. No announcement seems to have appeared in the newspapers, nor was the volume reviewed. In an attempt to clear Cave's warehouse, Johnson puffed the work in a two-part essay in the *Gentleman's Magazine* for March and November 1743.[3] The book did not sell well, and Cave was still advertising it as late as 1753.[4]

Johnson has not left a record of how he felt about the failure of the Crousaz projects. His work to help ready the *Examination* for publication may have been part of the editorial chores he per-

---

1. John Nichols says that the *Commentary* "was kept back until November 1741." See *Literary Anecdotes of the Eighteenth Century* (London, 1812), V.550. J. D. Fleeman, *Bibliography,* concurs. See no. 39.10CP/1a. The Yale University, Beinecke Library copy of the 1739 *Commentary* has an inscription in Elizabeth Carter's hand: "E Libris Elizae Carter."

2. Fleeman, *Bibliography,* no. 39.10CP/1b.

3. See pp. 379–86 below.

4. The work appears as item XXII, immediately below the listing of the *Examination,* in an undated advertisement, "Books Printed for E. Cave at St. John's Gate," bound at the end of *A General Index to the First Twenty Volumes of the Gentleman's Magazine* (London, 1753) in the Bodleian Library, Oxford. Although the advertisement is a separately printed gathering, it could not have been printed earlier than 1753, as it advertises the third edition of *The Entire Works of Dr. Thomas Sydenham,* to which SJ's life was prefixed, published that year. The advertisement reproduces all of the information on the title page except Crousaz's credentials and, of course, the imprint. Underneath Cave adds a comment: "The two foregoing proper to be bound with Mr. Warburton's defence of the Essay on Man."

A COMMENTARY

ON

Mr *POPE*'s

PRINCIPLES of MORALITY,

Or ESSAY on MAN.

By *Monſ.* CROUSAZ,
Member of the Royal Academies of Sciences at *Paris* and *Bourdeaux*, and Profeſſor of Philoſophy and Mathematics at *Lauſanne*;

In ANSWER to a LETTER of
REMARKS on his EXAMEN, &c.

CONTAINING ALSO

I. The LETTER of REMARKS to Monſ. CROUSAZ.
II. The Abbé DU RESNEL's Tranſlation of the ESSAY into FRENCH Verſe.
III. An Interlineary *Engliſh* Verſion of the ſame.
IV. M. DU RESNEL's Preface, with his Obſervations on the *French, Italian,* and *Engliſh* Poetry.
V. Some Annotations by the Tranſlator.

LONDON:
Printed for E. CAVE, at ST JOHN's GATE
M,DCC,XLII.

INTRODUCTION   xxxvii

formed for Cave, under some unknown payment scheme.[5] But for translating the *Commentaire* Johnson was probably paid by the sheet. The rate of payment for translation at this time ranged from ten shillings to a guinea a sheet.[6] Johnson seems to be providing a clue that he received a guinea per printed sheet when he translates *"Voilà du Grec qu'il faut traduire en Latin, on vous donnera un Ducat par feuille"* (p. 357) as *"Take this* Greek, *and translate it into* Latin, *and you shall receive a guinea a page"* (p. 330). A better translation for "feuille" would be *sheet;* receiving a guinea a *page* for translation would have meant riches beyond the dreams of avarice.[7] At a guinea per printed sheet Johnson would have received fourteen and one-half guineas. Perhaps there was some consolation for the failure of the projects in the money he received, although it was not a great deal of money and may well have been spent by the time he completed the translation.

The high hopes of becoming a tragedy writer with which Johnson had entered London in 1737 had been dashed by the rejection of *Irene* for the stage. His translation of Sarpi's *Istoria del concilio Tridentino,* with his name on the title page and which was to establish his reputation as a scholar, had ended in failure. If the translation of Crousaz's *Commentaire,* with its notes largely defending the poetry of the *Essay on Man* against misrepresentations and carping complaints, had been published in a timely fashion, it might have attracted favorable notice from Pope and his circle, leading to recognition for the anonymous translator and annotator. The cumulative effect of repeated failures to succeed as a writer had taken its toll, and in late summer 1739 Johnson left London in an attempt to secure a post at Appleby Grammar School in Leicestershire, "choosing rather to die upon the road, *than be starved to death in translating*

---

5. As part of his editorial work SJ wrote most, if not all, of the annotations for the *Examination.* See Brack, "Translations," pp. 78–84.

6. On the rate of payment for translation, see Kaminski, pp. 71–76, and pp. 166–70 for SJ's payment for editorial duties on the *Gentleman's Magazine.*

7. A *ducat* is worth considerably less than a guinea. Boyer defines it as "a gold or silver coin" and SJ defines it in the *Dictionary* as "A coin struck by dukes; in silver valued at about four shillings and six pence; in gold at nine shillings six pence." Earlier SJ translates "francs" as "shillings" (p. 49). Boyer defines a "Franc" as "twenty pence French" and SJ defines "Frank" only as "A French coin" (sense 3 in *Dictionary*). In this instance a franc and a shilling are near equivalents.

for the booksellers, which has been his only subsistance for some time past."[8]

IV

The antagonism of Cave and Johnson toward Edmund Curll should not obscure the fact that Curll's publication of a translation of the first epistle of the *Commentaire* influenced Johnson's *Commentary*. Curll's *Commentary* is, in fact, a translation and abridgement by Charles Forman of the first epistle of Crousaz, with Pope's lines substituted for the Du Resnel text, essentially vitiating Forman's attack on the verse translation since the reader has few examples of it. The "Remarks" in Forman's translation of the *Commentary* are in footnotes to the text. These notes, largely favorable to Pope, attack both Du Resnel's translation and Crousaz's commentary based on it.

Although Johnson had at least read over the *Commentaire* in anticipation of translating it before 27 November, as he cites the second line of the third epistle of Du Resnel's verse translation in a footnote to the *Examination*,[9] he could not have begun serious work on the first epistle of his *Commentary* before the publication of Forman's translation on 21 November 1738 for he clearly used it to make his own. Johnson's translation is superior to Forman's and includes the whole text; nevertheless there are a number of verbal parallels, several too close to be dismissed as coincidence. Johnson, for example, translated "à la gayeté" (p. 60) as "mirth and gaiety" (p. 61) and Forman as "gaiety and mirth" (p. 24). The French "on en prend ce qu'il faut pour se conserver en vigueur; & on n'a garde de se laisser séduire par des plaisirs qui émoussent l'attention & la vivacité de l'intelligence" (p. 103) is translated by Forman as "We take what is necessary for preserving us in *health and vigour;* but we

---

8. From a letter written by John Leveson-Gower, later first earl Gower, on 1 August 1739 to an anonymous correspondent asking him to write to Jonathan Swift in an effort to obtain a master of arts degree for SJ from Trinity College, Dublin (*Early Biographies,* p. 25). When in 1754 SJ wrote his "Life of Cave," he recalled that "the fortune which he left behind him, which though large, had been yet larger, had he not rashly and wantonly impaired it by innumerable projects, of which I know not that ever one succeeded." See *Early Biographical Writings of Dr Johnson,* ed. J. D. Fleeman (1973), p. 408.

9. *Examination,* p. 138; Brack, "Translations," p. 79.

INTRODUCTION   xxxix

also take care not to suffer ourselves to be seduced by pleasures that take off the attention, and blunt the vivacity of the *understanding*" (pp. 56–57) and by Johnson as "We take what is necessary to preserve *health and vigour*, but are not to give ourselves up to pleasures that weaken the attention, and dull the *understanding* (p. 95; italics added). Johnson is misled by taking a cue from Forman's translation of "alloit plus loin que la bêtise de cet animal" (p. 55). Forman, confusing "bêtise" with "bête," instead of "exceeded the stupidity of that animal," writes "was more a beast than that animal" (p. 20) and Johnson "was much more despicable than the brutality of that animal" (p. 57).

Curll's edition of the *Commentary* served Johnson not only while he translated the first epistle; it also suggested the tone and form his footnotes should take. Curll's remarks in the preface—"Impartiality and justice obliges us to ask Mr. *De Crousaz*, as he had two *French* translations of Mr. *Pope's* Essay on Man in his hands, why he did not take the prose to comment upon rather than the verse, since he did not understand *English*?"—provide the point of attack for both Forman and Johnson.[1] Both translators make numerous complaints about how Du Resnel's French verse translation distorted Pope's meaning and hence Crousaz's commentary, and in six instances Johnson has a footnote at or near the same point in the text as Forman, even though he does not always agree with him. On "*just balance*" Forman's footnote suggests, "This is the translator's way of rendering *equal Eye*, which he likewise has too in the next Line; or *sa juste* balance is a flight of his own" (p. 31). Johnson says, "These two lines that give occasion to these questions, are entirely inserted by the translator" (p. 68). Forman's "These six lines are not in the translation; how they came to be passed over, the translator knows best" (p. 33) is condensed by Johnson to "In this place six whole lines are omitted" (p. 69).[2] To a quotation of lines 99–108 of Pope,

---

1. I follow E. Audra in attributing the Preface to Curll. See *L'Influence Française dans l'oeuvre de Pope* (1931), p. 93. The Preface, unlike the notes, is hostile to Pope, calling the *Commentary* "a Critical Satire on the *Essay on Man*" and challenging Pope for "his Honour" to reply "to the heavy Charge brought against him by a *Frenchman*" (pp. viii–ix). Curll has adapted a portion of his Preface in his advertisement of the work in the *Daily Advertiser* for 21 November and later. See p. xxx above.

2. SJ makes a similar, but more expansive, observation later: "In this place the

which Forman has substituted for those of Du Resnel, he adds a footnote: "To these ten lines, the translator, tho' counted one of the French first rates, has hobbled out their meaning within the compass of twenty four of his own; but he has left their spirit behind him" (p. 33). Johnson, of course, includes Du Resnel's verses with a translation, so he takes a slightly different approach, in part answering Forman:

> Mr Pope, in the original, has not made use of the word *nature* in the passage here refer'd to; his expression being only
> *Lo! the poor* Indian, *whose untutor'd Mind.*
> But he has, indeed, us'd the word a few lines after,
> *Yet simple Nature to his Hope has given,* &c.
> to which, perhaps, all that Mr Crousaz has written may be apply'd with propriety. (pp. 71–72)

In another footnote Forman writes, "Mr. Pope has nothing to do with these words, they are one of the translator's flights, which the critick is only exposing at the same time that he thinks he is demolishing Mr. Pope" (p. 36). Johnson says, "Mr Crousaz is so watchful against impiety, that he lets nonsense pass without censure.... I take this opportunity of observing, once for all, that he is not sufficiently candid in charging all the errors of this miserable version upon the original author.... He had a prose translation in his hand, which he might have compared with Du Resnel's" (pp. 74–75). Then Forman writes, "Here we omit some of the criticism, because it is upon a few lines of the translation that neither shew Mr. Pope's words nor his meaning" (p. 48). Johnson, who reprints the lines in his text with a translation, also adds a footnote: "This couplet is an addition by the translator" (p. 87). Again, Forman writes, "The translator's vein is, no doubt, fertile enough sometimes; for it makes Mr. Pope say many things which he never thought of, tho' not in this place, which is the first of Mr. Pope's that has met with the commentator's entire approbation; notwithstanding the beauty of the original is quite lost in 23 lines of French" (p. 62). Johnson comments, "On this passage where sixteen lines are translated into thirty three,

---

translator has, with great fidelity and judgment, entirely omitted a paragraph of twenty-two verses, from the fifty-third to the seventy-fourth" (p. 203).

INTRODUCTION   xli

it is not necessary to make any other remark than may be made in
general on the whole work, that it is extremely below the original
in spirit, propriety, and notwithstanding the diffuseness of his expression, in perspicuity" (p. 102).[3]

Even such a Johnsonian-sounding note as "The address of one is
the exclamation of a freeman, that of the other the murmur of a
slave" (p. 37) echoes Forman's "Notwithstanding all Mr. Crousaz's
logick, this argument smells more of the slave than Mr. Pope's philosophy does of the poet" (p. 66). Forman even anticipates Johnson
in discussing the significance of words: "The translator takes *vile* to
signify *poor* and *wretched* as to worldly circumstances, and therefore
places the man in a *chaumiere* (a *cottage*); after which he gravely shews
that a *poor* man may *sometimes* have good qualities; but, it seems,
never such good ones as are enjoyed by the *rich*" (p. 69). A parallel
case is Johnson's discussion of "*end*" or "*destinée.*"[4]

Forman substitutes Pope's verses for those of Du Resnel throughout his translation of the first epistle of the *Commentary*. Johnson,
however, follows Crousaz in reproducing Du Resnel's poem in its
entirety, although adding his own line-for-line translation. But
when Crousaz repeats a line or lines of Du Resnel's poem in his text
for analysis, Johnson usually substitutes the lines of Pope. He also
cites Pope's verse in the footnotes. This helps Johnson reinforce his
point about the difference in quality between the verses of Pope and
Du Resnel.

V

Johnson, like other educated young men of his time, had been
forced to think about translation theory and practice early, at least
in an elementary way. Throughout school he had translated Latin
into English and English into Latin, agonizing, no doubt, over how
literal or free a translation might be and still please the master.
Among Johnson's early poems are several translations from Latin

---

3. In this instance SJ is taking issue with Forman as well as Du Resnel. Two notes
later SJ, like Forman, praises Du Resnel's translation (p. 114). SJ is referring to
ll. 207–22 of Pope but the passage in French is only twenty-three lines, as Forman
says

4. See p. 65 below.

and Greek, and a translation of Pope's *Messiah* into Latin verse.[5] Early in his career he became familiar with some of the theories of translation, especially those of John Dryden, the Earl of Roscommon, and may have known others.[6] Later, in *Idler* 68 and 69 and in the *Lives of the English Poets,* Johnson demonstrated his familiarity with theories of translation, with his own view best summed up in the final sentence of *Idler* 69: "Dryden saw very early that closeness best preserved an author's sense, and that freedom best exhibited his spirit; he therefore will deserve the highest praise who can give a representation at once faithful and pleasing, who can convey the same thoughts with the same graces, and who when he translates changes nothing but the language."[7] Obviously this represents an ideal view of translation, one possible to maintain, perhaps, when translating Homer, Horace, and Virgil in the comfort of a scholarly retreat, but more difficult to achieve by a professional author paid a certain amount for each printed sheet.

Translation, an art Johnson practiced throughout his life, clearly came so naturally to him that it is not surprising he would turn to it at age twenty-four when he found himself in need of money. Johnson, in the preface to *A Voyage to Abyssinia* (1735), states that his work is "by no means a translation but an epitome." As Joel J. Gold observes in his introduction to *A Voyage to Abyssinia,* volume xv in this series, a comparison of the French and English versions reveals "Johnson translating fairly closely in places, epitomizing in others, omitting some sections, expanding others, softening or adding asperity to the tone, rearranging elements for greater clarity, balancing phrases for smoother syntax, inserting transitions for easier

---

5. *Poems,* pp. 4–28, 40–49. Six of SJ's Latin school exercises have survived, four from Lichfield Grammar School and two from Pembroke College.

6. Among the books SJ took to Oxford were Dryden's *Juvenal, Virgil,* and *Fables,* all of which have discussions on the art of translation, although the fullest discussion is in the Preface to Ovid's *Epistles*. In Dryden SJ would have found a number of theorists mentioned, including the Earl of Roscommon, for whose *An Essay on Translated Verse* (1684), Dryden wrote a complimentary poem. See Aleyn Lyell Reade, *Johnsonian Gleanings* (1928), V.225. For a summary of theories of translation, see T. R. Steiner, *English Translation Theory, 1650–1800,* Approaches to Translation Studies, No. 2 (Assen: The Netherlands, 1975), pp. 7–60.

7. *Idler and Adventurer,* ed. W. J. Bate, J. M. Bullitt, and L. F. Powell (Vol. II, Yale Edition of the Works of Samuel Johnson, 1963), p. 217. See *Lives,* I.421–23 (pars. 223–26), I.446–54 (pars. 299–313), III.236–40 (pars. 345–52).

INTRODUCTION   xliii

reading, and even inserting editorial comments to point a moral." The reason, however, the French version was epitomized, Johnson states, was to reduce "the narration into a narrow compass."[8] Reducing the size of the work was a commercial consideration; undoubtedly Thomas Warren, the bookseller and printer, wanted to publish a volume he could sell for five shillings and make a profit. The decision was left to Johnson, presumably, as to how the work would be epitomized. For this translation and epitome he received five guineas, or about four shillings per sheet. Johnson had begun a life of professional authorship.

By at least 1734 Johnson had a good working knowledge of French. James Gray has carefully sifted the evidence on Johnson's knowledge and use of French and believes that he was largely self-taught, using two works by Abel Boyer: *The Compleat French Master* (1694) and the *Dictionnaire Royale Français et Anglais* (1699). In fact, evidence presented in the annotations indicates that he consulted Boyer's *Dictionnaire Royale* when translating the *Commentaire*. Also a number of the Lichfield clergy spoke French and, in addition to the Garrick family, there were others in the community of Huguenot origin or descent, any of whom may have tutored the young Johnson. That he early developed at least a good reading knowledge in French is supported not only by his abilities as a translator but by his wide knowledge of French writers.[9]

Since Johnson's *Commentary* is by no means an epitome but a translation, it differs in some ways from *A Voyage to Abyssinia*. His theory of translation, inasmuch as it comes up in the *Commentary*, is confined to noting that Du Resnel had read the Earl of Roscommon's *Essay on Translated Verse* but failed to profit from it.[1] His

---

8. *A Voyage to Abyssinia*, ed. Joel J. Gold (Vol. XV, Yale Edition of the Works of Samuel Johnson, 1985), pp. 6, xlviii.

9. James Gray, "Arras/Hélas! A Fresh Look at Samuel Johnson's French," *Johnson After Two Hundred Years*, ed. Paul J. Korshin (1986), pp. 87–90. A revised second edition of *The Compleat French Master* was published in 1699 and had reached an eleventh edition by 1733. Johnson owned a copy of the *Royal Dictionary*, although it is not known when he acquired it. It was not among the books he took to Oxford but was in his library at his death. He also acquired at some time after leaving Oxford a copy of the 1710 edition of Pierre Richelet's *Dictionnaire François*. See Donald Greene, *Samuel Johnson's Library, An Annotated Guide* (1975), pp. 40–41, 97.

1. See pp. 37, 73, 142, 351–52.

practice as a translator can be discovered by comparing his English with the French sources.

As in *A Voyage to Abyssinia* and the other translations he was doing about the same time, Johnson translates closely in places, rearranges elements in the sentence and, occasionally, in the paragraph, balances phrases, often by introducing doublets, and provides smoother transitions. Unlike *A Voyage to Abyssinia,* the omissions are few and the condensations slight. Editorial commentary is reserved for the footnotes. L. F. Powell in a note on the *Commentary* says, "The translation does not, I am bound to admit, exhibit a striking resemblance to Johnson's style, but the annotations, which are avowedly by the translator, are distinctly Johnsonian."[2] Had Johnson not written annotations to the *Commentary,* it is unlikely that the work would have been recognized as his. Hawkins offers a possible explanation. Speaking of Johnson's design to translate Thuanus's history of his own times, Hawkins observes, "It may be questioned whether, upon trial, he would not have found himself unequal to the task of transfusing into an English version the spirit of his author. Johnson's talent was original thinking, and though he was ever able to express his own sentiments in nervous language, he did not always succeed in his attempts to familiarise the sense of others."[3]

The work in reality has two styles of translation, one for Du Resnel's verse and the other for the prose. As Johnson's footnotes make clear, he is out of patience with Du Resnel's "miserable version" of Pope's *Essay on Man.* To point up the poor quality of Du Resnel's verse, Johnson provides an excruciatingly literal interlinear translation with each word or phrase of his own carefully spaced so that it falls immediately below the word or phrase of Du Resnel it translates. The result is to make Du Resnel's somewhat vague and muddled effort to produce an *Essay on Man* virtually incomprehensible. One only need turn to any page of verse in the text below and read a section of the poem in Johnson's English translation to receive the full, often humorous, effect. When Crousaz re-

---

2. *Life,* IV.495.
3. Hawkins, *Life,* pp. 540–41. Hawkins praises the Preface of *A Voyage to Abyssinia,* which he thinks "bears stronger marks of Johnson's hand than any part of the work," but adds, "were we to rest our judgment on internal evidence, Johnson's claim to the title of translator of this work would be disputable" (p. 22).

INTRODUCTION   xlv

peats a line or lines of Du Resnel for analysis, Johnson does not repeat his own translation, but substitutes the lines from Pope, as was demonstrated above, further demeaning by comparison Du Resnel's verse.[4]

On the whole, Johnson's translation of the prose in the *Commentaire* may be said to be close but not exact.[5] The annotations to the text of the *Commentary* provide the reader with what the editor considers significant, interesting, or humorous departures from the French original, but it may be useful to categorize them further. As Gold has pointed out, Johnson makes occasional errors with simple words, probably more out of carelessness than lack of familiarity. His frequent errors in translating numerical terms suggests that the books from which he learned French had few such terms.[6]

"cent"—"thousand"
"milliers"—"millions"
"quatre Chants"—"five cantos"
"un million de personnes"—"thousands and ten thousands"
"Cheval de Bataille"—"engine of war"
"bras"—"hands"
"plus"—"less"
"parfait"—"present"
"égalité"—"purity"
"reproche"—"remorse"
"forêts"—"desarts"

His confidence in his knowledge of French, which led him to feel it was unnecessary to consult a dictionary, created other difficulties. When Johnson translates "A cet égard, je suis très éloigné de ses idées, & je ne puis convenir de regarder non plus comme des présens de Créateur, qui ne trompe point, les diverses illusions par lesquelles les hommes s'étourdissent sur la mort, & se dérobent à ses frayeurs" (p. 205) as "I cannot, for my part, concur with this notion, or consider, as the gifts of God infinitely pure, those

---

4. See p. xli above.
5. John Lawrence Abbott, "Dr. Johnson's Translations from the French" (Ph.D. diss., Michigan State University, 1963), pp. 72–93 and "No 'Dialect of France': Samuel Johnson's Translations from the French," *University of Toronto Quarterly*, XXXVI (1967), 129–36.
6. Gold, *Voyage*, p. xlix.

vices with which men are infected, or those delusive imaginations by which men harden themselves against the fear of death, as the dictates of a God infinitely true and without deceit" (p. 183) he seems to have confused "s'étourdir," "to shake off the thoughts of a thing" with "s'endurcir," "to harden, or grow hard."[7] In another place he confuses "ôter," "to take away, or remove" with "oser," "to dare, to be so bold as to—," when he translates "de peur que la distance infinie de vous à lui ne vous effraye, ou du moins ne vous intimide, & ne vous ôte l'assurance d'en approcher" (pp. 276–77) as "lest the infinite distance between him and thee should affright, or at least discourage, thee from daring to approach him" (p. 253). He also confuses "éclairer," "to light, to give light to," or figuratively, "to enlighten" with "éclaircir," "to clear," or figuratively, "to instruct, to inform, or give information" when he translates a line from Du Resnel, "Ils eclairent nos yeux sur les defauts des autres" as "They clear up our eyes to the faults of others" (p. 296).

An idiosyncrasy of Johnson's translations, extensively documented by John Lawrence Abbott and found here, is his unusual treatment of "venir de" plus an infinitive, in which Johnson "chooses to render the meaning in a variety of ways" but not as "to have *just* done something."[8]

Another characteristic of Johnson's French translations is the extensive use of doublets, over ninety in this text, according to Abbott's calculations.[9] On a few occasions a doublet of Crousaz is reduced to a single word. These techniques usually bring a force and balance to the style.

---

7. The definitions are taken from Boyer.
8. Abbott, "Dr. Johnson's Translations," p. 23.
9. Abbott, "No 'Dialect of France,'" p. 135. Abbott suggests that the doublet "appears so frequently that it becomes a kind of signature and might be of value in identifying doubtful authorship" (p. 130). Forman, as has been indicated earlier, introduces doublets: "grossness and ignorance of the senses" (p. 34) for "la grossiéreté des sens" (p. 74); "for surmounting what tires and fatigues him" (p. 34) for "pour tromper ses ennuis" (p. 74); "proud, haughty intelligences" (p. 41) for "ces fieres intelligences" (p. 84); "gratifications and pleasures" (p. 58) for "douceurs" (p. 104), and a number of others. Perhaps an extensive study of translations might reveal that SJ uses doublets with greater frequency than other translators. Attributing a work on the basis of translation techniques is fraught with difficulties. See the discussion by O M Brack, Jr. and Thomas Kaminski in "Johnson, James, and the *Medicinal Dictionary*," *Modern Philology*, LXXXI (1984), 378–400.

INTRODUCTION   xlvii

Although the style of the *Commentary* on the whole does not have a particularly Johnsonian resonance, a comparison of the English with the French reveals a few favorite words from his early writings.[1] Perhaps, for example, the most obvious is his use of "darling," which has no equivalent in the French, as in "his darling passion" (p. 167) for "ses projets ambitieux" (p. 188) or "his darling god" (p. 235) for "son Dieu" (p. 256).[2] He also uses "desirous," usually without an equivalent in the French, as in "insatiably desirous of praise" (p. 151) for "insatiable d'éloges" (p. 167) or "desirous of debasing virtue" (p. 163) for "pour rabaisser le mérite de la virtue" (p. 184).[3] He is also fond of various forms of "exalt" and "exhibit" as well as "hitherto."[4]

The unevenness of the translation suggests that Johnson lost interest in the project, at least from time to time. The most conspicuous evidence for his flagging interest occurs in his footnotes where, as sometimes happens in his longer projects, his assiduity seems to falter in the latter half of the work: there are twenty-seven footnotes to the commentary on Epistle I, nineteen to Epistle II, only three to Epistle III, and one to Epistle IV, although there are three substantial notes to Du Resnel's "Discours Préliminaire du Traducteur," called by Johnson "Preface to his Translations of Mr Pope's *Essay on Man* and *Essay on Criticism*. Containing Observations upon the English and French Poetry, and the Different Tastes of the Two Nations," included at the end of the volume.

This discrepancy in the quantity and length of the footnotes, however, may have other explanations. Perhaps it is only the result of the haste imposed by the publication of Forman's competing translation. Perhaps it is Johnson's response to the structure of Crousaz's work. Crousaz, by choosing to comment on Du Resnel's French version line by line, is forced into repeating his commen-

---

1. For an analysis of SJ's early prose style, see Jacob Leed, "Samuel Johnson and the *Gentleman's Magazine:* Studies in the Canon of His Miscellaneous Prose Writings, 1738–1744" (Ph.D. diss., University of Chicago, 1958), pp. 38–40, 93–96.

2. Other examples of the use of "darling" appear on pp. 173, 210, 284, 338, and in one of SJ's footnotes, p. 175.

3. Other examples of the use of "desirous" appear on pp. 13, 21, 35, 86, 184, 375.

4. In what appears to be a particularly Johnsonian touch, "paresse" is exactly rendered as "*Indolence*" but with the capital and italics added for emphasis (p. 25).

tary, in more or less the same terms, each time an idea recurs in the poem, making for a great deal of redundancy. Johnson, recognizing the pattern of repetition, attempts to follow Crousaz through his commentary on Epistle I, but then may have decided not to continue to repeat himself. Johnson may have recognized that his decision to write a commentary on a translation had created difficulties for himself. In any case, toward the end of the commentary on Epistle III Johnson, in a remark directed at Crousaz, seems to recognize that after writing fifty footnotes the observation may be equally directed to himself: "To comment on a translation is a very adventurous task" (p. 230). After this footnote only one more appears in the remainder of the commentary on Epistle III and a final one in the commentary on Epistle IV.

Johnson's interest in the translation does not follow the same precipitous decline found in the number of footnotes, but waxes and wanes. For stretches Johnson is content to translate Crousaz's French prose more or less exactly, not bothering to change the syntax. In other instances he recasts the French to make it Johnsonian. Even in his translation of Du Resnel's "Discours Préliminaire du Traducteur" on English and French poetry, probably included in the volume on his recommendation, where a reader might expect him to insert critical commentary into the text, he follows the same technique. Perhaps he was recalling his work on the *Commentaire* and the "Discours Préliminaire" when he says in the Preface to the *Dictionary* that "No book was ever turned from one language into another, without imparting something of its native idiom; this is the most mischievous and comprehensive innovation; single words may enter by thousands, and the fabrick of the tongue continue the same; but new phraseology changes much at once; it alters not the single stones of the building, but the order of the columns." If "the licence of translatours," he adds, is "suffered to proceed" it "will reduce us to babble a dialect of *France*."[5]

No one page of Johnson's *Commentary* will show all of his translation techniques, but an analysis of a representative page will demonstrate, better than lists of examples, how he worked through Crousaz's French, turning it into English.[6] The passage begins, "Etre

5. Preface to the *Dictionary* (5 pars. from the end).
6. It is p. 28 of the *Commentary,* although the first sentence begins at the bottom of

curieux de percer dans l'avenir & d'être instruit par avance de nous les événemens qui se succéderont, c'est une curiosité qui ne nous convient point; & si on trouve à propos de lui donner le nom d'orgueil je ne m'y oppose pas." According to Boyer, "Percer l'avenir *ou* dans l'avenir" means figuratively "to foresee things to come"; Johnson renders the opening of Crousaz's sentence as "A curiosity to pry into futurity." Perhaps "percer," defined by Boyer as "to pierce, bore, or make a hole into," suggested "pry" but, in any case, Johnson's word choice shifts Crousaz's statement to a more negative and admonitory one since "pry" means not only "to peep narrowly," but also "to inspect officiously, curiously, or impertinently," as Johnson indicated in the *Dictionary*. Later in the same sentence Johnson translates "curiosité" as "temper" to avoid repeating "curiosity."[7] Johnson balances the next sentence by twice using "submission." He translates "vivre sous de certaines Loix" as "live in submission to certain laws," then rendering "quelles sont ces Loix à l'observation desquelles il nous a assujettis" as "what those laws are that we are bound to observe," and retaining "soûmission" as "submission" at the end of the sentence. Next Crousaz quotes line 100 of Du Resnel: "*Le Livre du destin pour Dieu seul est ouvert.*" Johnson, who had earlier translated the line as "The book of fate to God alone is open," does not look back a half page or so to his previous rendering but translates it anew as "*The book of fate is open only to God,*" then adding a footnote: "Mr Pope only says, Heaven from all Creatures hides the Book of Fate."

After translating the next two sentences almost exactly, although rendering "le style d'un Philosophe," for example, as "the style of philosophy," he ignores Crousaz's metaphor in the opening of the following sentence, rendering "Il n'est donc pas toûjours couvert de nuages épais pour nous, ce Livre" (p. 62) more directly as "It is plain then, that this book is not altogether shut from our eyes," before translating the remainder of the sentence closely. In the next sentence Johnson substitutes Pope's "*Who could suffer being here below?*" for Crousaz's paraphrase of two lines from Du Resnel. The next sentence is straightforward, but in the following one "Des Ames

---

p. 27; the corresponding passage in Crousaz appears on p. 62. The passage appears below on pp. 61–62.

7. *Temper:* "Disposition of mind" (sense 4 in *Dictionary*).

Héroïques" becomes "saints and martyrs" and "mais dans cette attente elles s'appliquoient sans trouble à remplir leur devoir" is rendered "but they nevertheless applied themselves to their duty with calmness and content."

VI

Johnson's major contribution to the *Commentary* is the footnotes. Altogether there are sixty-eight, nine of which appear in whole or in part in Du Resnel's original preface. In the majority of the remaining footnotes Johnson points out the disparity between Pope's original and Du Resnel's version of the *Essay on Man* on which Crousaz has based his *Commentaire*. By the time Johnson has translated only half of the commentary on Epistle I, he is out of patience with Crousaz and his critical approach: "Mr Crousaz is so watchful against impiety, that he lets nonsense pass without censure.... I take this opportunity of observing, once for all, that he is not sufficiently candid in charging all the errors of this miserable version upon the original author" (p. 74). Later in the same section, however, he makes an attempt to balance his attack by observing that "The same justice that has obliged me so often to censure, obliges me in this place to commend the *French* poet" (p. 114). Nevertheless, he continues to defend Pope's poem against unfair misrepresentation, even though it is clear that he does not approve of the poem, finding it heterodox, ambiguous, and incomprehensible in places. A more focused attack on the *Essay on Man* and its doctrines was to come later in his review of Soame Jenyns' *A Free Inquiry into the Nature and Origin of Evil,* reprinted below, and in the "Life of Pope."

When on rare occasions Johnson's translation of the *Commentaire* has attracted any attention at all, it has turned, understandably, on several lengthy footnotes which contain ideas to which Johnson would return in later writings, such as his attack on the dominance of the passion of love on the stage, reiterated in briefer form in the *Preface to Shakespeare* and the "Life of Dryden."[8] Indications of Johnson's later prowess as a literary critic, however, are slight.

---

8. See pp. 175–76 below. Perhaps SJ's bitter attack on love may have had some origin in his own deteriorating marital circumstances. See Gay W. Brack, "Tetty and Samuel Johnson: The Romance and the Reality," *Age of Johnson,* V (1992), 156.

Johnson not only fails to insert any of his own critical ideas into his translation of Du Resnel's "Discours Préliminaire" on English and French poetry, but adds only three lengthy footnotes. In the first he corrects Du Resnel's assertion that Pope's *Essay on Criticism* had not been attacked by critics by pointing out that the poem had been "animadverted upon by Mr Dennis, with great fury and malice"; in the second he questions a reading in Roscommon's *An Essay on Translated Verse*, although his critical commentary is mitigated by the fact that Du Resnel is quoting the first edition and Johnson the revised second edition; but in the third footnote he makes a perceptive comment on Italian poets, anticipating his definition of "wit" in the "Life of Cowley" and his praise of the *Rape of the Lock* in the "Life of Pope."[9]

More important are the notes relating to the problem of evil, particularly the ruling passion and the necessity of free will. Johnson does not examine these subjects in any systematic way; that would come later. Instead he is responding to particular points raised primarily by Crousaz and Du Resnel, although Pope is more or less in the background.[1] From these scattered observations it is clear that Johnson comes down firmly on the side of orthodoxy, believing that God created man for happiness but that both physical and moral evil entered the world because of Original Sin and, hence, that many of the miseries of life are mankind's own fault. His remarks on the ruling passion, mild compared to his later denunciation of it in the "Life of Pope" as a doctrine "in itself pernicious as well as false," do show that Johnson believes that freedom of the will is essential for morality.[2] As he later remarked in Sermon 5, "vir-

---

9. See pp. 344, 352, 356 below.

1. Richard B. Schwartz in *Samuel Johnson and the Problem of Evil* (1975) makes a somewhat hyperbolic claim that the footnotes on the role of love, the knowledge of futurity, the meaning of "Eternal Artificer," with the two notes on the ruling passion "constitute something like an early essay on issues surrounding the problem of evil in the eighteenth century" (pp. 94–95). See pp. 175–76, 64, 160, 145–46, 166 below.

2. SJ's remark appears in his discussion on *Of the Knowledge and Characters of Men. An Epistle to the Lord Cobham*, where this definition is given: "In this poem he has endeavoured to establish and exemplify his favourite theory of the 'Ruling Passion,' by which he means an original direction of desire to some particular object, an innate affection which gives all action a determinate and invariable tendency, and operates upon the whole system of life either openly or more secretly by the intervention of some accidental or subordinate propension" (*Lives*, III.173–74, pars. 202, 205).

tue is the consequence of choice" and "Men would be no longer rational, or would be rational to no purpose, because their actions would not be the result of free-will, determined by moral motives; but the settled and predestined motions of a machine impelled by necessity."[3] How many of these ideas were first brought to Johnson's attention or given focus by Crousaz cannot now be known, but it is certain that many of the ideas first given expression here were to occupy Johnson's mind for the remainder of his life.

CRITICAL ANNOTATION

Annotations for a translation differ significantly from those for an original composition. No attempt has been made here to annotate Crousaz's or Du Resnel's work; rather the focus of the annotations is on Johnson's translation. The assumption has been that this edition is for a scholarly audience with a reading knowledge of French. Annotations are largely limited to citations of significant departures from the meaning or narrative progression of the French text, and to a representative selection of citations which show Johnson's method of translation. A photocopy of the unique 1739 *Commentary* in the Beinecke Rare Book and Manuscript Library, Yale University, available in the Garland Press Popeiana series, has been compared with a photocopy of the French 1737 *Commentaire* in the Cornell University Library. The French in the annotations is reproduced exactly to enable the reader to see what Johnson saw as he translated. Crousaz quotes Du Resnel's poem in its entirety, except for an occasionally omitted line, and the references to Du Resnel are to the poem as it appears in Crousaz, unless otherwise indicated. The poem as it appears in Crousaz, however, has been compared with a photocopy of the 1737 first edition of Du Resnel's *Les Principes de la*

---

3. *Sermons,* ed. Jean H. Hagstrum and James Gray (Vol. XIV, Yale Edition of the Works of Samuel Johnson, 1978), p. 56. Sermon 5 is SJ's fullest treatment of the problem of evil. Other discussions of various aspects of the problem, particularly freedom of the will, appear in the review of Jenyns' *Free Inquiry* below, pp. 389–432; *Rambler* 29, 32, 41, 43, 52, 128, 150; *Adventurer* 120; *Idler* 11, 89; *Lives* ("Life of Milton"), I.136–38 (pars. 118–22); ("Life of Pope"), III.173–75 (pars. 202–6); ("Life of Gray"), III.433 (par. 26); *Life,* II.82, 104; III.290–91; IV.71, 328–29; V.117, 366. See also *Rasselas and Other Tales,* ed. Gwin J. Kolb (Vol. XVI, Yale Edition of the Works of Samuel Johnson, 1990), pp. 67, 81, 101–3, 112–13, 122–23, 164–65.

INTRODUCTION   liii

morale et du goût in the Columbia University Library with occasional departures given in the annotations. References to Charles Forman's translation are to the British Library copy of the *Commentary* reproduced in the Garland Press Popeiana series. When, for one reason or another, Johnson's translation of a French word seemed unusual, copies of Abel Boyer's 1699 *Dictionnaire Royale* were consulted in the British Library and the Huntington Library.[4] A few of his definitions are included in the annotations.

Du Resnel's poem is part translation, part original, so that an exact correspondence between it and Pope's *Essay on Man* cannot be worked out. Nevertheless, some passages from Pope are included in the annotations, especially when Johnson is making a point about Du Resnel's departure from the original. For convenience, all citations are from Maynard Mack's edition of the *Essay on Man* in the Twickenham Pope, given by line number in parenthesis. The second line number in the parenthesis is to the second volume of the *Works of Alexander Pope* (London: Printed for Lawton Gilliver, 1736), in the William Andrews Clark Memorial Library.[5] If only one line number appears, the reader should assume the line numbers are the same in both editions. Among the various editions of the *Essay on Man* available to Johnson, the 1736 *Works* seems the best choice as it contains many of the textual readings found in the *Commentary*. There are, however, several discrepancies in the textual readings. Either Johnson had a made-up copy of the *Essay* containing the variant readings or, as is highly probable, he is quoting from memory.

Johnson translated the *Commentary* in the winter of 1738–39, long before the publication of his major works. Therefore, only some particularly striking or interesting parallel in words or ideas between the translation of Crousaz's *Commentaire* or Du Resnel's "Discours" and one of Johnson's later works, including the *Dictionary*, has been recorded. Neither of these works by Crousaz or Du Resnel has much originality. Johnson shared a number of the ideas with both men, ideas which were the common property of many others at the same time and which were drawn, perhaps, from similar sources. No attempt has been made to determine in an anno-

4. See p. xliii, n. 9.
5. No. 430 in Reginald Harvey Griffith, *Alexander Pope: A Bibliography* (1927), Vol. I, Pt. II, p. 343.

tation whether or not an idea of Johnson's may have originated in one of these works. Johnson's own footnotes, however, are treated as original compositions and annotated in the usual way.

THE TEXT

As with many eighteenth-century works, the autograph manuscript of the *Commentary* has disappeared. The 1739 first edition of the *Commentary*, printed from Johnson's lost autograph manuscript, is the only authoritative text and has been chosen as copy-text for this edition. The first edition contains relatively few errors, suggesting that Johnson read proofs carefully. Before the work was reissued in late 1741 the leaf containing the 1739 title page was cancelled and replaced by a bifolium with a 1742 title page on the first leaf and an errata on the verso of the second leaf correcting four errors discovered by Johnson. These are corrected in the text and reported in the textual notes.

In the present edition no attempt has been made to achieve a general consistency in spelling and punctuation. The spelling and punctuation of the 1739 first edition have been retained except when they are clearly in error, or when they obscure meaning or distract the attention of the reader. Johnson follows Du Resnel's verse closely, placing his English word directly below the French. In the vast majority of cases the punctuation of the English line follows exactly that of the French line above. When occasionally the punctuation of the two lines differs, the 1737 first edition of Du Resnel's poem has been consulted. Even though hundreds of changes in punctuation and spelling were made from the first edition of Du Resnel when Crousaz reprinted the poem, in all but one or two instances it has been able to serve as a final arbiter. Johnson, as well as Cave's compositors, follows Crousaz's text closely, and the few differences in punctuation are likely errors in copying by Johnson or the compositor; they have been silently emended. Any changes in spelling or textual readings have been recorded in the textual notes. All emendations to the copy-text, except those listed by Johnson in the errata, have been made on the authority of the editor.

Capitalization and typography have been modernized following the editorial practice of the Yale Edition of the Works of Samuel

INTRODUCTION

Johnson. Hyphenated words at the line-end have been adjusted according to the usual practice of the first edition insofar as that practice could be ascertained from other appearances or parallels. All turned letters or wrong fonts have been corrected, the long *s* has been replaced by the modern *s*, and "ae" and "oe" have not been treated as digraphs. Display capitals have not been exactly reproduced. Quotations have been indicated according to modern practice, and the punctuation in relation to the quotation marks has been normalized. The length of dashes and the space around them have also been normalized according to modern practice. "Mr" (without a point) is the dominant form in the copy-text and has been adopted throughout. Capitals have been retained or added for all references to God, hence "Creator," "Supreme Being," "the Deity," "the Almighty," "Universal Father," and so on. Proper names in italics have been changed to roman. Book titles have been placed consistently in italics.

As John Smith notes in *The Printer's Grammar* (1755), "By the Laws of Printing, indeed, a Compositor should abide by his Copy, and not vary from it. . . . But this good law is now looked upon as obsolete, and most Authors expect the Printer to spell, point, and digest their Copy, that it may be intelligible and significant to the Reader; which is what the Compositor and Corrector jointly have regard to, in Works of their own language." The compositor peruses his copy but, before beginning to compose, "should be informed, either by the Author, or Master, after what manner our work is to be done; whether the old way, with Capitals to Substantives, and Italic to Proper names; or after the more neat practice, all in Roman, and Capitals to Proper names and emphatical words," and nothing "in Italic but what is underscored in our Copy."[6] Johnson, following Smith's scheme, would be both author and corrector. The *Commentary* is printed in the old way, with capitals to substantives and italic to proper names supplied by the compositor. Johnson, of course, like most writers, did not underline proper names, and was inconsistent in his use of capitals for substantives. In fact, Johnson uses capitals for substantives infrequently. Such capitals and italics

---

6. See pp. 199, 201–2, 209. Joseph Moxon makes a similar point in *Mechanic Exercises on the Whole Art of Printing* (1683–84), ed. Herbert Davis and Harry Carter (1962), pp. 192, 219, 250.

supplied by Johnson can, no more than the punctuation, be separated from those supplied by the compositor. To put it another way, Johnson may have had no control over these aspects of the text. He could, however, control the use of various typographical features for emphasis. Although it is the practice of the Yale Edition to modernize capitals and italics, on occasion, when Johnson is being emphatic about the relative merits of the English and French verse the italics on *English* and *French* have been retained. Apart from eliminating italics for most proper names, all others have been retained. The compositor would have had no idea what was intended for emphasis, and must have been supplied with a copy marked by Johnson. All words and passages in italics or in large and small capitals, therefore, must have been marked in the copy by Johnson for emphasis. It should be remembered that Johnson almost certainly corrected the work for the press, not only as one of his editorial chores for Cave, but as the author, and gave at least tacit approval to the formal presentation of the text.

In order to have all of Johnson's text in roman, his English translation of Du Resnel's verse is here in roman and the French in italics, reversing the usage of the copy-text. Cave habitually omitted accents when printing French, and this feature has been retained. In a small way the absence of accents, when coupled with his literal translation, perhaps reveals Johnson's contempt for Du Resnel's French verse. Also Johnson's inconsistent line numbers in the margins for Du Resnel's verse have here been normalized. The running heads in this edition of the *Commentary* reflect those in the copy-text.

The present edition has been printed from the copy of the 1739 first edition in the Beinecke Rare Book and Manuscript Library, Yale University. This copy was bibliographically collated against the eleven known copies of the 1742 issue.[7]

---

7. Copies: British Library, Bodleian, Cornell University, Harvard University, Yale University, University of Iowa, University of Illinois, University of North Carolina at Chapel Hill, Gerald M. Goldberg Collection, Hyde Collection (2).

SHORT TITLES

Boyer: *Dictionnaire Royale,* 1699.
Dictionary: Johnson's *Dictionary of the English Language,* 2 vols., 1755.
Fleeman, *Bibliography: A Bibliography of the Works of Samuel Johnson,*
    compiled J. D. Fleeman, 2 vols., 2000.
Letters: The Letters of Samuel Johnson, ed. Bruce Redford, 5 vols., 1992–94.
Life: Boswell's *Life of Johnson,* ed. G. B. Hill, revised and enlarged by L. F.
    Powell, 6 vols., 1934–50; vols. 5–6 (2d ed.), 1964.
Lives: Lives of the English Poets, ed. G. B. Hill, 3 vols., 1905.

A COMMENTARY ON MR. POPE'S PRINCIPLES OF MORALITY, OR ESSAY ON MAN

CONTENTS

Actions, in appearance virtuous, may spring from vice.	163
The present satisfactions and advantages of virtue illustrated by two examples.	164
An explication of Pope's doctrine of the ruling passion.	166
Virtue will guide the passions right.	167
The conduct of a man actuated only by present advantage.	169
The gradations by which men advance in false notions.	172
How little excusable in the sight of God.	173
Frenchmen always introduce love. Note	175
Men do not equally promote the general good.	176
Neither *shame, rashness,* nor *vanity* necessary.	180
The fear of death useful.	183
The *English* not enough afraid of it.	184
Discontent frequent in few states.	186
All conditions not equally happy.	187
Pride not a blessing.	189
Security in the highest degree dangerous.	191
Self-love implanted by God.	193

Epist. III.

Man the author of his own destiny.	197
Comparison between the natural system and society.	197
Nothing in reality annihilated.	198
The states of brutes and man with regard to their knowledge of futurity compared.	203
The superiority of reason to instinct.	207
Different orders of being not related to each other.	211
Nature, the term explained.	217
The primitive religion according to Pope.	218
The original of government.	228
Pope's meaning mistaken.	230
The causes of faction.	233
The original of depravities in religion.	234
Gradations by which men attain'd divine honours.	235
None but good men sincerely promote the good of others.	238
Self-love and the love of God concur to produce happiness.	244

Epist. IV.

Happiness, according to Pope, easily attainable.	249

Pope does not direct his reader to happiness.	251
Nature, the meaning of that term.	251
A man supposed to be sent into the world in the full strength of his reason.	252
How he would naturally reason.	252
How gladly he would receive information.	253
The exalted happiness of devotion.	254
Happiness attainable by different abilities.	259
How the balance of heaven is kept equal.	262
Men not always sollicitous about their own merit.	265
Men not wholly good or bad.	265
Character of a libertine.	266
Men not always desirous of esteem of the good.	267
Length or shortness of life no proofs of God's favour or anger.	270
Physical and moral events not connected.	272
If all actions are necessary, why is any suffering produced by them?	275
All difficulties removed by admitting free-will.	276
Resignation, a virtue produced by vice.	276

Persecution and malignity no characters of a Christian.	277
Providence for just reasons snatch'd away Titus as well as Caesar.	278
Miraculous assistance not the proper reward of virtue.	280
False notions of riches and honour.	285
Every man conscious of his liberty.	293
Necessary actions not punishable.	293
Pope's inconsistencies.	294
The abuse of power.	295
Superior parts, their value.	296
Contrast of benevolence and malignity in learned men.	297
True method of defeating envy.	298
A small number of pious families retiring to a desart island, their conduct.	304
Causes of the decay of families.	305
The virtues exerted in giving and receiving.	305
Happiness not the peculiar property of deep reasoners.	307
Pope's picture of a virtuous man.	310

CONTENTS.

Letter to Mr Crousaz.	21
The inconsistency of a position with an author's other tenets no proof that he does not maintain it.	21
The weakness of human understanding a common plea.	22
Language full of ambiguities.	23
From thence a confusion of ideas.	23
This the schools have not rectified but encreased.	23
Instance of opposite opinions.	24
Cause of ignorance.	25
The reigns of opposite systems.	26
The absurd philosophy of Leibnitz.	27
Negatives easy.	28
Reasons for which opinions are received.	29
Some brains adapted to absurdity.	29
Fatalism, an opinion favourable to interest.	30
Oppositions between fatalism and practice.	30
Fatalists never regulate their lives by their system.	31

The fluctuation of the mind inclined to fatalism.	31
Fatalists unjustly lay claim to the suffrages of the divines.	32
Free-will asserted by divines.	33
Man, if fatality be allowed, not a moral agent.	33

Comment on Epist. I.

Crousaz, formerly a cultivator of logic, now a reader of morality.	35
How Crousaz discovers Resnel's deviations from his original.	36
Two of Mr Pope's lines translated into eight.	37
Modesty a proper qualification of a moralist.	38
Comparison of retirement and publick life.	38
Enquiry what is to be understood by *nature*.	41
Enquiries instead of information.	45
The *first cause* absolutely necessary.	46
Perversion of the term *necessary existence*.	47
Creation an act of choice.	48
Different orders of being.	48
The perfection of the universe limited.	49
Therefore might have been different.	49

CONTENTS

Neither physical nor moral evils necessary.	52
The history of the *fall* to be considered.	53
Questions relating to moral agency.	53
The fall of the angels.	54
Man pitied because tempted.	54
God distinguishes errors from crimes.	55
Man has the power of exalting his nature.	55
The horse and ox made our teachers.	57
Many of our errors arise from vice.	58
The knowledge of the horse no standard.	59
Man, whether as perfect as he ought.	59
Description of Mr Pope and his associates.	60
Desire of prying into futurity culpable.	61
Mr Pope mis-interpreted by Crousaz. *Note*	64
Reasons for which God frustrates mens designs.	64
Uses of self-love.	66
Pope mis-represented. *Note*	65
The progress of the mind in divine truth.	66
Balance, the meaning of it in Pope.	67

Hero and *sparrow*, whether of equal value.	68
Nature, what Pope means by it.	71
Life not to be possessed with indifference.	72
Pope mis-represented. *Notes*	72, 73
Imperfection not in God but man.	75
A good man's gratitude for life.	77
Pope represented as a Catholic, why.	78
Devil's malice produces good effects.	80
False humility.	82
God not necessitated to the present form of the universe.	84
The elements and passions improperly compar'd.	86
God not the author of moral evil.	88
Desires of universal virtue not ridiculous.	89
Storms and crimes not parallel.	90
Good effects of sorrow for sin.	91
Picture of a fool.	92
Different imports of the word *nature*.	92
Pope's direction to happiness insufficient.	93
The true way to happiness.	94

CONTENTS

Picture of Pope's Indian consider'd.	97
Des Cartes's rule for reasoners.	100
Superiority of man to the brutes.	102
The universe not unalterable in its parts.	106
The power of acting, in men, *free*.	110
The virtue and happiness of the poor.	111
The parts of the universe not naturally tending to separation.	112
God not the author of evil.	113
The translation remarkably excellent.	114
Nature of submission to the Supreme Being.	115
Pope's inconsistency.	116
Chance not incident to God.	117
Vice universally an evil.	118
Some physical events imputable to vice.	119
In what sense *whatever is is right*.	120

Epist. II.

The necessity of studying ourselves.	121
Pope's picture of life considered.	123

Newton really an *ape* according to the Leibnitzian system.	130
Self-love and reason consistent.	134
Reason conducts us to religion.	135
Self-love sometimes errs.	136
Passions arise from self-love.	138
Stoical indolence.	140
Passions conduce to virtue.	140
Evils arising from the passions.	142
Nonsense imputed to Pope.	143
The notion of a *ruling passion* unjust. Note	145
Passions operate differently on different men.	147
Reason not chargeable with our faults.	148
Passions may be subdu'd——The Abbe de St Cyran.	151
The true method of conquering our passions.	155
Advantages of society.	156
Vices though not implanted by God, become his instruments of justice.	156
Eternal Artificer, the expression examined.	159
The true original and use of the passions.	161

CONTENTS 9

Actions, in appearance virtuous, may spring from vice.	163
The present satisfactions and advantages of virtue illustrated by two examples.	164
An explication of Pope's doctrine of the ruling passion.	166
Virtue will guide the passions right.	167
The conduct of a man actuated only by present advantage.	169
The gradations by which men advance in false notions.	172
How little excusable in the sight of God.	173
Frenchmen always introduce love. Note	175
Men do not equally promote the general good.	176
Neither *shame, rashness,* nor *vanity* necessary.	180
The fear of death useful.	183
The *English* not enough afraid of it.	184
Discontent frequent in few states.	186
All conditions not equally happy.	187
Pride not a blessing.	189
Security in the highest degree dangerous.	191
Self-love implanted by God.	193

Epist. III.

Man the author of his own destiny.	197
Comparison between the natural system and society.	197
Nothing in reality annihilated.	198
The states of brutes and man with regard to their knowledge of futurity compared.	203
The superiority of reason to instinct.	207
Different orders of being not related to each other.	211
Nature, the term explained.	217
The primitive religion according to Pope.	218
The original of government.	228
Pope's meaning mistaken.	230
The causes of faction.	233
The original of depravities in religion.	234
Gradations by which men attain'd divine honours.	235
None but good men sincerely promote the good of others.	238
Self-love and the love of God concur to produce happiness.	244

Epist. IV.

Happiness, according to Pope, easily attainable.	249

CONTENTS

Pope does not direct his reader to happiness.	251
Nature, the meaning of that term.	251
A man supposed to be sent into the world in the full strength of his reason.	252
How he would naturally reason.	252
How gladly he would receive information.	253
The exalted happiness of devotion.	254
Happiness attainable by different abilities.	259
How the balance of heaven is kept equal.	262
Men not always sollicitous about their own merit.	265
Men not wholly good or bad.	265
Character of a libertine.	266
Men not always desirous of esteem of the good.	267
Length or shortness of life no proofs of God's favour or anger.	270
Physical and moral events not connected.	272
If all actions are necessary, why is any suffering produced by them?	275
All difficulties removed by admitting free-will.	276
Resignation, a virtue produced by vice.	276

Persecution and malignity no characters of a Christian.	277
Providence for just reasons snatch'd away Titus as well as Caesar.	278
Miraculous assistance not the proper reward of virtue.	280
False notions of riches and honour.	285
Every man conscious of his liberty.	293
Necessary actions not punishable.	293
Pope's inconsistencies.	294
The abuse of power.	295
Superior parts, their value.	296
Contrast of benevolence and malignity in learned men.	297
True method of defeating envy.	298
A small number of pious families retiring to a desart island, their conduct.	304
Causes of the decay of families.	305
The virtues exerted in giving and receiving.	305
Happiness not the peculiar property of deep reasoners.	307
Pope's picture of a virtuous man.	310

CONTENTS	13
Benevolence how founded.	311
Orders of being for which we have no regard.	312
Enquiry (supposed) how much we love the inhabitants of *Saturn*.	313
How we are to regard the angels.	314
Consequences of a supposition that all the parts of the universe depend on each other.	315
Self-love unrestrained prejudicial to society.	316
The true motives to the love of others.	320
Pope's conclusive address to his patron.	321
Conjecture about the manner in which Pope compiled his essays.	321
Pope's contradictions.	321
The power of Pope's poetry.	322
His doctrines only received because they flatter pride.	323
The uncertainty of Mr Pope's reasonings.	325
Letter to Crousaz.	327
Crousaz's answer.	327
The principles of some Leibnitzians.	327
Stupidity of many of that sect.	328

14　A COMMENTARY

Reasons against their system.

First, it is not certain that God was determined to one only scheme of creation.	329
Second, a creation of free agents most worthy of God.	329
Third, it is inconsistent with philosophy.	329
Instances of this inconsistency.	330
Criminals according to this system unjustly punished.	331
Resnel not conscious of his own writings.	332
Every man transformed by every new object.	333
The motives that produced this system, and call in adherents to it.	334
The Leibnitzian system unworthy of a wise man.	335
A man according to it can only be sure of his own existence.	335
The Leibnitzians without any test of truth.	335
Ludicrous account of the contest between two controvertists, according to Leibnitz's system.	336
History of a man who denied the reality of human existence.	337
The ill consequence of indulging odd actions in private without communicating them.	339
Danger of romantic histories.	340

CONTENTS

Resnel's Preface.

Present taste in France.	343
Attacks of critics upon Pope.	344
Reasons for translating the *Essay on Criticism*.	344
Reasons for adding the *Essay on Man*.	344
Use of the *Essay on Man*.	345
General plan of the four epistles.	346
Pope a Catholic.	348
Pope's excellencies.	349
Poetry cannot be translated but into poetry.	351
Brevity of the English language.	351
Conciseness of Pope's essays.	352
How to be imitated.	353
Delicacy of the French.	353
Taste of the French complied with.	354
The propagation of the English language.	355
The writings of English and Italians compared.	356
General accounts have always many exceptions.	357
Difference between the English and French writers.	357

The English leave room for reflection.	357
The French exhaust their sentiments.	358
The English less delicate than the French.	358
The English do not allow the French to be poets.	358
England the *country of the spleen.*	359
Addison's character of the English.	359
The French strict observers of rules.	360
Not easy to decide between different nations.	360
Montaigne, la Bruyere, Bossuet, admired.	361
Pope's simile of the apothecaries.	362
Homer's descriptions defended.	363
Fontanini's defence of the Italians.	364
We have too little knowledge of foreign authors, and are too nearly acquainted with our own.	365
Opinions of the best critics different.	366
Quintilian's precept to critics.	368
The ancients to be reverenced and followed.	369
The laws of a strict translation.	370

CONTENTS

The disadvantages of close translations.	371
Charact. of Roboton's version of *Essay on Criticism*.	372
The stile of *didactic* writers.	373
Method of reading Mr Pope.	374
Bp Atterbury's opinion of imitation.	375

Cum habeant iter rectum, devios sequuntur anfractus.——*His consulendum est, ne contra se pugnent, velintque se tandem ab inveteratis erroribus liberari, quod utique facient, si quare sint nati aliquando perviderint. Haec enim pravitatis causa ignoratio sui, quam si quis cognita veritate discusserit, sciet quo referenda & quemadmodum sibi vita degenda sit. Cujus scientiae summam breviter circumscribo, ut neque religio ulla sine sapientia suscipienda sit, neque ulla sine religione probanda sapientia.* Lactant. Lib. I. Cap. I.

The meaning of Lactantius in these words is, that reason and revelation, religion and good sense should go together. He likewise traces our disorders to their source, *the ignorance of what we are.* The knowledge of ourselves will immediately shew the end to which we are to direct our steps, and the path that will lead us to it. We may see here to what a deplorable degree that man is blinded, who having the misfortune of being too much applauded by others, lives and dies without knowing himself. *Qui notus nimis omnibus, ignotus moritur sibi.*

Advertisement to the Reader.

The author of this little performance is very far from being asham'd of his zeal for the defence of religion. The reader will find in the following letter the reasons and the occasion of this commentary.

The Abbe du Resnel had certainly no intention of composing his poem for the gratification of libertines; but the heart of man having a strong tendency to infidelity, too much application cannot be used, to take away all pretences of forming doubts, and all occasions of strengthening them. To this end the writer of this commentary thought it might contribute.

A LETTER WRITTEN TO MR CROUSAZ
ON HIS *EXAMEN* OF
MR POPE'S *ESSAY ON MAN*.

Sir,[1]
I am too well acquainted with you to apprehend that I shall not give you pleasure, by informing you what has been thought of your work, in which you have applied yourself to free Mr Pope from the suspicion of adhering to the Leibnitzian system of fatality. Your strongest arguments against the justice of that imputation are drawn from the inconsistencies into which Mr Pope would fall: but some urge, that if this method of reasoning be followed, we must never allow ourselves to be persuaded that any author has embraced an erroneous opinion, and endeavoured to establish it in his writings, unless he be so fond of singularity as at once to renounce all truth; since there is no error, but what is inconsistent with a certain number of truths, either greater or less. This objection, Sir, makes your apology, in its present form, considered as discovering a way, by persuing which, authors may shield themselves from any accusation, what notions soever they may be desirous[2] of propagating in their works. For whatever opposition may be discovered between these new opinions and received principles, and however they may find their own consciences recoil, they may entirely get clear, by scattering here and there a few lines conformable to the notions which the world is prepossessed in favour of, or at least to expressions which custom has authorised, and with which mankind have been used to satisfy themselves. This objection, which, as you see, Sir, is not without its weight, appeared new to me, as well as others to whom I communicated it, and who, like me, on account of its novelty, suspected it of being sophistical.

---

1. The salutation is an SJ addition.
2. notions . . . desirous: "sentimens qu'ils ayent à coeur" (p. 2).

But when I came to consider it more nearly, and with greater attention, I thought it not so new as at first, and am assured that you yourself will immediately be of the same opinion.——A man maintains and reverences an opinion which to others appears horrible, and is desired by them to attend to the dreadful consequences which according to their notions flow naturally from it. The defender of the opinion, attack'd with these detestable deductions, answers without scruple;[3] *I condemn these consequences, and, like you, think them shocking and abominable, but deny that they follow from my principle.* Instruct us then, replies his opponent, on this important point, set us free from so tormenting a scruple, and shew us the real contrariety of your principles to these consequences which you yourself hold in detestation. That, alas, returns he, is not to be expected, our minds are not formed equal to subjects so great, nor are they able to comprehend them with the clearness of evidence; they are, in short, too weak to rise to that sublime light, which alone is capable of reconciling these consequences with these principles. If, after having returned an answer in this humble strain,[4] he sees himself still charged with these hateful consequences, he conceives himself unquestionably entitled to complain in the most open manner of injustice, and in private even of calumny. It appears that human weakness has for a long time pretended to the melancholy privilege of contradicting itself, at least, appearing to contradict itself with impunity: or, if this is not altogether the case, it comes very near it, and it is still with some degree of impunity. It is by virtue of this weakness and this miserable privilege, that those who have but a confused and imperfect view of things, imagine that they may justly demand the kind assistance of better eyes.[5]——These were almost the very words in which I expressed myself in my small company of friends, and this open'd the way to a conversation, of which

---

3. without scruple: "hardiment" (p. 3).

4. after having returned . . . strain: "Après cette humble réponse" (p. 4).

5. imagine . . . better eyes: "se comptent en droit d'exiger des yeux plus éclairés, un charitable support" (p. 5).

I think myself under an obligation to send you a short account.

The language of men is crouded with equivocal words, and with terms imperfectly defined, which have no clear or distinct ideas annexed to them. It is full even of forms of speech that express ideas destructive of each other, but of which we do not apply ourselves to observe the contrariety. On this point we all agreed, and no-body gave himself the trouble to produce instances, which he knew would be superfluous to the whole company.

It is therefore not at all surprising, if in the conversation of those who content themselves with speaking like other men, and make use of common terms as of current money, we meet with so many ill-coupled and inconsistent expressions,[6] more particularly when they give themselves leave to rise above their ordinary sphere of thought.[7] There are few that endeavour to make their ideas clear, to disentangle them from obscurity, and afterwards to select words that may express them properly, and present them clearly and distinctly such as they conceive them in their own minds.

We observed that the greatest part of the schools have been so far from producing remedies for this evil, that they have contributed to increase it. A set of maxims, there called *axioms* or *canons*,[8] must be looked on with reverence. The expression in these is equivocal, but considered as sacred, and appeal'd to as decisive;[9] in this respect each party is in possession of its own *codex*,[1] distinct from all others. In favour of a system new rules are contrived, which are commanded to be reverenced as the maxims of right reason. New bounds are set to the understanding, or, according to the present exigence, those that confin'd it before are overthrown. Terms stamp'd with the mark of the system are the only current coin, a man must be either content with them or be hooted at; to demand any

---

6. many ill-coupled . . . expressions: "tant de *galimatias*" (pp. 5–6).
7. "of thought" added by SJ.
8. *axioms* or *canons*: "Canons" (p. 6).
9. The expression . . . decisive: "C'est un langage équivoque, mais décisif & sacré" (p. 6).
1. *codex*: "*Code*" (p. 6).

explanation of words authorised by the author of the system, is to make an open declaration of ignorance. He distinguishes himself most eminently by his abilities, who best knows how to perplex the question in debate, and his only equal in reputation is he who understands how to evade his pursuit, by involving himself, in his turn, in darkness; as the gods of Homer wrapt their favourite heroes in a cloud to withdraw them from the war, when the danger was too great for human strength. On this head of the conversation we allow'd ourselves to allege a number of instances, which I shall not repeat, since your eyes and ears will supply you with too many. We then came back to the principal subject, the inconsistencies into which men fall without perceiving them, and the obstinacy with which they rather chuse to adhere to error, than quit it for the enjoyment of pure and simple truth, with which they have imprudently confounded it. He to whose turn it came to speak, from the place which he had by accident in the company, began his reflections in these very words:

Take a child of eight or nine years old, or if you please somewhat more, of whose education at least common care has been taken, and whose memory has been particularly cultivated.[a] If this child be of a bold and resolute temper, and practised in his lessons, he will answer all your questions without mistakes, and without confusion; but still the more periods he shall repeat, the less clear ideas shall he have of all that he has said. Would you have a clear and incontestable evidence of this, go to some great city where every communion of Christians has the liberty of educating their children in their own opinions. Ask any number among them,[2] if there is not beyond comparison a greater reverence due to the voice of God than to that of human reason, every one will answer without the least hesitation that undoubtedly there *is*.

Examine then every one of these children separately upon

---

a. cultivated,

---

2. Ask . ... them: "Demandez à deux, à trois, à quatre d'entr'eux" (p. 8).

each of the opinions that are subjects of dispute, and when you have heard his answer, ask him farther—but is this answer of yours agreeable[3] to that profound respect, and that entire preference which is due to the voice of God *above the voice of reason?* Undoubtedly, says one of them, for when God speaks, I oblige my reason to silence. But another will say, I should evidently fall short of the infinite respect which is due to God, if I should ascribe to the words of his revelation a sense contrary to reason. Here is then, according to one, a plain opposition between the respect due to God, and the interpretation given by the other to his words. But, says the other, you must pardon me, if I affirm that the opposition is on your side. Here is now a real contrariety on one side or the other, which neither is sensible of, for each denies the consequence that infers that contrariety. The number of contradictions will increase with the number of questions proposed, and of opinions by which the different communions of Christians are distinguished one from another. Want of ability to examine, reverence to parents, deference to the masters to whose care we have been committed by those to whom we owe our birth, and prepossession in favour of their instructions, are the reasons which make us adhere to particular modes of speech,[4] and flatter ourselves that we see with sufficient clearness what is entirely out of our sight. The same principles of prejudice and error follow our youth to the universities, where according to the opinions then prevailing every man forms his notions, and continues to maintain them all his life.

In our early years we are incapable of examining, and afterwards *Indolence*,[5] which takes away the courage necessary for such an attempt, represents the labour of it greater than it is, and makes us turn our thoughts from the harrassing design of surmounting it. You are now left, or going to be left, says a father to his son, to your own conduct, 'tis your busi-

---

3. but . . . agreeable: "*Mais cette Réponse que vous venez de faire, est-elle conforme*" (p. 9).

4. and prepossession . . . speech: "sont cause qu'on s'attache à des mots" (p. 10).

5. Capitalization and italics are added; the French is "paresse" (p. 10).

ness now to turn your thoughts and your endeavours to the attainment of glory, and the improvement of your fortune. I have put you into the hands of a great man, who is among the learned what your sovereign will be among kings. You will be heard and applauded proportionably to the care you take to repeat his notions. I have recommended you to *His Excellency,* and have obtained for you a promise of his protection. Remember to deserve his notice, deviate not from his measures to the right or to the left, his steps are the path of honour, and it is by being commended by him that you are to rise. Upon such principles as these the world has been successively devoted to Aristotle, to Descartes, &c.

There was a time, when to establish a reputation, and raise a fortune, it was necessary to speak in the same manner with Aristotle, and the most approved of his commentators, and complaints have been made that some terms, very little understood, were borrowed from philosophy by divinity, and having been treated with respect in the lower schools, became likewise formidable in the highest. The followers of Descartes did not oblige themselves to pursue with exactness the paths which he had open'd, and so strongly recommended. One part of his scholars contented themselves with[6] repeating his words, and applying them at random. The *materia subtilis* was the engine of war,[7] which was made use of to explain several phaenomena, in which it had not the principal part, and they gave each other authority, by mutual examples, to talk much without learning the subject of discourse.[8] When Sir Isaac Newton's philosophy became the fashion, we saw young gentlemen look down upon all others with contempt,[9] because they carried in their hands[1] the principles of that great man, which they understood very imperfectly, and were very

---

6. contented themselves with: "se borna" (p. 12).

7. engine of war: "Cheval de Bataille" (p. 12). SJ appears to be confusing "cheval de bataille" (charger or war-horse) with "cheval de frise" (engine of war).

8. without learning . . . discourse: "sans répandre que très peu de lumiére" (p. 12).

9. look down . . . contempt: "regarder tout au dessous d'eux" (p. 12).

1. in their hands: "sous leurs bras" (p. 12).

unsuccessful in their attempts to apply them. The philosophy of Mr Leibnitz has made a noise in the schools, and his party has exerted itself with great warmth and zeal to bring it into credit.[2] They have fixed *definitions* in their memories, without being much concerned whether they have any foundation in reason, or are merely arbitrary. They have filled their minds with *aphorisms, distinctions, propositions,* and *demonstrations* real or pretended.[3] With all this, his scholars have raised, in[b] their own imaginations, a throne,[4] from which they look with pity upon all who do not own the authority of their master. But after having rang'd the system in their memories, there was a necessity of fortifying it against objections. The consequences that necessarily arise from that philosophy with a force of evidence that compels assent (if any such evidence can be) are such as would be sufficient to over-turn the best-concerted system. Against these violent attacks his defenders furnish their scholars with an entrenchment, made invincible, like the enchanted castles of old, by a charm of words, NEGO CONSEQUENTIAM: spare not to repeat those two words,[5] and they will bring you off victorious from every dispute. This defence appears absurd, and in reality is so: but one must have had very little acquaintance with mankind, and made very few reflections upon their conversation, and their obstinacy, not to know that there are men (and in greater numbers than would be easily imagined) that are stupid enough to satisfy themselves with these words, and applaud themselves for their pretended victories which they gain by their assistance: it is entirely vain to tell them that, *Plus negaret asinus in hora,*

b. on

---

2. his party . . . credit: "son parti s'est empressé à la mettre en crédit, avec un zéle des plus vifs" (p. 12).

3. They have filled . . . pretended: "On en a gravé les *Définitions* dans sa Mémoire, fondées ou arbitraires, c'est de quoi on s'est peu embarrassé. *Aphorismes, Distinctions, Propositions, Démonstrations* vrayes ou prétenduës" (pp. 12–13).

4. With . . . throne: "A tout cela les Ecoliers ont élevé dans leur esprit un thrône" (p. 13).

5. NEGO CONSEQUENTIAM: spare . . . words: "*Nego Consequentiam.* Ne vous lassez jamais de repeter ces deux mots" (p. 13). NEGO CONSEQUENTIAM: of no importance; unimportant.

&c. "An ass may deny more propositions in an hour, than a philosopher can prove in his whole life." This maxim was not made for them, but for other people.[6]

The dullest genius's are generally the most obstinate; their dullness makes them slothful, and a man must be far from such dispositions, to re-examine a system which he has once adopted, on account of some difficulties that perplex it. A young man has been bred up from his childhood in some principles of virtue: he has heard a thousand[7] times that virtue will be rewarded, and vice punished, and punished with the utmost justice. These truths are so strongly supported by conscience, that is by certain sentiments which the Divine Providence has adapted the heart of man to the reception of, that many good people never suffer them to be effaced. When he is grown up, he enters the school, where he hears a doctrine, that strikes him with astonishment, boldly advanced from men of great reputation. *Don't be frighted* (say they to these young men who are to be initiated);[c] *contract the happy custom of denying consequences, keep the precepts that were dictated to you for the direction of your childhood, and add to them those which we now recommend; by these means you will enrich your mind with knowledge, without impoverishing it in virtue.* But these second lessons are directly contrary to the first. *Never perplex yourself about that appearance of contrariety, deny that there is any such, and act as if there were none.* This is the manner (says he, whose discourse I am now epitomising) in which I conceive that heavy souls, that have been early tinctured with principles of probity, which they still continue to preserve and esteem, may live at peace in themselves, notwithstanding the opposition between a speculative system, which they value themselves upon maintaining, and rules of practice, of which they do not deny the obligation. There are others of a more sprightly

---

c. initiated)^

---

6. This maxim . . . people: "C'est pour les autres, & non pour eux, qu'ils comptent que cette Maxime est reçûë" (p. 14).

7. thousand: "cent" (p. 14).

genius, who might be perplexed with ideas so opposite to each other, but that they resolve to take their choice among them, to adhere to some and refuse others.

Were men to determine themselves only by evidence (adds a third of my friends) it would be impossible that any one should be persuaded of the truth of a proposition to-day, and to-morrow admit one directly contradictory, without revoking his assent to the former. But it falls out that men make resolutions to affirm or to deny; in a word, they agree to propositions, and adopt them upon principles very different from demonstration. A man yields to an assertion because it pleases him, and it pleases him because it favours some private lurking inclination, or some passion which he is determined not to part with. He denies the truth of another, because he has conceived a dislike of the author of it.

There are some disorder'd brains adapted to wild opinions. There are families to be met with, distinguished by their taste for absurdities. I have known a man who maintain'd that the hour of death was inevitably fix'd, that all precautions against it were entirely fruitless,[8] and that if the last fatal moment were not yet arriv'd, a man might expose himself to destruction without hazard. *This,* said we, *is affirming that if you had this morning been thrown from a tower, you would have received no hurt, since we have you here safe and well; come take a leap from the window, the danger is nothing, for if your last hour be come, you must die immediately of an apoplexy.* "I am not," answer'd he, "in any apprehension of shortening my life by such an experiment, but the reason that hinders me from trying it is, that I am not inclin'd." Needs there any other proof[9] that there are many kinds and degrees of madness?

Great numbers would reject, in the strongest terms, a proposal of declaring in favour of an opinion, if they had not some interest to serve by appearing in its defence.[1] They per-

---

8. That all precautions . . . fruitless: "quelque précaution que l'on prit" (p. 17).

9. Needs there any other proof: "On voit par là" (p. 17).

1. Great numbers . . . defence: "Combien de gens rejetteroient avec hauteur la proposition de se déclarer pour un dogme, s'ils n'avoient aucun intérêt de le favoriser extérieurement, & qui

mit themselves to appear to the publick what their hearts disapprove. It is for their present advantage to think these appearances allowed them, and then they soon determine to allow them in themselves. Such illusions as these are common; such was that of the Bishop of St Papoul.[d2] Few men have, like him, the courage to examine their principles anew, and to come back to sincerity and plain truth.

A man, whose mind is filled with prospects of interest and ambition, imagines that, by declaring for *fatality*, he falls into a path that will lead him to the end in view. The hypothesis on this account gains his heart, he fixes his attention upon the arguments that tend to establish it, to these he confines his ideas, and familiarises them to his imagination. But his reason and his conscience remonstrate to him, that he is going by this doctrine to overthrow all the principles of morality in his auditors. For this inconvenience, says he, I shall find a good remedy. The morality of my adherents will be in no danger, when I have taught them to persist in denying consequences, and to intrench themselves impregnably in negatives. This conduct I will be always inculcating, and enforce it by shewing that their honour, their reputation, and even their honesty, depend upon it. Having made this resolution, he adopts this system without farther scruple.

There was only one in our little company who had hitherto been silent: he then took his turn to speak. I can, says he, give you a clearer account, than will frequently be met with, of the struggles between practice and speculation, which a man feels, when an opinion in theory has not yet suppress'd those fears which are excited by religion, nor stifled the reproaches with which our consciences torment us upon every deviation from our duty. These struggles I once experienced, when I suffered myself to be dazzled with the system of fa-

d. Papeul

---

se permettent de certains dehors que leur coeur desaprouve?" (p. 17). Perhaps SJ has taken "combien de" as "beaucoup de."

2. The Bishop of St. Papoul was Jean-Charles de Ségur.

tality. I could not suspect it of any latent ill consequences in the mouth of a severe divine. He did not carry his notions so far as to a fatality, distant[3] from the divine nature, and to which his will was subject. He was himself the original of it, and thus all that came to pass was conceiv'd to come to pass by inevitable necessity,[4] as well within my breast, as in any external events.

But when this position was laid down, what need was there of prayer, or of confession?[5] To ask what, without being asked, must certainly come to pass, was useless; to ask what could never possibly be obtained was still worse.[6] Why should pardon be intreated, when a man has done nothing but what he was inevitably determined to do? How can resolutions be formed, or promises made? A man has no power to execute them, if all events are the production of destiny.

To free myself from these perplexities, I forbore all thoughts of my hypothesis, and enjoyn'd myself a course of conduct, as if I never had entertain'd any notion of these principles, as if there were no fatality, and as if I were master of my own actions.

This is in effect the method by which the fatalists regulate themselves in the ordinary course of their lives. Their erroneous notions do not extinguish their faculties, they continue free, and they act freely. Only some of them apply to their system[7] for relief against any inquietudes of conscience, or fears of futurity, and I have known more than one of this stamp.

God was always so favourable to me, as not to permit me to give the system with which I was infatuated, so absolute an empire over me; but, it is true, it disordered my devotions; my meditations and my prayers were interrupted by troublesome

---

3. Perhaps this is an error for "distinct." The French is "Ses Idées n'alloient point à une *Fatalité* différente de Dieu" (p. 19).

4. thus all . . . necessity: "dès là tout ce qui arrivoit devoit arriver inévitablement" (pp. 19–20).

5. what need . . . confession: "pourquoi prier? pourquoi se reconnoitre coupable?" (p. 20).

6. to ask . . . worse: "Il est encore plus contre le respect, de demander ce qui n'arrivera jamais" (p. 20).

7. system: "Systême spéculatif" (p. 21).

distractions, and I was far from finding in myself those dispositions of mind, which St James so expressly recommends, viz. *Let him who wanteth wisdom ask it of God, and it shall be given him; but let him ask it in full assurance; if he doubt, let him not expect to receive any thing of the Lord. The double-hearted man is inconstant in all his ways.* James i. 5, &c.[8]

St James compares his thoughts to the *waves of the sea,* and such is the state of all the *fatalists,* who are not desperately harden'd in their destructive system.[9]

As for those who have proceeded so far, they only deny those consequences with their mouths which they admit in their hearts, and they recur to this negative for no other reason than that they may not have their system to defend against the whole body of mankind, by which it is opposed.[1]

They are likewise deficient in sincerity, when they support their notions by the authority of divines, who are so far from admitting the consequences imputed to them, that they hold them in detestation.

It is temerity, say these divines, to deduce the consequences of an opinion that transcends the capacity of man, and which, if we comprehended it fully, would appear more distant from those deductions than heaven from earth.

But the principle of our modern philosophers, from which we see these consequences evidently arise, is, if we take their word, a clear principle, which fully explains the union of the soul with the body, and which, upon the subject of Providence, has enlightened the world with informations, which it has wanted till now.

Divines acknowledge in man such freedom, as must be admitted to subject him to just punishment for any faults he is guilty of, and that freedom as full and complete as if there

---

8. SJ provides the citation. He is not following the text of James i.5–8 in the Authorized Version, preferring to follow the French text almost exactly.

9. destructive system: "mortelle hypothese" (p. 22).

1. they recur . . . opposed: "c'est uniquement pour n'avoir pas à essuyer le gros des hommes revolté contre leur Système, qu'ils ont recours à cette Négative" (p. 22).

were no prescience. This they believe, though, as they confess, they know not how to reconcile it with a position which man is not capable of understanding. But our fatalists maintain, that freedom, as we understand it, is incompatible with prescience; and so much are they enemies to it, that, rather than not set themselves free from all fear of punishment, and all apprehension of giving an account, they deny free-will in the Deity himself, and are so prejudiced against any such notion, that they speak of it as implying a contradiction.[2]

The divines own, that morality and duty are founded in free-will; but this foundation is entirely demolished by the fatalists. They indeed own such a liberty in words, but their definitions reduce it to nothing. No man determines his own actions; to think that he determines them is all illusion and fancy, and even this fancy is the effect of an external cause, distinct from the will, which imagines that it determines itself, because it is not sensible of the cause that directs it, and directs it, according to them, by a physical efficacy.

Whatever extravagancies a man happens to utter, or to do, in the paroxysms of a phrenzy, he is not accountable for, being then without liberty or choice, and rather a *passive* than an *active* being: his condition of *moral agent* is for that time suspended. Now if man passes his whole life without liberty, if that power be never granted him by his Creator from the hour of his birth to that of his death, he is to be considered as a *physical being*, which has only the appearance of a *moral* one, and every one of his determinations, however weak, is the result of a necessary and physical cause, no less than the most impetuous transport of a violent phrenzy. A degree of speed which carries a body the space of an inch in a minute, is as much the necessary and physical effect of its weak cause, as a degree of speed, that carries a body a hundred feet in the same time, is of a cause[3] twelve hundred times stronger.

---

2. and are so prejudiced . . . contradiction: "tant ils sont prévenus contre cette idée, & se croyent en droit de la traiter de contradictoire" (p. 23).

3. cause: "force" (p. 25).

This, Sir, is a sketch of a conversation with which I thought it necessary to make you acquainted. I have since seen some Leibnitzians not satisfied with Mr Pope, who has, say they, let fall many things, that discover a very imperfect knowledge of the system: and some of these gentlemen seem so far disgusted (for he that admits any part of their system is expected to swallow the whole)[4] that they incline rather to suspect him of *Spinosism*. But this is so horrid an accusation, that a man ought not to suspect it just, without being forced to it, and I find you are not the only person that has undertaken to clear him from it.

Give me leave, Sir, to inform you, in one word, what I have done since I read your *Examen:* I have laid aside, as far as I could, all prepossession, and every idea of a system, and, endeavouring to abstract my mind from notions I had already conceiv'd, I have confin'd myself to read Mr Pope's *Essay upon Man,* as a mere treatise of morality, of a new form; and, in that view, have applied myself to learn from it how to know and conduct myself.

You, Sir, have never denied me any request. I know that you abstract your thoughts from any object without difficulty, and that you have form'd a habit of employing your attention as you please. I intreat you to favour me so far as to read once again the essays of Mr Pope, with the same frame of mind that I have done, and communicate your objections to me:[5] I shall be extremely pleased to compare them with mine; I do not tell you for what end,[6] that I may avoid filling your mind with any prepossession.

---

4. (for he . . . whole): "(car ils veulent tout ou rien) (p. 25).

5. I intreat . . . me: "Ayez pour moi, je vous prie, la complaisance de lire une nouvelle fois l'*Essai de Mr.* POPE, dans le même esprit que je viens de le lire, & accordez-moi le plaisir de me faire part de vos Observations" (p. 26).

6. for what end: "dans quelles vûës" (p. 26).

MR CROUSAZ'S ANSWER TO THE LETTER; BEING A COMMENTARY ON MR POPE'S ETHIC EPISTLES, OR *ESSAY ON MAN*. ON EPISTLE I.

I find in myself an inclination to comply punctually with your request, as far as it is in my power. From the earliest years of my youth I found in myself a strong tendency to the study of LOGIC, and employ'd my time upon it, without yet repenting it. I have made advantage of maxims which I met with in books not written with an intention to teach them. I have perused all the writings that have fallen into my hands with that title, or a title of any affinity to it: I have not even neglected such as are entirely out of fashion. But to what purpose does a man learn to think justly, if his attainments do not enable him to regulate his conduct? Truth is of no value, if it does not lead us into the paths of wisdom, or fix us in them. For this reason, in whatever form, and in whatever manner any author has treated *morality,* I have thought myself under an obligation to profit by his instructions, and it is with this only view that I am about to read over again the essay of Mr Pope, and to enter myself among his scholars; but as a scholar desirous of improvement, I shall hear him with attention, and, that I may be the more improv'd, shall examine his precepts.[7]

With this design I have made choice of the poetical translation; this way of writing is agreeable to my taste, and will much add to my docility. I am indeed not easy to be pleased in my judgment of poetry, and not finding myself born a poet, for fear of making bad verses, never allow'd myself to make any. But I must assure you that I am nevertheless very well pleased with the version of the Abbe de Sept Fontaines.

---

7. but as a scholar . . . precepts: "mais Disciple attentif, qui veut profiter, & qui pour mieux profiter, examine" (p. 28).

Sors de l'enchantement,[8] *milord, laisse au vulgaire*
Break from th'enchantment, my lord, leave to the
 vulgar
Le seduisant espoir d'un bien imaginaire.
The seducing hope of a good imaginary.
Fui le faste des cours, les honneurs, les plaisirs;
Shun the pride[9] of courts, the honours, the
 pleasures;
Ils ne meritent point de fixer tes desirs.
They not merit at all to fix thy desires.
Est-ce a toi de grossir cette foule importune, 5
Is it for thee to increase that crowd importunate,
Qui court aupres des rois, encenser la fortune?
Which runs after kings, to offer incense to fortune?
Viens, un plus grand objet, des soins plus importans
Come, a more grand object, cares more important
Doivent de notre vie occuper les instans.
Should of our life employ the moments.

I do not understand *English,* and how loudly soever I might declare my approbation[1] of the judicious comparison of the poetry of the two nations made by Mr du Resnel,* my suffrage ought to be made no account of, being given upon a subject I do not understand.

I cannot however help observing an evident difference be-

---

*Mr Crousaz, who, as he says, understands not *English,* discovers du Resnel's variation from Mr Pope, by comparing his version with another in prose, on which he writ his *Examen,* lately translated by an ingenious hand.[2]

---

8. SJ quotes this opening passage to Hester Maria Thrale on 24 July 1783 (*Letters,* IV.180–81): "If ever therefore you catch yourself contentedly and placidly doing nothing, *sors de l'enchantement,* break away from the snare, find your book or your needle, or snatch the broom from the maid."

9. pride: "faste" (p. 29). Boyer gives authority for this in one of his definitions of "Faste": "stateliness, pride, vainglory."

1. I do not . . . approbation: "Je n'entens pas l'Anglois; & quelque approbation que je donnasse" (p. 29).

2. The prose translation of *The Essay on Man* is by Etienne de Silhouette and the translation of Crousaz's *Examen* is by Elizabeth Carter. See Introduction, pp. xxix–xxxv.

FIRST EPISTLE   37

tween the openings of the two* poems; the expressions of Mr Pope are more harsh, and those of Mr du Resnel more soften'd.

The author (Mr Pope) shews a dissatisfaction that amounts to ill humour, or indeed goes somewhat farther:

> (— —*Leave all meaner Things*
> *To low Ambition, and the Pride of Kings*)³

The translator (M. du Resnel) is content with remarking, that solid happiness is not to be found in a court-life.

---

*The address of one is the exclamation of a freeman, that of the other the murmur of a slave.⁴

——It is unnecessary here to remind the reader of Roscommon's observation upon the *English* poetry compared with the *French*,

> *One Sterling Line*
> *Drawn to* French *Wire will thro' whole Pages shine*.⁵

This translator cannot but recall it to his memory, by giving us 8 lines of 12 or 13 syllables for 2 lines of 10; as for the second couplet,

> *Let us, since Life can little more supply,*
> *Than just to look about us, and to die,*

he has totally omitted it;⁶ but it may be proper to observe, that du Resnel's version is entitled *Les* PRINCIPES *de la Morale; Traduits de l'*ANGLOIS *de Mr* POPE, *Par Mr* DU RESNEL *Abbe de* Sept-Fontaines, *de l'Academie des Inscriptions & Belles-Lettres:* that is, the PRINCIPLES OF MORALITY; a Poem *translated from the* English *of Mr* POPE, *by Mr* DU RESNEL, *Abbe de* Sept-Fontaines, *and Member of the Academy of Inscriptions and Belles-Lettres*.⁷

---

3. SJ substitutes the lines from Pope for Crousaz's quotation of Silhouette (p.[1]): "*Laissons les petits objets à la basse ambition & à l'orgueil des Rois*" (p. 30).

4. Forman (p. 66) places an asterisk at the beginning of a paragraph below, in SJ's translation "So in society . . . immediately imbroil'd" (p. 108), with a footnote registering a similar sentiment: "Notwithstanding all Mr Crousaz's logick, this argument smells more of the slave than Mr Pope's philosophy does of the poet."

5. *An* Essay on Translated Verse *in* Poems *by the Earl of Roscommon* (1717), p. 9. The second line should read "would thro' whole Pages shine." See Du Resnel's comments on Roscommon in his Preface and SJ's comments on Du Resnel, pp. 351–52 below.

6. Awake, my St. John! leave all meaner things
   To low ambition, and the pride of Kings.

7. For the complete title of the volume, see Introduction, p. xxi, n. 4.

A spirit of moderation in an author, who is about to teach *morality,* prejudices the reader in favour of his work. A magisterial accent only makes instruction more burthensome. Some restraint and modesty of style are decent,⁸ especially when great persons are mention'd, whose virtue such numbers conspire to assault, that they are more to be admired when they persevere in the right way, and more to be lamented when they wander from it.*

He that follows the court from motives of ambition, that he may enjoy the pleasure of tyrannising over others, and of receiving homage in any exalted station, instead of meeting with happiness at court, will find there a thousand disappointments, and be a prey to innumerable vexations. But the man that has no other view than of truly serving his country and his prince, who diligently takes every opportunity that occurs of prosecuting that design without regard to recompence or applause, who does his duty with the same zeal, on occasions which never can be known, as in affairs of which the whole world will be informed: such a man enjoys the happiness of a perpetual serenity in the possession of virtue, which nothing can dispirit, and which, however neglected, can support itself.

But if the tranquillity of solitude has more powerful charms than a life,⁹ which must expose a man to be every day the witness of a thousand detestable actions, and in which virtue must struggle with continued attacks, I conceive that it may be natural to grow weary of such embarrassments, and think of retiring.

Such I suppose to be the temper of a *fine genius,*¹ celebrated

---

*May it not be opposed to this soft language, that the vices of the great ought to be more severely censured, because they are committed in open day, because they set fashion on the side of wickedness, corrupt whole nations by their influence, and are out of the reach of any other punishment?

---

8. Some restraint . . . decent: "Un stile modeste & retenu sied bien" (p. 30). "Bienséant" is "decent."

9. But if . . . life: "Mais si la tranquil-lité de la retraite a plus d'appas qu'une vie" (p. 31).

1. *fine genius:* "*bel Esprit*" (p. 31).

for his writings, and of a *lord,* whose abilities have enabled him to shine in the administration.

To this retreat I resolve to follow them, and that I may attend more tractably to the new instructions which are to be received,[2] I suppose myself to be one of their attendants. Here my felicity will equal theirs, however inferiour it would have been at court.

> *Ce*[3] *grand object, c'est l'homme, etonnant labirinthe,*
> This grand object, 'tis man, astonishing maze,
> *Ou d'un plan regulier l'oeil reconnoit l'empreinte;*   10
> Where of a plan regular th'eye discerns the mark;
> *Champ second, mais sauvage, ou par de sages loix*
> A field fertile, but wild, where by wise laws
> *La rose & le chardon fleurissent a la fois.*
> The rose and the thistle flourish at the same time.[4]

Here are mixtures, and even contrarieties, which I cannot but acknowledge: with these contrarieties I am much perplexed, and promise myself the most agreeable peace of mind from seeing them laid open to the view.

> *Voyons a quel dessein le ciel nous a fait naitre;*
> Let us see for what intent heaven us has caused to be born;
> *Que l'homme dans mes vers apprenne a se connoitre;*
> Let man in my verses learn to know himself;

For this information I wait with impatience, and which I foresee is likely to continue, for my difficulties and fears are increased upon me by new antitheses. What am I to hear now?

---

2. To this retreat . . . received: "Je prens le parti de les suivre; & pour profiter avec plus de docilité des lumieres qu'ils vont acquerir" (p. 31).

3. Crousaz has "Leur" (p. 32); Du Resnel has "Ce" (l. 9).

4. Expatiate free o'er all this scene of Man;
  A mighty maze! but not without a plan;
  A Wild, where weeds and flow'rs promiscuous shoot,
  Or Garden, tempting with forbidden fruit. (5–8)

SJ comments on Pope's revision of l. 6 in the "Life of Pope," *Lives,* III.162 (par. 170).

De son coeur tenebreux sondons la profondeur; 15
Of his darksome heart let us sound the depth;
Jusques dans sa bassesse admirons sa grandeur.
Even in his lowness let us admire his grandeur.
L'un fier de ses talens, enfle de sa science,
One proud of his talents, puffed up with his knowledge,
Ne croit rien d'impossible a son intelligence.
Believes nothing impossible to his understanding.
Pour ces dons precieux l'autre plein de mepris,
For these gifts precious another full of contempt,
De sa propre raison semble ignorer le prix. 20
Of his own reason seems not to know the value.
Rappellons-les tous deux a sa pure lumiere,[5]
Let us recall them both to its pure light,
Et cherchons les sentiers[6] *ou marche la nature.*
And let us seek out the paths where marches nature.*

Here is a scheme of discoveries that awakens my impatience, I am all attention to every syllable, and find in the conclusion that, to attain the knowledge I desire so much,

---

*Eye Nature's Walks———v. 13.
The reader will observe with indignation the dull introduction, and common remarks which are interwoven with Mr Pope's animated sentiments. The translator is very injudicious in presuming to add any thing of his own, but may perhaps be more easily justified in his omission of these words.

> Shoot Folly as it flies,
> And catch the Manners living as they rise.[7]

---

5. Crousaz has "à la lumiere pure" (p. 33); Du Resnel has "à sa lumiere pure" (l. 21).

6. Crousaz has "chemins" (p. 33); Du Resnel "sentiers" (l. 22).

7. Lines 13b–14 are omitted:

> Together let us beat this ample field,
> Try what the open, what the covert yield;
> The latent tracts, the giddy heights explore
> Of all who blindly creep, or sightless soar;
> Eye Nature's walks, shoot Folly as it flies,
> And catch the Manners living as they rise. (9–14)

I must *eye* the *walks of nature,* and follow them;[8] grandeur is the delight of poetry,[9] but my heart is set upon clearness and simplicity. What idea am I to conceive from the term *nature?* NATURE is, it seems, the guide I am to follow. Is *nature* then that assemblage of bodies[1] with which I am surrounded? This sense, though very frequent, is not proper here. Is *nature* the bulk of mankind, whose example carries me along, and often draws me from the right way? Am I to give that appellation to any secret desires, which are sometimes good, and very often bad? Or to violent passions, which seldom benefit, and often hurt me?[2] Or shall I reserve that title for the light of reason? But nobody has yet settled a method for distinguishing its deceitful glimmers from its true light. Am I to follow nature, by walking in the way which all consent to approve? Where then am I to look for that consent, and what is it that meets with such general approbation?

By *nature* am I to understand the *universal cause* of all spirits, and of all bodies? Let me then be taught how I may assuredly know his *walks,* and distinguish his undoubted attributes from false imputations.[3]

*I have hopes given me, that the presumptuous, who think themselves capable of every thing, and the indolent, who, to free themselves from the necessity of labour, determine[e] to despise all that can be attained by it, will be now reconciled, and brought back to the pure light of truth. I expect a great deal, and hitherto attain nothing.[4]

*This paragraph relates only to Du Resnel's addition, v. 17, 18 &c. *L'un fier de ses talens,* &c.
e. determines

8. SJ omits the sentence "Ces derniers termes sont bien métaphoriques, *les chemins où marche la nature*" (p. 33).

9. grandeur . . . poetry: "La Poësie adopte le grand" (p. 33).

1. assemblage of bodies: "les Corps" (p. 33). Here "les corps" means all substance, organic and inorganic.

2. and often hurt me: "me nuisent ordinairement" (p. 34).

3. and distinguish . . . imputations: "& de démêler ce qu'on est fondé à lui attribuer, d'avec ce qu'on auroit tort de lui imputer" (p. 34).

4. I expect . . . nothing: "Je m'attendois à beaucoup, & je ne saisis encore rien" (p. 34).

Yet far from losing courage I feel it revive at the following lines.

> *Que par nous eclaire sur ses vraix interets,*
> Let, by us enlightened in his true interest,
> *L'homme rougisse enfin de ses voeux indiscrets;*
> Man blush at last for his wishes indiscreet;
> *Qu'il reconnoisse ici ses virtus & ses vices,* 25
> Let him acknowledge here his virtues and his vices,
> *Et bravant de l'erreur les dangereux caprices,*
> And defying of error the dangerous caprices,
> *Contre les vains discours de l'aveugle mortel*
> Against the vain reasoning of a blind mortal
> *Essayons de venger les loix de l'eternel.*
> Let us try to vindicate the laws of th'eternal.*

Here are promises yet more liberal.[5] I shall be taught to live, and, above all, to have just notions of my Creator, his will, and his laws. This is of infinitely greater value than barely to know him without going any farther.

> *Si tu veux eviter les ecueils ordinaires,*
> If thou wilt avoid the rocks common,
> *Ou se brise l'orgueil des esprits temeraires,* 30
> Where splits the pride of rash wits,
> *Sur des mondes sans nombre, eloignes de tes yeux,*
> On worlds without number, remote from thy eyes,
> *Garde-toi de porter des regards curieux.*
> Beware of carrying views curious.†

---

*Of these lines I need not say how distant they are from Mr Pope's sense, and how much inferiour to it.[6]

†Du Resnel's introduction would be dull in prose, and is very far from giving an idea of Mr Pope's fire and precipitation.[7]

---

5. Here are . . . liberal: "Les promesses croissent" (p. 35).

6. Laugh where we must, be candid where we can;
But vindicate the ways of God to Man. (15–16)

7. I. Say first, of God above, or Man below,
What can we reason, but from what we know? (17–18)

FIRST EPISTLE

I am disingaged from an endless toil, and congratulate myself upon finding that I may dispense with a labour[8] which, in all appearance, would have been without effect.

> *Cherchez Dieu dans ce monde, ou sa vive lumiere*
> Search God in this world, where his vivid light
> *S'offre de toutes parts a ta foible paupiere.*
> Itself offers from all parts to thy feeble eyes.[9]

This task I embrace, with the utmost satisfaction, to find how my searches are to be confin'd.

> *Tu ne peux d'un regard voir les divers ressorts,*[1]   35
> Thou canst not with a look view the different springs,
> *Dont le parfait concert entretient l'universe;*
> Of which the perfect concert maintains th'universe;
> *Penetrer par quel art la puissance supreme*
> Penetrate by what art the power supreme
> *Des tourbillons errans a regle le sisteme;*
> Of vortexes wandering hath regulated the system;
> *Parcourir les soleils, les globes radieux,*
> Run over the suns, the globes radiant,
> *Et les etres divers qui remplissent les cieux;*   40
> And the different beings which fill the heavens;
> *Et tu veux des decrets, qui formerent le monde,*
> And thou wilt of decrees, which have formed the world,
> *Comprendre clairement la sagesse profonde.*
> Comprehend clearly the wisdom profound.

I am more and more encouraged, by observing what limits my conductors set to their excursions, and am no longer in fear lest men of genius, each in his sphere so much superior to mine, should attempt to raise themselves to a height, whither I should be unable to follow them; they inspire me as they go on with new courage.

---

8. congratulate . . . a labour: "je me félicite de m'acquiter d'un devoir en me refusant à cette peine" (p. 35).

9. eyes: "paupiére" (p. 36).
1. Crousaz has "ressorts divers" (p. 36).

Dans les liens du corps ton esprit arrete,
Within the bands of body thy spirit detained,
Au celeste conseil a-t-il donc assiste?
At the heavenly council hath it then assisted?
Est-ce une main divine, ou toi, foiblesse humaine, 45
Is it a hand divine, or thou, human weakness,
Qui formas, qui soutiens cette invisible chaine,
Who hast formed, who sustainest that invisible chain,
Dont effort[2] *insensible attire tous les corps,*
Whose force insensible attracts all bodies,
Et qui les attirant dirige leurs ressorts?
And which attracting them directs their springs?*

These last ideas are borrow'd from Sir Isaac Newton's system, to which several allusions have been made, not all equally just; but too close an application to a system might have frozen the vein of poetry.

The effects of attraction must be very restrained, or the world would at once become a mass of compact and solid matter.[3]——But this is an episode which I, who am only their disciple in *morality*,[4] may pass over without obstructing my design.[5]

Presomptueux mortel! ta raison inquiete
Presumptuous mortal! thy reason restless
Voudroit approfondir quelle cause secrete 50
Would fathom what secret cause
T'a forme si petit, si foible, & si borne.

*Here verses 33, 34 are translated into six, and perhaps, when the numerous omissions are taken into the account, the whole *French* version will be found to preserve very near the same proportion.[6]

---

2. Crousaz has "l'effort" (p. 36).

3. must be . . . matter: "bornés & très modérés, sans quoi tout l'Univers se seroit d'abord réduit en une Masse très compacte" (p. 37).

4. their discipline in *morality:* "Auditeur de Morale" (p. 37).

5. without obstructing my design: "sans nuire à mon dessein" (p. 37).

6. Is the great chain, that draws all to agree,
And drawn supports, upheld by God, or thee? (33–34)

FIRST EPISTLE

    Thee hath formed so weak, so feeble, and so
        bounded.
Mais, d'abord, apprens-moi pourquoi tu n'es pas ne
But, first, inform me wherefore thou art not born
Plus foible, plus petit, plus borne, dans tes vues.
More weak, more little, more bounded, in thy views.
Fais, moi sentir pourquoi jusques au sein des nues
Make me perceive why even to the bosom of the
        clouds
Les chenes elevant leurs superbes rameaux   55
The oaks raising their proud branches
Laissent ramper sous eux les foibles arbrisseaux.
Leave to creep under them the feeble shrubs.
Tu vois de Jupiter les brillans satellites,
Thou seest of Jupiter the shining satellites,
Dis par quelle raison fixes dans leurs limites
Tell for what reason fixed within their limits
De l'astre qui les guide n'ont pas la grandeur.
Of the star which them guides they have not the
        bigness.

I am yet at a great distance from what I was in expectation of. I looked for some information upon the end of my being.[7] But before any light is afforded me I am overwhelmed with interrogatories, and condemn'd to languish in ignorance, till I have given an answer to these problems of natural philosophy:[8] after having said

> Thro' worlds unnumber'd tho' the God be known,
> 'Tis ours to trace him only in our own,[9]

they compel me to gaze upon the skies, in spite of my unwillingness to disobey so agreeable a precept.

---

7. upon the end of my being: "sur ma destinée" (p. 38). SJ omits a reference to l. 13 of Du Resnel: "*Voyons*, m'avoit-on dit pompeusement, *à quel dessein le Ciel nous a fait naître.*"

8. But . . . philosophy: "Mais avant que de me tenir parole, on m'assassine de questions, & on me refuse des lumieres, jusques à ce que j'aye résolu ces problêmes physiques" (p. 38).

9. SJ substitutes ll. 21–22 of Pope for Crousaz's quotation of ll. 31–32 of Du Resnel (p. 38).

Si des decrets divins la sage profondeur,   60
If of decrees divine the wise depth,
Au plan le plus parfait donnant la preference,
To a plan the most perfect giving the preference,
Doit enfanter un monde ou brille sa puissance;
Must produce a world wherein shines its power;
Ou quoique separe, rien ne soit disuni;[1]
Where, however separate, nothing is disunited;

Mr du Resnel had reason to remark[2] in his preliminary discourse, that *The English, even in their most inconsiderable writings, love to leave something to the reader's thoughts, and think they oblige him, by giving him an opportunity of making conjectures.*[3]

This is Mr Pope's conduct in the passage before us, for he compliments his readers so far, as to conceive, after barely having heard *that we are to trace God in our own world,*[4] they are capable of expanding that sentiment into its whole extent, of ascending to its first principles, and carrying it forward to its consequences.[5]

If this earth, and the objects upon it, presented nothing to the view, which the mind of man was not capable of immediately comprehending, the work would not carry sufficient marks of its infinite author. If every thing were incomprehensible, its author would be totally conceal'd, instead of being made known, as his perfections now are, to the human mind, even in its imperfect state. It appears mere madness, and a perfect deviation from reason, to ascribe such order, connexion, and symmetry to unintelligent causes, which had no intention in their operations, nor were conscious of their own effects.

If any notion can imply an absurdity, it is evidently absurd to suppose that the FIRST CAUSE *may* in reality *exist*, but that at

---

1. Crousaz has correctly "désuni" (p. 38).
2. had reason to remark: "a raison de remarquer" (p. 38).
3. See p. 357 below.
4. SJ substitutes a paraphrase of l. 22 of Pope for Crousaz's quotation of ll. 33–34 of Du Resnel (p. 39).
5. they are capable...consequences: "Il les compte capables de développer cette pensée, de remonter à ses principes, & de la pousser plus loin" (p. 39).

the same time it might possibly *not exist*. For, in that case, some cause must have determined the *first cause* to exist, rather than not exist. The *first cause* could not then be the *first*, since it must owe its existence to some *antecedent cause*. It is therefore only in itself that we must enquire for the grounds of its existence. Should it be demanded, why the *first cause* exists, we must answer, Because, that it should not exist, implies an absurdity. It is reality itself, perfect reality; it is that perfect eternal being, in which no real perfection is wanting. We are forced, irresistibly forced, to acknowledge that it exists, and thence it is that we call its existence *necessary:* an expression and sentiment, which in one sense is true, just, and proper, but is capable of being perverted to a bad meaning, and in reality is perverted, when it is used to countenance a supposition that God is subject to any necessity. He is subject to nothing, nor is he dependent on any thing, being perfectly and infinitely self-sufficient. As his power is infinite, he can do whatever he wills: as his wisdom is infinite, he is conscious of his own infinite perfection. He has ideas of every thing, to which his omnipotence can give existence. And when he sees those beings which he hath chosen to create, he receives no new impression; all operations of the creature being only the result of his divine power. He contemplated in himself the whole creature and all its powers, while it was yet nonexistent.

As being self-sufficient, he stands in need of nothing, his perfections did not of necessity determine him to exert rather than not exert any act[6] of creation. No created being can make the least addition to his felicity, for in that case he must, if he had not created it, have wanted something essential to his happiness.

It is by choice, a choice infinitely free, that he was deter-

---

6. In all copies consulted, a number of the letters after "act" have been pulled out, leaving a space before "aion" at the end of the sentence. The word "least" from the line below has drifted into the space. The French says, "Suffisant à lui-même, n'ayant besoin de rien, ses perfections ne l'ont point nécessairement déterminé à former des Etres" (p. 41). "Act of creation" is a good translation and fits the space. SJ uses the phrase again p. 48.

mined of his unbounded goodness to call other beings into existence. When it was his pleasure to form the universe, he saw that a more perfect work was more worthy of himself, than one less compleat: but we must not rashly conclude[7] that, among all the ideas that his wisdom might form of many systems of creation, there must of necessity arise *one* so perfect, that infinite knowledge could not form another of equal excellence: it is therefore still by a free choice that he has produced that universe of which *we* are a part.

It has pleased his infinite wisdom to give being to creatures answerable to the infinite diversity of his ideas. He has created beings insensible, and unconscious of their own existence; on others he has confer'd the power of sensation; to a third order he has given intelligence, freedom of will, and power of action; and proportion'd the different degrees of perfection in their intellectual and active powers, and in their liberty of choice, to the different classes in which they are ranged.

It was put in the power of the intelligent part of the universe to make a good or bad use of freewill. Men have made a bad use of it. The knowledge of this truth discovers the original of that astonishing mixture of perfections and imperfections, light and darkness, virtue and vice, which we find in the world.

So that these words,

> *Of Systems possible, if 'tis confest,*
> *That Wisdom infinite* must *chuse the best*,[8]

may be understood in too great a latitude; which must be avoided; *first,* by rejecting any supposition, that the perfections of the eternal being were necessarily determined to exert rather than not exert any act of creation, or to form the universe such as we find it, rather than another different from

---

7. but we must . . . conclude: "Mais c'est une conclusion trop hardie & trop téméraire" (pp. 41–42).

8. SJ substitutes ll. 43–44 of Pope for Crousaz's quotation of ll. 60–61a of Du Resnel (p. 43). The second line should read "form the best."

this, which yet, upon the whole, that is, compared in every respect, might have been equally perfect.

It is impossible that what was formed from *nothing,* and owes its existence to some superior agent, should equal the perfection of the ETERNAL CAUSE that never had a beginning. *The perfection of the universe is therefore limited,* and where an assemblage of beings consider'd in general is perfect only to a certain degree, another assemblage may possibly be perfect in the same degree.[9]

We are, *in the second place,* not to conceive that every portion of the universe is so essential to it, that the want of it would be any reproach to the infinite wisdom of the creator, or any disadvantage to his work. Would a worm, a horse, or a mountain, more or less, destroy the beauty of the world?[1] The islands are represented as *scatter'd over the sea by the hand of the Almighty.* Was it not at his choice to scatter more or fewer? The truth of this assertion will reach to the planets, and all the habitable inhabited globes. Nothing is more agreeable to the nature of the first cause, supreme and self-sufficient, than a perfect freedom; since whatever choice is made by him, his holiness, power, happiness, and wisdom, continue always infinite, always the same.

A prince thinks it proper to stamp gold coins of thirty, fifteen, ten, and five shillings: his neighbour coins pieces of forty, twenty, ten, and five; another furnishes his subjects with gold money of six, twelve, twenty-four, and thirty shillings. Now, as each of these was wholly at liberty in this affair, would it not be madness for a man to disturb his brain with long calculations, to demonstrate which of these three discover'd most wisdom, and the greatest compass of thought. It is a matter of mere choice, and by no means a subject of argument.

---

9. *The perfection* . . . degree: "Or dès qu'un Tout est fini en perfection, il peut y en avoir d'autres, dont l'assemblage montera à un degré égal de perfection" (p. 43).

1. Would a worm . . . world: "Un Ciron de plus, un Ciron de moins; un Cheval de plus, un Cheval de moins; une Montagne de plus, une Montagne de moins, défigureroit-elle l'Ouvrage?" (p. 44).

A man ought likewise to think himself indispensably oblig'd to distinguish between those effects which flow immediately from the supreme cause, and those which are produced by created intelligences that make an ill use of their liberty.

Mr Pope's expressions are indeterminate, and therefore are capable of a sense agreeable to truth; and his excellent[2] translator, to shew likewise what our language could perform in poetry, has borrow'd the vague and indeterminate ideas of his original, and express'd them in the same manner, so that the reader is under no necessity of taking them in a bad sense.

He goes on to speak of the gradations of the world;

> *Ou croissant par degres jusques a l'infini,*
> Where increasing by degrees even to infinity,
> *Les etres differens, sans laisser d'intervale,*   65
> The beings different, without leaving an interval,
> *Gardent dans leur progres une justesse egale:*
> Keep in their progress an exactness equal:
> * *Si pour remplir ce tout que Dieu forme a son gre,*
> If to fill up that hole which God forms after his will,
> *Parmi les animaux l'homme occupe un degre,*
> Among animals man possesses a degree,

    *Mr RESNEL varies here from his author's reasoning, by assuming as one of his premises, what in the original is inferr'd as a conclusion, viz.

> Then *in the scale of life and sense 'tis plain, There* must *be somewhere such a rank as* Man.

Perhaps it might be not improperly alter'd thus,

> *Il faut que dans ce tout*——[3]

---

2. excellent: "habile" (p. 45).
3. Lines 64–70 of Du Resnel correspond to ll. 45–50 of Pope:

> Where all must full or not coherent be,
> And all that rises, rise in due degree;
> Then, in the scale of reas'ning life, 'tis plain
> There must be, somewhere, such a rank as Man;
> And all the question (wrangle e'er so long)
> Is only this, if God has plac'd him wrong?

In his note SJ has the earlier reading "Life and Sence" for l. 47.

FIRST EPISTLE

Le seul point est de voir, si le ciel equitable
The only point is to see, if equitable heaven
L'a place dans un rang qui lui soit convenable.   70
Him has placed in a rank which to him is suitable.

Here then the question is stated, and brought down from general terms to a particular point. God, as sovereign, and unrestrain'd, has regulated, according to his own pleasure, the gradations of the several parts that compose the universe. Our only business is to convince ourselves that man is in possession of that place, in this regular gradation, which he is best adapted to, and which is most agreeable to the justice as well as liberty of his Creator.[4] To this question Mr Resnel answers after his author.*

Dans l'homme, tel qu'il est, ce qui paroit un mal
In man, such as he is, that which appears an evil
Est la source d'un bien dans l'ordre general.
Is the source of a good in the order general.
L'oeil, qui ne voit d'un tout qu'une seule partie,
The eye, which sees not of a whole but one only part,

---

*Mr RESNEL is very far from giving his author's answer. The first of these couplets is indeed as good a translation of the *English* as perhaps his language will admit, but nothing can excuse his total omission of the seven following lines, which, if not essential to the argument, contain an hypothesis, that, if admitted, will contribute very much to illustrate it, and must at least be allow'd one of the ornaments, if not one of the pillars of this philosophical structure.[5]

---

4. Our only business . . . Creator: "Il ne s'agit plus que de faire comprendre que, dans cette gradation, l'Homme occupe une place qui lui convient, & sur tout qui convient à l'Equité, autant qu'à la Liberté de son Créateur" (p. 46).

5. Respecting Man, whatever wrong we call,
May, must be right, as relative to all.
In human works, tho' labour'd on with pain,
A thousand movements scarce one purpose gain;
In God's, one single can its end produce;
Yet serves to second too some other use.
So Man, who here seems principal alone,
Perhaps acts second to some sphere unknown,
Touches some wheel, or verges to some goal;
'Tis but a part we see, and not a whole. (51–60)

Pourra-t-il la juger bien ou mal assortie?
Will it be able to judge it well or ill disposed?

I must own that, in my opinion, the man, whom this answer can send away satisfied, is very cheaply contented.[6] There are in man both physical and moral evils or imperfections. These evils make us interested in the present question, and are indeed the subject of astonishment. Let us begin with those of a physical nature, which the more we observe, the more improbable it will appear, that the headach,[7] gravel, stone, gout, and palsy, the weakness of infancy, the infirmities of old age, the dulness of some, the distractions of others, and the chimeras of the inhabitants of the madhouse, should be circumstances that turn to the advantage of the whole system of things, and extend their beneficial influences through all the universe.[8]

At the view of *moral evil* our difficulties redouble; for what advantage can the most inventive imagination conceive arising to the universe in general from cheats, poysoners, calumniators and assassins, from rapes, perjuries and unnatural lusts? Were all these gradations necessary to prevent a *void*, and obviate the ill effects of too wide a step?[9]

Mr Pope seems strongly inclined to consider the universe as a *whole* consisting of many parts, so exactly link'd one to another, that no single part can be displaced without leaving the rest unsupported, and endangering the overthrow of the creation.[1] This is carrying the notion of a system too far, nor would it be easy to conceive a scheme of natural philosophy, from which this universal concatenation would result. A very complicated piece of machinery, of which all the parts depended reciprocally upon each other, would be the effect of

---

6. I must . . . contented: "Il me paroit qu'il faut être bien facile pour trouver cette réponse satisfaisante" (p. 47).

7. SJ omits "les douleurs de dens" (p. 47).

8. that turn to the advantage . . . universe: "dont la totalité de l'Univers profite, & qui portent si loin leurs influences" (p. 47).

9. and obviate . . . step: "& qu'il ne s'y fit aucun faut trop brusque" (p. 48).

1. and endangering . . . creation: "& le mettre en risque d'être bouleversé" (p. 48).

FIRST EPISTLE

great art, and long consideration; but could we, amidst our applause, forbear regretting the time spent in forming a work that however excellent might so easily be destroy'd?[2]

When any one proposes to study *man,* and penetrate into the recesses of his breast,[3] it is not improper to retire to solitude, because we can then more easily attend to the inclinations of our own minds, and consider them without distraction:[4] but the knowledge of a man that has only observed himself, is commonly very much confin'd, and leaves many things uncomprised. Matters of fact are only known by experience, and they who are not inclined to use that method of information must apply to those that have used it, and make advantage of their discoveries. As for past events, whoever would know them must consult history. If our illustrious travellers, whom I conceive to be mere philosophers, confin'd to the conjectures which reason is capable of striking out, after having left the court for the sake of studying the nature, duties, and end of man,[5] had followed this reasonable maxim, they would have consulted an ancient history, which many men of the first class have shewn to be highly credible, for an account of the FALL.

Before they entertain'd a supposition that God at first form'd man, such as he appears at present, they ought to have enquired *for what reason the primitive*[6] *man, the original of humankind, was not form'd, at his first production, without the unhappy power of abusing his liberty?*

To this question it may easily be answered, That the Creator is the supreme arbiter of his own gifts, and may limit them in his distributions as he pleases. It was enough that man had it in his power to use his liberty and the gifts of his Creator to

---

2. but could we . . . destroy'd: "mais on plaindroit le tems employé à un ouvrage si facile à être entiérement dissous" (p. 48).

3. Crousaz has a paraphrase of l. 15 of Du Resnel: *"sonder la profondeur de son coeur ténébreux"* (pp. 48–49).

4. because we can . . . distraction: "on s'y rend plus aisément attentif aux inclinations de ce coeur, & on lit dans son intérieur avec moins de distraction" (p. 49).

5. SJ omits "(suivant le projet annoncé dans la 23. 24. & 25ᵉ. ligne de ce Poëme)" (p. 49).

6. *primitive: "premier"* (p. 50).

good purposes, and his Sovereign Lord conferr'd upon him a great and infinite honour, in chusing to be obey'd by him freely and voluntarily.[7]

But why are infants born with minds distorted from their just rectitude, and disposed to chuse evil rather than good?[8] *Why do they fall into hands so far from rectifying these inclinations, that they suffer them to strengthen by their negligence, and increase them by their own examples, and all the consequences of a bad education?*

A whole order of intelligences, of great abilities, and active powers, have withdrawn themselves from the submission due to their Creator, and chosen to conduct themselves wholly by their own will. Perhaps their creation[9] and rise from nothing appeared to them an event beyond credibility, perhaps they imagined it the effect of destiny. But, however it came to pass that they deserted their station, the Supreme Being thought it not proper to divest them of existence,[1] but chose rather to display his wisdom, his power, and, in the conclusion, his justice, by defeating all their measures; which will produce events quite contrary to their intention, and end only in their own confusion.

The disobedience of man has not been unpunish'd, for it was reasonable that sin should deprive man of that felicity which was decreed as a reward for his perseverance in innocence. But as man was seduced and tempted from his innocence, he is become in his fallen state an object of compassion, and the design of the tempter was disappointed. The life of man was prolong'd, that he might by repentance obtain a better state, and perpetuate among his posterity the memory of the event of which he had been witness.

The infinite knowledge, and perfect justice of God distin-

---

7. It was enough . . . voluntarily: "Il suffisoit à l'Homme d'être né en pouvoir de faire un bon usage de ses dons & de sa liberté, & c'étoit un grand honneur, un honneur immense, que son souverain Maître voulut bien se plaire à en être aimé & obéi par choix & volontairement" (p. 50).

8. *distorted from their just rectitude* . . . *good:* "*dérangés & disposés à choisir mal*" (p. 50).

9. Perhaps their creation: "Peut-être que la merveille de leur création" (p. 51).

1. But, however . . . existence: "Mais de quelque maniére que se soit fait leur dérangement, l'Etre suprême n'a pas trouvé à propos de les anéantir" (p. 51).

FIRST EPISTLE 55

guish with the utmost exactness,[2] in all the misbehaviour of children and older persons, between what is to be imputed to them as a crime, and what is to be lamented as their misfortune;[3] and the balance in this distinction inclines always to the side of mercy. It would be impious to imagine that God is the author of moral evil, and causes vice that he may draw good from it. Moral evil is not produced by him, though it give occasion to a new exertion of his attributes.

The blessed spirits have seen, from that time, birth given to a new order of creatures, which enter upon their existence amidst the darkness of ignorance,[4] and live in the midst of a thousand infirmities and imperfections, which sufficiently evidence that a great part of their behaviour is culpable and irregular.[5] But they are born with the wonderful ability of enlightening their minds, correcting their manners, and advancing in knowledge and virtue; in a word, of supplying their natural defects, and promoting, by their endeavours, their own perfection. They enquire after the original of their existence; they enquire indeed as it were in the dark, but yet discover it, and though they *trace* it *only in their own world*,[6] they find sufficient evidence of it there. They are instructed in the will of their Creator by the motions of their own minds. These are arguments, that God calls them to please him, and offers them his grace; and the assistances which he grants them upon their petitions, are a full conviction that he accepts their service.

I now resume my first supposition, and imagine myself enter'd into the service of these two exalted philosophers,[7] and expect that in recompence of my affection and fidelity, they

---

2. The infinite . . . exactness: "La parfaite Intelligence de Dieu & son infinie Equité discernent très exactement" (p. 52).

3. between what is . . . misfortune: "ce qui peut leur être imputé, d'avec ce qui les rend à plaindre" (p. 52).

4. darkness of ignorance: "ténébres & l'ignorance" (p. 52).

5. which sufficiently . . . irregular: "c'est une preuve que leur vie a beaucoup d'endroits condamnables" (p. 53).

6. SJ substitutes a paraphrase of l. 22 of Pope for Crousaz's paraphrase of ll. 33–34 of Du Resnel (p. 53) and adds the remainder of the sentence in his own words.

7. these two exalted philosophers: "ces deux grands Génies" (p. 53).

will favour me with the knowledge of their discoveries. May I not take the liberty to remind them of their proposal? You promised to lay open to the view of man his virtues, his vices, and the folly of his desires; but have been transported by your heat of genius[8] to a very great distance from that important plan. I intreat you to keep your word, and to admit me as your first scholar; inform me what are the rules from which I must not deviate: shew me for what I ought to wish, at what end I am to aim, and what fate I have to expect.

What answer do I receive? One that fills me with surprize,[9] and almost extinguishes my hopes.

> *Lorsque le fier coursier saura pour quel dessein*   75
> When the proud courser shall know for what design
> *L'homme l'assujettit a recevoir un frein,*
> Man him subjects to receive a bridle,
> *Precipite sa course au travers de la plaine,*
> Precipitates his course across the plain,
> *Le modere a son gre quand la fougue l'entraine;*
> Him curbs at his will when the mettle him hurries;
> *Lorsque le boeuf tardif, presse par l'aiguillon,*[1]
> When the slow ox, pricked by the goad,
> *Saura*[2] *pour quel usage il ouvre un dur sillon,*   80
> Shall know for what use he opens a hard furrow,
> *Par quel noble destin, couronne de guirlandes,*
> By what noble destiny, crowned with garlands,
> *Du peuple de Memphis il reçoit les offrandes;*
> Of the people of Memphis he receives the offerings;
> *Nos esprits affranchis de folles visions*

---

8. heat of genius: "*feu*" (p. 54).

9. One that fills . . . surprize: "Une Réponse qui me terrasse" (p. 54).

1. Crousaz has "l'éguillon" (p. 54); Du Resnel has "l'aiguillon" (l. 79), which SJ adopts.

2. Du Resnel has "sçaura" here and five lines above. Crousaz has "Sçaura" here and "saura" five lines above (p. 54, ll. 75, 80). SJ repeats the first spelling he found in Crousaz.

FIRST EPISTLE

> Our minds freed from foolish visions
> *Ne verront plus en nous de contradictions;*
> Shall not see more in us of contradictions;

I am now sent far enough away. I have the horse for my preceptor, and am to pursue my enquiries under the tuition of the ox, being doom'd to remain in utter ignorance of my condition, till those two learned doctors have acquainted themselves with the reasons of their master's proceedings.[3] The madness of that emperor who chose his horse consul, was much more despicable than the brutality of that animal;[4] and the ox surrounded by his Egyptian worshippers, was less stupid than those kings who have assumed divine honours.

Will not those absurdities, which are the reproach of man, find an end till the horse and the ox shall cease to be brutes? And is man to be so long without knowing whether he contradicts himself? Have poets so extensive a privilege as that they may boldly assert the wildest paradoxes, provided they utter them in sounding language?

> *L'orgueil humain alors aura droit de connoitre*   85
> Human pride then shall have a right to know
> *Pourquoi, de ses panchans & l'esclave & le maitre,*
> Wherefore, of his inclinations both the slave and
>   the master,
> *Avec tant de foiblesse il joint tant de grandeur;*
> With so much of weakness he joins so much of
>   greatness;
> *Pourquoi, toujours en guerre avec son propre coeur,*
> Why, always in war with his own heart,
> *Tantot il se rabaisse au dessous de lui-meme,*

---

3. I have . . . proceedings: "On m'assigne pour Précepteur le Cheval & pour Curé le Boeuf, & je dois compter de vivre dans l'ignorance de mon sort, pendant que ces deux Docteurs ne verront goute dans les raisons de ce qu'on leur fait faire" (p. 55).

4. was much more . . . animal: "alloit plus loin que la bêtise de cet animal" (p. 55). Perhaps SJ took his cue for translating "bêtise" from Forman, who confuses the word with "bête" and translates the phrase, "was more a beast than that animal" (p. 20), instead of "exceeded the stupidity of that animal."

> Sometimes he himself debases below himself,
> *Et s'eleve tantot jusqu'a l'etre supreme.*   90
> And himself exalts sometimes even to the being supreme.

I need not wait till the horse and ox make a discovery of their reasoning abilities, to know what passes within myself. I am conscious, that it is in my power to make a good use of my liberty, and that I may likewise abuse it to bad purposes. I act one way or the other, according as I apply myself with greater or less diligence, or observe with more or less care, the precepts of the wise, and examples of the good. From what passes in myself, I can guess what passes in the breasts of others. When a man gives himself up to sensuality, or abandons himself to pride, he forgets his nature, and his duty, and degrades himself to the life of a brute; he sets himself free from all restraint, and acknowledges no superior direction. Proceeding from one excess to another, he carries his sensuality beyond the brutes, or demands the respect and honours due to a divinity.[5] The Christian religion has enlarged our knowledge on this point, by informing us, that when a man has disobey'd God to a certain degree, he is forsaken by him, and deliver'd into the hands of the cursed spirits, whose whole endeavour is to drive virtue and order out of the world.[6]

> *Ne soutenez donc plus que l'homme est imparfait:*
> Don't maintain then more that man is imperfect:
> *Le ciel l'a forme tel qu'il doit etre en effect,*[7]
> Heaven him hath formed such as he ought to be in effect,
> *Tout annonce dans lui la sagesse profonde*
> All declares in him the wisdom profound
> *Du Dieu qui l'a cree pour habiter ce monde.*

---

5. or demands . . . divinity: "& on exige des hommes des respects qui vont jusqu'à l'adoration" (pp. 56–57).

6. The Christian religion . . . world: "La Religion Chrétienne étend là-dessus nos lumiéres; elle nous apprehend que Dieu abandonne ceux qui lui ont tourné le dos jusqu'à un certain point, & que les Esprits malheureux qui n'aspirent qu'à tout renverser chez nous s'en emparent" (p. 57).

7. Crousaz has "effet" (p. 57).

FIRST EPISTLE 59

Of God who him hath created to inhabit this world.
Un etat plus parfait ne lui conviendroit point; 95
A state more perfect to him would *not* agree at all;
Son tems n'est qu'un moment, son espace qu'un point.
His time is but as a moment his space but a point.

This is a very hasty conclusion. The horse and the ox are entirely ignorant of the reasons for which they are made to act in the manner they do. We therefore cannot arrive at knowing whether we are perfect or imperfect, or what are our degrees of perfection. I know not the sentiments of the horse, or the ox; I therefore am unacquainted with my own sentiments, and all endeavours to enlighten my mind will be to no purpose.

Upon what is this decision founded? *Man,* says Mr Pope, *is perfect as he ought.*[8] Whence arises this profound knowledge? Has he forgot the *weakness, littleness,* and *blindness of man? Can a part contain the whole? Has his soul pervaded and look'd through the universal system?*[9] His expressions are indeterminate and equivocal. Man was created such as he ought to be; he has degraded himself, not by the will of God,[1] but by his own fault. Those impressions that are still discoverable of the wisdom of his Creator are the remains of his primitive state.

——*Man's as perfect as he ought.*[2]

---

8. SJ substitutes part of l. 70 of Pope ("Man's as perfect as he ought") for Crousaz's quotation of l. 92 of Du Resnel (p. 58).

9. Has he forgot . . . *system?*: "A-t-il oublié que l'esprit de l'homme est *petit & aveugle? Au céleste Conseil a-t-il donc assisté?* (p. 58). Crousaz is alluding to ll. 43–51 of Du Resnel. Pope's lines are,

> But of this frame the bearings, and the ties,
> The strong connections, nice dependencies,
> Gradations just, has thy pervading soul
> Look'd thro'? or can a part contain the whole?
> Is the great chain, that draws all to agree,
> And drawn supports, upheld by God, or thee?
> II. Presumptuous Man! the reason wouldst thou find,
> Why form'd so weak, so little, and so blind? (29–36)

1. will of God: "l'ouvrage de Dieu" (p. 58).

2. SJ substitutes l. 70 of Pope for Crousaz's quotation of l. 95 of Du Resnel (p. 58).

Can a bolder assertion be easily met with? Or one more exposed to the frequent censures thrown, by Mr Pope, upon rash conclusions? Are all men equally perfect, either in a physical or a moral sense? Can it be said of a lame or a blind man,[3] of a drunkard, a cheat, or a perjur'd villain, that *he is as perfect as he ought?* Very strong proofs were necessary for the support of such a position, so new and unexpected as this. But Mr Pope puts us off with crying out,

> *His Time a Moment, and a Point his Space.*[4]

Is so exaggerated an assertion to be made good by figurative terms, and expressions yet more hyperbolical, and in a literal sense evidently false? If offering such arguments to the reader is not throwing dust into his eyes, I know not what kind of writing falls properly under that censure.

Was it not worth while to

> ——*leave all meaner Things*
> *To low Ambition,*

for so noble a discovery?[5] Life is but a moment, and we are too blind to know if what is transacted about us be good or bad. Let us then make use of the moment while it lasts, and since we cannot attain any solid knowledge of truth, let us give up our lives to diversions and inattention;[6] and for such a scheme what place more proper than a court?

I survey in my imagination a circle of these pretended philosophers, who being engaged in the study of man, and having toil'd a long time at the subject,[7] conclude that he is an assemblage of contradictions, that if he must not be owned imperfect, it is because *he is as perfect as he ought,* and he would in a state of greater perfection have been ill-adapted to his

---

3. lame . . . man: "d'un Boiteux, d'un Bossu" (p. 58).

4. SJ substitutes l. 72 of Pope for Crousaz's quotation of l. 96 of Du Resnel (p. 58).

5. Was it not . . . discovery: "Valoit-il la peine de quitter la Cour pour s'élever à une si belle découverte?" (p. 59). SJ incorporates parts of ll. 1–2 of Pope here.

6. let us give . . . inattention: "terminons nos inquiétudes en nous livrant aux dissipations" (p. 59).

7. having toil'd . . . subject: "avoir longtems battu la campagne" (p. 60).

place;[8] his life is to be accounted only a moment, since it fleets away with such rapidity. If in the moment in which they determine upon this conclusion, from which the heart can receive so little satisfaction, a servant comes to tell them that dinner is upon the table, up rise all the philosophers, and run in haste to another entertainment.[9] There will they lay aside all their speculations, for mirth and gaiety,[1] without feeling any interruption from perplexing scruples, for such are unknown to this philosophy.

> *Au milieu des transports que ton orgueil t'inspire,*
> In the midst of the transports with which thy pride thee inspires,
> *Dans le sombre avenir tu voudrois pouvoir lire.*
> In dark futurity thou would'st be able to read.
> *De nuages epais pour toi toujours couvert*
> With thick clouds to thee always covered
> *Le livre du destin pour Dieu seul est ouvert.* 100
> The book of fate to God alone is open.
> *Ce qu'il cache a la brute, a l'homme il le revele;*
> That which he hides from the brute, to man he it reveals;
> *Et ce qu'il cache a l'homme, a l'ange il le decele.*
> And that which he hides from man, to an angel he it discloses.
> *Quel etre ici pourroit, sans cette obscurite,*
> What being here could, without this obscurity,
> *Couler ses tristes jours avec tranquillite?*
> Spend his sad days with tranquillity?

These last verses are only a heap of equivocal words.

A curiosity to pry into futurity, and inform ourselves beforehand of distant events, is a temper that does not become

---

8. it is because . . . place: "c'est que tel qu'on le voit il est ce qu'il doit être; il ne convenoit pas qu'il fut rien de plus" (p. 60).

9. run in haste to another entertainment: "pour courir au solide" (p. 60).

SJ's phrase *"another* entertainment" is puzzling since "au solide" simply means "to the food."

1. mirth and gaiety: "à la gayeté" (p. 60). Forman translates the phrase "gaiety and mirth" (p. 24).

us, nor shall those who term it pride meet with any opposition from me. But an ardent desire to know clearly whether our Creator has sent us into the world to live in submission to certain laws, and what those laws are that we are bound to observe, is neither pride nor rashness, but humility, duty and submission.

> * *The Book of Fate is open only to God.*

This is not the style of philosophy,[2] but the language of Homer, who makes even the divinity subject to destiny.

> *WHAT is hid from Brutes is reveal'd to Man.*

It is plain then, that this book is not altogether shut from our eyes,[3] and the knowledge of what God thinks fit to reveal ought to be the object of our desires.

But without this happy ignorance

> —*Who could suffer being here below?*[4]

Why might we not, if we relied upon God, and resigned ourselves wholly to his will? It was well known to saints and martyrs,[5] that they exposed themselves to a death painful and ignominious in the eyes of the world, but they nevertheless applied themselves to their duty with calmness and content.[6]

> *Cet innocent agneau que ta* faim *meurtriere*   105
> That innocent lamb which thy murdering *hunger*

*Mr Pope only says,

> *Heaven from all Creatures hides the Book of Fate.*[7]

---

2. of philosophy: "d'un Philosophe" (p. 61).

3. It is plain . . . eyes: "Il n'est donc pas toûjours couvert de nuages épais pour nous" (p. 62).

4. But without . . . *below:* "Mais, *sans cette ignorance de l'avenir pourroit-on vivre tranquille?*" SJ substitutes l. 80 (76) of Pope for Crousaz's paraphrase of ll. 103–04 of Du Resnel (p. 62).

5. saints and martyrs: "Des Ames Héroïques" (p. 62).

6. but they . . . content: "mais dans cette attente elles s'appliquoient sans trouble à remplir leur devoir" (p. 62). SJ omits "dans cette attente," "in that expectation."

7. Just above SJ translates DuResnel's line as "The book of fate to God alone is open." The corresponding line of Pope, given in the footnote, is 77 (73).

FIRST EPISTLE

Condamnera ce soir a perdre la lumiere,
Shall condemn this evening to lose the light,
S'il avoit ta raison, s'il prevoyoit son sort,
If he had thy reason, if he foresaw his lot,
Dans une paix tranquille attendroit-il la mort?
In a quiet peace would he wait death?
Jusqu'a instant[8] fatal qui termine sa vie,
Until the fatal instant which ends his life,
Il pait en bondissant l'herbe tendre & fleurie,   110
He feeds, in frisking, the grass tender and flow'ry,
Sans crainte, sans soupçon, au milieu du danger.
Without fear, without suspicion, in the midst of danger.
Il caresse la main qui le doit egorger.
He caresses the hand which is to cut his throat.
Heureux aveuglement! heureuse incertitude!
Happy blindness! happy uncertainty!
Qui cache l'avenir a notre inquietude!
Which hides the future from our uneasiness!
Mistere que le ciel renferme dans son sein,   115
A mystery which heaven reserves in its bosom,
Pour conduire tout etre a remplir son destin!
To conduct every being to fulfil his destiny!

Beasts give very evident proofs that they are afraid of blows and of pain, but it no way appears that they have any idea of death, or any apprehensions about it.

But with regard to man, a frequent[9] reflection upon the certainty of death will very much assist him to conduct his life wisely, and conclude it happily. In this religion and common sense agree; and as man must equally divest himself of both to cry out,[1]

---

8. Crousaz has "l'instant" (p. 62).
9. SJ adds "a frequent."
1. man must . . . cry out: "il faut faire également abstraction des lumiéres de l'une & de l'autre pour s'écrier." SJ substitutes below ll. 85–86 (81–82) of Pope for Crousaz's quotation of ll. 113–16 of Du Resnel (p. 63). The lines should read "kindly giv'n" and "may fill."

O blindness to the future, wisely giv'n![2]

when he adds that it is giv'n us,

That each might fill the Circle mark'd by Heaven,

he supposes that, if men were inform'd of their end, and of *the circle mark'd out for them,* they might avoid it or deviate from it,[3] since it is by means of this ignorance that heav'n conducts every being to the end proposed. But if man cannot employ his powers, and direct his actions according to his own will, this consequence is evidently ill-grounded.[4] But the doctrine of fatality is productive of contradictions; and if once we lose sight of it, plain reason carries us away into notions very remote from it. Every page of the writings of the Stoicks is a confirmation of this; the beauty of their morality is founded upon principles that interfere one with another.*

God has favour'd man with abilities sufficient for making, upon things not altogether beyond their power, or wholly separated from the circumstances that encompass them, such conjectures, as capacitate them to conduct themselves with prudence and success, and to give good advice to such as want it.

But God, whose views of futurity are infinitely more clear than man's, and who has the sovereign disposal of all events, very often mercifully disappoints human designs, because the disappointment is more to our advantage than success. He

---

*Mr Crousaz, in this reflection, seems to have forgotten either the candour of a moralist, or the sagacity of a commentator; for he either evidently perverts, or mistakes his author's expressions, and animadverts upon that mistaken sense. Every man perceives how much it contributes to his quiet in the present state, to be ignorant of the time and manner of his death. Every man will find, upon the least reflection, that the knowledge of futurity would make such a change in the face of human affairs, that we might be accounted almost another order of beings: nor could he, if he had attended to his author, have imagined, that he meant to insinuate that a knowledge of its end would enable any being to avoid it, since both the original and the translation include all other animals as well as man in the assertion.

---

2. SJ adds the quotation from Pope. The line (85) should read "kindly giv'n" and the following line (86) "may fill."

3. avoid . . . it: "l'éviter" (p. 64).

4. consequence . . . ill-grounded: "conséquence qui ne sauroit avoir lieu" (p. 64).

FIRST EPISTLE

often brings to nothing the pride and rashness of their undertakings, and suffers them to fall into the calamities they deserve. Men, with regard to futurity, make an ill use of their freewill, sometimes persuading themselves, without just grounds, of the certainty of what they wish for; and sometimes, when they are inform'd of the approach of misfortunes, disregarding advice because they do not like it: of this we have an affecting instance in the conduct of the Israelites a little before the[5] captivity.

There is yet another kind of testimony,[6] concerning which it is of infinite consequence that they should attain the clearest knowledge, which God will not fail to grant them, if they ask it with ardent zeal and true sincerity.

By the confession of Mr Pope himself, evidences of goodness and wisdom shine in all his works, and particularly in man: this truth he proclaims in his poetical strain, that is, in a style to the utmost degree pompous and magnificent.[7]

Wisdom always tends to some end. As our Maker has bestow'd feet upon us, he evidently intends that we should walk upon them, and convey ourselves by the help of them to any place where our presence is required: the eye was given us to see with, and the organs of voice invite us to conversation. We need only observe ourselves and the objects about us, and we may make infinite additions to the knowledge of our end.*

---

*Mr Crousaz seems to impose upon his readers, or at least upon himself, by the equivocal and variable import of the word *end*, [or *destinee*] which signifies either the period of our being, or intentional end for which we are sent into the world. So that his argument against Mr Pope seems to stand thus: *Heaven*, says the author, conceals from all earthly beings their *end*, or time of their dissolution. *Heaven*, says the commentator, discovers clearly to man his end, or the intention for which he was created.

---

5. SJ's text has "the." Perhaps this is a slip of the pen or a compositorial error as the French is "leur" (p. 65).

6. There . . . testimony: "Mais il y a une autre destinée" (p. 65). "Destinée" is "divine disposition," which SJ may have misread in his dictionary as "deposition." Boyer, however, defines "Destinée" the substantive as "destiny, fate," and "Destinée" the adjective as "born, designed, devoted, destinated, appointed."

7. this truth . . . magnificent: "Ce sont des vérités qu'il énonce dans ses Vers, c'est à dire très pompeusement" (p. 66).

If self-love were not implanted in our natures, the infinite and almighty goodness of God would have heap'd his gifts upon us in vain, since we should be insensible of his benefits. He would have us love ourselves; that is, according to the strictest sense of the word, he would have us esteem ourselves, and employ our utmost diligence to improve our condition. But what can we find estimable in ourselves? those gifts which God hath conferr'd upon us. We ought to reverence and love ourselves as we are his work. This is a sufficient reason why we should be afraid of dishonouring ourselves. We perceive ourselves capable of gratitude; and what object is so worthy of our gratitude and thanks as the Supreme Being from whom we have receiv'd all that we enjoy? What ought we more ardently to wish, than that we may perform our duty to him? For surely we can propose to ourselves no advantage that can be compared with the true, the glorious and transporting pleasure of devoting ourselves to his service: such devotion will be approved and accepted by that infinite wisdom, power and goodness that enables us to offer it. Is not this a new subject of thanksgiving and admiration? He had made us capable of attaining knowledge; and certainly no knowledge can contribute to the perfection of our nature like that of his will. Nor can it be conceived that his infinite goodness would refuse to let us succeed in our enquiries after that obedience which is the proper expression of our zeal and devotion. For this happy discovery we need not soar to the skies, or plunge into the deeps. His laws are engraven on our hearts, and our first duty is to acquaint ourselves with them: we shall thus be brought on to love and adore the fountain of this inestimable knowledge, and to found our highest satisfaction in a submission to his holy commands. We may, indeed, make an offer to him of ourselves as we are, but we can give him nothing, nor add any thing to the fulness of his felicity, which is incapable of want. But he gives us an opportunity of assisting our fellow-creatures. Every man has a claim to our love and esteem, since he, like ourselves, is the work of that being whom we worship; a creature of the same order, and equally favour'd with his regard. Thus, as we pursue our enquiry, morality unfolds itself by degrees, and the heavenly transports which its author has made attendant on[8] the knowledge and practice of his commands, convince us fully of the end of our being, and of the intention with which we were created. Our condition, therefore, as well as our knowledge, is infinitely above that of the horse and the ox, and the bounty[9] of the Creator well deserv'd to be celebrated by the utmost efforts,[1] and the whole capacity of the poet I am studying; whose verses, with a very little inclination in the reader to take them in a bad sense, tend wholly to discourage our endeavours, and to lull us in indolence.

> *Ainsi tout obeit a ce pouvoir immense,*
> Thus every thing submits to that power immense,
> *Qui pese l'univers en sa juste balance;*
> Who weighs th'universe in his just balance;
> *Qui voit d'un oeil egal, dans un parfait repos,*
> Who sees with an equal eye, in a perfect repose,
> *Un passereau tomber, ou perir un heros;* 120
> A sparrow fall, or perish a hero;
> *Des nuages legers en vapeurs se resoudre,*
> Thin clouds into vapours themselves resolve,
> *Ou des cieux ebranles a grand bruit dissoudre;*[2]
> Or the heavens shaken with a great noise dissolve;
> *De fragiles roseaux plier au gre du vent,*
> Frail reeds bend at the will of the wind,
> *Ou des mondes entiers rentrer dans neant.*[3]
> Or worlds entire fall back into nothing.

Perhaps Mr Pope confines himself to write to minds of greater penetration than mine, and for that reason some things may be obscure to me, which to his favourite readers are perfectly clear. By the *just balance*[4] does he mean, in this place, that by which vice and virtue are duly recompensed?

---

8. its author . . . attendant on: "son Auteur nous fait la grace de goûter" (p. 69).
9. bounty: "Bonheur" (p. 69).
1. utmost efforts: "veine" (p. 69).
2. Crousaz has "se dissoudre" (p. 70).
3. Crousaz has "le Néant" (p. 70).

4. *just balance:* Forman has a footnote at this point in the text similar to SJ's immediately below: "This is the translator's way of rendering *equal Eye*, which he likewise has too in the next line; or *sa juste balance* is a flight of his own" (p. 31).

Or, by the *balance** does he only intend the *equilibrium* preserved by the Creator between the parts that compose this structure[5] of the world? This would be making the idea of the Supreme Being too much like those of a mechanick. Does, then, *the death of a sparrow*, or *the fall of a hero*, engage his attention lest the balance should be destroy'd?[6]

Is it Mr Pope's opinion, that every thing is the immediate act of God, and he directs equally the dagger by which the hero dies, and the shot that brings a sparrow from the wing? The more reputation an author is arriv'd at, the more cautious ought he to be, that nothing drops from his pen,[7] from which men of corrupt inclinations may take advantages in opposing religion.

If he affirms nothing more, than that the unchangeable felicity of the Supreme Being suffers no more interruption from the murder of a *hero*, than the fall of a *sparrow*, his notion ought to be that of all mankind.

But if he intends to insinuate, that these two events are indifferent in his sight, he throws a very injurious imputation on his justice. To kill a bird is allow'd by the Creator;[8] to attempt the life of an innocent man, is criminal in a high degree; it is still more criminal to attempt a life, in which the rest of the world has so great an interest.[9]

The lines that follow could have been written only for the sake of filling this performance with striking antitheses. They are not very consistent with Mr Pope's own system of the de-

---

*The two lines that give occasion to these questions, are entirely inserted by the translator.

---

5. this structure: "la grande Machine" (p. 70).

6. Does . . . destroy'd: "se rendroit-elle attentive à empêcher que la mort d'un Passereau, ou celle d'un homme ne rompit cet équilibre" (p. 70). SJ may be taking his cue for translating this passage from Pope:

>Who sees with equal eye, as God of all,
>A hero perish, or a sparrow fall.
>(87–88; 83–84)

7. SJ adds "from his pen."
8. SJ adds "by the Creator."
9. to attempt . . . interest: "mais il est criminel d'attenter à la vie d'un homme innocent, & à plus forte raison à une vie, qui a tant d'influence sur le bonheur des autres" (p. 71).

pendence of each part of the universe upon the rest. The breach of a single link of that great chain, would, it seems,

> *Make Nature tremble to the Throne of God;*[1]

would he then behold, with absolute indifference, worlds after worlds falling into nothing?[2] May we not add, that the conceit of those ingenious ladies, that were so charm'd with Des Cartes's falling worlds, is now wholly out of fashion?[3]

> **Joignons donc a l'espoir une humble defiance;*   125
> Let us join then to hope an humble distrust;
> *Et craignons les ecarts ou* jette *la science,*
> And let us fear the errors on which knowledge
>   throws,
> *Attendons que la mort, ce maitre universel,*
> Let us wait till death, that master universal,
> *Decouvre a nos esprits les loix de l'eternel.*
> Discover to our minds the laws of th'eternal.

---

*In this place six whole lines are omitted.[4]

---

1. SJ substitutes l. 256 (248) of Pope for Crousaz's paraphrase of l. 374 of Du Resnel (p. 72). The line should read "And Nature."

2. nothing: "le néant" (p. 72).

3. May we not . . . fashion: "Ajoutons que la mode de ces Précieuses, qui admiroient sur tout les Mondes tombans de DES CARTES, ne subsiste plus" (p. 72).

4. Hope humbly then; with
    trembling pinions soar;
Wait the great teacher Death, and
    God adore!
What future bliss, he gives not
    thee to know,
But gives that Hope to be thy
    blessing now.
Hope springs eternal in the
    human breast:
Man never Is, but always To be
    blest. (91–96; 87–92)

SJ comments on l. 95 in an entry for 10 April 1775 in the *Life:* "that *the present* was never a happy state to any human being; but that, as every part of life, of which we are conscious, was at some point of time a period yet to come, in which felicity was expected, there was some happiness produced by hope" (II.350–51). These four lines of Du Resnel correspond, more or less, to lines 97–98 (93–94) of Pope:

> The soul uneasy and confin'd from
>   home,
> Rests and expatiates in a life to
>   come.

In a footnote Forman also observes that six lines (93–98; 89–94) are missing: "These six lines [inserted into the text of his translation] are not in the translation; how they came to be passed over, the translator knows best" (p. 33).

Let us be cautious of waiting so long: such indolence is far from innocence.[5] As God, when he created us, impress'd self-love upon our minds, let us not be ungrateful for his gifts, by an obstinate unconcern about our own interests; nor let us any more apply to the stupidity and extravagance of the Indian for example and instruction, than to the ignorance of the ox or of the horse.[6]

> *Regarde l'Indien, dont l'esprit sans culture*
> Behold th'Indian, whose mind without culture
> *N'a point l'art d'alterer les dons de la nature;*   130
> Hath not th'art of altering the gifts of nature;
> *Il voit Dieu dans les airs, il l'entend dans les vents;*
> He sees God in the air, he hears him in the winds;
> *Son savoir[7] ne va point au dela de ses sens.*
> His knowledge goes not beyond his senses.
> *Il s'arrete avec eux aux seules apparences.*
> It stops with them at bare appearances.
> *Sa raison n'etend point ses foibles connoissances*
> His reason extends not his weak notions
> *Au de la[8] du soleil, & des corps radieux*   135
> Beyond the sun, and the bodies shining
> *Que son oeil apperçoit dans la voute des cieux.*
> Which his eye discerns in the vault of heaven.
> *Cependant secouru par la simple nature*
> Nevertheless assisted by simple nature
> *Pour tromper ses ennuis, il croit, il se figure*
> To cheat his sorrows, he believes, he imagines
> *Un sejour plus heureux, conforme a ses desirs,*
> An abode more happy, conformable to his desires,
> *Ou sans aucune[9] melange il attend plaisirs.*   140
> Where without any allay he expects pleasures.

---

5. such indolence . . . innocence: "Cette indolence est trop criminelle" (p. 72).

6. nor let us . . . horse: "ne soyons pas moins éloignés de prendre pour modéle la stupidité & les extravagances de l'Indien, que l'ignorance du Cheval & du Boeuf, & refusons de nous aller instruire à ces Ecoles" (pp. 72–73).

7. Crousaz has "sçavoir" (p. 73).

8. Crousaz has "delà" (p. 73).

9. Crousaz has correctly "aucun" and "des plaisirs" (p. 73).

FIRST EPISTLE

Au dela de ces monts que terminent sa vue
Beyond these mountains which terminate his sight
Il imagine un monde, une terre inconnu,[1]
He imagines a world, a land unknown,
Que de vastes forets mettront en surete
Which vast forests shall place in safety
Contre les attentats d'un vainqueur redoute.[2]
Against the attempts of a conqueror formidable.
Il se peint dans les mers une isle fortunee,   145
He fancies in the sea an island fortunate,
Ou maitre de lui-meme & de sa destinee,
Where master of himself and of his destiny,
Quelque Dieu bienfaisant enfin rompra ses fers,
Some God beneficent at last shall break his fetters,
Et le consolera des maux qu'il a soufferts.
And him shall comfort for the evils which he hath suffered.
Les esprits infernaux, dans l'horreur des tenebres,
The spirits infernal, in th'horror of darkness,
Ne l'y troubleront plus sous formes funebres;   150
Shall there trouble him no more under forms dismal;
Dans ces paisibles lieux les armes des chretiens
In these peaceful regions the arms of christians
N'iront plus lui ravir son repos ni ses biens.
Shall come no more to rob him of his rest nor his goods.

I found at verse 23, a great difficulty in annexing a reasonable meaning to the term *nature*. Has Mr Pope given, in this place, a clearer explication of it?* This nature, whose voice

---

*Mr Pope, in the original, has not made use of the word *nature* in the passage here referr'd to; his expression being only

---

1. Crousaz has correctly "inconnue" (p. 73).

2. formidable: Crousaz has "redouté" (p. 73), meaning "feared, dreaded." The omission of the accent may have misled SJ. Boyer defines "Redoutable" as "dreadful, formidable." This definition appears immediately above that for "Redoute."

is to be reverenced, and whose steps are to be followed, and whose gifts are not to be changed, is, it seems, that state of the *mind* in which it lies, unimproved, tho' formed with a capacity of improvement, of endeavouring after perfection, and of acquiring true notions. Are the instructions of nature never to extend beyond the gross informations of sense? Is this blissful state of nature the condition of a man who, without condescending to call in the assistance of reason, alleviates the troubles of life,³ by giving up himself to the wildest chimeras? And tho' we should suppose that God looks down with pity upon the poor Indian's darkness, must we judge with equal favour of their obstinate and voluntary blindness, whom sensuality and pride, and aversion from restraint persuade to shut their eyes against that light, which cannot guide them without their own consent?

Our lives are given us by God, and are therefore not to be enjoy'd with indifference. Are they not to be valued as his gifts? If we esteem and love them as we ought, shall we not desire the continuance of the favour? Does he that desires the continuance of a good, turn his knowledge of it to an ill use? Can a desire of preserving our existence, that we may advance in the knowledge of his will, and submit to it with just respect, be unbecoming the nature of man,⁴ or displeasing to the goodness of God? He has created us with abilities to im-

---

Lo! the poor Indian, whose untutor'd Mind.

But he has, indeed, us'd the word a few lines after,

Yet simple Nature to his Hope has given, &c.

to which, perhaps, all that Mr Crousaz has written may be apply'd with propriety.⁵

---

3. alleviates the troubles of life: "tromper ses ennuis" (p. 74). SJ has made a literal translation of an idiomatic phrase meaning "whiles away his time."

4. submit to it . . . man: "à s'abandonner à la soumission dont elle est digne, sont-ce des desirs qui ne nous conviennent pas" (p. 75).

5. Crousaz seems to be referring to l. 22. See p. 46 above. SJ quotes lines 99 (95) and 103 (99). In a footnote Forman takes a harsher view of the same passage (99–108; 95–104): "As to these ten lines [inserted into the text of his translation], the translator, tho' counted one of the French first rates, has hobbled out their meaning within the compass of twenty four of his own; but he has left their spirit behind him" (p. 33).

prove our understanding; shall we be ravish'd with gratitude for this inestimable gift, and lost in admiration of it,[6] and at the same time scruple to make use of it? And will God be displeas'd with prayers offer'd up with equal fervor and humility for a fuller knowledge of him, that we may admire[7] him with more purity? Can any man prohibit us to indulge such ideas, and set them on a level with the dreams of the blind Indian? Every man that shall give his heart up to desires so reasonable, and so worthy of the nature with which God has endued us, will find,[8] by happy and never-failing experience, that his desires are such as he was created to entertain.

Mr Pope continues to say, in praise of his Indian favourite,[9]

> *Que content d'exister, il attend l'heureux jour,*
> But content to exist, he waits the happy day,
> *Ou porte tout a coup dans un autre sejour*
> When carry'd on a sudden into another abode
> *Il ira, jouissant d'une plus douce vie,*   155
> He shall go, rejoicing in a sweeter life,
> *Habiter des humains la commune patrie.*
> To inhabit of mankind the common country.*

---

*Mr Pope only says,

> TO BE *contents his Natural Desire,*
> *He asks no Angel's Wing, no Seraph's Fire.*[1]

Three of these lines, and the latter of the next couplet, so justly animadverted on by the commentator, are Mr Du Resnel's; who, as he has read Roscommon, ought to have remembered

> *That 'tis much safer to leave out than add.*[2]

By omitting a just sentiment, we only suppress part of an author's virtues; by adding an improper thought, we charge him with faults of which he is not guilty.

---

6. shall we be ... it: "pleins d'admiration & de reconnoissance pour ce rich présent" (p. 75).

7. admire: "adorer" (p. 76).

8. the nature ... find: "la nature que nous avons reçu de Dieu, & si conformes à son infinie bonté, éprouvera" (p. 76).

9. SJ adds "favourite."

1. SJ quotes lines 109–10 (105–06) of Pope. SJ, or the compositor, made a happy emendation in line 110 (106). According to Maynard Mack in the Twickenham Edition (p. 28), the text read "or" or "nor Seraph's" until the Pope and Warburton collected edition of 1743 when it was changed to "no Seraph's."

2. *An Essay on Translated Verse* in *Poems by the Earl of Roscommon* (1717), p. 29.

If Mr Pope had intended, by assisting the Indian with his own notions and his poetry, to raise his chimeras[3] to an equality with the persuasions of a Christian, could he have spoken in any other terms? Two lines higher he seems to give him the preference.

> *Il ne desire point cette celeste flamme,*
> He desires nothing of that celestial flame,
> *Qui des purs Seraphins devore & nourrit l'ame.*
> Which of pure Seraphim consumes and nourishes
>   the soul.

Mr Pope, fir'd by an antithesis, has, by the way, thrown ridicule upon the happy spirits. The Indian, wiser than they, is content to want a flame which consumes at the same time that it supports.*

*Mr Crousaz is so watchful against impiety, that he lets nonsense pass without censure: can any thing consume and nourish at the same time?[4] I take this opportunity of observing, once for all, that he is not sufficiently candid in charging all the errors of this miserable version upon the original author. If he had no way of distinguishing between Mr Pope and his translator, to throw the odium of impiety, and the ridicule of nonsense entirely upon the former, is at least *stabbing in the dark*,[5] and

---

The line should begin with "And." See Du Resnel's comments on Roscommon in his Preface and SJ's comments on Du Resnel, pp. 350–54 below.

3. chimeras: "imaginations" (p. 76). Lines 53–54, "Il ne desire . . . l'ame," of Du Resnel have been shifted to lines 57–58 by Crousaz.

4. Forman has a footnote at the same point in the text: "Mr. Pope has nothing to do with these words, they are one of the translator's flights, which the critic is only exposing at the same time that he thinks he is demolishing Mr. Pope" (p. 36). In the Preface to Forman's translation, Edmund Curll asks: "The same impartiality and justice obliges us to ask Mr De Crousaz, as he had two *French* translations of Mr Pope's *Essay on Man* in his hands, why he did not take the prose to comment upon rather than the verse, since he did not understand *English?*" (p. ix).

5. Perhaps the image of *stabbing in the dark* was suggested to SJ by his own "Life of Father Paul Sarpi," published in the November 1738 issue of the *Gentleman's Magazine:* "But their [Romans'] malice was chiefly aimed against F. Paul, who soon found the effects of it, for as he was going one night to his convent, . . . he was attack'd by five ruffians armed with stilettoes, who gave him no less than fifteen stabs, three of which wounded him in such a manner that he was left for dead" (VIII.583). The destruction of a person's reputation compared to a *stabbing* occurs again in SJ's "Life of Dr Herman Boerhaave," in the installment published in the February 1739 issue of the *Gentleman's Magazine:* "Those who cannot strike with force, can however

> *Va, plus sage qui lui, dans ta prevention,*[6]
> Go, wiser than him, in thy conceit,
> *Imaginer en tout quelque imperfection.* 160
> Fancy in all some imperfection.

Who is it that searches for imperfection, and supposes it where there is none, but he that set[7] the most enlightned minds below the darkness of a rude savage?

In the conduct of God, let us neither suppose nor look for imperfection; but in the behaviour of men, we shall find a great deal of imperfection, and something worse, when they appear indolent with regard to that which ought to awaken them to the highest ardour, and lavish the warmth of the passions upon things which at best can claim nothing more than a careless wish, to which we ought very often to be wholly indifferent, and which we ought yet more often to detest.[8] These disorders and irregularities we behold with regret: the tranquillity of our lives is interrupted by them; and if we endeavour after any comfort, we must expect it from our care not to imitate them, from our sollicitude to extricate those who are involved in them, and to hinder others from falling into them whenever we have an opportunity. Will any one pretend to maintain, that such conduct, as this, is less wise than that of a mere animal, that is wholly engross'd by the present moment, and only possess'd with idle notions, that serve to divert him from the troubles of life.[9]

---

wounding, for ought he knows, an innocent character: but this seems not to be, in reality, the case. He had a prose translation in his hand, which he might have compared with Du Resnel's: he has, therefore, done a voluntary wrong to the *English* poet. What can be the reason of this conduct? Or what can be said in justification of it? Could it be fear of Mr Du Resnel? Mr Pope seems much the more formidable enemy. Could it be friendship for him? The friends of a philosopher and Christian ought to be justice, charity, and truth.

---

poyson their weapon, and, weak as they are, give mortal wounds, and bring a hero to the grave . . ." (IX.73).

6. conceit: "prévention" (p. 77).
7. set: "compte" (p. 77).
8. lavish the warmth . . . detest: "tout de feu pour ce qui ne mérite que de foibles desirs, souvent même de l'indifférence, & plus souvent encore un grand éloignement" (p. 78).

9. only possess'd . . . life: "seulement mêlée de quelques imaginations

I must, by the way, say one word of those peaceful habitations, where

> ————*No Christians thirst for Gold.*[1]

Can Mr Pope find any fault with those who look with horror upon persecution and inhumanity, which dishonour the Christian religion by a conduct entirely opposite to all its precepts?*

> *Prends*[2] *follement en main ton injuste balance;*
> Take foolishly in hand thy unjust balance;
> *Parle, eleve ta voix contre la providence.*
> Speak, raise thy voice against providence.
> *Dis que le createur, en ses dons inegal,*
> Say that the creator, in his gifts partial,
> *La te paroit avare, ici trop liberal.*
> There seems to thee sparing, here too liberal.
> *Renverse pour toi seul les loix de la nature,* 165
> Reverse for thy self alone the laws of nature,
> *Fais*[3] *divers changemens en chaque creature;*
> Make various alterations in every creature;
> *Arbitre souverain des biens & des plaisirs,*
> Arbitrary sovereign of wealth and of pleasures,
> *Reforme l'univers au gre de tes desirs;*
> Reform th'universe to the pleasure of thy desires;

*This remark I cannot understand; this persecution and inhumanity are evidently condemn'd in the *English,* and no less evidently in the *French.*

---

sans preuves, pour tromper des ennuis, c'est-à-dire pour se repaître d'illusions" (p. 78).

1. SJ substitutes l. 108b (104b) of Pope for Crousaz's paraphrase of ll. 151–52 of Du Resnel (p. 78).

> Yet simple Nature to his hope has giv'n
> Behind the cloud-topt hill, an humbler heav'n;
> Some safer world, in depth of woods embrac'd,
> Some happier island in the wat'ry waste,
> Where slaves once more their native land behold,
> No fiends torment, no Christians thirst for gold! (103–08; 99–104)

2. Crousaz has "Pren" (p. 79).
3. Crousaz has "Fai" (p. 79).

FIRST EPISTLE 77

> *Ose accuser du ciel l'eternelle sagesse,*
> Dare to accuse of heaven th'eternal wisdom,
> *S'il n'epuise pour toi ses soins & ses*[4] *tendresse.* 170
> If it exhausts not for thee its cares and its tenderness.

To whom does Mr Pope speak in this long period? To those presumptuous disputers,[5] who are putting themselves continually to the stretch, and exhausting their fruitful imaginations, to perplex Christians with objections against Providence; their hastiness and impatience of rules well deserve all those censures which Mr Pope throws out upon them. But when he adds,

> *S'il ne joint aux faveurs que te fait sa bonte*
> If it adds not to the favours which its goodness does thee
> *L'irrevocable sceau de l'immortalite,*
> Th'irrevocable seal of immortality,

he seems to go too great a length, or, at least, his expressions appear to imply more than he designs: with those who accuse and deny the wisdom and justice of Providence, he joins,[6] in the same period, those who acknowledge and adore its goodness; those who confess, that if God had many[7] years ago taken their lives from them, he had only treated them according to their deserts; but conclude, that since he continues to preserve them, and to give them new proofs of his regard, they are not irreversibly condemned, or detested by him, but regarded with kindness and compassion. Their Supreme Master seems to them to prolong their lives, that their repentence may be continued, and their virtues improved. Their former wanderings of thought are succeeded by a fervent love of God, and admiration of his goodness. Then looking upon these sentiments which they feel now predominant within them, as evidences of his favour and reconciliation, they

---

4. Crousaz has "sa" (p. 79).
5. those presumptuous disputers: "ces présomptueux" (p. 79).
6. Providence, he joins: "Providence, pour en conclure qu'il n'y en a point, il joint" (p. 80).
7. many: "plusieurs" (p. 80). Boyer defines "Plusieurs" as "many."

make, with equal ardor and humility, such requests as are permitted, and even commanded by him.

Is any allusion made here to the faith of Christians, declared by St Paul *to be* sealed *by the* HOLY SPIRIT to the day of redemption? And does not he that ascribes to a spirit of pride the inestimable effects of divine grace, approach to blasphemy of the highest kind?⁸* Has Mr Pope never read the scripture? Or has he read it like a libertine, with a spirit of cavil and opposition?⁹ Has he read it for the sake of extracting passages to be ridiculed by profane allusions? The sacred writings never mention our expectations without comparing them with our unworthiness; nor do they found them upon any other grounds than the free mercy of God, and the certainty of his promises,¹ which cannot be sufficiently admired. Even under the Old Testament,² these were the sentiments of believers, who always accompanied their hopes and prayers with acts of humility. *O my God,* said Nehemiah, imploring a blessing upon himself, and upon the good he had done, *remember me and pardon me, according to the multitude of thy mercies.*³

Mr Pope is introduced by his translator under the character of a *good Catholick,* perhaps with the same notions with which some men endeavour to make converts, by such applications as these: *Do but stick fast to the trunk of the tree, enlist*

---

*The English reader, whom we desire to compare, on all occasions, this *Commentary* with the original, will not need to be inform'd, that this word, which gives Mr Crousaz so much offence, is not Mr Pope's. Nor, indeed, does it seem in the French liable to such a dreadful construction as this writer, whose expression we have soften'd in this translation, endeavours to fix upon it.

---

8. And does not . . . kind: "en ce cas n'approche-t-on pas du crime irrémissible des Pharisiens qui imputoient les Miracles de J. C. à Béelzebul, quand on attribue à un Esprit d'orgueil les plus précieux effets de la Grace Divine?" (p. 81).

9. with a spirit . . . opposition: "que dans un esprit de Critique" (p. 81).

1. promises: "promesses de sa Grace" (p. 82).

2. the Old Testament: "l'ancienne Alliance" (p. 82), literally the pact concluded between God and the Jewish people.

3. *the multitude of thy mercies:* "la grandeur de ta Misericorde" (p. 82). SJ did not consult the Authorized Version of Nehemiah i.11 and v.19 to provide his translation. His phrase, "the multitude of thy mercies," appears in Psalms lxix.13 and cvi.7; "the multitude of his mercies" is found in Psalms cvi.45 and Lamentations iii.32.

yourself but under the same denomination with us, and for the rest act and think as you are most inclined. There is nothing that a Christian ought to be more apprehensive of than of contributing to the fall of those whose faith is yet weak. Why should they be exposed by flights of poetry[4] and magnificent expressions, to grow familiar[5] with prophane ideas? There are in many that call themselves Christians latent seeds of infidelity. A corrupt mind easily embraces any thing that tends to set it free from restraint, and they that would not be the authors of certain daring[6] expressions feel no reluctance against hearing them from another. The eagerness of mankind for scandalous and infectious writings, gives a great deal of pain to those whose concern for the good of others ought not to subject them to such mortifications.

> *Sois le Dieu de ton Dieu; ne suis que ton caprice,*
> Be the God of thy God; follow only thy caprice,
> *Place-toi sur son trone, & juge sa justice.*
> Place thyself upon his throne, and judge his justice.

These are horrible expressions, which can only be ascribed to libertines, who have declared open war against Providence.

> *Aveugle en ses desirs, l'orgueil ambitieux*   175
> Blind in its desires, *ambitious pride*
> *Veut sortir de sa sphere, & s'elever aux cieux;*
> Would go out of its sphere, and exalt itself to the heavens;
> *L'orgueil de tout erreur fut la cause premiere;*
> Pride of every error was the first cause;
> *Les Anges, eblouis par sa fausse lumiere,*
> The Angels, dazzled with its false light,
> *Au Dieu qui les crea voulurent s'egaler;*
> To God who them created would equal themselves;
> *Aux Anges, a son tour, l'homme veut ressembler,*   180

---

4. flights of poetry: "Vers hardis" (p. 82).

5. to grow familiar: "au danger de se familiariser" (p. 82).

6. SJ has added "daring."

> To Angels, in his turn, man would be like,
> *Changer l'ordre etabli par la cause supreme;*
> Change the order establish'd by the supreme cause;
> *C'est pretendre comme eux s'egaler a Dieu meme.*
> That is to pretend like them to be equal to God himself.

Those arrogant spirits, which we call *devils,* being uneasy under a submission which they thought too burdensome, chose rather to govern themselves by their own inclinations, and to admit no laws but their own. God looks with compassion upon the miserable state of man whom their subtilty and malice have reduced, and determines to do him infinitely more good than they have attempted to do him injury; and to place him out of all danger of being seduced, and falling a second time, decrees to exalt him to a nature and perfection far superior to his original rank. Standing out against so just a submission, and following the call of God with the utmost admiration and devotion, in hopes of living to all eternity in obedience and submission to his laws,[7] are such different states of the heart, that no man can help looking with equal pity and indignation upon the disorder of that mind, which can think of setting such contrarieties in parallel with each other.

> *Pourquoi se presentant a nos voeux tour a tour*
> Wherefore presenting themselves to our wishes by turns
> *Les Astres dans les cieux brillent-ils nuit & jour?*
> The Stars in the heavens shine they night and day?
> *Pourquoi sur ses pivots la terre inebranlable*   185
> Wherefore on its axis the earth immoveable
> *Offre-t-elle par tout l'utile & l'agreable?*
> Offers it throughout the useful and the agreeable?
> *Je suis, repond l'orgueil, l'objet de tous ces dons;*
> I am, answers pride, th'object of all these gifts;

---

7. in hopes . . . laws: "dans l'espérance de voir éternellement ses Loix regner en nous & sur nous" (p. 84).

FIRST EPISTLE

La nature pour moi, dans ses efforts feconds
Nature for me, in its *fruitful endeavors*
Sans jamais s'epuiser[f] *veille,*[8] *conçoit, enfante;*
Without ever exhausting itself labours, conceives, brings forth;
C'est pour mes seuls besoins que sa main bienfaisante   190
It is for my alone occasions that her *bounteous hand*
Fertilise les champs, embellit les jardins,
Fertilises the fields, embellishes the gardens,
Fait eclore la rose, & meurir[9] *les raisins;*
Makes *the rose to bud,* and the grapes to ripen;
Les mines, les metaux, les tresors de la terre,
The mines, the metals, the treasures of the earth,
Sont des biens que pour moi dans son sein elle enserre.
Are goods which for me in her bosom she locks up.
Les vents impetueux qui soulevent les mers,   195
The *boisterous winds* which raise the seas,
Sont faits pour me porter en des climats divers;
Are made to carry me into different climates;
Ce soleil, qui fournit sa brillante carriere,
This sun, which describes its shining course,
Ne repand que pour moi ses feux & sa lumiere;
Displays only for me his fires and his light;
Et ce vaste univers, mon superbe palais,
And this vast universe, my proud palace,
M'offre un trone eclatant, dont les cieux sont le dais.   200
Affords me a glittering throne, of which the heavens are the canopy.

This is the language of *pride,* carried to the most excessive extravagancies, and can hardly be supposed to have been ever utter'd unless it were in jest.

---

f. l'epuiser

---

8. Boyer defines "Veille" in a figurative sense as "(grande & longue application qu'on donne à l'etude & aux affaires) labour, study, business."

9. Crousaz correctly has "mûrir" (p. 85).

That we form some idea of the immensity and exalted nature of God, we say, in figurative terms, that *the heaven is his throne, and the earth his footstool;*[1] images, which, taken together, represent the whole universe as the temple of his glory.

Upon that part of the universe, which is called the earth, we are placed by our Creator, surrounded with external good, and enriched with internal gifts. Weak as we are, we see ourselves encompassed with a thousand assistances, and are in possession of such an *industry* as may secure us from every thing that can hurt us, and produce every thing that can conduce to our advantage. A reasonable man remarks these mercies with a heart fill'd with gratitude, he feels himself unworthy of them, and his gratitude is doubled; he then bows down with thanksgivings under the hand of that almighty power, to whom he is indebted for his existence, and in this temper of mind is convinced that to know his laws and obey them is the utmost heighth of felicity.

With this condition, so suited to the nature of man, but pretended to be the aim only of pride, let us compare the modesty and humility of those who, to set themselves free from such a number of obligations as hinders them from being entirely at ease, debase themselves to the level of brutes, confine themselves to the pleasures[2] of animal life, and, that they may enjoy the present moment without disturbance from any apprehensions of futurity, admit chimerical notions unsupported by argument, and lull themselves in a tranquillity without foundation. Such modest philosophers suffer[3] themselves to be carried along by their appetites, and are only restrained in their conduct by the dread of transportation, a gaol, or a gibbet, and (if that be not too severe a check) by some concern for continuing their lives, and preserving their health.

---

1. Pope's line is, "My foot-stool earth, my canopy the skies" (140; 136). Crousaz (p. 86) is paraphrasing Silhouette: "la terre est mon marchepié, & le Ciel est mon dais" (p. 12).

2. pleasures: "douceurs grossiéres" (p. 87).

3. Such modest philosophers suffer: "se laissent" (p. 87).

FIRST EPISTLE

Mais lorsqu'un vent, porte sur des ailes rapides,
But when a wind, carry'd on rapid wings,
Soufle de toutes parts des vapeurs homicides;
Blows up from all parts deadly vapours;
Lorsque la terre ouvrant ses gouffres redoutes,
When the earth, opening its dreadful caverns,
Avec leurs habitans engloutit les cites;
With their inhabitants swallows up the cities;
Lorsque pour submerger des nations entieres,   205
When, to drown whole nations,
La mer s'enfle, mugit, & force ses barrieres;
The sea swells, roars, and forces its barriers;
Lorsque tout est en bute a de si rudes coups,
When all is exposed to such rude attacks,
Repondez, la nature agit-elle pour vous?
Answer, doth nature act for you?
Oui sans doute, & toujours la cause universelle,
Yes doubtless, and always the universal cause,
A ses premieres loix attentive & fidelle,   210
To its first laws attentive and faithful,
De l'ordre general maintenant le lien,
Of the general order preserving the connexion,
Permet un mal leger pour produire un grand bien.
Permits a slight evil to produce a great good.
Si des exceptions rares & passageres
If exceptions rare and transient
Derangent de son cours les regles ordinaires,
Disturb of its course the ordinary rules,
Ce desordre apparent l'entretient en effet.   215
That seeming disorder maintains it in effect.

Supposing any connection in Mr Pope's periods, or any continued chain of thought, one would imagine the lines now quoted to be a satire[4] still carried on against those men who

---

4. satire: "censures" (p. 88). SJ's translation is consistent with his definition of "satire" in the *Dictionary:* "a poem in which wickedness or folly is *censured.*" Boyer defines "Satyre" as "(Ouvrage en prose *ou* en vers pour censurer les vices) a *satyr* or *lampoon.*"

conceive themselves to be distinguished from brutes by the more particular care of Providence; but there is not the least force in any thing alleg'd by him to prove it.

The punishments which God inflicts upon men are not such events as contribute to keep up order and connexion between the different parts of the universe[5] while they appear to throw them into confusion, they are not physical goods necessary for the preservation of the whole. The intent of them is the chastisement and correction of mankind.[6]

Est-il rien ici bas qui puisse etre parfait?[7]

Into what difficulties is a man thrown by a system hastily taken up, and an hypothesis destitute of any solid foundation! God, says the system, was inevitably determined to create an universe, and to create it such as it now is. And for what reason? Because it must necessarily be created in conformity with the most perfect idea that could be formed by divine wisdom. But must an universe of such consummate perfection as made it necessarily prefer'd to any other system, be exposed to plagues, deluges, and famines?[8] Why should it not, says the poet,

For what created perfect?[9]

Had God been able to have formed a perfect system of creation, he would have done it; but Omnipotence with its utmost efforts could perform no more. Would then the void, the original nothing, or the matter produced from it admit no greater perfection?[1] But *slight evils were necessary for the produc-*

---

5. The punishments . . . universe: "Les fleaux de Dieu ne sont point des événemens qui servent à entretenir la laison des parties de l'Univers" (p. 88).

6. The intent . . . mankind: "Leur destination est de punir, de châtier, de corriger les hommes" (p. 88).

7. SJ provides a translation of l. 216 of Du Resnel below.

8. exposed . . . famines: "exposé à des inondations, à des bouleversemens, à des pestes, à des famines" (p. 89). SJ omits "bouleversemens," "upheavals."

9. SJ substitutes l. 148a (144a) of Pope for Crousaz's quotation of l. 216 of Du Resnel given above (p. 89). The line begins "And" rather than "For."

1. Would then . . . perfection: "Et pourquoi encore? Est-ce que le Néant, est-ce que la Matiére tirée du néant, refusoit de se prêter à une plus grande perfection?" (p. 89).

FIRST EPISTLE

tion of great good. The most agreeable and beneficial parts of the world, the light of the sun, the order of the sky, the most delicious fruits, and the most salutary medicines, owe their beauty, and their continuance to these plagues, famines, and desolations;[2] by such evils as these are the greatest blessings necessarily preserved, the order of things could not be constituted otherwise, an eternal dependence must always subsist between one part and another, nor could a *headach,* or a *cold* be left out of the system without breaking the chain, and confounding the universe.

> *Est-il rien ici bas qui puisse etre parfait?*
> Is there nothing here below which can be perfect?
> *Pour tout etre cree cette regle est egale;*
> For every being created that rule is equal;
> *L'homme doit-il sortir de la loi generale?*
> Man, ought he to go free from the general law?
> *Si tout dans l'univers, sujet au changement,*
> If every thing in the universe, subject to change,
> *Se combat, se detruit, & change incessamment;*   220
> Clashes, decays, and alters continually;
> *Si de l'etre eternel la sagesse infinie*
> Since of the eternal being the infinite wisdom
> *Du monde, par le trouble, entretient l'harmonie,*
> Of the world, by confusion, preserves the harmony,
> *Pourquoi pretendez vous qu'exempt de passions*
> Why do you pretend that exempt from passions
> *L'homme soit insensible a leurs impressions?*
> Man should be insensible to their impressions?

Mr Pope lets drop, ever and anon, such paradoxical principles, so widely different from what would be expected, not only from a Christian but from a reasonable man, accustomed to live in subjection to laws, and to regulate his conduct by the rules of morality,[3] that no man can help refusing his as-

---

2. desolations: "à ces bouleversemens qui nous étonnent" (p. 90).

3. and to regulate . . . morality: "& de se plaire dans une régularité morale" (p. 90).

sent to the notions he seems desirous of establishing. I should gladly find some reason for thinking that he does not give us his own sentiments. But the system appears here too plainly.[4]

——All subsists by elemental Strife,
And Passions are the Elements of Life.[5]

The strife between the different elements of the world has always beneficial consequences.[6] The passions are at variance among themselves, and, if ever they unite, it is in opposition to reason. But since it is so, it evidently ought to be so, the construction of the universe requires; that whatever *is*, *should be*.[7]

The different nature of the particles dispersed through the air, the earth, and the waters, produces fermentations, and those fermentations contribute to the support of plants and animals. These are the means ordain'd for this end by the creation. But how would the world suffer, if men were constantly to follow the light of their reason, without being disconcerted by their passions? But by being thus disconcerted, they bring no *physical* confusion into the world, nor do they in the least contribute to the harmony or union of its parts: such irregularities are only *moral* evils, which might and ought to be prevented by acts of the will, and for which therefore man deserves to be punished.

> *Si l'ordre soit affermi par d'affreuses tempetes,*   225
> If order be established by horrible tempests,
> *Pourquoi donc croirez-vous que de coupable tetes,*
> Why then will they believe that guilty heads,
> *Qu'un Neron, qu'un Cromwel, puissent le renverser?*
> As a Nero, a Cromwell, can subvert it?

---

4. But the system . . . plainly: "Mais le Systême se découvre ici plus clairement qu'on ne souhaiteroit" (p. 91).

5. SJ substitutes ll. 169–70 (161–62) of Pope for Crousaz's paraphrase of l. 222 of Du Resnel (p. 91). Line 169 begins "But."

6. SJ omits "*Pourquoi l'Homme ne renfer-meroit-il pas aussi des contradictions?*" He also omits a question after the next sentence: "*Pourquoi en seroit-il autrement?*" (p. 91).

7. But since . . . should be: "Puisque cela a lieu, il faut bien que cela soit. L'Univers exige que tout ce qui est, soit" (p. 91).

FIRST EPISTLE 87

> *C'est un secret orgueil qui vous le fait penser.*
> It is a secret pride which makes you think so.

Storms and tempests neither break nor preserve the order of the universe, which is kept up without any dependence on these irregularities, nor do they contribute to maintain the course of natural motions, but to raise our admiration of that unvaried regularity which subsists without suffering any interruption from [8] those rare [9] and inconsiderable disorders.

Criminals[1] (for criminals Mr Pope is at length willing to allow, though how a man can be criminal, who had it not in his power to keep the laws he has broken,[2] or to resist the motions that impelled him to measures contrary to his duty, is hard to tell) may be the occasion of great disturbances to society, and of great prejudice to the members of it. But God, who permits, not causes them, suffers them to happen for the punishment of the wicked, and the tryal of the good, and restrains them within such bounds as he pleases. Mr Pope introduces pride here without any necessity.

> *Mais Dieu ne peut-il pas a assujettir le vice*
> But God can he not subject vice
> *A servir aux desseins formes par sa justice?*   230
> To serve designs formed by his justice?*

Mr Pope thought these verses too fine to be left out of his poem.

What follows seems not very consistent with what we have just been reading.

*This couplet is an addition by the translator.[3]

---

8. without suffering any interruption from: "nonobstant" (p. 92).

9. rare: "clair-semées" (p. 92). Boyer defines "Clair-semée" as "Adj. (rare) thin-sown, thin, scarce."

1. *Criminals:* "Les têtes *coupables*" (p. 92). Boyer defines "Coupable" as "Adj. (qui a commis quelque faute ou quelque crime) guilty, culpable, faulty, in fault."

2. criminal . . . broken: "coupable, si on n'a point de liberté, & si l'on n'est pas en pouvoir d'observer les Loix qu'on viole" (p. 92).

3. Forman has a footnote at this point in the text: "Here we omit some of the criticism, because it is upon a few lines of the translation that neither shew Mr. Pope's words nor his meaning" (p. 48).

> *La raison doit porter un jugement egal*
> Reason ought to pass an impartial judgment
> *Sur l'ordre naturel, & sur l'ordre moral.*
> Upon the order natural, and upon the order moral.

This would be very bad reasoning. God is either ultimately[4] or immediately the author of natural order. A second motion is the consequence of a first, and a third of a second. But of moral evil there is no necessity, nor is God either immediately or by consequence the author of it.

> *Le ciel dans le premier vous paroit equitable;*
> Heaven in the first to you appears just;

Without doubt, for heaven is the author of it.

> *Pourquoi dans le second seroit-il condamnable;*
> Why in the second should it be blameable?

Heav'n cannot be justly charged in this case, for heav'n has no share in those disorders, nor can they be imputed to it without impiety.

> *Sur ces points, au dessus de notre entendement,*   235
> On these points, above our understanding,
> *L'esprit ne peut former qu'un vain raisonment.*[5]
> The mind can frame but a vain argument.

Why then does Mr Pope aspire so high, reason so freely, and decide so boldly upon the greatest of all subjects? If we take his word, the Supreme Being was inevitably determined to create *this* universe because the most perfect that he could conceive, yet there is nothing perfect in that part which is assigned for our habitation; it is full of imperfections, which God is the author of, and could not avoid. He takes care not to proceed to the ill use made by man of his liberty, the original of all the evil that surrounds us, suitably enough to that state of disorder in which men live by their own fault.

---

4. ultimately: "médiatement" (p. 93).
5. Crousaz correctly has "raisonnement" (p. 94).

> *A suivre nos projets, tout seroit en ce monde*
> To follow our schemes, every thing should be in this world
> *Dans un concert parfait, dans une paix profound;*
> In a perfect harmony, in a profound peace;
> *Nous voudrions que l'homme, ami de la vertu,*
> We would that man, the friend of virtue,
> *De desirs vicieux ne fut point combattu.* 240
> With vicious desires might never be encounter'd.

And what is there blameable in such desires as these? Desires and ideas! which we ought, instead of extinguishing and suppressing, to raise, encourage and entertain.[6] Every man ought to labour with vigorous and constant endeavours after so desirable a state, without suffering himself to be divided from his prospects by a madrigal, that tends only to sink the ardour of his most lawful wishes into indolence and indifference.[7]

> *Que l'air ne fut jamais obscurci de nuages,*
> That the air might never be darkened with clouds,
> *Ni le calme des mers trouble des orages;*
> Nor the calm of the seas disturbed by storms;
> *Et que le coeur, conduit par la loi du devoir,*
> And that the heart, guided by the law of duty,
> *Jamais des passions n'eprouvat le pouvoir.*
> Might never of the passions experience the power.

To draw a parallel between things of a nature entirely different, is mere sophistry, and sophistry so much the more delu-

---

6. And what is . . . entertain: "Et qu'y a-t-il de répréhensible dans ces souhaits, ou de fanatique dans ces idées? Loin d'étouffer ces desirs, ce n'est pas assez de les laisser naître & de les entretenir" (p. 95).

7. without suffering . . . indifference: "on se rend coupable, en se laissant séduire par des Chansons qui font succéder l'indifférence à des souhaits si légitimes" (p. 95). In the *Dictionary* SJ defines "madrigal" as "a pastoral song; any light airy short song" but in the first illustrative quotation Bailey calls it "a little amorous piece." Boyer also defines it as "a kind of amorous song."

sive and contemptible, as there is greater difference between those things which are supposed in a state of purity.[8]

Rains are necessary, and consequently clouds, which we are often much pleased to see gathering in the sky. Of winds, natural philosophy demonstrates the benefit. Storms are objects of terror, and man in his fallen state deserves to be terrified.

A reasonable man would not desire the utter extinction of his passions, which are of use under the government of reason, and which he raises and regulates with this view.

> *Mais des fiers*[9] *elemens l'eternal discorde*　　　　245
> But of fierce elements the eternal discord
> *Fait que le monde entier se conserve & s'accorde.*
> Causes that the world keeps itself entire, and
> 　　in harmony.

These ideas, invented by Ovid in his description of the chaos, and borrow'd by Scarron, are extremely poetical; but natural philosophy is not my business.

> *Et sans les passions qui viennent l'agiter,*
> And without the passions which rise to shake him,
> *L'homme insensible a tout pourroit-il subsister?*
> Man, insensible to every thing, could he subsist?

What would become of an intelligent being that should not love itself, and should look upon every thing with mere indifference? But though strong and constant inclinations are necessary parts of our constitution, can it be concluded from thence, that tumultuous and impetuous desires are equally necessary, by which we are sometimes animated to compassion and justice, but sometimes transported to cruelty and oppression?

---

8. purity: "égalité" (p. 96).

9. SJ translates "fiers," usually meaning "proud," as "fierce." Boyer gives authority for this in one of his definitions of "Fier": "fierce, cruel, barbarous." The corresponding line in Pope is, "But ALL subsists by elemental strife" (l. 169; 161).

> *Mais quel est son objet? Que ses voeux sont etranges!*
> But what is his object? How strange are his wishes!
> *Quelquefois, afflige d'etre au-dessous des anges,* 250
> Sometimes, grieved to be below angels,
> *Il aspire a leur sort; que dis-je? Ses souhaits,*
> He aspires to their condition; what do I say? His desires,
> *S'il n'est au-dessus d'eux, ne sont point satisfaits.*
> If he is not above them, are by no means satisfied.

That man who thinks the state of a sinner a melancholy state, who is affrighted[1] at the remembrance of his past faults, at the remains of them which he is still sensible of, and at the apprehension of falling into them as before, thinks nothing but what he ought to think; and his thoughts, afflicting as they are, lead him back to the right way. But he neither envies the happiness of more exalted natures, nor the extensive powers of holier beings. He aspires not to the same rank of existence, but would account himself happy at a great distance below it, were but his obedience perfect.

> *Quelquefois, peu content des dons de la nature,*
> Sometimes, little contented with the gifts of nature,
> *Il se plaint que de l'ours il n'a pas la fourrure,*
> He laments that of the bear he hath not the fur,
> *La vitesse du cerf, la force du taureau.* 255
> The swiftness of the stag, the strength of the bull.
> *Homme trop aveugle! toi qui des le berceau*
> O Man too blind! for thee, who from the cradle
> *Crois que les animaux sont faits pour ton usage,*
> Believest that the animals were made for thy use,
> *Quand tous leurs attributs deviendroient ton partage,*
> Since all their qualities might become thy share,
> *Par les dons que le ciel a repandu sur eux,*
> Through the gifts which heaven hath bestowed upon them,
> *Serois-tu plus parfait, serois-tu plus heureux?* 260

---

1. affrighted: "s'afflige" (p. 97).

> Wouldst thou be more perfect, wouldst thou be
>   more happy?

Mr Pope in these lines diverts himself with drawing the picture of a fool, that he may remark upon him, and extend these remarks to mankind in general.[2] But such fools are rarely to be met with, and I question whether one can be found infatuated to a degree like this.

> *De leurs corps differens l'admirable structure*
> Of their different bodies the admirable structure
> *Annonce la bonte de la sage nature.*
> Declares the goodness of wise nature.

In this line,[3] by the word *nature*, is evidently imply'd the *Author of nature,* by a figure much in use. All the metaphysicks of Spinosa are employed in confounding these two terms.

> *Liberale pour tous, mais sans profusion,*
> Bountiful towards all, but without profusion,
> *Elle a pour chacun d'eux la meme attention.*
> She hath for each of them the same care.
> *Dans l'un l'agilite compense la foiblesse;*   265
> In one agility compensates weakness;
> *L'autre a reçu la force au defaut de l'adresse;*
> Another hath received strength for the want of
>   subtilty;
> *Et mesurant en eux les secours aux besoins,*
> And dispensing among them helps to necessities,
> *Le createur fait voir sa sagesse & ses soins.*
> The creator displays his wisdom and his care.
> *Il forma leurs ressorts, il regla leur figure,*
> He made their springs, he proportion'd their
>   shape,
> *Sur les diverses fins qu'ils ont dans le nature.*   270
> For the different ends that they serve in nature.

---

2. that he may . . . general: "pour se donner le plaisir de le censurer, & de faire tomber sa censure sur l'Homme en général' (pp. 98–99).

3. SJ omits "& dans le 253. de ceux qui le précédent" (p. 99).

FIRST EPISTLE 93

Here the word *nature* can mean nothing more than the assemblage of beings that compose the universe, and particularly those that are placed on the earth.

> *L'insecte le plus vil, le plus lourd animal,*
> The insect the most vile, the most sluggish animal,
> *Ont pour y parvenir un avantage egale;*[4]
> Have to arrive thereat an equal advantage;
> *Chacun d'eux est heureux & jouit dela*[5] *vie,*
> Each of them is happy, and enjoys life,
> *Sans que l'etat d'un autre attire son envie.*
> Nor the condition of another draws his envy.
> *Pour oser accuser le ciel de durete,* 275
> To dare accuse heaven of rigour,
> *De la commune loi l'homme est-il excepte?*
> From the common law is man excepted?
> *Quoi l'homme qui se dit sage & raisonable,*[6]
> How shall man, who is called wise and rational,
> *Mecontent de son sort vivra seul miserable?*
> Discontented with his condition live alone miserable?
> *S'il ne possede tout, il croira n'avoir rien.*
> If he possesses not all, he will believe he has nothing.

Here is another picture of a man bewildered in extravagance; he is undoubtedly to be blamed, but all are not like him.

> *Homme!*[7] *pour etre heureux tu n'as que un*[8] *seul moyen;* 280
> Man! for to be happy thou hast but one only means;
> *C'est de vivre content des dons de la nature.*
> It is to live content with the gifts of nature.

In this place Mr Pope seems to express a great deal in a few words, but upon reflection, we learn nothing from him. He

---

4. Crousaz correctly has "égal" (p. 99).
5. Crousaz correctly has "de la" (p. 100).
6. Crousaz correctly has "raisonnable" (p. 100).
7. The exclamation point is an SJ addition.
8. Crousaz has "qu'un" (p. 100).

tells us that to be *happy* we must be *content;* this is amusing us with a repetition of words that have the same meaning, for it might be said, with equal truth, that to be *content* a man must be *happy*.⁹ But Mr Pope will shew us the way to this happiness and content. Every man will attain to them, that shall rest satisfied with the gifts that *nature* has bestowed, without desiring any thing beyond them. But who is this *nature*¹ to whom such deference is to be paid, and who is to set limits to our wishes? Is it the Author of our existence? The precept is then indisputable, but very extensive, and ought to be very accurately explained.

The abilities which our Maker has given us, and the internal and external advantages with which he has invested us, are of two very different kinds. Those of one kind are bestow'd in common upon us and the brute creation, but the other exalt us far above other animals. To disregard any of these gifts would be ingratitude; but to neglect those of greatest excellence, to go no farther than the gross satisfactions of sense, and the functions of mere animal life, would be a far greater crime. We are formed by our Creator capable of acquiring knowledge, and regulating our conduct by reasonable rules; it is therefore our duty to cultivate our understandings, and exalt our virtues. We need but make the experiment to find, that the greatest pleasures will arise from such endeavours.

It is trifling to allege, in opposition to this truth, that knowledge cannot be acquired, nor virtue pursued without toil and efforts,² and that all efforts produce fatigue. God requires nothing disproportion'd to the powers he has given, and in the exercise of those powers consists the highest satisfaction.

Toil and weariness are the effects of vanity; when a man has formed a design of excelling others in merit, he is disquieted by their advances, and leaves nothing unattempted, that he

---

9. For SJ's distinction between happiness and contentment, see, for example, *Rambler* 63, and *Adventurer* 111.

1. But who ... *nature:* "Mais que faut-il entendre par cette *Nature*" (pp. 100–01).

2. It is trifling ... efforts: "En vain on opposeroit à cette vérité, que l'acquisition des connoissances, & la persévérance dans la vertu, demande des efforts" (p. 102).

FIRST EPISTLE

may step before them; this occasions a thousand unreasonable emotions, which justly bring their punishment along with them.

But let a man study and labour to cultivate and improve his abilities,[3] in the eye of his Maker, and with the prospect of his approbation; let him attentively reflect on the infinite value of that approbation, and the highest encomiums that men can bestow will vanish into nothing at the comparison. When we live in this manner, we find that we live for a great and glorious end.

To live in this manner, is the way to use our senses in a manner perfectly agreeable to the precepts of religion.[4] We open our eyes, and behold with extasy and admiration[5] the beauties which Divine Providence has displayed before them; we wish we could communicate to them our ideas and sensations, that they might join their adorations and thanksgivings with ours.

When this is our frame of mind, we find it no longer difficult to restrain ourselves in the gratifications of eating and drinking, the most gross enjoyments of sense. We take what is necessary to preserve health and vigour,[6] but are not to give ourselves up to pleasures that weaken the attention, and dull the understanding.

This temper will set us beyond the reach of envy and malice, and those vexations that flow naturally from them. Whatever be our rank in the universe, and our station in society, we are content with it, and endeavour to perform the duties of it in the sight of God, with a full assurance that we[g] shall obtain the approbation of the Sovereign of the World, who shall perform what his condition makes his duty.

---

g. he

---

3. cultivate . . . abilities: "à cultiver ses talens, & à les enrichir" (p. 102).

4. To live . . . religion: "Vivre dans cette attention, c'est le moyen de répandre une parfaite régularité sur l'usage de nos sens" (p. 103).

5. behold . . . admiration: "lasser d'admirer avec ravissement" (p. 103).

6. health and vigour: "vigueur" (p. 103).

I have already given my sentiments upon the use that we ought to make of our ability to obtain true notions of our future state.

I am willing to believe, that we should wrong Mr Pope, (and certainly we should wrong[7] ourselves) if by the gifts of nature, which we are advised to content ourselves with the enjoyment of, we should understand only the gift conferred upon *us* in common with other animals, though what he has just now been saying seems to tend that way, and the picture he has drawn of the Indian is no improper introduction to such a sentiment.*

> *C'est de vivre content des dons de la nature,*
> It is to live content with the gifts of nature,
> *Et de te conformer a leur juste measure.*[8]
> And to conform thyself to their just measure.

If this advice be confin'd to the senses and the gross pleasures which they afford, the precept is plainly[9] given; but the practice is almost impossible, unless foreign assistance be called in. Give up yourself to luxury,[1] you impair your health; resist the temptations of that vice, you feel the inconveniences of restraint. No man falls into excess without endeavouring to gratify his taste, and for that end, nature must be assisted by art, in a thousand different ways. These pleasures produce expences, these expences require an estate, and that estate makes rank and power necessary to secure the owner in the possession of it.[2]

---

*Mr. Pope's words are

> The Bliss of Man (could Pride that Blessing find)
> Is not to act, or think, beyond Mankind.
> No Pow'r of Body or of Soul to share,
> But what his Nature and his State can bear.[3]

---

7. wrong: "très grand tort" (p. 104).
8. Crousaz has "mesure" (p. 104).
9. plainly: "bientôt" (p. 104).
1. luxury: "plaisirs de la bouche" (p. 105).
2. nature must be . . . it: "il faut ajoûter art sur art à la Nature. Alors les gros revenus deviennent nécessaires, & on a besoin de l'autorité du rang pour se soûtenir dans la possession des richesses" (p. 105).
3. Lines 189–92 (181–84). Line 191 (183) should read "pow'rs."

FIRST EPISTLE   97

Mr Pope has drawn, according to his own imagination, the picture of an Indian temperate and contented. Mr Bayle, in the same manner, has given us pictures of men without any religion, fill'd with touches that raise esteem, but copied only from his own fancy, and, that he might more easily attain his end, has placed in contrast with them the portrait of a bad Christian.

The savage lies under a necessity of maintaining himself, and of securing his fields and his possessions,[4] he must be a skilful huntsman, he must run the hazard of falling into the hands of his neighbours, and being devoured by them, when he is obliged to make incursions into their district to procure slaves by rapine and violence,[5] whom he afterwards obliges to serve* him by force.

Does not Mr Pope think those Indians to be pitied, when their *gold* and their quiet are invaded by the *thirst* of merciless and cruel Christians?[6] Would not a society well compacted and regulated[7] have secured them from such ravages? But can society be form'd and continued without inequality, de-

*Though Mr. Pope's picture of the Indian be undoubtedly liable to very just objections, both with regard to the justness of the draught, and the light in which he has placed it, yet perhaps Mr. Crousaz's contrast may be no less unjustifiable. India in its most extensive signification comprehends a great part of the globe, and includes a multitude of nations, some barbarous and savage to a degree that almost degrades them from the rank of men; some such as the commentator describes, crafty, malicious, provident, and rapacious; some human and civilized almost to politeness, or perhaps to a generosity and good nature far preferable. But I recollect no authentick relation from which it does not appear, that civility and religion promote each other. No regulated polity can, I believe, be produced, which does not include or presuppose a religious institution; nor is there any people much superior to their dogs in this world, that imagine they shall be placed on a level with them in the next.[8]

---

4. possessions: "provisions" (p. 105). Boyer defines "Provision" as "(Fourniture des choses nécessaires) provision."

5. obliged . . . rapine and violence: "obligé de faire des courses pour se procurer, par la violence" (p. 106).

6. Does not . . . Christians: "Mr. POPE ne les trouve-t-il pas à plaindre, lors qu'ils se voyent enlever leurs biens & leur repos par des avides & impitoyables Chrêtiens" (p. 106). This alludes to ll. 151–52 of Du Resnel. SJ's emphasis on *gold* and *thirst* reflects the parallel line of Pope (108b; 104b) quoted earlier (p. 76).

7. compacted and regulated: "réglée" (p. 106).

8. SJ's comments on India anticipate remarks made to Boswell at Dunvegan in Skye, 14 September 1773, beginning, "Nay, don't give us India" (*Life*, V.209).

pendance and care? A heart enlighten'd with religion and resign'd to Providence[9] is the surest foundation of tranquillity in all perplexities.

> *Si l'oeil, du microscope imitant les effets,*
> If the eye, of the microscope imitating the effects,
> *Dans le meme degre grossissoit objets,*[1]
> In the same degree did enlarge objects,
> *De quoi nous serviroit une semblable vue?*   285
> For what would serve us such a view?
> *Sur de petits objets bornant son etendue,*
> On small objects bounding its extent,
> *L'oeil verroit d'un ciron les ressorts curieux,*
> The eye would see of a maggot the curious springs,
> *Et ne jouiroit plus du spectacle des cieux.*
> And would no more enjoy the sight of the heavens.
> *Donnez a tous les sens plus de delicatesse,*
> Give to all the senses more of delicacy,
> *Du toucher par degres augmentez la finesse,*   290
> Of feeling by degrees increase the fineness,
> *Sensible au moindre choc, tremblant au moindre effort,*
> Sensible to the least shock, shaking at the least impulse,
> *L'homme craindroit toujours la douleur ou la mort.*
> Man would fear always pain or death.
> *Que des corps odorans les fleches invisibles*
> Let of odorous bodies the invisble darts
> *Fissent sur le cerveau des effets plus sensibles,*
> Make on the brain effects more sensible,
> *Des parfums les plus doux la violente odeur*   295
> Of perfumes the sweetest the violent smell
> *Deviendroit le tourment de la tete & du coeur.*
> Would become the torment of the head and of the heart.

---

9. A heart . . . Providence: "La résignation d'un coeur éclairé & plein de Religion" (p. 106).

1. Crousaz correctly has "les objets" (p. 106).

FIRST EPISTLE   99

> *D'un sentiment plus vif si l'oreille munie*
> With a sensation more quick if the ear endowed
> *Des spheres dans leurs cours entendoit l'harmonie,*
> Of the spheres in their courses did hear the harmony,
> *Comment parmi ce bruit trouver quelques plaisirs*
> How amidst that noise could it find any pleasure
> *Au murmure des eaux, au souffle des zephirs?*   300
> In the murmur of waters, in the whisper of zephyrs?
> *Reconnoissez enfin la sagesse eternelle*
> Acknowledge finally the eternal wisdom
> *Dans les dons qu'en naissant chaque etre reçoit d'elle,*
> In the gifts which at birth each being receives of it,
> *Dans ceux qu'elle refuse adorez sa bonte.*
> In those which it refuses adore its goodness.

These lines discover at once the imagination of a poet and the accuracy of a philosopher, if we take away *the musick of the spheres*,[2] which is not consistent with the knowledge we have at present of the nature and causes of sound.

The *musick of the spheres*[3] was one of the wildest notions of antiquity, and still finds a place in poetry, where the mind is to be strongly moved by grand images; but all the harmony of this poetry consists in the cadence.[4]

> *Parmi les animaux quelle diversite!*
> Among animals what variety!

---

2. *musick of the spheres:* "*l'harmonie des Sphéres dans leurs cours*" (p. 107).

3. *spheres:* "Sphéres célestes" (p. 107).

4. Forman's footnote at this point in the text is worth reprinting: "Mr. Crousaz is not here much out of the way in speaking of the French verses; they are not even the skeleton of Mr. Pope's: if they are harmonious in the critick's ear, they rumble in ours like a parcel of empty casks on a dray driving up Holborn-Hill" (p. 60). Pope's lines are,

> If nature thunder'd in his op'ning ears,
> And stunn'd him with the music of the spheres,
> How would he wish that Heav'n had left him still
> The whisp'ring Zephyr, and the purling rill? (201–04; 193–96)

> *Quelle gradation trouvons-nous etablie,* 305
> What gradation shall we find established,
> *Depuis les vermisseaux, dont la terre est remplie,*
> From worms, whereof the earth is full,
> *Jusqu'a l'homme, ce chef, ce roi de l'univers!*
> Even to man, that head, that king of the universe!

Here *man's imperial race* are allowed that honour and precedence which have been denied them in other passages, because it serves to heighten and embellish the gradation.[5] Mr Pope forgets, almost in every line, one of the chief rules laid down by Mr Des-Cartes,[6] in his philosophy, that a reasoner should upon every new proposition take an accurate review of the whole argument, to be certain that he has not admitted suppositions without foundation, and that his system is consistent with itself. There are several instances of a bad memory in the parts already considered, and in the following parts more will be remarked by the reader, without being pointed out.

> *Entre leurs facultes que degres divers!*
> Among their faculties what different degrees!
> *Sous les voiles obscurs qui couvrent sa paupiere*
> Under the dark veils which cover his eyelid
> *La taupe ne peut voir l'eclat de la lumiere;* 310
> The mole cannot see the glare of the light;
> *Mais rien n'echape au linx; a ses yeux penetrans*
> But nothing escapeth the lynx; to his piercing eyes
> *Les corps les plus epais deviennent transparens.*
> Bodies the most dense become transparent.
> *Dans l'ombre de la nuit, par le seul bruit guidee,*
> In the shade of night, by the noise alone directed,
> *La lionne poursuit la biche intimidee.*

---

5. Here *man's* . . . gradation: "Cette place d'honneur qu'on lui refuse ailleurs, on la lui assigne ici, parce qu'elle sert à embellir la gradation" (p. 108). SJ adds l. 209b (201b) of Pope.

6. Mr. Pope . . . Des-Cartes: "A tout coup Mr. POPE oublie une des grandes régles, & des plus essentielles que Mr. DES-CARTES ait donné" (p. 108).

The lioness pursues the fearful hind.
L'odorat dans le chien, par un prompt judgment,[7]   315
Smelling in the dog, by a quick determination,
Sur d'invisibles pas le conduit surement.
On invisible steps him conducts surely.
Des oiseaux aux poissons, pour la voix, pour la ouie,
From birds to fishes, as to voice, as to hearing,
Raprochez, s'il se peut, la distance infinie.
Bring near, if possible, the infinite distance.
Contemplez l'araignee, en son reduit obscur;
Contemplate the spider in her obscure retreat;
Que son toucher est vif, qu'il est prompt, qu'il est sur!   320
How lively is her feeling, how quick is it, how sure is it!
Sur ses pieges tendus sans cesse vigilante,
On her snares laid continually watching,
Dans chacun de ses fils elle paroit vivante.
In each of her threads she seems alive.
Par quel art marveilleux l'abeille dans nos champs
With what wonderful art the bee in our fields
Va-t-elle s'enrichir des tresors du printems!
Goes on to enrich herself with the treasures of the spring!
Par quel discernment sait-elle nous extraire   325
With what discretion knows she to extract for us
Des sucs les plus mortels un present salutaire.
From juices the most deadly a wholesome present.
Dans ce qu'on nomme instinct que de variete!
In that which we call instinct what variety!
Elephant! si connu par ta docilite,
Elephant! so noted for thy docility,
Toi qui de la raison parois avoir l'usage,
Thou who of reason seemest to have the use,
Combien sur le porceau[8] *n'as-tu pas d'avantage!*   330

---

7. Crousaz correctly has "jugement" (p. 109).
8. How Instinct varies in the grov'ling swine, Compar'd, half-reas'ning elephant, with thine. (221–22; 213–14)

How much above the swine hast thou not the
advantage!⁹*

Mr Pope opens a vast field for reflections without end, to which a man may and ought to return every day of his life; the habit of indulging them neither makes them less efficacious nor agreeable. They feast and exalt the soul, they fill it with solid satisfaction, and with ardent gratitude. To be most affected by them is the character of the most amiable mind: by them the desire of superfluities may be totally extinguish'd. It depends only upon men to make a happy experiment of this truth, and there are few subjects so worthy of the exuberant imagination of Mr Pope and his translator.[1]

> *Comment par l'homme meme un instinct admire,*
> How by man himself an instinct admired,
> *Si pres de la raison, en est-il separe?*
> So near to reason, from it is it separated?
> *O! qu'entre l'un & l'autre on voit peu de distance!*
> O! how little between the one and the other see we
>   of distance!
> *Pouvez vous concevoir la secrette alliance,*
> Can you conceive the secret alliance,
> *Qui joint le souvenir a la reflexion?* 335

*On this passage where sixteen lines are translated into thirty three, it is not necessary to make any other remark than may be made in general on the whole work, that it is extremely below the original in spirit, propriety, and notwithstanding the diffuseness of his expression, in perspicuity.[2]

These lines come up in a discussion of a learned pig in *Life*, IV. 373–74. Crousaz correctly has "Pourceau" (p. 109).

9. The exclamation point is an SJ addition.

1. there are few . . . translator: "il y a peu de sujets également dignes d'exercer la fécondité d'une veine aussi riche & aussi distinguée que celle de M. POPE, & celle de son Traducteur" (p. 110).

2. SJ is referring to ll. 207–22 (199–214) of Pope but the passage in French is only twenty-three lines. The four lines of Du Resnel quoted immediately above also belong to this section of Pope's text. Forman also singles out this passage for comment in a footnote: "The translator's vein is, no doubt, fertile enough sometimes; for it makes Mr. Pope say many things which he never thought of, tho' not in this place, which is the first of Mr. Pope's that has met with the commentator's entire approbation; notwithstanding the beauty of the original is quite lost in 23 lines of French" (p. 62).

FIRST EPISTLE

Which joins memory to reflection?
Ou commence, ou finit la separation,
Where begins, where ends the separation,
Qu'entre les sens grossiers & la pure pensee
Which between the gross senses and simple thought
La main du createur a pour jamais placee?
The hand of the creator hath for ever placed?
Donnez un meme instinct a tous les animaux,
Give a like instinct to all animals,
Si par les facultez[3] vous les rendez egaux, 340
If by the faculties you them render equal,
Vous rompez les liens de cette dependance,
You break the tyes of that dependence,
Qui fait regner entr'eux l'ordre & l'intelligence;
Which makes to reign among them order and intelligence;
Ils ne pourront alors s'accorder & s'unir,
They will not be able then to agree and unite,
Et vous verrez sur eux votre empire finir.
And you will see your empire over them to end.

In these latter verses, I meet with some obscurity, which I am not surprized at, as the subject is little understood.[4] I have treated it in my *Examen du Pyrrhonism*, and shall return to it in another work.

Que peuvent contre vous leur force & leur addresse? 345
What avail against you their strength and their subtilty?
Le ciel de la raison arme votre foiblesse;
Heaven with reason arms your weakness;
Il met dans ce present qu'il reserve pour vous,
He bestows in that present which he reserves for you,
L'infallible[5] moyen les subjuguer tous.

---

3. Crousaz has "facultés" (p. 110).

4. the subject is little understood: "Le sujet sur lequel ils roulent n'est pas assez connu" (p. 110).

5. Crousaz correctly has "L'infaillible" and "Moyen de les" (p. 111).

The infallible means of subjecting them all.*

These are very distinguishable privileges, and this sovereignty is very evident, which it would be a horrid degree of ingratitude not to be sensible of, and which argues that man guilty of a very criminal meanness of spirit, that places himself upon the level with creatures to which his creator has made him far superior. We are therefore indispensably obliged to act as becomes reasonable beings.

> *Dans le vague des airs, sur la terre, dans l'onde,*
> In the open space of air, on the earth, in the water,
> *Voyez en mouvement la nature feconde*   350
> You see in motion fruitful nature
> *Travailler sans relache a peupler l'univers.*[6]
> To work without remissness in peopling the universe.
> *Commencez par le Dieu, qui leur donne la vie;*
> Begin with God, who gives them life;
> *Quel spectacle etonnant! quelle chaine infinie!*
> What astonishing object! what infinite chain!
> *Esprits purs dans les cieux, hommes, poissons, oiseaux,*   355
> Pure spirits in the heavens, men, fishes, birds,
> *Habitans de la terre, & des airs, & des eaux,*
> Inhabitants of the earth, and of the air, and of the waters,
> *Insectes differens, que l'oeil decouvre a peine!*
> Insects various, which the eye with difficulty discovers!

*In these lines, which it is not our province to reconcile with the other parts of the poem, man is evidently acknowledged the master of the other creatures.[7]

---

6. The following line (352) is omitted:

> Parcourez, rassemblez tous les Etres divers; (p. 111).

7. SJ is referring to both the lines of Du Resnel and Pope:

> The pow'rs of all subdu'd by thee alone,
> Is not thy Reason all these pow'rs in one? (231–32; 223–24)

FIRST EPISTLE

Mr Pope returns to his magnificent gradations, and shews that this inexhaustible subject enlarges upon us, and discovers new wonders, in proportion as we dwell upon it: but when he adds;

> *Brisez un des anneaux qui forment cette chaine,*
> Break one of the links which make that chain,
> *De l'assemblage entier l'equilibre est perdu,*
> Of the whole composition the equilibrium is destroy'd,
> *Et tout dans le cahos se trouve confondu.* 360
> And all in a chaos lies confounded.
> *Si chaque tourbillon, ou nagent les planettes,*
> So each vortex, where swim the planets,
> *Se meut differemment selon des loix secrettes;*
> Moves differently according to secret laws;
> *Si conservant toujours un ordre merveilleux,*
> So preserving always a wonderful order,
> *Il forme, il affermit l'assemblage des cieux.*
> It constitutes, it confirms the system of the heavens.
> *Qu'une seule planette en rompe l'harmonie,* 365
> Let one only planet of it break the harmony,
> *Des autres tourbillons tout a coup desunies,*
> From the other vortexes instantly disjoined,
> *Elle entraine en tombant tous les globes divers,*
> It draws in falling all the other globes,
> *Qui par leur union forment cet univers.*
> Which by their union form this universe.
> *De son centre ebranle la terre derangee*
> From its shaken center the earth disorder'd
> *Sera dans le cahos au meme instant plongee.* 370
> Will be in the chaos at the same instant plunged.
> *Les astres, les soleils, l'un sur l'autre entasses,*
> The stars, the suns, one on another heaped,
> *Par les globes voisins ne sont plus balances;*
> By neighbouring globes are no longer balanced;
> *Dans le trouble & l'horreur la nature expirante*

> In the confusion and horror nature expiring
> *Jusqu'au trone de Dieu porteroit l'epouvante.*
> Even to the throne of God would carry the fright.
> *Pour repondre aux desirs de l'homme ambitieux,*   375
> To answer the desires of ambitious man,
> *Faudra-t-il renverser & la terre & les cieux?*
> Must the earth and the heavens be overturned?

Mr Pope's natural philosophy seems somewhat infected by his poetry.[8] The most compleat piece of workmanship is not such as by its weakness, and its duration notwithstanding that weakness, displays the great dexterity of the maker. Supposing equal beauty and equal usefulness, solidity is always preferable to slightness, and simplicity to composition.[9]

Besides the fancied chain of dependencies,[h] this endless connection is not agreeable to experience. We meet with no appearances of a concatenation in which the least link cannot be broken without endangering the whole.[1] Ramparts are blown up by the force of mines; earthquakes overthrow a city, and destroy the adjacent country; lightning may by setting fire to a magazine of gunpowder[i] shake the ground to a certain extent, and throw down the walls built upon it; but a few miles off every thing will go on as usual. We change the course of rivers, join seas together by new canals, dig mines, and level mountains; we root up forests, and plant new ones; yet the earth moves round just as it has always done, nor have any alterations in its surface affected its motion.[2]

Have the comets that traverse part of our solar vortex and enter[3] more or less into it, hastened or retarded the revolution of a single year? Some alterations are observed in the

---

h. dependencies^   i. gunpower

---

8. Mr. Pope's . . . poetry: "La Physique de Mr. POPE se ressent du Poëte" (p. 113).

9. solidity . . . composition: "le solide doit toûjours l'emporter sur le subtil, & le simple sur le composé" (p. 113).

1. endangering the whole: "la totalité en souffre, jusques à être entiérement bouleversée" (p. 113).

2. nor have . . . motion: "la régularité de son tournoyement ne souffre aucune altération" (p. 114). SJ seems to have conflated "souffre" with "surface."

3. enter: "s'y enfoncent" (p. 114).

FIRST EPISTLE   107

satellites of the planets after the near approach of some other,
but every thing recovers of itself, and these alterations and re-
establishments are explained by the settled laws of pressure
and attraction, or by the centripetal and centrifugal powers.
A relapse into nothing, *nature trembling to the throne of God,
ruling angels hurl'd from their spheres, being wreck'd upon being, and
world upon world,* are expressions exaggerated and hyperbolical to the last degree, which the poet makes use of to shew
his own force by frighting his readers.[4]

> *Si dans le corps humain chaque membre rebelle*
> If, in the human body, each member rebellious
> *A ce que lui prescrit une loi naturelle,*
> Against that which to it prescribes a law of nature,
> *A d'autres fonctions se vouloit attacher;*
> To other functions itself would apply;
> *Si le pied vouloit voir, si l'oeil vouloit marcher,*   380
> If the foot would see, if the eye would walk,
> *Si la main au travail uniquement bornee,*
> If the hand, to work only confined,
> *Pretendoit de la tete avoir la destinee;*
> Did pretend of the head to have the disposal;
> *Enfin si chacun d'eux se faisoit un tourment*
> In short, if each of them makes it a torment
> *D'obeir a l'esprit, dont ils sont l'instrument,*
> To obey the mind, whereof they are the
>   instrument,
> *Quelle confusion! N'en est-il pas de meme,*   385
> What confusion! is it not the same thing,
> *Quand l'homme revolte contre l'etre supreme*
> When man rebelling against the supreme being
> *De tout etre cree le mobile & l'esprit,*
> Of every being created the first mover and the soul,

---

4. A relapse . . . readers: "Le retour dans le néant, le risque d'un bouleversement porté jusqu'au Throne, sont des expressions infiniment exagérés, par lesquelles un Poëte prouve le pouvoir de ses Vers à répandre l'effroi dans l'imagination foible de ses Lecteurs" (p. 114). SJ incorporates part of Pope's lines 253–56 (245–48) here.

Veut sortir de la regle & de l'ordre prescrit?
Would break from the rule and from the order established?

This reasoning is inconclusive, and[5] founded on the vulgar notions of a certain degree of power given to the soul for regulating the motions of the body.

If the sun, moon, and other parts of the universe were intelligent and free agents, and the sun should shorten the night, or prolong it according to his present inclination; if the moon in her turn should think it proper to direct the course of the sun, if the clouds should only afford rain in a good humour, and winds only blew as fancy and caprice should incite them, without any regard to the advantage or concern for the sufferings of the earth,[6] universal confusion would soon follow instead of the wonderful order that we now behold.

Of this truth the heathens were convinced, and took occasion from it to invent the fable of the farmer, to whom Jupiter gave the privilege of calling rain or sunshine upon his own land at pleasure.

Nor was King Alphonso less mistaken, if that be true which is imputed to him: that he thought himself able to place the orbs of heaven in a better order, conceiving these orbs to be very different from what they are in reality.

So in society, if every man, instead of applying himself to the duties of his own station, and contenting himself with performing them, should amuse himself with animadverting upon the conduct of the government, and employ his time in directing his superiors, confusion would encrease with such presumption, and society would be immediately embroil'd.[7]

---

5. inconclusive, and: "sans force, ou" (p 115).

6. if the clouds . . . earth: "Si les Nuées ne versoient la pluye que par fantaisie, & que les vens ne soufflassent que par caprice, sans faire attention ni aux utilités, ni au préjudice, qu'en pourroit recevoir la Terre" (pp. 115–16).

7. confusion . . . embroil'd: "les désordres s'y multiplieroient avec la présomption qui les feroit naître" (p. 116); "and society would be immediately embroil'd" is an SJ addition. For Forman's footnote to this passage, see p. 37, n. 4 above.

> *De ce vaste univers les diverses parties*
> Of this vast universe the different parts
> *Sont, pour former un tout, sagement assorties;*   390
> Are, to constitute one whole, wisely disposed;
> *De ce tout etonnant la nature est le corps,*
> Of this amazing whole nature is the body,
> *L'eternel en est l'ame, en conduit les ressorts.*
> The Eternal of it is the soul, of it he regulates the springs.

These expressions are very metaphorical, and taken literally would imply a very odious meaning productive of detestable consequences.

> *Et s'il se cache aux yeux, les traits de sa puissance*
> And if he conceal himself from the eyes, the traces of his power
> *Annoncent a l'esprit son auguste presence;*
> Declare to the mind his awful presence;
> *En fabriquant la terre, en construisant les cieux,*   395
> In framing the earth, in forming the heavens,
> *Il est egalement puissant & glorieux;*
> He is equally powerful and glorious;
> *En tous lieux il s'etend, sans avoir d'etendue;*
> In all places he is extended, without having extension;

That is, his immensity is very different from the extension of bodies, having neither the same gross nature nor imperfections.

> *Sans etre divise, par tout il s'insinue;*
> Without being divided, into all he insinuates;

Of this we have some representation in that space which contains, and by turns receives and forsakes them,[8] without suffering any change in its place or nature, and which full or not full is for ever the same.

---

8. contains . . . them: "contient tous les Corps, les abandonne & les reçoit" (p. 117).

Des esprits & des corps c'est l'invisible appui,
Of spirits and of bodies he is the invisible support,
Et tout etre vivant respire, agit en lui. 400
And every living being breaths, acts in him.

We should pervert these pompous expressions to a very bad purpose,[9] if we should allow ourselves with Spinosa to confound our own substance with that of the deity, and to imagine that the substance of created beings is the same with that of him who created them. Men have thought fit, say those idle reasoners,[1] to call particular modifications of the one eternal substance by the name of *creatures;* whereas they ought to say, that men have been guilty of a very unhappy and wicked sentiment, in calling created beings modifications of the eternal substance.[2]

It is not sufficient to believe that the substance of created beings is wholly distinct from that of God; we must add, that intelligent beings have received from him a real power of action distinct from his. By representing them to ourselves as theatrical machines that appear to act upon the stage, when they are only put in motion by a foreign impulse, what employments do we not assign to the most holy, happy and perfect being? Was it beyond the limits of Omnipotence to produce beings endued with some power of action? They are not less indebted to the almighty and benevolent being for permanent strength and existence, than if they were renewed by him at every instant; nay, their obligations are greater, for the more they have received, the more they owe.

This assertion once laid down, we read the following verses with more pleasure, and the sense is more clear and beautiful.

Il donne, & ne perd rien, il produit, il opere,
He gives, and loses nothing, he produces, he operates,

---

9. We should pervert . . . purpose: "On feroit un criminel abus de ces expressions pompeuses" (p. 118). In the next sentence "criminellement abusé" is translated as "wicked sentiment."

1. Men have thought . . . reasoners: "On s'est avisé, disent-ils" (p. 118).

2. the eternal substance: "la Substance unique & éternelle" (p. 118).

FIRST EPISTLE

> *Sans que jamais sa force ou se lasse, ou s'altere;*
> Nor does ever his strength either tire, or change;
> *Il se montre a nos yeux, aussi sage, aussi grand,*
> He shews himself to our eyes, as wise, as great,
> *Dans le moindre ciron, que dans un elephant;*
> In the least worm, as in an elephant;

Particular relations, demonstrative of this great truth, may be found in the memoirs of Mr De Reaumur, in which he inspires his readers with the same admiration which he feels himself, from his great and accurate acquaintance with operations that justly produce it.[3]

> *Dans un homme ignore sous une humble chaumiere,*   405
> In an ignorant Man under a low thatch'd roof,
> *Que dans le seraphin rayonnant de lumiere.*
> As in the seraph radiating with light.

In persons of the lowest rank may be sometimes found a high degree of piety[4] and resignation, that demands our respect. Their knowledge reaches but a little way, yet is sufficient to guide their actions: steady to their views, and not subject to any doubts, they have the full sovereignty over their own minds, and by governing themselves are under the government of God.[5]

Spirits exalted to degrees of knowledge and perfection, even above our comprehension, will rejoice to see what appeared so contemptible on earth approaching, by the infinite goodness of God, to their own splendour and elevation.[6] God has given proofs of his omnipotence in this respect in the sudden illumination of the apostles, who were so ignorant till they were visited by him on the day of Pentecost.[7]

---

3. with operations . . . it: "cause" (p. 120).

4. piety: "probité" (p. 120). Boyer defines "Probité" as "(integrité de vie & de moeurs) probity, honesty, integrity, uprightness, goodness."

5. steady . . . God: "fermes & au dessus de tout doute, elles régnent dans leur esprit, & Dieu y régne par elles" (p. 120).

6. splendour and elevation: "élévation" (p. 120).

7. God has given . . . Pentecost: "Dieu a donné, à cet égard, des preuves de

> *La foible & le puissant, le grand & le petit,*
> The weak and the strong, the great and the small,
> *Tout, devant ses regards, tombe, s'evanouit.*
> All, before his sight, falls, vanishes.
> *Sa substance penetre & le ciel & la terre,*
> His substance penetrates both heaven and earth,
> *Les remplit, les soutient, les joint, & les resserre.* 410
> Them fills, them sustains, them unites, and them binds fast.

These ideas are magnificent, but not all equally clear; they are express'd in terms proper to give verse an air of sublimity, and which occur of themselves to a poet. He is pleased with them, and makes use of them. A philosopher[8] does not admit them so easily, nor can comprehend any necessity of a continual exertion of divine power to keep up the union of the parts of the universe. They have no natural tendency to a separation,[9] for they have no properties but what they have received from the Creator; and if he by one act of his power determines them to separate and recede one from the other, why does he by a second act oppose and destroy the effects of the first?

> *Rougis donc, O mortel, de ta presomption,*
> Blush then, O mortal, for thy presumption,
> *Et ne nomme plus l'ordre une imperfection.*
> And no more call order an imperfection.
> *Ce qui paroit un mal a notre foible vue,*
> That which appears an evil to our weak view,

---

sa Toute-puissance dans les Apôtres, si grossiers au commencement, mais tout d'un coup si éclairés, dès que l'Esprit de Dieu fut répandu sur eux dans le jour de la Pentecôte" (p. 120). SJ omits the next paragraph: "Nous trouvons une image de ces changemens bien dignes d'attention, dans les Chenilles, nées dans une classe si voisine des vers les plus rampans, & passant par degrés à une espéce approchante de celle des Oiseaux. C'est ainsi que l'Homme deviendra semblable aux Anges" (p. 121).

8. philosopher: "Physicien" (p. 121). Boyer defines "Physicien" as "(qui sçait la physique) a natural philosopher, a physicien."

9. to a separation: "à se séparer & à s'éloigner l'une de l'autre" (p. 121).

FIRST EPISTLE

> *Est de notre bonheur une source inconnue.*
> Is of our happiness an unknown source.

This is true in natural events brought to pass by Providence, and of this truth, whatever our *degrees of blindness*[1] may be, we are often convinced by experience. The order of the world makes such events necessary for punishing or reforming sinners, or trying the patience of the good, and giving new lustre to their virtues.

But let us beware of reckoning among those events, which the order of the world requires, the bad actions, or wicked customs of men. God indeed may sometimes display his power by producing good from them. He that could call beings out of *nothing* into existence, can make the most beautiful regularity arise from confusion, but he does not cause that confusion that he may have an opportunity of reforming it. It is the consequence of human blindness and depravity, and the malice of the devil by whom men are seduced: but he makes it conducive to his own designs, and to the disappointment of those wicked spirits[2] that oppose them.

God does not infect[3] the heart of man with ambition or envy, or that rage with which they mutually labour to undo one another; but being left by him to themselves and their own criminal passions, they are punished by the hands of one another, and are the instruments of God, to execute his just decrees, without having themselves any such intention.

> *Rentre enfin dans toi-meme, & d'un esprit soumis*   415
> Re-enter at length into thyself, and with a mind submissive

---

1. SJ substitutes Pope's phrase for Crousaz's quotation of l. 413 of Du Resnel (p. 122). Pope's lines are,

> X. Cease then, nor ORDER Imperfection name:
> Our proper bliss depends on what we blame.
> Know thy own point: This kind, this due degree

Of blindness, weakness, Heav'n bestows on thee. (281–84; 273–76)

2. disappointment . . . spirits: "confondre les Intelligences criminelles" (p. 123).

3. infect: "fait naître" (p. 123).

Contente-toi du rang ou l'eternel t'a mis.
Be contented with the rank where the eternal hath placed thee.
Sois sur que dans ce monde, ou dans quelqu' autre sphere,
Be sure that in this world, or in some other sphere,
Dans les bras de ton Dieu tu trouveras un pere;
In the arms of thy God thou shalt find a father;
Et qu'en lui soumettant ton esprit & ton coeur,
And that in submitting to him thy spirit and thy heart,
Chaque pas que tu fais te conduit au bonheur.   420
Every step that thou makest conducts thee to happiness.
Dans le moment fatal qui finit ta carriere,
In the fatal moment which finisheth thy course,
Ainsi que dans l'instant ou tu vois la lumiere,
As well as in the instant when thou seest the light,
Toujours cher a ses yeux, ne crains rien pour ton sort,
Always dear to his eyes, fear nothing for thy lot,
S'il preside a ta vie, il preside a ta mort.
If he presides over thy life, he presides over thy death.*

    The mind gives itself up captive to the pomp of these lines, and to the exalted hopes excited by the perusal of them, which we are directed by the poet to entertain without the least uncertainty or doubt.[4]

---

*The same justice that has obliged me so often to censure, obliges me in this place to commend the *French* poet, whose paraphrase is here exceedingly beautiful, and his additions to the original not superfluities but ornaments; the last couplet of this quotation is particularly elegant.[5] In his version of the four next verses he has fallen below his author, but what translator could have been more successful?[6]

---

4. The mind . . . doubt: "Le coeur se livre à la magnificence de ces Vers, & aux grandes espérances dont ils font naître l'idée, & auxquelles le Poëte ordonne de s'attendre avec la plus ferme certitude" (p. 124).

5. Pope's next four lines are,

Submit–In this, or any other sphere,
Secure to be as blest as thou canst bear:
Safe in the hand of one disposing Pow'r,
Or in the natal, or the mortal hour.
(285–88; 277–80)

FIRST EPISTLE 115

By this frame of mind we not only enter upon those mere hopes which men may persuade us to form, but those assured and confident expectations to which our Supreme and Almighty Master incites us.⁷ But we must not delude ourselves, or think of taking what we like, and refusing what we are less pleased with;⁸ we must necessarily subject our hearts⁹ to God, and consequently our conduct.

These pleasing and consolatory ideas¹ give me occasion to ask Mr Pope, Whether he formed them by mere reasoning without the assistance of religion? If the light of nature discovered them to him, why may not the Indian attain them by the same light? And if he declines the labour of searching for them, will his negligence be a full excuse for all the absurdities of his notions, and the faults of his conduct?

This passage is of great importance. Mr Pope and his elegant translator would be grieved to throw their readers into any dangerous illusion. Men easily admit them;² they love to flatter themselves. As a zealous commentator, therefore, I propose to clear up all ambiguities.

If the submission required³ by Mr Pope be obedience, a submission to laws, implying the study of them, and a desire⁴ of conforming to them; in a word, if the submission mentioned by Mr Pope be a careful and circumspect conduct, it is a just foundation of comfortable hope.

But if the submission, so strongly recommended as the sure way to everlasting happiness, consists in looking undisturb'd and careless upon every thing that passes, in an indolent and

---

Cf. the closing lines of SJ's own *The Vanity of Human Wishes* (ll. 355–68).

6. See below p. 119 for the lines by Pope.

7. By this frame . . . us: "Par cette attente, on répond effectivement, non aux simples espérances qu'un Homme nous fait concevoir, mais à celles où nôtre Grand & Tout-puissant Maître nous invite" (p. 124).

8. we are . . . less pleased with: "ce qui pése" (p. 124).

9. hearts: "son esprit & son coeur" (p. 124).

1. pleasing and consolatory ideas: "consolantes idées" (p. 124).

2. The "them" refers to "dangerous illusion" which in Crousaz is plural, "illusions dangereuses" (p. 125).

3. If the submission required: "Si la soûmission de l'esprit & du coeur, que demande" (p. 125).

4. a desire: "une affection de coeur" (p. 125).

supine unconcern about our actions and those of others, it is a fatal calm, an ill-grounded security that tends to the total overthrow of morality and religion.[5]

Yet this is the most rational conduct, upon the supposition that every thing is the act of God operating as well on the bad as the good. But discontent and submission would in that case go together, nor would he that acquiesces and approves be more innocent than he that murmurs and complains.[6]

If men do not determine their own actions, if they have only the appearance of liberty, and receive impressions from some other cause, which impells them without being perceiv'd, while they imagine themselves acting by their own powers, nothing is more superfluous than to give them advice; since whatever they do, they act rightly, nor can be censured without imputing evil to the Supreme Cause.

The lines therefore upon which I have been remarking, are instructive in the mouth of a good man, but impious, offensive, and profane in that of a libertine.

Should Mr Pope be ask'd, Why the desire of immortality, which in verse 172, (116 of the *original*)[7] was pronounced the effect of human pride and impatience, is here celebrated and encouraged;[8] would he say that only to shew the fruitfulness of his genius he praises and condemns the same thing, or that since he wrote the former lines he has received new information?

> *La Nature n'est pas une aveugle puissance,*   425
> Nature is not a blind power,

---

5. But...religion: "Mais si la soûmission de l'esprit & du coeur, que recommande Mr. POPE, comme le chemin qui conduit à l'Eternité bien-heureuse, se réduit à regarder tout ce qu'on voit faire & tout ce qu'on fait, avec une tranquillité constante; si elle réduit à une espéce d'indolence, à ne s'inquiéter point de ce que font les autres, & à ne s'allarmer point de ce qu'on fait soi-même; c'est une sécurité qui va au renversement de la Morale & de la Réligion" (pp. 125–26).

6. he that murmurs and complains: "Celui qui condamne & qui trouve à redire" (p. 126).

7. SJ adds the parenthetical reference. Pope's line is,

> Alone made perfect here,
>   immortal there (120; 116).

8. is here . . . encouraged: "est présentement célébré" (p. 127).

> *C'est un art, qui se cache a l'humaine ignorance;*
> It is an art, which is hidden from human ignorance;

The meaning is, that the universe is not governed by a cause which acts without consciousness of its own operations, but that the mind of man is not sufficiently enlarged to comprehend how all the motions are performed.

> *Ce qui paroit hazard est l'effet d'un dessein,*
> What appears chance is the effect of design,
> *Qui derobe a tes yeux son principe & sa fin.*
> Which conceals from thy eyes its principle and its end.

An effect not above the ordinary powers of the cause that produces it, and which was intended and foreseen by that cause, is not attributed to chance.

When, for example, a man puts his hand before or behind him, to the right or left, he acts with knowledge and choice; but when his fingers take hold of a white or yellow ball, the event is not the effect of choice, but may be contrary to what he intended; we then attribute it to chance, that is, to a cause that acted without any view of the consequence.

But nothing of this kind can be imputed to the Supreme Being, who has always distinct ideas of what he proposes to do, and whose operation is exactly conformable to his ideas. The reasons for which he chooses to produce one effect rather than another, or at a particular time rather than sooner or later, or in this or that form rather than another; the reason likewise for which he permits, or retards, or wholly frustrates the execution of designs not in themselves above the common strength of man, are often out of the reach of our penetration, and where we attempt to guess at them our conjectures are at least uncertain, if not too daring.

> *Ce qui dans l'univers te revolte & te blesse,*
> What in the universe rebels against thee and offends thee,
> *Forme un parfait accord qui passe ta sagesse.* 430
> Makes a perfect harmony which surpasses thy understanding.
> *Tout desordre apparent est un ordre reel;*

Every seeming disorder is a real order;
Tout mal particulier un bien universel;
Every particular evil an universal good;

When the *discord* or *disorder* is a moral breach of order, an irregularity by which men infringe the laws of God, and the rules which their own consciences prescribe, it is real *discord*, though God by his wisdom and power may make order and harmony succeed it, by which the proper course of things may be re-established. But that harmony is the effect of God's wisdom and power, not of discord and confusion,[9] which of itself did not at all contribute to it.

Vice[1] is therefore neither a particular good to the man that is guilty of it, nor a general good extending its influence to the rest of the world.

Mr Pope has already given us a representation of the confusion that would arise in the human body, if the different members, instead of applying themselves to their proper functions, should each of them invade the province of another: such is the disorder of society when men, instead of minding their own business, interrupt that of others.[2]

I know that a certain order of men, ranked by their own suffrages among wits of a higher class, have thought it proper to display the advantages arising to society from the vices of mankind. These are the sophistries which the ingenious author of *Alciphron* has exposed, this is the justification of vice in which Mr Baile intrenches himself.[3] I shall not repeat here the remarks which I have made in my *Examen du Pyrrhonism*.

---

9. *discord* or *disorder* . . . order and harmony . . . discord and confusion: "desordre . . . ordre . . . desordre" (pp. 129–30).

1. Vice: "Les fautes de l'homme" (p. 130).

2. such is the disorder . . . others: "il nous a, dis-je, donné dans cette confusion une image du desordre qui a lieu dans la Société humaine, à proportion que les hommes, qui la composent, s'écartent de la tâche qui leur est assignée, pour troubler celle des autres" (p. 130).

3. the sophistries . . . has exposed . . . himself: "des Sophismes . . . fait sentir le faux & le ridicule. Mr. *Baile* avoit aussi appuyé sur cette Apologie du Vice" (p. 131). George Berkeley, bishop of Cloyne from 1734, published *Alciphron*, seven dialogues in defense of morality and religion, in 1732. The major work of

FIRST EPISTLE 119

If we should imagine any imperfections in the world around us, it is not wholly our fault; Mr Pope has himself reminded us of them, by his question,

> *And what created perfect?*[4]

Even among physical events, produced either consequentially or immediately by God himself, there are some that deviate from the original order of things: but they are to be imputed to the faults of men, who deserved to be put in mind by some disorders in nature that they are criminals, and who are by objects of terror to be awaken'd to a reformation.

> *Et bravant de tes sens l'orgueilleuse imposture,*
> Then defying of thy senses the proud imposture,
> *Conclus que* tout est bien *dans toute la nature.*
> Conclude that *all is right* in all nature.*

* Mr. POPE *thus concludes his first* EPISTLE.

> All nature is but art, unknown to thee;
> All chance, direction which thou canst not see:
> All discord, harmony not understood:
> All partial evil, universal good:
> And spight of pride, in erring reason's spight,
> One truth is clear; Whatever *Is*, is Right.[5]

Pierre Bayle, French Protestant scholar and philosopher, was the *Dictionnaire historique et critique* (2 vols., 1695, 1697; 2d ed., revised and enlarged 1702; English translations in 1710, revised 1734–38, and in 1734–41 *A General Dictionary, Historical and Critical,* "Supplement to Bayle," directed by Thomas Birch). See Lawrence Lipking, *The Ordering of the Arts in Eighteenth-Century England* (1970), pp. 76–83. SJ owned a set of the revised and enlarged 1702 second edition. See Donald Greene, *Samuel Johnson's Library: An Annotated Guide* (1975), p. 34. The entries are largely biographical articles on biblical, classical, and modern historical personages divided into two parts: the first a succinct historical account running across the top of the page, often no more than a few lines, and the second a series of discursive footnotes, often applying a skeptical critical analysis to theological and philosophical questions. Crousaz examined Bayle's skepticism in *Examen du Pyrrhonisme ancien et moderne* (1733). On 6 July 1763 SJ remarked, "Bayle's *Dictionary* is a very useful work for those to consult who love the biographical part of literature, which is what I love most" (*Life,* I.425).

4. SJ substitutes l. 148a (144a) of Pope for Crousaz's paraphrase of l. 216 of Du Resnel (p. 131).

5. Lines 289–94 (281–86). SJ comments on Pope's revision of l. 293 (285) in the "Life of Pope," *Lives,* III.162 (par. 177).

I should rather say, *in spight of self-love and thy*[6] *inclination to a false tranquillity, this truth is clear, That men have many vices to reform.*

We may say however in one sense, that

——*Whatever is,*[j] *is right.*[7]

A sacred and adorable order[8] is established in the government of mankind. These are certain and unvaried truths:[9] he that seeks God, and makes it his happiness to live in obedience to him, shall obtain what he endeavours after, in a degree far above his present comprehension. He that turns his back upon his Creator, neglects to obey him, and perseveres in his disobedience, shall obtain no other happiness than he can receive from enjoyments of his own procuring; void of satisfaction, weary of life, wasted by empty cares, and remorses equally harrassing and just, he will experience the certain consequences of his own choice. Thus will *justice* and *goodness* resume their empire, and that order be restored which men have broken. That state to which each man has devoted himself, shall be allotted to him: *affliction and despair to every one that has given himself to evil, but to every one that does well, glory and peace.* So will order be established, and such are the irrevocable decrees of ETERNAL JUSTICE, WISDOM and GOODNESS.[1]

---

j. *is*^

---

6. *thy:* in Crousaz "*son*" is "his," referring to the poet (p. 132).

7. SJ substitutes l. 294b (286b) of Pope for Crousaz's quotation of l. 434 of Du Resnel (p. 132).

8. A sacred . . . order: "Un ordre très sacré & très respectable" (p. 132).

9. certain and unvaried truths: "vérités constantes" (p. 132).

1. Capitalization has been added.

COMMENTARY ON THE SECOND EPISTLE

Ne sonde point de Dieu l'immense profondeur;
Sound not of God the immense depth;
Travaille sur toi-meme, & rentre dans ton coeur,
Work upon thyself, and enter into thy heart,
L'etude la plus propre a l'homme est l'homme meme.
The study the most proper for man is man himself.

Mr Pope in the first of these verses expresly warns us against the temerity of building our theology, philosophy, or morality, upon the supposition that God has inevitably determined by his infinite perfection to create, furnish, and govern the universe in the manner we behold, and that the design and the work were the necessary consequences of his own attributes.

Instead of soaring so high, and tow'ring[2] after incomprehensible objects, we are exhorted to descend into ourselves. The sentiment is entirely just, and the advice the best that can be given. To view and to know ourselves, the mind needs not be distracted with a multiplicity of outward objects, nor is it necessary that a man should be consider'd in his own mind as an object different from himself. How do we know that we exist? By perception.[3] How do we know that we are free? By perception. How do we know that we are created with a capacity to attain knowledge, and to improve in virtue? How are we certain of truth, and how do we learn what is virtue, and what are the passions, which sometimes assist, and sometimes oppose it, but by the same means, a continual attention to ourselves?

Mr Pope, after having invited his reader to a study capable of informing him of every thing that it is of most consequence to him to know in this life, warns him at first, that this study is

---

2. tow'ring: "monter hardiment" (p. 134).   3. SJ omits "Comment fait-on que l'on pense? Par sentiment" (p. 134).

not extremely easy, but must be followed with great circumspection. Then proceeding to a particular account of the difficulties, he recounts so many, and paints them so formidable, that the reader is terrified, and conscious of his own inability, is disposed to attend with docility and gratitude to any one that will be so charitable as to assist him.

> *Quel melange etonnant! quel etrange probleme!*
> What an astonishing medley! How strange a problem!
> *En lui que de lumiere, & que d'obscurite;*   5
> In him what light, and what obscurity;
> *En lui quelle bassesse, & quelle majeste!*
> In him what meanness, and what majesty!
> *Il est trop eclaire pour douter en sceptique,*
> He is too enlighten'd to doubt as a sceptic,
> *Trop foible pour s'armer de la virtu stoique.*
> Too weak to arm himself with a stoical virtue.
> *Seroit-il en naissant au travail condamne?*
> Could he be at his birth condemn'd to labour?
> *Au douceurs du repos seroit-il destine?*   10
> To the sweets of repose could he be destin'd?
> *Tantot de son esprit admirant l'excellence,*
> Sometimes of his mind admiring the excellence,
> *Il pense qu'il est Dieu, qu'il en a la puissance;*
> He thinks that he is God, that he hath his power;
> *Et tantot gemissant des besoins de son corps,*
> And sometimes lamenting the necessities of his body,
> *Il croit que de la brute il n'a que les ressorts.*
> He imagines that of a brute he has no more than the springs.
> *Ce n'est que pour mourir, qu'il est ne, qu'il respire;*   15
> It is only to die, that he is born, that he breathes;
> *Et toute sa raison n'est presque qu'un delire.*
> And all his reason is little more than raving.
> *S'il ne l'ecoute point, tout lui devient obscur;*
> If he hearkens not to it, all to him becomes obscure;
> *S'il la consulte trop, rien ne lui paroit sur.*
> If he consults it too much, nothing to him appears certain.

Cahos de passions, & de vaines pensees,
A chaos of passions, and of vain thoughts,
Admises tour a tour, tour a tour repoussees;   20
Admitted by turns, by turns repulsed;
Dans ses vagues desirs incertain, inconstant,
In his wandering desires uncertain, unconstant,
Tantot fou, tantot sage, il change a chaque instant;
Sometimes a fool, sometimes wise, he changes every moment;
Egalement rempli de force & de foiblesse,
Equally filled with strength and with weakness,
Il tombe, il se releve, & retombe sans cesse.
He falls, he rises, and falls again without ceasing.
Seul il peut decouvrir l'obscure verite,   25
Only he can discover obscure truth,
Et d'erreur en erreur il est precipite;
And from error into error he is precipitated;
Cree maitre de tout, de tout il est la proie;
Created master of all, of all he is the prey;
Sans sujet il s'afflige, ou se livre a la joie;
Without occasion he grieves, or gives a loose to mirth;
Et toujours en discorde avec son propre coeur,
And always at variance with his own heart,
Il est de la nature & la honte & l'honneur.   30
He is of nature both the shame and the honour.

I am inclined to believe, that the Abbe Du Resnel would not have engag'd in so long a course of antitheses, but that he obliged himself to render every thought of his original, that his poem might correspond exactly with the English, and be more readily compared with it. Antitheses have been formerly in greater credit among the French than they are at present, nor have they been degraded from that esteem by meer caprice or change of fashion, but by rational motives;[4]

---

4. nor have they . . . motives: "& ce n'est pas un esprit de légéreté & de mode qui les a décréditées" (p. 137).

for though they strike the imagination, and strongly affect the passions, they do not enlighten the reason in the same degree. Besides, by heaping them together, an author falls into contradictions, and overthrows in the second part of his sentence, what he had been establishing in the first. Mr Pope's figures are so much the more surprising, and less comprehensible, as by speaking of man in the singular number, he inclines his reader to look for all these defects in a single person, which are distributed among numbers, and which, for that reason, men allow themselves to ascribe in general to human nature.

I confess, that having neglected this distinction, I was once of opinion,[5] that Mr Pope contradicted himself. *Man* has, according to him, *too much knowledge* to be quite a *sceptick;* yet he has strange doubts, and chimerical apprehensions about his own nature,[6] for he is sometimes

In doubt to deem himself a God or Beast.[7]

Of what can that man be certain, who lives in doubt whether to rank himself among deities or brutes? But these are two opposite follies,[8] which do not happen to one and the same man. A disciple of Spinosa entertains a notion, that his nature is part of the divinity; a materialist fancies that *his* is of the same kind with that of a brute.

These antitheses rather raise emotions than convey knowledge; and for this reason, because they are carried beyond nature. *Was man at his birth sentenced to perpetual fatigue, or may he allow himself to slumber in softness and indolence?*[9]* What an af-

---

*Mr Pope has only these words,

——*In doubt to act or rest.*[1]

Of which, whether the translator or any other of his readers have discovered the true meaning, I cannot determine.

---

5. I was once of opinion: "il m'est arrivé de soupçonner" (p. 137).

6. *Man* has . . . nature: "*L'Homme*, selon lui, est *trop éclairé* pour ne rien croire, & donner dans un *Scepticisme* universel" (p. 137).

7. SJ substitutes l. 8 of Pope for Crousaz's allusion to ll. 11–14 of Du Resnel (pp. 137–38).

8. follies: "égaremens" (p. 138).

9. *perpetual fatigue . . . softness and indolence?*: "au travail? Doit-il se permettre la mollesse & le repos?" (p. 138).

1. Line 7b.

flicting and discouraging prospect should we have before us, if there were no choice between these two opposite extremes: but we are happily neither design'd for sluggish inactivity, nor sentenced to insupportable or over-burthensome fatigues.[2]

It would be an irrational and ungrateful notion, to conceive that life was only given us, that we might breathe a short time, and see our breath stopped for ever.[3] We are born for immortality, and Mr Pope insinuates our future existence in the strongest terms, at the end of his first epistle. Should we do him any injury by suspecting that he wrote them only to shew that his imagination is so fruitful and exuberant, as to be able to furnish happy sentiments upon subjects of every kind?

Man is so far from

Reasoning but to err,[4]

that he only errs in proportion as he departs from reason.

He that rather chuses to live in ignorance than to hearken to instruction, or undergo the trouble of reading, contemplating, and discoursing with temper, may be justly blamed:[5] but he likewise may be blamed, who gives up himself to a wild ambition of knowledge,[6] and without considering his own strength, exhausts himself by continual efforts,[7] and denies himself the necessary intervals of repose: each of these extremes is condemn'd by reason, and he that endeavours it in earnest, may easily avoid both the one and the other.

He that neither desires to know nor to observe rules, and who, instead of observing himself, and keeping up those resolutions, which the light of reason guides him to, will put no

---

2. nor sentenced . . . fatigues: "ni condamnés à un travail accablant & inhumain" (p. 138).

3. It would be . . . ever: "Il y auroit de l'ingratitude à croire que la *Respiration* ne nous ait été donnée que pour la voir s'éteindre" (p. 138).

4. SJ substitutes l. 10b of Pope for Crousaz's quotation of l. 16 of Du Resnel. Because SJ substitutes the line from Pope for Du Resnel's "Et toute sa raison n'est presque qu'un délire," he translates "réver" as "err" later in the sentence. Crousaz reads: "qu'au contraire on n'approche de réver qu'à mesure qu'on s'écarte de la Raison" (p. 139).

5. He . . . may be justly blamed: "On a tort" (p. 139).

6. who gives . . . knowledge: "s'abandonner à un desir ambitieux de connoissances" (p. 139).

7. continual efforts: "des efforts" (p. 139).

force upon his own inclinations, nor make any efforts to continue in the right way, rises and falls alternately, and is nothing but inequality and inconstancy.[8]

But he that resolves to act as reason directs, will consider himself as living and acting under the inspection of God:[9] this notion determines him to perseverance. If he takes care to return him thanks, as it is doubtless reasonable, and if the happy effects which he experiences from such a course of life determine him to beg a continuation of it, and to implore with confidence and humility the assistance of infinite goodness, he will soon see his present weakness succeeded by new strength, which will enable him to persevere in his conduct.

In the 25th and 26th[1] lines there is nothing inconsistent, if the different characters there described are supposed to relate to different persons. There are undoubtedly some men that have obliged the world by discovering, illustrating, confirming, and extending certain valuable truths: of this[2] we have every day new demonstration. But there are likewise ambitious tempers, men naturally opinionative, who think it necessary for their honour to be the authors of new notions, to oppose the opinions of others, and never to recede from what they have once asserted. Errors as well as truths are connected with each other, and when a man has once set out in the wrong way, he goes forward in it, and with greater expedition than in the right; because in *that* it is necessary to be continually upon the watch, to distrust himself, to hear other men without prejudice, and never to desist from reviewing his steps, and examining his progress.

I cannot conceive how the same person can be at once the honour and reproach of nature.[3] But there are indeed men, with whom the wise and the good think it an honour to be ranked, and at the sight of whose behaviour they exult and re-

---

8. and is nothing . . . inconstancy: "& toute sa constance se réduit à ces inégalités" (p. 140).

9. will consider . . . God: "s'attache à vivre en la présence de Dieu" (p. 140).

1. SJ adds "and 26th."

2. this: "ce que je viens de dire" (p. 140).

3. nature: "Nature humaine" (p. 141).

SECOND EPISTLE

joice: there are also men who shock and disgust all who interest themselves in the honour of humanity:[4] and, to conclude, there are men, who, after having been led aside from their duty, return to it, and become the subjects of applause.

Mr Pope, after having confounded good with bad, in order to present his reader with a chaos in mankind, where nothing distinct is to be discovered, thinks himself intitled to insult these wretches upon follies and miseries.[5]

> *Va, sublime mortel, fier de ton excellence,*
> Go, high-flown mortal, proud of thy excellence,
> *Ne crois rien d'impossible a ton intelligence,*
> Think nothing impossible to thy understanding,
> *Le compas a la main mesure l'univers,*
> With compass in hand measure the universe,
> *Regle a ton gre le flux & le reflux des mers;*
> Regulate at thy will the flux and the reflux of the seas;
> *Fixe le poids de l'air, & commande aux planetes,*   35
> Fix the weight of the air, and command the planets,
> *Determine le cours de leurs marches secretes;*
> Determine the course of their secret marches;
> *Soumets a ton calcul l'obscurite des tems,*
> Submit to thy calculation the obscurity of time,
> *Et de l'astre du jour conduis les mouvenens.*
> And of the star of the day conduct the motions.
> *Va, monte avec Platon jusques a l'empiree,*
> Go, mount with Plato even to the empyreum,
> *Cherche la verite dans sa source sacree;*   40
> Search truth in its sacred source;
> *Et joignant la folie a la temerite,*
> And adding folly to rashness,
> *Plonge-toi dans le sein de la Divinite;*

---

4. exult and rejoice . . . honour of humanity: "se félicitent; Comme il en est aussi dont la vuë présente un objet mortifiant à ceux qui prennent intéret à la Nature humaine" (p. 141).

5. to insult . . . miseries: "d'insulter à ces infortunés" (p. 142).

Plunge thyself into the bosom of the Godhead;
Dans ton aveugle orgueil instruis l'etre supreme,
In thy blind pride instruct the supreme being,
Apprens a gouverner a la sagesse meme;
Teach government to wisdom itself;
Et dechu de l'espoir qui seduisoit ton coeur,   45
And fallen from the hope that seduced thy heart,
Rentre dans ton neant, rougis de ton erreur.
Return into thy nothingness, blush for thy error.*

Who is it that he thus reproaches and contemns? Is it the whole body of mankind? That cannot be without supposing, that every particular man is irrational, self-conceited, and a fool. He must be more a madman[6] than any to whom that name has been given, that should pretend to measure the universe with a compass. Where is the man so blind as not to perceive the wide difference between making curious observations on the time and height[k][7] of the tides, and registering

---

*Go, wond'rous Creature! mount where Science guides,
  Go measure Earth, weigh Air, and state the Tides,
  Shew by what Laws the wand'ring Planets stray,
  Correct old Time, and teach the Sun his Way.
  Go soar with *Plato* to th' empyreal Sphere,
  To the first Good, first Perfect, and first Fair;
  Or tread the mazy Round his Follow'rs trod,
  And quitting Sense call *imitating God,*
  As eastern Priests in giddy Circles run,
  And turn their Heads to imitate the *Sun.*
  Go, teach eternal Wisdom how to rule—
  Then drop into thyself, and be a Fool![8]

    The particular superfluities and defects of the *French* version of the passage, as they are obvious to the reader, need not be mention'd; but it is necessary to observe, that the last and most important line, in which the assertion is contained, which the next paragraphs are inserted to prove, is evidently misinterpreted, in such a manner as to make the whole introductory part of this poem much more obscure to a *French* than it is to an *English* reader.
k. weight

---

  6. He must... madman: "Il faudroit en effet surpasser en extravagance" (p. 143).

  7. The text reads "weight" and the French is "les hauteurs" (p. 143). Probably a typographical error since SJ translates the word correctly below (p. 151).

  8. Lines 19–30.

SECOND EPISTLE

them exactly, which is very possible, and regulating at pleasure the flux and reflux of the ocean.

We may say of an excellent clock, in figurative language, that it rectify'd the sun; and the expression is not liable to any exception,[9] since, tho' there be some exaggeration in the language, no-body can possibly be deceived by it. But after having taken, or appeared to take, these expressions in a literal sense, should we have a right to censure an honest clockmaker, who had invented a method of ascertaining the motions of his clocks, as if he was mad, and set himself up as a rectifier of the course of the sun?[1]

Can a man, who is persuaded that ideas offering themselves to the mind with resistless evidence discover to him the truth of any proposition, and consequently make it appear to him in the same manner as it appears to God, be censured as unreasonable?[2] Can he who is convinced that God neither denies his blessing nor his direction to such as ask it, not with a view of outshining others, but with a sincere desire to attain a certain and clear knowledge[3] of those truths which are to regulate his conduct, be charged with entertaining an ill-grounded notion?[4] Can such men be said to act like fools? Or to plunge themselves enthusiastically into the bosom of the Divinity?

Let any man, that pleases, insult those that conceive the Deity inevitably determined to create the universe such as it now is, with parts that must produce, or seem to produce, the effects which we now observe: such philosophers as these may justly be charged with regulating[5] the designs and operation of the Almighty, and with reason may they be directed to *sink*

---

9. "and the expression ... exception" is an SJ addition.

1. who had invented ... sun: "qui a trouvé moyen d'ajoûter quelque chose à l'exactitude des Montres, comme s'il prétendoit à la gloire de régler le cours du Soleil" (p. 143).

2. "be censured as unreasonable" is an SJ addition.

3. certain ... knowledge: "connoître sûrement" (p. 144).

4. "be charged ... notion" is an SJ addition.

5. such philosophers ... regulating: "qu'on leur reproche, dis-je, la témérité de régler" (p. 144).

into their nothing, that state of non-existence from which God call'd them by the free choice of his infinite goodness.

> *Des celestes esprits la vive intelligence*
> Of celestial spirits the quick intelligence
> *Regarde avec pitie notre foible science.*
> Regards with pity our weak science.
> *Newton, le grand Newton, que nous admirons tous,*
> Newton, the great Newton, whom we all admire,
> *Est peut-etre pour eux ce qu'un singe est pour nous.* 50
> Is, perhaps, to them what an ape is to us.*

The heavenly spirits have so great and tender a concern for the happiness,[6] of mankind, that, amidst the inconceivable felicity which they enjoy, the conversion of a single sinner is capable of increasing their satisfaction: nor is our pride itself more despised than compassionated by them. But as to that part of us which is the work of God, the more enlighten'd they are, the greater subject of admiration do they discover there; they are astonished to see so much greatness in such weak beings, and adore with new raptures their Creator and their King. This notion Mr Pope has insinuated in Ep. I. verse 404.[7]

The great Newton, *who unfolded all nature's law*, was in reality but an ape in their sight, if the Leibnitzian system be true, and which, if it be true, they must follow.

Neither the hand nor the tongue of Newton received, according to this system, any direction from his soul. His machine was formed in such a manner, that, by the concurrence

---

*Mr Pope asserts, that the celestial intelligences *admired* the knowledge of Newton; and the translator, that they *pitied* it.[8]

---

6. happiness: "sort" (p. 145).
7. This notion . . . 404: "Mr. POPE lui-même fait naître cette idée, quand il dit: *Il se montre à nos yeux* (Ep. I. v. 404. & les trois suivantes.)" (p. 145). SJ adds the paraphrase of l. 32 of Pope in the next paragraph.

8. Superior beings, when of late they saw
A mortal Man unfold all Nature's law,
Admir'd such wisdom in an earthly shape,
And shew'd a NEWTON as we shew an Ape. (31–34)

SECOND EPISTLE 131

of the whole universe, it performed motions of which the traces or impressions⁹ are still extant in his books: and the machines of his readers receive, without knowing it, impressions, which their *monads* or souls imagine that they perceive rising in themselves. Thus the ideas of Newton are in them, as they were in¹ him, the effects of a series or chain of causes, that have acted for an immense number of ages, and from which those ideas inevitably resulted at the moment in which Newton imagined that he had produced them in himself by his study and enquiries.

> *Toi, qui jusques aux cieux oses porter ta vue*
> Thou, who even to the heavens darest carry thy view,
> *Qui crois en concevoir & l'ordre & etendue;*¹
> Who thinkest of them to conceive both the order and extent;
> *Toi, qui veux dans leur cours leur prescrire la loi,*
> Thou, who wouldst in their course prescribe them law,
> *Sais-tu regler ton coeur, sais-tu² regner sur toi?*
> Knowest thou to regulate thy own heart, knowest thou to rule thyself?
> *Ton esprit qui sur tout vainement se fatigue,*   55
> Thy spirit which about all vainly wearies itself,
> *Avide de savoir,*³ *ne connoit point de digue.*
> Greedy of knowing, admits of no restraint.
> *De quoi par ses travaux s'est-il rendu certain?*
> Of what by its labours has it made itself certain?
> *Peut-il te decouvrir ton principe & ta fin?*
> Can it discover to thee thy beginning and thy end?*

---

1. in in

*Nothing is more remote than this translation from the sense and design of the author, whose meaning in this couplet,

---

9. traces or impressions: "vestiges" (p. 146).
1. Crousaz correctly has "l'étenduë" (p. 146).
2. Crousaz has "Sçais" (p. 146).
3. Crousaz has "sçavoir" (p. 147).

If we except the manner in which these sentiments are expressed, which is too figurative to afford any ground for censure, it must be own'd that, how great soever the knowledge may be, which is attained by a mind capable of labour and attention, such a genius deserves rather censure than applause, if it has been employ'd in speculations of useless curiosity, or idle subtilty, when he ought to have been endeavouring to know himself, to regulate his conduct, and to satisfy himself about *his own beginning and his end*.[4] Much less is he to be applauded, if, instead of good-nature, benevolence, and an obliging disposition, virtues so worthy of human nature, his heart is full of envy, ambition, and a furious ardor for precedency, which have broken out into shameful and scandalous consequences,[5] of which the world has too frequently been witness. But from these faults Sir Isaac Newton liv'd and died entirely free.[6]

> *Deux puissances dans l'homme exercent leur empire,*
> Two powers in man exercise their empire,
> *L'une est pour l'exciter, l'autre pour le conduire.*   60
> One is to excite him, the other to conduct him.
> *L'amour propre dans l'ame enfante le desir,*
> Self-love in the soul produces desire,
> *Lui fait fuir la douleur, & chercher le plaisir:*

> *Could he whose Rules the whirling Comet find,*
> *Prescribe or fix one Movement of the Mind,*[7]

seems to be this, *Could he who has* laid down the laws of motion, by which the comets and heavenly bodies are directed in their courses, explain the operations of the soul? Could he give a physical or mechanical account of our passions or sensations? — Nor does the author cast any reflection upon the knowledge of Newton, or upon his studies, which the translator insults without mercy; tho', indeed, it is not plain, that he refers this paragraph to the former, or makes any connection between them.

---

4. SJ substitutes part of l. 38 of Pope for Crouzaz's paraphrase of l. 58 of Du Resnel (p. 147).

5. a furious . . . consequences: "une fureur de primer, dont des emportemens & des rancunes ont été des effets scandaleux" (p. 147).

6. entirely free: "très éloigné" (p. 147).

7. The lines (35–36) should read "Comet bind," "Describe or fix," and "his Mind." The Twickenham Edition gives "whirling" instead of "rapid" for l. 35 in the 1735a–43a text.

SECOND EPISTLE

Causes him to avoid pain, and seek pleasure:
La raison le retient, le guide, le modere,
Reason him restrains, him guides, him moderates,
Calme des passions la fougue *temeraire.*
Calms of the passions the rash *heat.*
L'un & l'autre d'accord nous donnent le moyen   65
The one and the other in concert afford us the means
Et d'eviter le mal, & d'arriver au bien.
Both to avoid evil, and to attain good.
Bannissez l'amour propre, ecartez ce mobile,
Banish self-love, get rid of that moveable,
L'homme est enseveli dans un repos steril.[8]
Man is buried in a useless repose.
Otez-lui la raison, tout son effort est vain,
Take from him reason, all his endeavour is vain,
Il se conduit sans regle, il agit sans dessein;   70
He orders himself without rule, he acts without design;
Il est tel qu'a la terre une plante attachee,
He is like a plant set in the earth,
Qui vegete, produit, & perit dessechee;
Which grows, fructifies, and withering perishes;
Ou tel qu'un meteore enflamme dans la nuit,
Or like a meteor blazing in the night,
Qui courant au hazard, par lui-meme est detruit.
Which running at random, by itself is destroy'd.
L'amour propre en secret nous remue & nous presse,   75
Self-love in secret stirs us and presses us,
Et toujours agite, nous agite sans-cesse:
And always agitated, acts on us without ceasing:
La balance a la main la raison pese tout,
With balance in hand reason weighs all,
Compare, reflechit, delibere, & resout.
Compares, reflects, deliberates, and resolves.

---

8. Crousaz correctly has "stérile" (p. 148).

The necessity both of self-love and reason is, in these verses, not less evidently proved than beautifully expressed. It was then only to fright us, or to make us more cautious, that he[9] fell so roughly upon reason in the beginning of his epistle.[1]

But lest the reader should be deceived by these prosopopoeias of reason and self-love, and be led by these abstracted ideas to suppose a greater difference than there really is, between the soul of a man that loves itself, and the soul of the same man that reasons, it may be proper to take notice that, by carrying this distinction too far, a man may impose upon himself, as much as if he should conceive the soul represented by a man in a chariot drawn by self-love and guided by reason. The human soul loves itself: this love of itself makes it eager after happiness, and in order to attain it, attentive to its own ideas, which, being in themselves evidently true, point out the way to it. All these acts, though different in appearance, are operations of the same soul, which lives,[2] desires, reasons and examines, moves itself, and is the directress of its own motions. To form just notions, we must neither confound different things, nor make distinctions where there are no differences.

Mr Pope still continues the prosopopoeia of the acts of the mind, and adds,

> *Par l'objet eloigne la raison peu frappee,*[3]
> With the distant object reason little smitten,
> *Est d'un bien a venir foiblement occupee;*[4]   80
> Is on a good to come weakly employ'd;
> *Par le plaisir present l'amour propre excite*
> By the present pleasure self-love excited

---

9. Pope.
1. his epistle: "cette deuxiéme Epitre" (p. 149).
2. All these acts . . . lives: "c'est elle qui fait tout cela, qui s'aime" (p. 149).
3. Crousaz has incorrectly "frapée" (p. 150) but Du Resnel has "frappée" (l. 79).

4. Pope's lines are:

> Reason's at distance, and in prospect lie:
> That sees immediate good by present sense;
> Reason, the future and the consequence. (72–74)

SECOND EPISTLE

> *Le desire, & s'y porte avec vivacite;*
> It desires, and is carry'd to it with eagerness;
> *Tandis que la raison conjecture, examine,*
> While reason conjectures, examines,
> *L'amour propre, plus prompt, veut, & se determine.*
> Self-love, more ready, wills, and determines itself.

If the soul attends only to the impressions made upon it by the senses, and to the effects of those impressions, or the thoughts, which owe their rise entirely to the senses, distant objects will have but little power to influence its determinations. But if it applies itself to reason with attention, events to come will be more interesting, and have in every resolution a weight proportioned to their importance. A man sunk in sensuality gives up himself to the pleasures of a luxurious table, and refuses to attend to the idea of the miseries and diseases that may be the consequences of his dainties.[5] But the reasoner makes no difficulty of preferring a lasting tranquillity to transient enjoyments, however great, and easily to be obtained.[6]

> *Du panchant naturel les secrets mouvemens*   85
> Of the natural bent the secret motions
> *Sont plus frequens, plus forts, que les raisonnemens.*
> Are more frequent, more strong, than ratiocinations.

This is very true of the man who abandons himself wholly to mere *animal* satisfactions. But reason deserves to be accounted natural to man, as much, and more, than those appetites[7] which man and beast have in common.

> *La raison, dans sa marche, est prudente & timide;*
> Reason, in its march, is prudent and timorous;
> *Le vol de l'amour propre est ardent & rapide.*
> The flight of self-love is ardent and rapid.

---

5. A man sunk . . . dainties: "Un homme sensuel se livre à la bonne chére, & se refuse aux idées des maux qui en naîtront" (p. 150).

6. easily to be obtained: "actuellement en sa disposition" (p. 151).

7. appetites: "panchans" (p. 151).

> *Mais pour en moderer la vive impulsion,*
> But to moderate its quick impulse,
> *La raison le combat par la reflexion;* 90
> Reason opposes it by reflection;
> *L'habitude, le tems, les soins, l'experience,*
> Habit, time, care, experience,
> *Repriment l'amour propre, & reglent sa puissance.*
> Restrain self-love, and regulate its power.

The meaning of this passage is, That man always loves himself, but that sometimes for want of sufficient circumspection, he suffers impatience to take hold of his faculties, and determines before he has examined. And though he even then does not love himself less, he yet brings misfortunes upon himself by his eagerness of good. But in these cases the misfortune is no less than the *good* at other times, to be imputed to self-love. A man when he makes a bad choice loves not himself less[8] than when he chooses well: neither in the latter case does he love himself in a greater degree, tho' more rationally.[9]

> *Qu'un Scholastique vain, cherchant a discourir,*
> When a vain Schoolman, seeking to argue,
> *Cache la verite, loin de la decouvrir;*
> Hides the truth, far from discovering it;
> *Que par un long tissu d'argumens inutiles,*[1] 95
> While by a long thread of useless arguments,
> *Voulant tout diviser jusques a l'infini,*
> Willing to split every thing even to infinity,
> *Il separe avec art ce qui doit etre uni;*
> He separates with art that which ought to be united;
> *Laissons-le par des mots obscurcir la matiere.*
> Suffer him by words to darken matter.

A poet may express himself with more elegance than a Schoolman without arriving at more justness or accuracy.

---

8. less: "plus" (p. 152).

9. neither . . . rationally: "Dans ce dernier cas, on ne s'aime pas plus encore, mais on s'aime mieux" (p. 152).

1. The following line (96) is omitted:

"Par des tours ambigus, par des raisons subtiles" (p. 152).

SECOND EPISTLE 137

> *Sur nos raisonnemens jettons plus de lumiere;* 100
> On our arguments let us cast more of light;
> *La^m raison, l'amour propre, avec le meme effort,*
> Reason, self-love, with the same endeavour,
> *Tendant au meme but, doivent marcher d'accord.*
> Tending to the same end, ought to march in consort.
> *Ils ont pour la douleur une invincible haine,*
> They have to pain an invincible hatred,
> *Un attrait naturel au plaisir les entraine.*
> A natural attractive to pleasure them draws.
> *Mais l'amour-propre, ardent a l'aspect du plaisir,* 105
> But self-love, kindled at the sight of pleasure,
> *Devore avidement l'objet de son desir:*
> Devours greedily the object of its desire:
> *La raison le menage, & d'une main habile*
> Reason manages it, and with a skillful hand
> *Prend, sans blesser le² fleur, le miel qu'elle distille.*
> Takes, without wounding the flower, the honey which it distills.
> *L'homme doit discerner, s'il veut se rendre heureux,*
> Man ought to discern, if he would make himself happy,
> *Du plaisir innocent le plaisir dangereux.* 110
> From innocent pleasure dangerous pleasure.

In these last verses there will be no obscurity, and it will appear that Mr Pope keeps his promise with great exactness,[3] if we consider the mind of man always loving itself, and, in consequence of that love, sometimes[4] inflamed too much at the sight of a pleasing object, and sometimes proceeding with more caution, and making, from a sense of duty, a very great difference between innocent and dangerous pleasures.

m. Lu

---

2. Crousaz correctly has "la fleur" (p. 153).

3. Mr. *Pope* . . . exactness: "Mr. POPE tient exactement parole" (p. 153).

4. SJ translates "souvent" as "sometimes" here and later in the sentence (p. 153).

This necessary distinction contributes very much to the illustration[5] of what Mr Pope has asserted in another place, That

> *Whatever is, is right.*[6]

He would be guilty of very great inconsistencies should he assert that, *Whatever is, is innocent.*[7] This last period[8] is much less obscure in the poetical, than in the prose translation.

> *Que sont les passions? L'amour-propre lui-meme,*
> What are the passions? Proper self-love,
> *Evitant ce qu'il hait, & cherchant ce qu'il aime.*
> Avoiding that which it hates, and seeking that which it loves.
> *D'un bien faux ou reel la prompte impression,*
> Of a good false or real the quick impression,
> *Les frappant vivement, les met en action.*
> Them striking briskly, puts them in action.
> *Lorsque, sans offenser les interets des autres,* 115
> When, without injuring the welfare of others,
> *Leur mouvement se borne a contenter les notres,*
> This motion is confin'd to provide for our own,
> *La raison les adopte, & leur donnant ses soins,*
> Reason them adopts, and taking them under its care,
> *Emprunte leur secours dans nos justes besoins.*
> Borrows their help in our lawful occupations.

The passions are the different states, the different[9] manners of thinking and willing of a soul, which being always actuated by self-love, endeavours with more than ordinary efforts either to obtain something or avoid it. If the object of its de-

---

5. This necessary ... illustration: "Ce discernement si nécessaire répand un grand jour" (p. 153).

6. SJ substitutes part of the last line of Epistle I by Pope for Du Resnel's *"Tout est bien"* (p. 153).

7. SJ recasts "tout est innocent" to echo Pope (p. 153).

8. period: "Période" (p. 154). *Period:* "A complete sentence from one full stop to another" (sense 7 in *Dictionary*). Boyer defines it as "(Portion d'un discours) a period, a perfect sentence."

9. SJ adds "different" here and later in the sentence (p. 154).

SECOND EPISTLE

sires may be obtained without any injury to others, and is to itself the means of happiness, the ardour of its wishes, and the eagerness of the pursuit, only improve and exalt its virtues; and much more if it be the means of happiness to others.[1]

> *Mais lorsque d'un mortel elevant le courage*
> But when of a mortal raising the courage
> *Elles ferment ses yeux sur son propre advantage,*   120
> They shut his eyes on his self-interest,
> *La raison applaudit a leurs nobles transports,*
> Reason applauds their noble transports,
> *Et du nom de vertu couronne leurs efforts.*
> And with the name of virtue crowns their efforts.

This, doubtless, happens too frequently, but no man ought to allow it in himself.

> *Que le Stoicien, se croyant insensible,*
> Let the Stoic, thinking himself insensible,
> *Travaille follement a se rendre impassible;*
> Labour foolishly to render himself impassible;
> *Que sa fausse vertu, sans force, & sans chaleur,*   125
> Let his false virtue, without strength, and without heat,
> *Reste sans action, concentree dans[2] son coeur;*
> Remain without action, concenter'd in his heart;
> *Plus notre esprit est fort, plus il faut qu'l agisse;*
> The stronger our mind is, the more it must needs act;
> *Il meurt dans le repos, il vit dans l'exercise;*[3]
> It dies in repose, it lives in exercise;
> *C'est par les passions que l'homme est excite;*
> It is by the passions that man is excited;
> *L'ame en tire sa force & son activite.*   130

---

1. If the object . . . others: "Si ce où elle tend ne fait tort à personne, si c'est un bien pour elle, & à plus forte raison, si c'est en même tems un bien pour les autres, la véhémence de ses désirs, & de sa poursuite donne de nouveaux degrés à sa vertu" (p. 154).
2. Crousaz has "en" (p. 155).
3. Crousaz correctly has "l'exercice" (p. 155).

The soul from them derives her strength and her activity.

The indolence of the *Stoicks* may be the effect of their constitution, or it may be the consequence of some delusive principle. They allow nothing but virtue the appellation of *good*, and therefore, if they ever assisted others, it was always without warmth or emotion.[4]

But, said they, *the avenues of the breast*[5] *are always to be kept shut against the passions; for if they are once open'd, those enemies to our repose very easily slip in, disturb the tranquillity of reason, and, either by the fear of missing our aims, or the grief for having missed them, destroy*[6] *our happiness.*

To this reasoning, it was answer'd, That the passions are so far from destroying our virtue, that they produce opportunities for the more perfect practice of it.

Loin qu'un trouble naissant l'epouvante & l'arrete,
Far from being terrify'd and hinder'd by a rising trouble,
Elle met a profit une utile tempete:
She turns to advantage the useful storm:
La vie est une mer, ou sans cesse agites,
Life is a sea, where incessantly tossed,
Par de rapides flots nous sommes emportes.
By rapid waves we are driven.

This world is to be considered not as the seat of present[7] content, or compleat happiness; it is a place of exercise and probation, a field in which we are to contend for happiness,[8] and in which, if we run our race well, and surmount the obstacles that oppose us, every step we take brings us nearer to perfect and eternal felicity.

La raison, que du ciel nous eumes en partage,   135
Reason, which from heaven we had in share,
Devient notre boussole au milieu de l'orage;

---

4. without warmth or emotion: "trop nonchalamment" (p. 155).

5. *the avenues of the breast:* "la porte aux passions" (p. 156).

6. *destroy:* "sappent" (p. 156).

7. present: "parfait" (p. 156).

8. exercise . . . happiness: "exercice, une carriére" (p. 156).

SECOND EPISTLE 141

> Becomes our compass in the midst of the tempest;
> *Et son flambeau divin, pret a nous eclairer*
> And its divine taper, at hand to enlighten us
> *A travers les ecueils, peut seul nous rassurer:*
> Through the rocks, can alone set us in safety:

The author once more sets reason on the throne, and recommends her to us as a faithful protectress,[9] and as the power from which our strength and our succours are to be expected; he even acknowledges that she is ready to afford her light to illuminate our obscurity.*

> *Mais de nos passions les mouvemens contraires*
> Yet of our passions the contrary motions
> *Sur ce vaste ocean sont des vents necessaires.*   140
> On this vast ocean are the necessary winds.

If the passions are compared to winds which impel us forward in our way with greater velocity, provided they blow from the right point,[1] and the pilot knows how to make a good use of them, the comparison is just; but when the passions oppose each other, when the second gust destroys the effects of the first, our life becomes a state of inconstancy and irregularity.

> *Dieu lui-meme, Dieu sort de son profond repos,*
> God himself, God goes forth from his profound rest,
> *Il monte sur les vents, il marche sur les flots.*
> He rides upon the winds, he walks upon the waves.

These expressions are extremely poetical; the idea of God quitting his profound repose, is such as we cannot dwell upon. And the instance of God presiding over the storms, and directing the course of the waves, does not give the least countenance to the tumults of our passions.†

---

*This is only said by the translator.
†The last couplet of this paragraph is misrepresented by the version, and the

---

9. faithful protectress: "azyle [asile] assûré" (p. 157).

1. the right point: "coté du Port" (p. 157).

Le desir, & l'amour, la joie & l'esperance,
Desire and love, joy and hope,
Cortege du plaisir, qui leur donne naissance;
Retinue of pleasure, which gives them birth;
La crainte, le soupçon, la haine & le chagrin, 145
Fear, suspicion, hatred and sorrow,
Que la douleur enfante, & nourrit dans son sein;
Which pain brings forth, and nourishes in its bosom;
Toutes ces passions, entre elles combinees,
All these passions, among themselves combined,
Au bonheur des humains ont ete destinees.
For the happiness of mankind were appointed.

This assertion I cannot entirely agree with, and Mr Pope only supposes without proving it. There are few passions which do not owe their excesses to a bad state of mind; they afford a confirmed and steady virtue opportunities of triumph, but a weak and wavering disposition to goodness is shaken by them, and often overthrown.[2] And what is it but the passions of bad men that interrupts and destroys the happiness of the good? I know not by what kind of fatality it is, that in reading Mr Pope, a man must be always upon his guard against the notion of a physical constitution of things,

---

whole passage very much injured. The lines, *Que le Stoicien,* &c. seem not only an imperfect translation of the *English,* but almost entirely *unideal* in themselves; the ten lines are wiredrawn into twenty, and yet part of the sentiments is lost.[3]

---

2. they afford . . . overthrown: "Si elles fournissent des occasions de victoire à une vertu très affermie, elles ébranlent celle qui est encore foible, & souvent la font trébucher" (p. 158).

3. In lazy Apathy let Stoics boast
 Their Virtue fix'd; 'tis fix'd as in a frost,
 Contracted all, retiring to the breast;
 But strength of mind is Exercise, not Rest:
 The rising tempest puts in act the soul,
 Parts it may ravage, but preserves the whole.
 On life's vast ocean diversely we sail,
 Reason the card, but Passion is the gale;
 Nor God alone in the still calm we find,
 He mounts the storm, and walks upon the wind. (101–10)

SECOND EPISTLE

by which moral evil is forced into the world like natural, and is therefore not moral evil.[4]

> *De leur combats divers resultent des accords*
> Of their several jarrings results the harmony
> *Qui forment l'union & de l'ame & du corps.*   150
> Which constitutes the union both of soul and of body.

This union is beyond my comprehension: every man is not equally subject to passions, but the soul of those who have subdued them is not less united to their bodies, than that of those in whom they reign without opposition in their full force.[5]*

> *Reglez vos passions, songez a les reduire.*
> Regulate your passions, take care to restrain them.
> *Ce qui forme le coeur, pourroit-il le detruire?*
> What forms the heart, can it destroy it?

---

*Mr Crousaz ought, at least, when he met with nonsense, to have consulted Mr Pope in the prose version. To attribute such an uncommon sentiment, *as that the passions constitute the union between the soul and body*, to a wrong author, is such injustice as no man ought either willingly or negligently to be guilty of. What effects might not this wonderful notion produce if carefully inculcated, firmly believed, and diligently pursued? It might perhaps, in time, produce a sect of philosophers, who might be continually endeavouring to strengthen this union, and exploding the antient means of longevity, temperance and chastity, might grow immortal by indulging their passions.[6]

---

4. by which moral . . . evil: "où le mal moral entre comme le bien, & cesse par là d'être mal moral" (p. 159).

5. the soul . . . force: "Il en est même chez qui elles ont perdu leur empire. Leur ame cependant n'en est pas moins unie à leur corps" (p. 159).

6. Pope's lines are:

> Passions, like Elements, tho' born to fight,
> Yet, mix'd and soften'd, in his work unite:
> These 'tis enough to temper and employ;
> But what composes Man, can Man destroy? (111–14)

Silhouette's version reads, "Les passions, ainsi que les élémens, quoique nées pour combattre, cependant mêlées & adoucies s'unissent dans l'ouvrage de Dieu: modérez les & faites en usage; ce qui compose l'homme peut-il détruire l'homme?" (pp. 35–36).

The passions do not constitute the mind, and he that regulates them, is so far from destroying his faculties, that he advances their perfection.

> *Tenir leur mouvemens dans un sage milieu,*
> To keep their motions in a prudent mean,
> *C'est suivre la nature & les desseins de Dieu.*
> Is to follow nature and the designs of God.

They are then not intended to form by their oppositions the union between the soul and body.

> *De l'amour du plaisirs notre ame possedee*   155
> With the love of pleasures our soul possessed
> *En joint⁷ en effet, ou les goute en idee;*
> Enjoys them in reality, or tastes them in idea;
> *Elle agit sans relache, ou pour les retenir,*
> She acts without intermission, either to retain them,
> *Ou pour s'en preparer au moins dans l'avenir.*
> Or to procure them at least for the future.
> *Mais de ces passions la seduisante amorce*
> But of these passions the seducing bait
> *A sur le coeur de l'homme ou plus ou moins de force,*   160
> Hath over the heart of man either more or less power,
> *Selon que les esprits, repandus dans le corps,*
> According as the spirits, diffused in the body,
> *Sont plus ou moins nombreux, plus foibles ou plus forts.*
> Are more or less plentiful, weaker or stronger.

In this passage I find nothing but what is agreeable to experience.

> *De la se forme en nous la passion regnante,*
> Thence is formed in us the reigning passion,
> *Qui toujours combattue, & toujours triomphante,*
> Which always opposed, and always victorious,

---

7. Crousaz correctly has "jouït" (p. 160).

SECOND EPISTLE 145

> *Semblable a ce serpent du grand legislateur,*   165
> Like to that serpent of the great legislator,
> *Qui brava d'un tiran le prestige enchanteur,*
> Which defy'd of a tyrant the juggling enchanter,
> *Des autres passions soumet l'orgueil rebelle,*
> Of other passions subjects the rebellious pride,
> *Les domte, les devore, & les transforme en elle.*
> Them tames, them devours, and them transforms into itself.

In this elegant description of that which is called the *ruling passion*, which is not the same in every man, but generally more strong than any other, I shall only remark that it is too general an assertion to say that it is *always opposed:* there are men so far from always opposing it, that they live in a state of habitual subjection to it. There are others who sometimes attempt[n] an opposition, but soon remit their efforts, and leave it unmolested, under a plea of weakness, which they are not uneasy at, because it gratifies their laziness and their appetites. There are others who weaken its influence, and there are some who utterly destroy it.*

---

n. atempt

*There seem to me to be many reasonable objections against this system, of a *ruling passion* interwoven with the original constitution, and perpetually presiding over its motions, invariable, incessant, and insuperable. I have at present no design of entering into an accurate discussion of the question, which is perhaps rather a question of fact and experience than of reason. The author may, perhaps, be conscious of a *ruling passion* that has influenced all his actions and designs. I am conscious of none but the general desire of happiness, which is not here intended, so that there appears equal evidence on both sides. Men, indeed, appear very frequently to be influenced a long time by a predominant inclination to fame, money or power; but perhaps if they review their early years, and trace their ideas backwards, they will find that those strong desires were the effects either of example or instruction, the circumstances in which they were placed, the objects which they first received impressions from, the first books they read, or the first company they conversed with. But there are others who do not seem to act in pursuance of any fix'd or unvaried principle, but place their highest felicity sometimes in one object sometimes in another, and these make undoubtedly the gross of mankind. Every observer however superficial, has remark'd, that in many men the love of pleasures is the *ruling passion* of their youth, and the love of money that of their advanced years. However this be, it is not proper to dwell too long on the resistless power, and despotick authority of this tyrant of the soul, lest the reader should, as it is very natural,

> *L'homme en venant au jour, porte dans son berceau*
> Man coming to the light, carries in his cradle
> *Le principe de mort qui le mene au tombeau;* 170
> The principle of death which brings him to the tomb;
> *Ce* germe *destructeur dans le cours de sa vie,*
> That destructive *bud* in the course of his life,
> *Se mele avec son sang, y croit, y se*[8] *fortifie.*
> Mixes with his blood, there grows, there gathers strength.
> *Ainsi la passion qui doit nous gouverner,*
> Thus the passion which is to rule us,
> *Acquiert sur notre esprit le droit de dominer.*
> Acquires over our mind the right of dominion.
> *Elle y verse en secret sa maligne influence,* 175
> It there sheds in secret its malign influence,
> *Elle y transforme tout en sa propre substance;*
> It there transforms all into its own substance;
> *L'imagination seconde ses efforts,*
> Imagination seconds its efforts,
> *Et la rend souveraine & de l'ame & du corps.*
> And makes it the arbitress both of the soul and of the body.

Here is another elegant description of the state of too many persons. It is scarce necessary to remark, that the great power which a passion at length gains by long continuance, cannot, but in very figurative terms, be called a *right* of dominion. And when we read, that

> *Each vital Humour that should feed the whole,*
> *Soon flows to this in Body and in Soul,*[9]

take the present inclination however destructive to society or himself, for the *ruling passion,* and forbear to struggle when he despairs to conquer.[1]

---

8. Crousaz has "s'y" (p. 161).
9. SJ substitutes ll. 139–40 of Pope for Crousaz's quotation of l. 176 of Du Resnel (p. 162). The first line should read "humour which" and the second should have a comma after "this."
1. See introduction, p. li.

the language is yet more raised above literal exactness, and is such as would be utterly unpardonable in a prose-discourse, unless it were a translation from poetry. The same observation may be made of the following lines, in which imagination is affirmed to finish the work, and make the passion absolute over soul and body.

> *Chaque jour l'habitude & nourrit & fait croitre*
> Every day habit both nourishes and increases
> *Ce panchant qu'avec nous la nature fit naitre.*   180
> That inclination which with us nature gave
>   birth to.*

I have already observed, that the term *nature* is susceptible of various meanings: here it signifies the disorder'd state of human nature since the *fall,* which is the cause that children come into the world with bad dispositions. But our inclinations to evil are, by no means, to be imputed to the Supreme Being, for he does not produce them.

> *Lorsque sa force agit, loin de lui resister,*
> When its force acts, far from resisting it,
> *L'esprit & les talens ne font que l'irriter.*
> The mind and the faculties do but irritate it.

There are, in reality, some men so settled in their resolutions, either by constitution, habit, or bad examples, and the pernicious conversation of those about them, or by impatience of advice, which they owe to their pride, as they owe their pride to their rank and their riches, that any endeavours to cure only inflame their vices: they think it would injure their honour to allow that any part of their behaviour wants amendment. But to conclude from particulars to generals, is to reproach human nature. There are others, who are grateful for advice, make use of it, apply it to themselves, and sac-

---

* *Nature* its Mother, *Habit* is its Nurse,
  Wit, Spirit, Faculties but make it worse.[2]

---

2. Lines 145–46.

rifice their passions, even their *ruling passions,* to their duty;³ at first, indeed, not without painful and toilsome struggles; afterwards, with less trouble; and, at last, with hearts equally filled with zeal and content.

> *Que dis-je? la raison dans le secret de l'ame*
> What do I say? reason in the recesses of the soul
> *Flatte cet ennemi, le soutient, & l'enflamme;*
> Flatters this enemy, maintains it, and inflames it;

There is nothing that gives a man more pain, than to lie under a necessity of condemning himself; and he seldom fails to employ all his powers in finding reasons for what he is resolved to do. Our ideas rise partly from one another, and partly from our sensations.⁴ When a man loves or hates, he produces in himself modes of thinking, which represent the object of his passion as amiable or detestable; and then persuades himself, that the objects deserve to be so esteemed; for a man willingly, and without resistance, acquiesces in those notions that suit his inclination;⁵ and when he desires an opinion should be true, very seldom examines it with exactness. But reason is not to be charged with those faults, into which no man is led by his reason, but falls into them for want of consulting it.

> *Telle que le soleil, qui souvent par ses feux*   185
> Just as the sun, which often by his fires
> *Rend des sucs corrompus encor plus dangereux.*
> Renders corrupt juices yet more dangerous.
> *Quelle que soit enfin la passion regnante,*
> Whatever be in short the reigning passion,
> *Contre elle la raison est souvent impuissante.*
> Against it reason is often impotent.

---

3. sacrifice their passions . . . duty: "qui font des sacrifices de leurs passions les plus dominantes à leur devoir" (p. 163).

4. sensations: "sentimens" (p. 164).

5. for a man . . . inclination: "parce qu'on acquiesce volontiers à ce qui plait" (p. 164).

To this assertion, we must once more subjoin, that man only wants strength, because he neglects, or sometimes absolutely refuses, to make use of his real powers.[6]

Orgueilleuse raison! tu soutiens mal tes droits.
Proud reason! thou ill maintainest thy rights.
Foible reine! crois-tu nous prescrire des loix?   190
Weak queen! thinkest thou to prescribe us laws?
A quelque favori toujours abandonee,
To some favourite always abandoned,
Tu lui laisses le soin de notre destinee.
Thou leavest to it the care of our destiny.
A quoi donc se reduit ton pouvoir si vante?
To what then amounts thy power so boasted?
De tes dures leçons quelle est l'utilite?
Of thy hard lessons what is the use?
Tu veux, que du plaisir nous redoutions les charmes;   195
Thou willest, that of pleasure we should dread the charms;
Mais pour en triompher nous donnes-tu des armes?
But to subdue it dost thou give us weapons?
Ta voix sur nos defauts nous force a reflechir;
Thy voice on our faults forces us to reflect;
Mais que peut ton secours pour nous en affranchir?
But what avails thy help to free us from them?
De reproches amers en vain tu nous accables;
With bitter reproaches in vain thou loadest us;
Sans nous rendre meilleurs tu nos rens miserables.   200
Without making us better thou makest us miserable.
Le flambeau, qu'a nos yeux tu viens sans cesse offrir,
The torch, which to our eyes thou art continually presenting,
Sert a nous tourmenter, non a nous secourir.
Serves to torment us, not to help us.

---

6. SJ omits the first sentence of this paragraph: "Dans ce dernier Vers, le mot de *souvent* est essentiel; il y est placé par opposition à *toûjours*" (p. 165).

150   A COMMENTARY

> *Tu sais justifier nos differens caprices,*
> Thou knowest to justify our different caprices,
> *Et du nom de vertu tu decores nos vices.*
> And with the name of virtue thou honourest our vices.
> *Tu fais dans notre coeur, par les soins que tu prens,*   205
> Thou makest in our heart, by the pains which thou takest,
> *A de foibles defauts succeder de plus grands.*
> To weak defects succeed greater.
> *C'est ainsi qu'aux humeurs faisant changer de route*
> 'Tis thus that causing the humours to change course
> *L'art a des maux legers fait succeder la goute;*
> Art to *slight* ailments makes succeed the gout;
> *Et que le medecin, fier de ce changement,*
> And that the doctor, proud of that alteration,
> *Croyant nous soulager, accroit notre tourment.*   210
> Thinking to comfort us, increases our torment.

What have I been reading?[7] Sentiments entirely opposite to those which gave me so much pleasure, in ver. 107. and 135.[8]* Does Mr Pope divert himself with blowing hot and cold? With presenting us by turns with sweet and bitter, that we may not know upon what to determine? Or do these contradictions arise from no ill design, but merely from an imprudent custom, establish'd in schools, of making young persons compose on both sides of the same question,[9] and praise and satirise the same thing, only for the reputation of a fruitful and almost inexhaustible imagination?

*98th of the original.

---

7. What . . . reading?: "Que viens-je de lire?" (p. 166).

8. The French reads, "dans le Vers 107. & les trois suivans, & encore plus dans le 135. & les trois qui le suivent" (p. 166). These passages correspond, more or less, to ll. 87–92 (77–82) and 105–08 (95–98). Line 108 (98) is "Reason the card, but Passion is the gale."

9. of making . . . question: "de faire composer les jeunes gens, qu'on y envoye, sur le pour & sur le contre" (p. 166).

'Tis said, that the Cardinal Du Perron having made an oration to prove the existence of the Deity, with great applause both of the king and the whole court, still insatiably desirous of praise,[1] invited them to hear, on the day following, the proofs of the opposite opinion; but, to the disappointment of his pride, his proposal was rejected with horror.[2]

But, without dwelling long upon what I do not certainly know to be true, I shall attempt to examine, without prejudice, this paragraph,[3] which contains a satire of the severest kind. The first question to be asked on this occasion, is, What is the subject of these reproaches? And I discover, without difficulty, that they are pointed, not at reason, but at the stupid negligence of those men, who either never consult, or refuse to obey, her.

It is to no purpose, that *reason* is introduced as a person, with all the unbounded freedom of poetry,[4] we must not suffer ourselves to be dazzled by elegancies. *Reason* is not a person that enters into us as an haughty guest into an inn, to behave imperiously, and controll the house. What is the sight? Is it not the man that has the power of seeing? What is a man's shape, his height, his bulk? Is it not the man himself? What then is reason, but the reasonable man? The man who can think justly, in conformity to truth, and to his duty. This position once establish'd, what becomes of that severe and galling satire?[5] Does it not sink into this short exclamation, *Unhappy mortals, whose only duty it is to be reasonable, why are you not so?*[6] This comment, short as it is, seems to me sufficient to obviate the ill use that might be made of this passage.

The whole world has heard of the impetuous and despotick passions of the celebrated Abbe De St Cyran; yet, when he

---

1. still...praise: "insatiable d'éloges" (p. 167).

2. his proposal...horror: "ses offres firent horreur" (p. 167).

3. this paragraph: "vingt & un vers" (p. 167). The same translation is given at the end of the next paragraph. There are twenty-two lines.

4. the unbounded...poetry: "la liberté que se donne la Poësie" (p. 167).

5. what becomes of that severe and galling satire: "à quoi se réduit cette longue & atterrante censure" (p. 168).

6. *why are you not so:* "*pourquoi donc ne le veux-tu pas être*" (p. 168).

sincerely attempted the conquest of them, he accomplish'd it in the compleatest manner.[7]

In vain do some attempt to countenance the idleness of human kind, and the negligence and insincerity of their conduct, by making a distinction between the virtues of nature and of grace. No reasonable man can imagine,[8] that our Creator will refuse us those abilities that are necessary to make our devotion acceptable to him, if we implore them with constancy and sincerity, if we highly value, and ardently desire them; and sure nothing else equally deserves our esteem, and our wishes.[9] These hopes are not empty chimeras, but equally elevated and real; at least, not to be willing to try the experiment, is to rise to the very summit of wickedness.

> *Cedons, conformons-nous aux loix de la nature;*
> Come, let us conform ourselves to the laws of nature;
> *La route qu'elle trace est toujour[1] la plus sure.*
> The road which she marks is always the safest.
> *Le but de la raison n'est pas de nous guider;*
> The scope of reason is not to guide us;
> *Son principal emploi se borne a nous garder.*
> Its chief business is confin'd to the guarding us.
> *C'est un maitre prudent, charge de nous instruire,*   215
> It is a wise master, commission'd to instruct us,
> *Qui doit regler nos gouts, mais non pas les detruire;*
> Which ought to rectify our tastes, but not to destroy them;
> *Et de la passion qui regne dans le coeur,*
> And of the passion which reigns in the heart,
> *Etre moins l'ennemi que le moderateur.*

---

7. in the compleatest manner: "avec la plus parfaite édification" (p. 168). Jean du Vergier de Hauranne, known as Saint-Cyran, Abbé of the Monastère de Port-Royal, who incurred the hostility of Cardinal Richelieu and was imprisoned.

8. SJ adds this opening clause.

9. if we highly ... wishes: "si nous en faisons l'objet de nôtre estime & de nos soûpirs? Et qu'y a-t-il au monde qui les mérite mieux?" (p. 169). Sure: "adv. [*surement*, French.] Certainly; without doubt; doubtless. It is generally without emphasis; and, notwithstandings its original meaning, expresses rather doubt than assertion" (*Dictionary*).

1. Crousaz correctly has "toujours" (p. 169).

SECOND EPISTLE

To be less the enemy than the moderator.
Par cette passion le ciel nous determine
By this passion heaven disposeth us
Aux desseins qu'a forme sa sagesse divine. 220
To designs which its divine wisdom hath formed.

This single sentence has almost disconcerted me.[2] I resume once more the character I at first took upon me, and suppose myself resolutely determined to serve my masters, in hopes of receiving new lights, with respect to my nature and my duty, by attending to their discoveries. But such is my unhappy fate, that, for once that I receive any improvement from them, I am obliged at least twice to shut my ears against them, to avoid discouragement and perplexity.

This, certainly, is one of the perplexing passages, nor have I any expedient to solve the difficulty, but the supposition that Mr Pope thought such sentiments as these sufficiently exposed by a naked recital, and that nothing more was necessary to make those men ridiculous and detestable, who were capable of talking seriously in this manner. Nor shall I injure his translator so much as to imagine he had any intention, when he gave us a version of such lines, as, taken in a literal sense, lead us unavoidably to the most shocking consequence.[3]

To make these notions appear in a stronger light,[4] let us put these words into the mouth of a confessor, who sees, at his confessional, sometimes a cheating gamester, sometimes a glutton and debauchee, and sometimes a robber and murderer. A little attention will shew us, that what he is at liberty to say to one of these, he is equally at liberty to say to the

---

2. This single . . . me: "Pour le coup me voila presque tout-à-fait dérouté" (p. 169).

3. This, certainly . . . consequence: "Voici sans doute un de ces endroits; & l'unique ressource qui me reste, c'est de supposer dans Mr. POPE la persuasion, qu'un simple exposé suffiroit pour faire sentir le ridicule & l'horreur de ceux qui pensent en effet conformément à ses Vers, & qui se conduisent conséquemment à ces injustes & affreuses pensées; & je croirois faire tort à Mr. l'Abbé de *Sept-Fontaines,* si je ne comptois qu'il les a traduit dans cette intention" (p. 170).

4. To make . . . light: "Pour sentir plus parfaitement ce ridicule & cette horreur" (p. 170).

other, if once we admit the notion, That God has implanted in every man his ruling passion, for the sake of producing the effects which naturally result from it.

Take courage, my son, says this charitable and philosophical physician of the conscience,[5] under the secresy of confession, *give way to these terrors no longer, your scruples are carried too far, I absolve you from your imaginary crimes, and dismiss you to pass the rest of your days in tranquillity.*

> *Yes, Nature's Road must ever be preserv'd;*
> *Reason is here no Guide, but still a Guard.*[6]

The meaning of this, is, That you are to live with some degree of prudence and caution, that you may not fall into the hands of some implacable and merciless magistrate, of some ensnaring and extravagant mistress, or some thief more artful than yourself, or suffer your pleasures to betray you to all the miseries of a ruin'd constitution.[7]

> *'Tis her's to rectify, not overthrow,*
> *And treat this Passion more as Friend than Foe.*[8]

That is, to take care not to impair the organs that contribute to the gratification of this ruling passion, *to teach you to be nice in the choice, and circumspect in the enjoyment, of your pleasures;*[9] *but not, by any means, to prohibit or diminish them.* For,

> *A mightier Power*[1] *the strong Direction sends.*

---

5. *Take courage . . .* conscience: "*Prenez,* dira à chacun d'eux, l'un après l'autre, dans le secret de la Confession, ce charitable & Philosophe Consolateur" (p. 171).

6. SJ substitutes ll. 161–62 of Pope for Crousaz's quotation of ll. 211–14 of Du Resnel (p. 171). The first line should read "ever be prefer'd."

7. *The meaning . . . constitution: Cela signifie qu'il faut vivre avec quelque précaution & quelque prudence, pour ne pas tomber entre les mains de quelques Magistrats* implacables, *de filoux plus fins que vous, ou de quelques maitresses ruineuses, & d'une santé dérangée*" (pp. 171–72).

8. SJ substitutes ll. 163–64 for Crousaz's quotation of ll. 215–16 of Du Resnel (p. 172).

9. *to teach you . . . pleasures:* "*Vous rendre plus fins, par example, & plus circonspects dans le choix de vos plaisirs*" (p. 172).

1. SJ substitutes l. 165 of Pope for Crousaz's quotation of ll. 217–18 of Du Resnel. He omits "*Afin qu'elle dure davantage*" and a quotation of ll. 219–20 of Du Resnel (p. 172).

SECOND EPISTLE   155

With these shocking and impious sentiments let us now compare the sober advice of a good man, acquainted with our duties, our weakness, and our strength. He will counsel in this manner any one that shall apply to him on the same occasion:[2] *Oppose,* says he, *the violence of your* ruling passion, *by frequent reflections upon the nature of God, the reasonableness of his commands, the greatness of his rewards, and the severity of his punishments.*[3] *You have long continued in the violation of his laws,*[4] *ask his pardon with the confusion and shame*[5] *that becomes you; form resolutions, and implore his assistance to put them in practice.*[6] *But take heed, above all, lest you hinder the effect of your wishes and your prayers, by acting in a manner entirely contrary to what you seem to desire, and do really desire from time to time.*

And, doubtless, nothing so much hinders men from obtaining a compleat victory over their *ruling passion,* as that all the advantages gain'd in their days of retreat, by just and sober reflections, whether struck out by their own minds, or borrow'd from good books, or from the conversation of men of merit, are destroy'd in a few moments by a free intercourse and acquaintance with libertines;[7] and thus the work is always to be begun anew. A gamester resolves to leave off play, by which he finds his health impaired, his family ruin'd, and his passions inflamed; in this resolution he persists a few days, but soon yields to an invitation, which will give his prevailing inclination an opportunity of reviving in all its force. The case is the same with other men; but is reason to be charged with these calamities and follies,[8] or rather the man who refuses to listen to its voice in opposition to impertinent solicitations?

---

2. With . . . occasion: "A ces horreurs, opposez les conseils d'un homme de bien, qui connoit les devoirs de l'homme, avec ses foiblesses & ses forces" (p. 172).

3. *Oppose . . . punishments:* "Aux attraits de vôtre passion dominante, opposez, dira-t-il, *l'idée de Dieu, la justice de ce qu'il vous commande, ce qu'il vous est permis d'en espérer, & ce que vous en devez craindre*" (pp. 172–73).

4. *his laws:* "*ses saintes Loix*" (p. 173).

5. *confusion and shame:* "*profonde confusion*" (p. 173).

6. *to put . . . practice:* "*pour les remplir avec exactitude*" (p. 173).

7. free intercourse . . . libertines: "commerce avec des vauriens" (p. 173).

8. but is reason . . . follies: "Est-ce la Raison qu'on doit accuser" (p. 174).

Elle veut,[9] *pour remplir ses augustes projets,*
It wills in order to fulfil its grand purposes,
Que chaque homme s'attache a differens objets.
That every man apply himself to different objects.

These words offer several meanings to our consideration, as it is very frequent; we may extend them to a larger, or restrain them to a more confined import. They are capable of a sense which would be extravagant and injurious to Providence, but they are likewise susceptible of a meaning strictly true and worthy of our regard.

Man is born[1] subject to a great number of wants, and society is the great instrument of supplying them. Mankind are divided into a prodigious multiplicity of employments, and yet among all that diversity, it is scarce possible to name any innocent occupation that is not useful, at least their number is very inconsiderable in comparison of those that are advantageous to the world: even the meanest offices are necessary, and such as we should feel most inconvenience from the omission of.

This is a wonderful instance of that providence which takes care of mankind. Yet it is not true that God has implanted in every single man a prevailing inclination to a particular trade. There are great numbers whose trade is by no means their *ruling passion;* they have only an habitual temper, that in some degree resembles it. But the dispositions implanted in us by our Creator, and which discover his regard for mankind, are always innocent, and sufficiently distinguished from vicious inclinations, which cannot without impiety be ascribed to God. He has no need to call in the assistance of vice for the execution of his designs: if ever he makes use of men to bring those events to pass which he has decreed, he can do it by means of their virtue, even without their concurrence he can do it: neither do their vices break his measures, but are made by him the instruments of his just designs. It is

---

9. Crousaz has in parentheses after this word "*la Sagesse Divine*" (p. 174).

1. Man is born: "Les hommes vivent" (p. 174).

SECOND EPISTLE 157

in his power to punish mankind by famines, or to send diseases upon them that shall destroy them by millions;[2] inundations and earthquakes are the instruments of his justice. He can subject them to their enemies, who will in that case do but their duty in treating them with severity, as the Israelites by divine command treated the inhabitants of Canaan. And when two neighbouring nations give themselves up to pride, envy, or inhumanity, he permits them to make war upon each other, and makes them reciprocally the instruments of his just vegence.

> *De cette passion la force imperieuse*
> Of that passion the domineering power
> *De tout autre panchant se rend victorieuse.*
> Over every other inclination makes itself victorious.

This indeed is always the case with those men who will not do what is in their power to restrain it within its proper bounds.

> *A l'objet qu'elle suit elle arrive toujours,*   225
> At the object which it follows it always arrives,
> *Et qui veut l'arreter precipite son cours.*
> And whoever would stop it hastens in course.

This is by no means universally true, I have already mentioned[3] in what cases it may be admitted.

> *Qu'un desir effrene de gloire & de puissance,*
> Let an unbridled desire of honour and of power,
> *Que la soif des tresors, le gout de la science,*
> Let a thirst after riches, a taste for knowledge,
> *Que l'amour du repos, quelquefois plus touchant,*
> Let the love of ease, sometimes more affecting,
> *S'etablisse en un coeur, en forme le panchant.*   230
> Establish itself in a heart, thereof it forms the bent.

---

2. millions: "milliers" (p. 176).
3. SJ omits the reference, "(*v.* 82)" (p. 177).

> *Chacun suit son attrait, chacun lui sacrifie*
> Every one follows his attractive, every one sacrifices
>   to it
> *Ses biens & son honneur, souvent meme sa vie.*
> His goods and his honour, oftentimes even his life.

This likewise is generally true, tho' not by necessity but by the negligence of mankind, who are not sufficiently careful to watch over themselves, and regulate their own conduct.

> *Qu'au fond de sa retraite un moine enseveli*
> In the depth of his retirement let a monk bury'd
> *Coule ses jours en paix dans un modeste oubli;*
> Waste his days quietly in a modest oblivion;

If solitude be his *ruling passion,* it may be entirely innocent, and he may have very good reasons for preferring that kind of life before any other.

> *Qu'un heros affame de perils & d'allarmes*   235
> Let a hero greedy of dangers and alarms
> *Mette tout son bonheur dans la gloire des armes;*
> Place all his happiness in the glory of arms;
> *Que le sage se plaise en son oisivete,*
> Let the philosopher please himself in his leisure,
> *Et l'avide marchand dans son activete;*[4]
> And the covetous merchant in his toil;
> *Ils trouveront toujours la raison complaisante,*
> They will find always reason complying,
> *Prete a favoriser le gout que les enchante.*   240
> Ready to favour the taste which charms them.

When a man has once determined to lay no constraint upon himself, but to comply with his inclination whatever it be, his mind soon falls upon some notion or other that appears to him a sufficient justification. He is convinced of the justness of his opinion,[5] by his desire that it should be just, and be-

---

4. Crousaz correctly has "activité" (p. 178).

5. He is convinced ... opinion: "son esprit fait bientôt naître des idées qui lui

SECOND EPISTLE 159

cause he is too fond of it to subject it to an examination, or to weigh the arguments for the contrary opinion.

> *L'eternel artisan qui tira tout de rien,*
> Th'eternal artist who drew all from nothing,
> *Et qui du sein du mal fait eclore*[6] *le bien,*
> And who from the womb of evil makes to spring good,
> *De ce panchant secret employant la puissance,*
> Of this secret inclination using the power,
> *Decide notre coeur, en fixe l'inconstance.*
> Determines our heart, of it fixes the inconstancy.

If Mr Pope did not write this poem with a good design, that is, such a design as the laws of Christianity approve; and foresaw, while he was writing, that some of his readers would apply their utmost attention, and exert all their sagacity to give his expressions a favourable interpretation, he had good reason to divert himself with a prospect of the labours they were to undergo; and my toilsome explications, in particular, must have been an unexhaustible fund of merriment.[7] However as I do not find myself yet quite disabled,[8] I shall proceed, while I have any strength left, upon the same scheme[9] that I begun.

The Eternal Artificer—There is a contrast in this expression, which has given offence to many persons of understanding, who look upon the word *artificer* as too low a term to be associated with so grand an epithet. It seems likewise to insinuate, that the artificer and his work are of equal duration, and

---

paroitront justifiantes, parce qu'elles lui plaisent, & que par là il se dispense de les examiner, & de les comparer avec ce qu'on pourroit y opposer" (p. 178). SJ omits the next paragraph: "J'oberverai encore qu'un Sage qui se plait dans l'oisiveté, & qui s'y renferme, me paroit une contradiction. La sagesse n'est pas donnée afin d'en garder pour soi tous les fruits, sans les répandre sur les autres" (p. 178).

6. Crousaz wrongly has "éclorre" (p. 178).

7. and my toilsome . . . merriment" "& les miennes en particulier auront dû le faire bien rire" (p. 179).

8. disabled: "épuisé" (p. 179).

9. upon the same scheme: "sur le pié" (p. 179). Boyer defines the phrase "at the [same] rate" or "on the same basis."

the world by consequence eternal.* There are at this time persons who do not indeed allow themselves to affirm this in plain terms, but would be well enough pleased to have such an opinion prevail. If every thing in the world was merely machinery, that is, if every thing that relates either to mind or body was the consequence of an uninterrupted chain of unalterable determinations, the appellation of *Eternal Artificer* would be more consistent with those of the Supreme Being, and the First Cause.

I cannot but own these expressions,

> *Th'* Eternal Art, *educing Good from Ill,*
> *Grafts on this Passion our best Principle:*
> *'Tis thus the Mercury of Man is fixt*——¹

carry, if closely examined, a sense which one cannot but dislike; but poetical language is not to be so nicely inspected. In a style of less liberty it would be sufficient to say, that the Creator of the World has favoured man with the gift of liberty, and the power of action: that there are some men who, by an ill use of that liberty, obstinately persist in their incli-

---

* It is of great misfortune to have too great an inclination to draw consequences, and too strong a desire to search deeper than the rest of mankind. This temper is undoubtedly of great use in abstruse learning, and on some important occasions; but when carried into the scenes of common life, and exerted without any necessity, only makes the unhappy reasoner suspicious and cautious, shews every thing in a false light, and makes his discoveries the sport of the world. What common reader would infer the eternity of the world from the expression of the Eternal Artificer? If the word be taken in its common acceptation, the first idea that naturally occurs is, that the artificer is prior to his work.² If we admit it, as here we certainly must, in a figurative sense, it will imply no more than Creator, which would probably have given no offence. What objections might not such a disposition to cavil have raised against such an expression as Divine Geometrician, *which would have confined the operations of the Supreme Being to this poor despicable spot of earth?*

---

1. SJ substitutes ll. 175–77 of Pope for Crousaz's "l'*Eternel Artisan déploye sa Toute-puissance, en produisant dans chaque homme une inclination dominante, & par là décide d'eux, & y fixe l'inconstance des passions*" (p. 180).

2. *Artificer:* "An artist; a manufacturer; one by whom any thing is made" (sense 1 in *Dictionary*). The second illustrative quotation from Robert South refers to the "*great artificer.*" Du Resnel calls God "L'Eternel Artisan." Boyer defines "Artisan" in a figurative sense as "(celui qui est l'auteur, la cause de quelque chose) an artificer, author, contriver."

SECOND EPISTLE 161

nations; that there are others who change them with more or less difficulty, and that there are likewise[3] some who act upon principles of duty, and act consistently and steadily.[4]

> *Du sein des passions ne voit-on sortir* 245
> From the seat of the passions don't we see proceed
> *Les[5] vertus dont l'effet peut moins se dementir?*
> Virtues whose effect cannot at all bely itself?
> *Comme d'un sauvageon, par une greffe utile,*
> As from a wild stock, by a profitable graft,
> *En fruits delicieux sort un arbre fertile.*
> Delicious in its fruits proceeds a fertile tree.

A mind enlightned with truth and wisdom, and mistress of its own motions, feels a passionate desire of discharging the duties of our present state, and, by the help of that passion, performs with more ease, chearfulness, and perseverance, without struggle or reluctance.[6] A man of this disposition does not owe his virtues to his passions, but his passions at once strong and well governed arise from his virtues.

Man loves himself: this inclination is neither vice nor virtue, but merely physical; as he loves himself, he endeavours to procure his own happiness; this again is only physical. But he is afraid of directing his endeavours wrong, and of erring in his choice: here begins the right use of his liberty. In this right use he makes continual advances by attentive examination, and still gains new strength and activity by devoting himself to that which he finds to be his duty.

The first dispositions, which are only physical, seem to be well enough represented by a wild stock that may receive good or bad grafts; and the moral choice may be emblemati-

---

3. difficulty ... likewise: "légereté ... enfin" (p. 180).

4. consistently and steadily: "constamment" (p. 180).

5. Crousaz has "Des" (p. 181).

6. A mind ... reluctance: "Un esprit éclairé, sage & maître de ses mouvemens, se passionne pour son devoir, & avec ce secours parvient à s'en acquiter plus aisément, sans effort, & avec plus de vivacité & de persévérance" (p. 181).

cally pointed out by the grafts, which ill-chosen produce bad fruits,[7] or, if selected with judgment, bear products equally beneficial to health, and grateful to the palate.

> *Combien de fois l'orgueil, & la haine, & l'amour,*
> How often have pride, and hatred, and love,
> *A de nobles exploits ont-ils donne le jour!*[8]   250
> To noble exploits given birth!
> *La colere supplee au zele, a la vaillance;*
> Anger supplies zeal, valour;
> *L'avarice est souvent mere de la prudence.*
> Covetousness is often the mother of prudence.
> *Arretant dans leur*[9] *cours nos bouillantes ardeurs*
> Stopping in their course our boyling passions
> *La paresse entretient la sagesse des moeurs.*
> Sloth maintains a soberness of manners.
> *L'envie adoucissant son impuissante rage*   255
> Envy sweetening its impotent rage
> *Sert d'emulation, & soutient le courage.*
> Turns to emulation, and upholds courage.
> *Est-il quelque vertue*[1] *qui se fasse admirer,*
> Is there any virtue which makes itself admired,
> *Que la honte ou l'orgueil ne nous puisse inspirer?*
> Which shame or pride cannot inspire in us?

Vicious inclinations are not implanted by Divine Providence in the heart of man; nothing can be more horrible than a system that insinuates such a doctrine.[2] But that the creation may not be thrown into confusion by the vices of men, God's wisdom and power make them subservient to good ends. A man who would have been, for his life, but an useless

---

7. the grafts . . . fruits: "des greffes d'où naîtront de mauvais fruits, par l'abus de la liberté qui choisit mal" (p. 182).

8. Crousaz has "jour?" (p. 182).

9. Crousaz has correctly "leurs" (p. 182). His mistranscription leads to an error in his translation.

1. Crousaz correctly has "vertu" (p. 182).

2. nothing . . . doctrine: "On ne peut s'empêcher de frémir à l'idée d'un Systême qui conduit là" (p. 182).

SECOND EPISTLE   163

burden to the earth, is dragged out of his dream of indolence by the desire of riches and of honours. Pride and avarice are criminal in themselves, but a proud or covetous man³ will do his neighbour services in hopes of recompence or acknowledgments. The most stupid and most abandoned of mankind may easily discover, that they have more to hope and less to fear than other men in proportion as they are more virtuous. Every man lies in some degree either greater or less, under the necessity of receiving assistance from others; and, to obtain it, must endeavour to be thought a man of worth: if therefore he is not so in reality, he finds himself obliged to assume the appearance of it. But this appearance is not virtue, it is only the show of it, and is of no other efficacy than to make those men inexcusable, who acknowledge the excellence of it, and pay it the outward homage which is required, yet never love it in reality, but pass their lives in imposing equally upon themselves and others.

It is to no purpose, that some, desirous of debasing virtue⁴ by ascribing it to mean principles, alledge, that

> *No Virtue Male or Female can we name,*
> *But what may grow on Pride or grow on Shame.*⁵

That which rises from these principles, however it may raise our admiration, is very different from virtue, and could we see the hearts of men thus superficially good, we should look upon them with detestation, and find nothing there conformable to the excellencies we admire. There is always something mean and contemptible in disguise, and when a man is surprized without his mask, nothing can preserve him from the most shameful confusion.

---

3. a proud . . . man: "un paresseux ou un voluptueux" (p. 183).

4. desirous of debasing virtue: "pour rabaisser le mérite de la vertu" (p. 184). SJ seems to have nodded here. The sense is that even a slothful or voluptuous person is ready to offer services in return for money or prestige.

5. SJ substitutes ll. 193–94 (183–84) of Pope for Crousaz's quotation and elaboration of l. 258 of Du Resnel (p. 184). The lines should read "Nor Virtue" and "will grow."

> *Du vice a la vertu qu'il est peu de distance!*
> From vice to virtue how small is the distance!
> *Entre eux l'homme sans cesse & chancele & balance.*   260
> Between 'em man continually both reels and wavers.*

The distance between vice and virtue is surely very great, and it is astonishing that men waver and deliberate between the two extremes. But their inconstancy is the effect of their insincerity; they are not good at the bottom, and have no regard but to the appearance of virtue.

The man, who, in the service of a master of great wisdom, lives temperately and without any excess, free from pride, and indifferent about any thing but the necessaries of life, always usefully employed, and ready to do good, without making a trade of his good offices, or setting his credit to sale; if, under these specious appearances, he concealed a corrupt heart, and inclinations not agreeable to his profession, as soon as his former master shall be succeeded by one of a different conduct, given over to pleasures and expences, impatient of solitude and reflection, and without any inclination but to riot and extravagance, immediately will this hypocritical slave adopt all the faults of his new master,[6] and make much more expeditious advances in them than he made before in virtue.

---

*The *English* is,

> Thus Nature gives us (let it check our Pride)
> The Virtue nearest to our vice ally'd;[7]

which the translator has so misrepresented as to make it bear little relation to the foregoing paragraph, and, as in a multitude of other passages, lies open to censures which are far from equally affecting the original.

---

6. The man . . . master: "Tel qui, au service d'un Maître très sage, vit dans une parfaite tempérance, & un éloignement exact de toute débauche, sans donner dans le faste, & ne marquant pour le superflu que de l'indifférence, actif, officieux, & n'ayant garde de vendre ses services & de mettre à prix son crédit; si, sous des dehors si beaux, il cache un coeur, dont les inclinations n'y soient pas conformes, dès que son premier Maître sera succédé par un voluptueux, un dépensier, sans goût pour la retraite, & uniquement porté à la dissipation, on verra ce faux vertueux adopter tous les vices de son nouveau Maître" (pp. 184–85).

7. Lines 195–96 (185–86).

SECOND EPISTLE

Thus it appears evidently, that the advantage, which men receive from solid unaffected virtue, is very different from that which empty appearances afford.

This subject is of such importance, that it deserves to be illustrated by another example. Let us suppose a state flourishing, by the wisdom of its monarch, with all the felicities of peace, justice, plenty and religion; and a neighbouring kingdom filled with pride, envy, discord, and tumults, where impiety, dishonesty, brutality, and debauchery reign without constraint, and every thing is set to sale. The king of this detestable race enters with fire and sword into his neighbour's dominions: but with what prospect of success? His unjust attack is opposed by bodies of men well instructed, and superiour by right notions to the fear of death: men who would lose many lives rather than be subject to so hateful a government.[8] In this case every man that can secure victory, union, order, intrepidity, sobriety, and its consequences, health, and vigour, will all unite on the side of justice.

To assemble great numbers of soldiers of this character, must be acknowledged to be no easy matter; and there is a necessity of enlisting such as offer themselves, and whom idleness, debauchery, the desire of living without restraint, and the hopes of plunder have incited to make choice of that kind of life. These vices are not willingly promoted by a society, but since there are such, they are turn'd to advantage where there is an opportunity. So it is that vice is of advantage; but it can by no means be admitted to be necessary to a community, since virtue would procure the same benefits, with less difficulty, and greater certainty.

Dans un panchant egal, lui servant de soutien,
In equal poise, him serving to suspend,

---

8. The king . . . government: "Le Maître de ce second Etat, entre à main armée dans celui du premier. Ici on oppose à l'injuste aggresseur des troupes, qui, bien instruites & bien convaincuës de la vérité, ne craignent point la mort, & qui aimeroient mieux perdre cent fois la vie, que de la passer sous une domination si odieuse" (p. 186).

166   A COMMENTARY

Le[o9] poids de la raison change le mal en bien.
The weights of reason change evil into good.
En l'ecoutant, Neron, vertueux & sans vices,
By listening to it, Nero, virtuous and without vices,
Comme Titus, du monde eut ete les delices.
Like Titus, of the world had been the delight.
Cette fougue d'esprit, cette fierte de coeur,   265
That fierceness of temper, that stubborness of heart,
Que dans Catilina je vois avec horreur,
Which in Catiline I see with horror,
Me charme en Decius; me ravit & m'etonne,
Charms me in Decius; ravishes me and surprises me,
Quand Curtius, par elle, a la mort s'abandonne.
When Curtius, by it, to death himself devotes.

At these verses I pause with great satisfaction.* A passion may be employ'd well or ill; for this reason, a wise man considers its nature, all its degrees, and possible effects; and accordingly endeavours to extinguish, preserve, or regulate it. Nero needed only to have acted thus, and he had equall'd

---

o. De

* *If the critic acknowledges the truth and beauty of these verses, which only contain an explanation of the foregoing passage, it will be reasonably thought that many of his censures might have been spared, which, tho' doubtless well intended, are sometimes thrown out with too little reflection. Mr Pope's assertion, in plain prose, seems to be this: there are many different virtues, equally necessary to the happiness of mankind, but which can hardly exist, in the highest degree, in one and the same person; the Supreme Being has, therefore, allotted to every individual a ruling passion, or strong tendency to some particular end, which generally may be attained by either good or bad means; and by which of the two he will obtain it, is left to his choice. The ruling passion, the natural byass of the mind, is equally powerful in both cases, and will hurry forward to its favourite object with equal rapidity, either thro' the paths of virtue or of vice. Thus the desire of being distinguished above the rest of mankind, while it was directed by reason, made* Nero, *in the first years of his reign, an excellent emperor; and afterwards, when he neglected to consult any guide but his appetites, the same passion made him an extravagant debauchee, &c. This system, whether true or not, seems hitherto innocent at least; and besides, as Mr* Crousaz *might have noted, contains an evident assertion of free-will.*

---

9. Crousaz correctly has "Le" (p. 187).

SECOND EPISTLE   167

Titus: that magnanimous contempt of death, which was madness in Catiline, who chose rather to perish than not disturb the tranquillity of the publick, engages our admiration in Decius and Curtius, who died for no other end than the preservation[1] of their country.

> *La meme ambition sauve & perd les etats;*
> The same ambition saves and ruins states;
> *Aux bons comme aux mechans fait braver le trepas;*   270
> The good as well as the wicked makes to brave death;
> *Change un foible soldat en guerrier intrepide,*
> Changes a faint-hearted soldier into an undaunted warrior,
> *Et le plus grand hero en citoyen[2] perfide.*
> And the greatest hero into a knavish citizen.*

An experienced and ambitious warrior may controul all the success of an usurper,[3] and place the lawful prince upon the throne, but the ambition of this deliverer of his country may as well incite him to mount the throne himself. Thus it appears, that he who is guided by the dictates of ambition, and forms his designs without consulting his duty, will never consider the justice or injustice of an attempt, when that consideration opposes the gratification of his darling passion.[4]

But the man who makes it his glory to perform his duty, and obtain the approbation of his Creator, and of those who understand and reverence the divine laws, acts upon sentiments that will effectually stifle, in the birth, all false ambi-

---

* *The same Ambition can destroy or save,*
And makes a patriot as it makes a Knave.[5]

---

1. preservation: "l'amour" (p. 187).

    The fiery soul abhor'd in Catiline,
    In Decius charms, in Curtius is
    divine. (199–200; 189–90)

2. Crousaz correctly has "Héros en Citoien" (p. 188).

3. may controul . . . usurper: "détruira l'ouvrage d'un traitre & d'un usurpateur" (p. 188).

4. darling passion: "ses projets ambitieux" (p. 188).

5. Lines 201–02 (191–92). In the Twickenham edition the second line reads "makes a patriot."

tion, which may break out in good or evil actions, as chance shall determine.[6]

> *Que peut donc, si ce n'est le Dieu qui nous conduit,*
> Who can then, except the God who governs us,
> *Donc la voix separa le jour d'avec la nuit,*
> Whose voice separated the day from the night,
> *Demeler ce chaos de raison, de caprices,* 275
> Discover that chaos of reason, of caprices,
> *Ce chaos qui confond les vertus & les vices?*
> That chaos which confounds virtues and vices?

Before the nature of a passion, the principles from which it rises, and the end to which it tends, are discovered by the event, God only can tell whether it is consistent with virtue, how great a distance it is from it, or in what instances it is incompatible with it.

> *Comme dans les tableaux d'un peintre ingenieux,*
> As in the pictures of an ingenious painter,
> *Des ombres & des jours l'accord industrieux,*
> Of shades and lights the artful agreement,
> *Unissant des coleurs[7] la teinte imperceptible,*
> Uniting of colours the tint imperceptible,
> *Rend des bruns & des clairs la passage insensible;* 280
> Makes of dark and light the transition insensible;
> *De meme en nous, cachant leurs veritables traits,*
> Even so in us, concealing their genuine traces,
> *Le vice & la vertu se touchent de si pres,*
> Vice and virtue border so nearly,
> *Qu'en vain on chercheroit le point de la distance,*
> That in vain should we look for the point of distance,

---

6. acts upon sentiments . . . determine" "est dans des sentimens, qui s'opposent directement à la naissance d'une ambition équivoque" (p. 188). SJ adds "which may . . . determine."

7. Crousaz correctly has "couleurs" (p. 189).

SECOND EPISTLE

Ou la vertu finit, ou le vice commence.
Where virtue ends, or vice begins.

A motive not wicked in the most atrocious degree, but partaking of a vicious taint,[8] produces effects, so nearly approaching to those which rise from the most pure and virtuous intentions, that they may, with propriety enough, be compared to those shades in a picture,[9] where it is impossible to mark out the end of one colour, or the beginning of the other. But this only relates to exterior effects, in which the disguises which men assume to impose upon others, and sometimes to delude themselves, make it difficult to determine whether they are to be ascribed to virtue, or imputed to vice.

> *Mais quoique entre eux leur traits[1] paroissent confondus,*   285
> Yet though among them their traces seem blended,
> *Pretendrez-vous qu'il n'est ni vices ni vertu?*[2]
> Will you pretend that there are neither vices nor virtues?
> *Que le blanc que le noir avec art s'assortissent,*
> Let white and black with art associate,
> *Qu'entre[3] elles ces couleurs se melent, & s'unissent;*
> Among themselves let these colours mingle, and unite;
> *Sur les simples dehors vous laissant decevoir,*
> By the bare outsides suffering yourselves to be deceived,
> *Direz-vous qu'il n'est point ni de blanc ni de noir?*   290
> Will you say that there is no such thing as white or black?

The beginning of this passage is more harsh in the prose translation, and even more obscure; the expressions appear

---

8. A motive . . . taint: "Un motif vicieux, ou peu éloigné des excès qui le rendent tel" (p. 189).
9. shades . . . picture: "à ces nuances" (p. 190).
1. Crousaz has "quoiqu'entr'eux leurs fruits" (p. 190); Du Resnel has "traits" instead of "fruits" (l. 285).
2. Crousaz correctly has "Prétendez-vous" and "vertus" (p. 190).
3. Crousaz has "Qu'entr'elles" (p. 190).

to be more indeterminate, and the meaning less easy to be settled.[4]

> *L'esprit veut-il prouver une telle chimere,*
> The wit would it prove such a chimera,
> *Le coeur le contredit, & le force a se taire.*
> The heart contradicts it, and forces it to be silent.

These two lines are a sufficient preservative against all the idle imaginations of libertines, and all that they alledge to weaken the obligations of morality, and lay their consciences asleep. The inward sentiments of our hearts rebel against all their sophistries, how subtil and specious soever, and an innate probity, of which we cannot divest ourselves, makes us always suspect them as fallacious and delusive.[5]

> *Le vice est regarde comme un monstre odieux,*
> Vice is look'd on as an odious monster,
> *Dans*[6] *le premier instant qu'il paroit a nos yeux.*
> At the first instant that it appears to our eyes.

We will suppose a man who has nothing at heart but his own interest, who considers every thing as it affects himself, and loves no man, but as he can make him useful to his purposes: being a man of capacity, he discovers, that it will be for his interest to promote certain laws or regulations[7] in

---

4. Fools! who from hence into the notion fall,
That Vice or Virtue there is none at all.
If white and black blend, soften, and unite
A thousand ways, is there no black or white?
Ask your own heart, and nothing is so plain;
'Tis to mistake them, costs the time and pain. (211–16; 201–06)

Silhouette's version reads, "O! quelle folie! de vouloir de là tirer cette conséquence, qu'il n'y a ici-bas ni vices ni vertus. Parce que le blanc & le noir seront mêlangés, adoucis, fondus ensemble de mille manières différentes, n'y aura-t-il plus pour cela ni noir, ni blanc? Consultez votre propre coeur, rien n'est plus évident: c'est pour les confondre qu'il en coûte & de la peine & du tems" (p. 44).

5. an innate probity . . . delusive: "un fonds de probité nous les fait soupçonner d'erreur" (p. 191).

6. Crousaz has "Dès" (p. 191).

7. laws or regulations: "établissemens" (p. 191).

the society of which he is a member; to this end, he applies all his faculties, and makes use of his eloquence, his credit, and all his arts of insinuation: the world is easily prevailed upon to believe, that he has no view but the interest of the publick. Thanks are paid him, encomiums are heaped upon him, and acknowledgments returned from every hand. But as new prospects of interest rise up before him, and engage his predominant self-love, his schemes become quite opposite to those he had lately been prosecuting. He has now something to propose that will be attended with inconveniencies, and followed by consequences which will hurt the commonwealth:[8] this gives him very little trouble, he puts his design in execution, and acting always under the disguise of a pretended zeal, never reflects on the events of his projects, while he is only in pursuit of his own private advantage. If through that cloak of imposture with which he deludes the prejudiced, you could penetrate to his heart, and take a survey of his real sentiments, could you help considering him as a monster?[9] Unhappily for mankind, what we are now going to read is true; vice always deserves to be seen with horror,

> *Mais l'horreur qui le suit, par degres diminue,*   295
> But the horror which follows it, by degrees lessens,
> *Nous-nous accoutumons a soutenir sa vue;*
> We accustom ourselves to endure its sight;
> *Bien-tot le coeur pour lui se laisse interesser.*
> Soon the heart comes to be concerned for it.
> *Et notre aveuglement va jusqu'a l'embrasser.*
> And our blindness goes so far as to embrace it.
> *L'homme fixe a son gre l'extremite du vice,*
> Man fixes at his pleasure the extremity of vice,
> *Blame par passion, approuve par caprice;*   300
> Blames by passion, approves by fancy;
> *Aveugle sur lui-meme, il ne voit point en lui*

---

8. and followed . . . commonwealth: "on aura sujet de s'en repentir" (p. 192).

9. If through . . . monster: "Si à travers tous ces dehors, qui imposent aux esprits qu'il a prévenus, vous lisiez dans le fond de son coeur, vous ne pourriez vous empêcher de le regarder comme un monstre" (p. 192).

> Blind to himself, he sees not in him
> *Les exces vicieux, qu'il condamne en autrui.*
> The vicious excesses, that he condemns in another.

> *Yet, seen too oft familiar with her Face,*
> *We first endure, then pity, then embrace.*[1]

This is the practice of the world, but it is what ought not to be practised. Men make an ill use of their liberty, they chuse to live according to their own humour, and this temper becomes in time habitual, then gains new strength every day, and at length grows, perhaps, too much confirm'd to be ever changed.

These disorders, therefore, are only to be charged upon mankind. If any man should impute them to fatality, or should be weak enough to think,[2] or daring enough to assert, that God was inevitably determined, by the perfection of his nature, to create an universe, in which every thing should fall out exactly and necessarily as we find it: when any man endeavours to establish such chimerical opinions, we must then attend to the opposition which our own hearts will make, and which are the dictates of pure uncorrupted sense; and silence these mad[3] reasoners, either by not attending to their sophistries, or giving them a full view of the dangerous consequences of their systems.[4]

This danger is certainly much greater than is generally imagined. There are rules which we ought to observe with reverence, and which we deserve to be punished for disregarding. The secret whispers of our conscience tell us our duty, and the universal consent of mankind concurrs with the inward motions of our hearts. Where can be the danger of acting upon principles at once so natural, and so generally received? Whosoever shall make the experiment, will find this

---

1. SJ adds ll. 219-20 (209-10) from Pope. The medial comma in the first line should be after "oft."

2. or should . . . think: "si quelqu'un s'avise de penser" (p. 193).

3. mad: "téméraires" (p. 193).

4. SJ adds "consequences of their systems."

SECOND EPISTLE   173

way both safe and easy; the greatest difficulties are at the beginning, and grow less as he advances farther. Besides, he will have the satisfaction of guiding others in the right way, of promoting the interest of virtue, and seeing the world grow better by his example. For the sight of the regular and amiable behaviour of a good man naturally incites others to the love of virtue, as a frequent and familiar intercourse with vice makes us less sensible of its deformity, and betrays, at last, to complaisance and imitation.[5]

But to how different a condition does he expose himself, who suffers his esteem and his attention to be engrossed by the daring authors and promoters of a system, which naturally tends to discourage all vigilance and attention[6] to the consequences of his own conduct, and inclines him to give up his life to the direction of chance, and to act wholly in pursuance of his present temper of mind, without fear, solicitude, or remorse![7]

What answer will such a wretch be able to make to the Eternal, the Supreme, the Infinite Being? That being, to whom we cannot be too fearful of imputing any thing unsuitable to his nature: when he shall be at length convinced of the falsehood of his darling notions;[8] when he shall find that God was not necessitated by his own nature to create the universe, or inevitably determined by his own perfections to constitute the present order of things? When he shall find that all the cor-

---

5. The secret whispers . . . imitation: "Une voix intérieure nous le dit, & le Genre humain en convient. Que risque-t-on de se conduire sur ces principes? Qu'on en fasse l'essai, on éprouvera qu'on le peut, & que cette estimable route deviendra toûjours plus aisée. On se procurera encore, par un choix de vie si raisonnable, une des plus douces & des plus constantes satisfactions, d'occuper les yeux des autres par de bons exemples, qui leur feront sentir le prix de la Vertu, & la leur rendront aimable; au lieu que la vuë fréquente du Vice, en fait peu à peu évanouïr la laideur, & entraine à l'imiter" (p. 194).

6. vigilance and attention: "vigilance" (p. 195).

7. remorse: "reproche" (p. 195).

8. What answer . . . notions: "Que répondra-t-on à l'Etre éternel, à l'Etre adorable, à l'Etre qu'on ne sauroit jamais estimer & aimer autant qu'il le mérite, à qui on ne sauroit trop craindre d'imputer ce qui ne convient pas, quand on sera convaincu qu'il n'est pas vrai" (p. 195).

poreal parts of the universe are not machines, or parts of a machine, which play on in concurrence with others, pursuant to an eternal and unalterable destiny; and that men are not beings merely passive, and condemned to a perpetual delusion, in imagining, that they receive impressions from their bodies, and influence their motions, when there is nothing real in this opinion, nor any thing more than inclinations and perceptions, of which they idly believe that they contribute to the production?

> *Ainsi sous cette zone, ou le cruel Boree*
> Thus under that zone, where the cruel Boreas
> *Aux fougueux aquilons donne une libre entree,*
> To the furious north-winds gives a free entrance,
> *Le Lapon s'endurcit, & n'est point malheureux;*   305
> The Laplander hardens, and is not at all unhappy;
> *Il imagine ailleurs un ciel plus rigoureux.*
> He imagines elsewhere a sky more severe.

In these lines we have a picture of those men who live immersed in ignorance, without any inclination after a clearer light,[9] and, without enquiring into the principles of morality, have no other guides than prejudice and custom.

> *Il est peu de vertus dans un degre supreme;*
> There are few virtues in a supreme degree;
> *Peu de vices aussi sont portes a l'extreme.*
> Few vices likewise are carry'd to the extreme.
> *Mais toujours notre coeur au-dedans divise,*
> But still our heart within itself divided,
> *De vices, de vertus, se trouve compose.*   310
> Of vices, of virtues, finds itself compounded.

Too scrupulous an exactness of expression would defeat the end of poetry; but, however, we must oblige ourselves to interpret one passage by another, for fear of injuring a writer, by ascribing to him sentiments which would be injurious to

---

9. without any inclination . . . light: "sans s'aviser d'en sortir" (p. 196).

his character. When it is affirmed, that *few men* are *virtuous in the extreme;*[1] or, that there are few men that carry their virtues to such a height as human nature admits of; it is insinuated, that there may be such persons, and even, that there are *some* such, and that, therefore, the heart of man is not always a composition of vice and virtue.

> *Les fous, les scelerats, dans leur profonde yvresse,*
> The fools, the rogues, in their deep debauch,
> *N'ont-ils pas des lueurs d'honneur & de sagesse?*
> Have they not glimmerings of honour and of wisdom?
> *Le sage dont le coeur par l'amour est surpris,*
> The wise man whose heart by love is surprised,
> *N'est-il pas pour lui-meme un objet de mepris?*
> Is he not to himself an object of contempt?
> *Les hommes ne sont bons ou mechans qu'en partie.*   315
> Men are neither good nor bad but in part.
> *Aux loix des passions notre ame assujettie*
> To the laws of the passions our soul subjected
> *Change a chaque moment, & passe tour a tour*
> Changes at every moment, and passes by turns
> *Du vice a la vertu, de la haine a l'amour.*
> From vice to virtue, from hatred to love.*

*Tho' I shall not mention all the defects in the translation of this passage, I cannot, however, forbear observing, in the second couplet, the evident marks of a *Frenchman*'s genius, who snatches every opportunity of talking of love, and misses not the least hint that can serve to guide him to his darling subject. Is the mind of man never disordered by any other passion? Is not a wise man sometimes surprized by envy or cowardice, by ambition or resentment? Is all weakness and folly the consequence of love? But it is the general genius of that airy people; debar them from love, and you debar them from poetry. This prevailing inclination to gallantry has given rise to such numbers of novels, and filled the world with romances, these bulky follies, which have served to crowd the closets and imaginations of studious ladies. It had indeed been happy if the infection had stopped here, without extending itself to poetry, and filling the stage with amorous madness, or refined obscenity. If tragedy

---

1. SJ substitutes a paraphrase of Pope's:
    VI. Virtuous and vicious ev'ry Man must be,
Few in th' extreme, but all in the degree. (231–32; 221–22)
for Crousaz's quotation of l. 307a of Du Resnel (p. 197).

This is true of a mind inflamed by passions,

> *Tous sans distinction, le fou comme le sage.*
> All without distinction, the fool as well as the
>   wise man,
> *Ne connoissent de but que leur propre avantage.*   320
> Know no end but their own advantage.

With this assertion I cannot entirely concur, it is expressed in terms too general, and places the fool and wise man in the same rank with too little scruple. Fools are a kind of atheists, or of idolaters at least, that assume in some degree the place of the Deity, and conduct themselves by their own choice; that consider nothing in any other respect than as it regards themselves and have no regard to any laws but such as are dictated by their own interest. But the wise man acts upon

---

be, as it certainly ought to be, a representation of human nature, and real life, why is all good or bad fortune made the effect of this single passion? Why does this alone exalt the virtue, or inflame the vices of their heroes or princes? It is evident, that it is far from operating so powerfully or so universally in the world as it appears to do upon the stage.p2

p. upon the stage *errata*

---

2. Pope's lines are,

> The rogue and fool by fits is fair
>   and wise,
> And ev'n the best, by fits, what
>   they despise.
> 'Tis but by parts we follow good or
>   ill,
> For, Vice or Virtue, Self directs it
>   still. (233–36; 223-26)

Cf. the *Preface to Shakespeare* where SJ remarks that "love is only one of many passions, and as it has no great influence upon the sum of life, it has little operation in the dramas of a poet, who caught his ideas from the living world, and exhibited only what he saw before him. He knew, that any other passion, as it was regular or exorbitant, was a cause of happiness or calamity" (*John-son on Shakespeare*, ed. Arthur Sherbo [Vol. VII, Yale Edition of the Works of Samuel Johnson, 1968], pp. 63–64). He observes that *All for Love* "has one fault equal to many, though rather moral than critical, that by admitting the romantick omnipotence of love, he has recommended as laudable and worthy of imitation that conduct which through all ages the good have censured as vicious, and the bad despised as foolish" ("Life of Dryden," *Lives*, I.361, par. 78). "Of the passion of love he remarked, that its violence and ill effects were much exaggerated; for who knows any real sufferings on that head more than the exorbitancy of any other passion?" (*Life*, 2.122). Here Boswell appears to be paraphrasing SJ's *Preface to Shakespeare*.

settled principles, and in pursuance of just notions, and of right reasoning. He is conscious that every thing that is good and estimable in him is the gift of God, to whom he therefore devotes himself, and expects no happiness but from his favour. This is either the immediate or the remoter end of all his endeavours, nor does any thing obviate his approbation that has not this tendency.[3]

> *Chacun cherche son bien; mais tous, d'un pas egal,*
> Each seeks his own good; but all, with equal pace,
> *Marchent, sans y penser, vers le bien general.*
> March, without thinking of it, towards the general good.

It is possible, that the reader having read the foregoing observations, will agree to some restriction of these general expressions.

If every man was to do his duty, he would contribute in a very different manner to the good of the *whole,* of which, it is very far from being true, that all men equally promote it.

I have already observed, that the need in which every man stands of the assistance of others, obliges men, whose dispositions are far from friendship or benevolence, to assist others in hopes of a return: an artisan who works with no other view than to get money, is still of use to the community, and the desire of growing rich incites him to serve his neighbours as well as he can.

> *C'est a ce grand design*[4] *que le maitre supreme*
> It is to this grand design that the supreme master
> *Fait servir les efforts de la malice meme,*
> Makes subservient the efforts of malice itself,
> *Les complots les plus noirs, le caprice, l'erreur,*   325
> The blackest conspiracies, caprice, error,
> *Les defauts de l'esprit, les foiblesses du coeur.*
> Defects of mind, weaknesses of heart.

---

3. This is either . . . tendency: "C'est à ce but que tous ses soins se rapportent immédiatement ou médiatement. Tout ce qui ne va pas là, il le desavouë & le reconnoit condamnable" (p. 198). Perhaps "obviate" should be "obtain."

4. Crousaz correctly has "dessein" and "suprême" (p. 199).

What good ends are promoted by error or conspiracies I am at a loss to conceive,* unless it be that of punishing those whose obstinate adherence to vice justly exposes to the anger of their maker, or those who, finding truth unfavourable to their designs, studiously seek for pretences to shut their eyes against it, and withdraw themselves from its influence.[5]

> *C'est pour ce grand dessein que Dieu, dans sa sagesse,*
> It is with this great design that God, in his wisdom,
> *En[6] chaque homme a place quelque heureuse foiblesse:*
> In every man hath placed some happy frailty:
> *La honte de ceder aux traits du suborneur*
> The shame of yielding to the tricks of the debaucher
> *Dans le coeur d'une fille est l'appui de l'honneur.*   330
> In the heart of a virgin is the fence of honour.
> *Dans l'esprit de la femme une fierte severe*
> In the mind of the matron a severe pride
> *L'empeche de bruler d'une flame[7] adultere.*
> Prevents her from burning with an adulterous flame.
> *Qui conduit les guerriers? C'est temerite.[8]*
> What conducts the warriors? It is rashness.
> *Qui fait fleurir les arts? Souvent la vanite.*

*Mr POPE only says,

> This counterworks each folly and caprice,
> This disappoints th' effect of every vice.[9]

He is far from saying that good effects naturally rise from vice or folly, and affirms nothing but what may be very easily admitted, that God superintends the world in such a manner, that they do not produce all those destructive consequences that might reasonably be feared and expected from them.

---

5. What good ends . . . influence: "Je ne vois pas à quoi servent *les complots les plus noirs*, ni *l'erreur*, si ce n'est à punir ceux qui méritent d'être chatiés, par leur persévérance dans le Vice, ou ceux qui importunés par la vérité, en détournent leur attention, & cherchent des prétextes pour se dérober à sa lumiére & à ses ordres" (pp. 199–200).

6. Crousaz has "Dans" (p. 200); Du Resnel has "En" (l. 328).

7. Crousaz correctly has "flamme" (p. 200).

8. Crousaz has "la témérité" (p. 200).

9. Both ll. 239 (229) and 240 (230) should begin with "That." Pope has "counterworks" and "ev'ry."

SECOND EPISTLE 179

What makes to flourish arts? Oftentimes vanity.
Et cette vanite secrete[1] *& delicate,* 335
And that secret and delicate vanity,
Sans qu'un vil interet nous anime & nous flate,
Without our being animated or allur'd by a sordid interest,
En charmant notre esprit par ses illusions,
While it charms our spirit by its illusions,
Enfante quelquefois de nobles actions.
Gives birth to sometimes noble exploits.

As human nature is constituted in general, I cannot but think these lines capable in several places of a sense which would be not much approved by the author of them, and, perhaps, less by the translator.

Modesty is a virtue directly opposite to unchastity. Shame is one of the outworks or fortifications[2] of virtue, of which it has no need in its confirmed state. The fear of suffering in the opinion of men is a motive to goodness, of which none but the most hardened can divest themselves. A man who tramples and despises it is blameable in the highest degree,[3] but neither is he much to be commended whom nothing but the fear of reproach withholds from wickedness.

Mr Bayle, who seemed carried away by an affectation of raising doubts concerning the necessity and efficacy of the Christian religion, has, instead of the motives which that suggests, supplied us with others, more real, in his opinion, and more forcible.

Heaven has, it seems, given

Rashness to the Chief.[4]

---

1. Crousaz wrongly has "secrette" (p. 200); Du Resnel has "secrete" (l. 335).

2. Shame . . . fortifications: "La *honte* est une barriére" (p. 200).

3. A man . . . degree: "On est souverainement blâmable quand on la foule aux piés" (p. 201).

4. SJ has substituted l. 243b (233b) for Crousaz's quotation of l. 333 of Du Resnel (p. 201), and paraphrased l. 238 to provide the link. SJ has created an ambiguity here since "all" in the next sentence refers to "*Qui conduit les Guerriers.*"

Is this to be understood of all? Are all branded alike at one stroke? Is it then lawful to fall upon men without provocation, and take away their lives for diversion? Surely there are occasions on which we are not only permitted but obliged to take arms in defence of our right, and in opposition to unjust aggressors.

I do not deny that, in war, use is sometimes made of the temerity of a daring adventurer: but in a commander it is generally of more danger than advantage, and, to conclude, whatever be its consequences, is by no means the gift of God.

Neither is vanity to be ascribed to his influence. A man that has a true sense of his duty, that loves mankind, and fears God, will, from these motives, think himself obliged to use his utmost application to attain perfection in those employments which he has reason to believe assigned him by Divine Providence, and, without proposing to himself to outshine others, will of course excel them by his industry and perseverance.

Vanity gnaws a man within, it takes up his mind,[5] and retards his progress, nor would he without the influence of that vice be of less, but of far greater use to mankind, he would more readily communicate his knowledge to others, he would be more willing to direct them in their pursuits,[6] nor would ever be guilty of these hateful, but frequent artifices, by which men are often robbed of their deserved reputation, and those advantages which they might justly claim. The conclusion therefore,

> *Ainsi du createur la sagesse profonde*
> Thus of the creator the profound wisdom
> *Se sert de nos defauts pour le bonheur du monde,*   340
> Makes use of our defects for the happiness of the world,

deserves to be considered.[7] Nothing can be more impious than to imagine that God[8] is the cause of men's vices, for the

---

5. gnaws a man ... mind: "ronge un homme intérieurement, l'use" (p. 202).
6. he would ... pursuits: "il leur serviroit volontiers de modéle" (p. 202).
7. SJ adds "deserves to be considered"; Crousaz ends his sentence with the word "monde" of Du Resnel (p. 203).
8. God: "Dieu très saint" (p. 203).

sake of making them subservient to good ends, which would be more effectually produced by virtue. But the world is constituted in such a manner by his infinite wisdom, that good consequences sometimes flow from vices, which he not only not causes but expressly forbids, and which naturally tend only to the disadvantage of the world: these providential consequences can therefore by no means afford any plea or alleviation of their guilt to wicked men.[9]

> *Pour conserver leurs biens, pour defendre leurs jours,*
> To preserve their goods, to defend their lives,
> *Tous les hommes entr'eux se doivent des secours;*
> All men to one another owe assistance;
> *Pour s'aider tour a tour le ciel les a fait naitre*
> To help one another in turn heaven made them to be born
> *Le pere, les enfans, les esclaves, le maitre.*
> Father, children, slaves, master.
> *Foibles separement, ils font de vains efforts;*   345
> Weak separately, they make vain efforts;
> *Ils sont en s'unissant plus heureux & plus forts.*
> They are while united more successful and stronger.
> *Ainsi, soit passion, soit besoin, soit foiblesse,*
> Thus, be it passion, be it business, be it frailty,
> *Pour la societe tout homme s'interesse,*
> For the community every man is concern'd,
> *Et chacun s'empressant a procurer son bien*
> And every one forward to procure his own good
> *De l'interest[1] commun resserre le lien.*   350
> Of the common interest closes the tye.

Did men love one another less than they really do, did every man solely regard his own interest without concerning himself about that of others, his own wants would nevertheless engage him to lend others what assistance he was able.

---

9. But the world . . . men: "Mais sa sagesse a tellement rangé les choses, que de ces vices qu'il ne fait point, & où l'on tombe contre ses commandemens, de ces vices, qui ne tendent qu'au mal, il en arrive des biens, dont le vicieux auroit tort de se féliciter" (p. 203).

1. Crousaz correctly has "l'intérêt" (p. 203).

> *De la le tendre amour, l'amitie veritable,*
> Thence tender love, friendship sincere,
> *Et ce charme secret qui rend la vie aimable.*[2]
> And that secret charm which makes life desirable.

As men interchangeably receive and confer benefits, those breasts which are not entirely void of humanity feel some sparks of gratitude: men soon perceive that where they love, it is less trouble to be kind and serviceable;[3] by degrees this tenderness increases, and more generous and elevated minds rise to a pure and a true benevolence, and make no distinction between their own interest and that of the publick, so that it might be said, that two souls are mingled together in one person.*

> *De la vient que touchant a la fin de ses jours,*
> Thence comes it that approaching the end of his days,
> *On renonce sans peine aux plaisirs, aux amours;*
> Man bids farewel without regret to pleasures, to loves;

The connection of these two verses with the foregoing passage is not at first sight very easily perceived: the concern which we naturally feel at parting with life is rather increased than alleviated by the sweets of friendship, since the loss of life is more deplorable in proportion as it was more happy.

---

*This expression is extremely obscure, figurative, and unphilosophical.

---

2. This paragraph of Du Resnel corresponds to Pope's

> Heav'n forming each on other to depend,
> A master, or a servant, or a friend,
> Bids each on other for assistance call,
> 'Till one Man's weakness grows the strength of all.
> Wants, frailties, passions, closer still ally
> The common int'rest, or endear the tie:
> To these we owe true friendship, love sincere,
> Each home-felt joy that life inherits here:
> Yet from the same we learn, in its decline,
> Those joys, those loves, those int'rests to resign:
> Taught half by Reason, half by mere decay,
> To welcome death, and calmly pass away. (249–60; 239–50)

3. kind and serviceable: "de rendre service" (p. 204).

SECOND EPISTLE

But these lines do not depend upon the last couplet, but on the passage above. We have received from our Creator, if we believe Mr Pope, our follies, our weaknesses, and even our vices: and the reason for which he has bestowed upon us such dangerous, and, which is more astonishing, such detestable gifts, is this, that he may make them the means of producing greater and more extensive good. I cannot, for my part, concur with this notion, or consider, as the gifts of God infinitely pure, those vices with which men are infected, or those delusive imaginations by which men harden themselves against the fear of death, as the dictates of a God infinitely true and without deceit.[4]

> *Que ne leur trouvant plus leur attrait ordinaire,* 355
> That no more finding in them their ordinary
>   attraction,
> *On se fait un honneur d'une loi necessaire;*
> He does himself an honour from a necessary law;
> *Qu'on s'attend sans murmure a recevoir la mort;*
> That he waits without murmuring to receive death;
> *Qu'apres un long orage on la voit comme un port;*
> That after a tedious storm he views it as a haven;
> *Qu'on trouve, par raison, ou par decrepitude,*
> That he finds, through reason, or through
>   decrepidness,
> *Et le jour moins aimable, & le trepas moins rude.* 360
> Both life less desirable, and death less shocking.

Here is a quick and easy method of reconciling mankind to the thought of death. But such reasonings, as these, are rather for show than use; they may furnish out a declamation, but will be of little service on a death-bed. Mr Pope may have

---

4. I cannot . . . deceit: "A cet égard, je suis très éloigné de ses idées, & je ne puis convenir de regarder non plus comme des présens du Créateur, qui ne trompe point, les diverses illusions par lesquelles les hommes s'étourdissent sur la mort, & se dérobent à ses frayeurs" (p. 205). He omits Crousaz's quotation of l. 354 of Du Resnel. An important omission, as the "plaisirs" and "amours" constitute the "leur" of the next quotation. Perhaps SJ has confused "s'étourdir" with "s'endurcir."

seen, perhaps, in England, some instances of this disregard for life, and willingness to resign it, but I much doubt whether it be even there the general temper. It were much for the advantage of that nation to fear death more, they would then live better; so that the fear of death would contribute more to the general good of the world than that indolence pointed out by Mr Pope as the favour and indulgence of heaven, and I am inclined to believe that his elegant translator and I do not much differ in our sentiments.

The loss of pleasure is one great cause of the moroseness and ill-humour of part of the old men: others, instead of those pleasures which age has not left them sprightliness enough to enjoy, attach themselves to other pursuits, which make them equally desirous of longer life; so that, in my opinion, the matter of fact here asserted is very disputable.

Experience indeed will inform every man, that makes any reflection upon mankind or upon himself, that the attention withdraws itself from disagreeable ideas, and that, to keep it employed, men naturally search for pleasing objects, and generally dwell upon them much longer than they deserve. It is melancholy to observe the greatest part of mankind turning away their thoughts from those real evils of which Providence has put the remedy in their own hands, and opposing nothing to the fear of death but flattering chimeras, stubborn obstinacy, or amusing fancies; when they might obtain, by that steady application which God requires, a solid satisfaction, a settled calm, and the happiness of looking on the approach of death without affright and without illusion.[5]

The author still goes on to take a review of mankind, who all agree, however their tempers or circumstances may differ, in imposing upon themselves with flattering ideas. But in what he is going to tell us, we must beware of imagining that Providence contributes to these delusive visions, or per-

---

5. It is melancholy . . . illusion: "Il est triste de voir à quel point les hommes détournent leur vûë des maux réels dont ils pourroient se guérir, se procurer, par de si justes & si indispensables soins, une tranquillité solide, & le bonheur de penser à la mort sans effroi & sans illusion; au lieu que la plûpart n'y opposent que chiméres flateuses, distractions & étourdissemens" (p. 207).

suades men to believe that they possess what they really have not.

> *Mais, jusqu'a ce moment l'erreur, dans tous nos maux,*
> However, even to that moment error, in all our ills,
> *Au defaut de*[6] *vrais biens nous en donne de faux.*
> In default of real good presents us with counterfeit.
> *Tant que nos respirons, l'opinion flateuse,*
> As long as we breathe, flattering opinion,
> *A charmer nos ennuis toujours ingenieuse,*
> To charm our toils always industrious,
> *Dore par ses rayons les nuages charmans*   365
> Gilds with its rays the delectable clouds
> *Qui versent sur nos jours de trompeurs agremens.*
> Which shed on our days deceitful graces.
> *Satisfait de ses gouts, content de sa science,*
> Satisfy'd with his judgment, content with his knowledge,
> *Chacun a pour soi-meme un oeil de complaisance.*
> Each hath for himself an eye of complaisance.

The man who exchanges his person for that of another, does not think what it is he consents to; but there are in reality very few who would consent[7] to such an exchange.

> *Feuilletant, nuit & jour, des volumes poudreux*
> Turning over, night and day, dusty volumes
> *Dans un reduit obscur, un savant est heureux.*   370
> In a dark confinement, a learned man is happy.

The jealousy which often seizes upon men of this character, and the high passions that are occasioned by it, are strong testimonies against their felicity.

> *L'ignorant, affranchi d'un travail si penible,*
> The ignorant, freed from a work so painful,
> *Dans un lache repos trouve un plaisir sensible.*
> In a dull repose finds a sensible pleasure.

---

6. Crousaz correctly has "des" (p. 208).

7. would consent: "ne voulût changer" (p. 208).

I grant it, if he can keep himself free from that disgust and weariness that attend a life of inactivity, and can exempt himself, by the assistance of money and flattery, from that contempt to which his idleness justly exposes him.[8]

> *Regardant l'avenir avec tranquillite,*
> Regarding the future with tranquillity,
> *Le riche de son bien fait sa felicite.*
> The rich man of his wealth makes his happiness.

Mr Pope makes no scruple of supposing and asserting, for the convenience of his system, what facts he pleases; but experience declares against him.[9] There are perhaps among the rich more men uneasy and anxious than happy and contented.

> *Rassure par les soins que prend la providence,*   375
> Encouraged by the care which providence takes,
> *Le pauvre vit content malgre son indigence.*
> The poor lives content in spight of his poverty.

I leave it to every man's observation to inform himself how many there are among the poor thus resigned to Providence, and how many there are that give every day some proofs of their discontent and impatience, by their murmurs at their condition, by the envy with which they look upon the rich, and by the little scruple which they make of seizing upon the revenues of other men, when they have a prospect of doing it with impunity.

> *Voi l'aveugle danser; se plaint-il que ses yeux*
> See the blind dance; complains he that his eyes
> *Soient pour jamais fermes a la clarte des cieux?*
> Are for ever closed to the brightness of the heavens?
> *Voi le boiteux qui chante; en est-il moins tranquille,*

---

8. I grant . . . him: "Oui, s'il n'étoit pas traversé par l'ennui, ou si ses dépenses & les flateurs qu'elles lui attirent, ne le déroboient pas au mépris, que sa lâche oisiveté mérite" (p. 209).

9. declares against him: "instruit du contraire" (p. 209).

SECOND EPISTLE

>   See the cripple who sings; at it is he less easy,
>   *Quoi qu'a former des pas son pied soit moins agile?* 380
>   Though to form steps his foot be less pliable?

The reader, carried away by the beauty of the poetry, reads with eagerness, and supposes, often contrary to truth, that facts are as the poet represents them. If the blind beggers are content with their condition, it must be owned that they are great hypocrites to stun those that approach them with outcries to excite their compassion. Some men born blind have, when they had obtained their sight, asserted with perpetual repetitions, that the pleasure was not to be expressed; nor is there a cripple, who, if he was rich, would not give half his fortune for the feet of a healthy and active man.[1]

There is a medium between afflicting one's self perpetually on account of one's condition, between repining with the utmost impatience that it is no better, and thinking that the state of another is no way preferable.

These wild sportings of imagination tend to no less than the utter extinction of all gratitude. Should a father whose sons, except one, were all born blind, admonish that one to return his thanks to God for the gift which he has been blessed with, and to make a good use of it; the son might answer, upon these principles, *What have I to be thankful for more than my brothers?*[2] *Do they dance less, or are they less happy?* Should a father represent to his son the care he has taken, and the money he has expended, for the sake of procuring him a learned education, might he not answer, What is the obligation?[3] Are not those as happy who know less?

>   *Dans les vapeurs du vin, le mendiant est Roi;*
>   In the vapours of wine, the begger is a King;
>   *Et le sot en tout tems vit satisfait de soi.*
>   And the sot at all times lives satisfy'd with himself.
>   *Le chimiste ebloui de l'or qu'il voit en songe,*

---

1. feet . . . man: "pour marcher comme font les plus agiles" (p. 211).
2. SJ adds this question.
3. SJ adds this question.

> The chymist dazzled with the gold which he sees
>   in a dream,
> *Prend pour realite ce qui n'est qu'un mensonge;*
> Takes for reality what is no more than a cheat;
> *Et meme en deplorant son destin rigoureux,*   385
> And even while deploring his hard fate,
> *Dans le sein de sa muse un poete est heureux.*
> In the bosom of his muse a poet is happy.

Are the chimeras of madmen to be numbered among the gifts of a gracious Providence? In the last couplet, the author, by pursuing too eagerly the insidious charms of an antithesis, is drawn unawares into a contradiction.[4] A poet that laments his fortune, and thinks it happy at the same time, is either chargeable with madness or falsehood.* There are many followers of the muse, whose temper is extremely sour, and who cannot with the least patience bear any disapprobation of their performances.

> *Par tout, ou du bonheur on regrette l'absence,*
> In every place, where of happiness we bewail the
>   absence,
> *Ne voit-on pas voler la facile esperance?*
> See we not flying commodious hope?

---

*It may be proper to observe once more, that this contradiction, whether real or supposed, is wholly the translator's, who has been very unfortunate in his version of this whole paragraph.[5]

---

4. In the last . . . contradiction: "Et, dans les deux derniers de ces Vers, l'appas d'une Antithése, fait tomber l'Auteur en contradiction" (p. 212).

5. Pope's paragraph reads:

> Whate'er the Passion, knowledge,
>   fame, or pelf,
> Not one will change his neighbor
>   with himself.
> The learn'd is happy nature to
>   explore,
> The fool is happy that he knows
>   no more;
> The rich is happy in the plenty
>   giv'n,
> The poor contents him with the
>   care of Heav'n.
> See the blind beggar dance, the
>   cripple sing,
> The sot a hero, lunatic a king;
> The starving chemist in his golden
>   views
> Supremely blest, the poet in his
>   muse. (261–70; 251–60)

SECOND EPISTLE   189

> *Du secourable orgeuil les soins compatissans,*
> Of helpful pride the compassionate cares,
> *Manquent-ils de remplir le vuide du bon sens?*   390
> Do they fail to fill up the void of good sense?
> *La subite lueur de la raison severe,*
> The sudden light of strict reason,
> *Vient-elle dissiper une aimable chimere,*
> Comes it to dissipate one lovely chimera,
> *Vient-elle nous priver d'un plaisir imposteur,*
> Comes it to deprive us of one fallacious pleasure,
> *Un autre au meme instant renait dans notre coeur.*
> Another at the same instant springs up in our heart.

In reading these lines I call readily to mind the conduct of the world, a conduct very different from that which reason requires. Men, instead of applying themselves with ardour and assiduity to solid knowledge, to the attainment of just notions, to a life of virtue, and to the duties which may procure the approbation of God, trifle away their lives in the poor amusement of forming a perpetual succession of schemes, uncertain in their own nature, and which, tho' they should not be disappointed, would yet be far from bringing the satisfaction that is expected from them.[6] What sense shall we put upon these lines?

> *Each Want of Happiness by Hope supply'd,*
> *And each Vacuity of Sense by Pride.*[7]

Does the poet intend to insinuate, that *pride* is one of the gifts which men enjoy by the mercy and compassion[8] of their Creator, that they may among their real miseries receive comfort from imaginary blessings; or that they are given over to the excess of their vanity, to punish them for the little regard they have shewn to right reason, which, when they cannot rec-

---

6. trifle away . . . them: "s'amusent misérablement à rouler dans leur esprit des projets incertains, & dont le succès même ne les satisferoit pas" (p. 213).

7. SJ substitutes ll. 285–86 (267–68) of Pope for Crousaz's quotation of ll. 394–95 of Du Resnel (p. 213).

8. mercy and compassion: "compassion" (p. 213).

oncile it to their inclinations, they utterly discard, and turn their eyes away from her clear and steady light, to fix them upon *painted clouds,* and deceitful glimmers?[9]

> *Est-il destin si triste, etat si miserable,* 395
> Is their lot so sad, state so miserable,
> *Que le secours du tems ne rende supportable?*
> That the assistance of time renders not supportable?
> *Regardez des humains le grand consolateur,*
> Behold of mankind the great conforter,
> *L'orgueil, leur presenter son secours enchanteur.*
> Pride, offer them its enchanting succour.
> *Voyez la passion convenable a chaque age,*
> See the passion agreeable to every age,
> *Pour regner sur nos coeurs, nous attendre au passage.* 400
> To reign over our hearts, attend us to our passage.

Pride once more appears upon the stage, as the great consoler of the miseries of man, whose unhappiness is indeed very deplorable,[1] if he is reduced to fly for consolation to one of the most odious vices; nor can Mr Pope be very easily acquitted of ingratitude, in giving vent to so many severe reproaches against this kind, this pleasing enchanter. We are now told of *some fit passions which supply every age,*[2] of which I cannot yet determine whether we are here taught to reckon them among our blessings or calamities.

---

9. when they . . . glimmers: "Ils en sont importunés, & se dérobent à sa lumiére, pour se livrer à des *lueurs trompeuses, & à des plaisirs imposteurs*" (p. 214). SJ substitutes "painted clouds" of Pope (284; 266) for Crousaz's *"plaisirs imposteurs."*

1. consoler . . . deplorable: "consolateur. Quelle allusion! En vérité la destinée des hommes est bien déplorable" (p. 214). SJ illustrates *consoler* in the *Dictionary,* defined as "One that gives comfort," with this passage: "Pride once more appears upon the stage, as the great *consoler* of the miseries of man. *Comment. on Pope's Ess. on Man."*

2. SJ substitutes a paraphrase of Pope's "See some fit Passion ev'ry age supply" (273; 263) for Crousaz's (p. 214) paraphrase of Silhouette (p. 49).

SECOND EPISTLE

> *L'esperance est constante a marcher sur nos pas,*
> Hope is constant in marching on our steps,
> *Sans meme nous quitter a l'heure du trepas.*
> Without even quitting us at the hour of departure.
> *N'offre-t-elle a nos yeux qu'une confuse image*
> Does it offer to our eyes but a confused image
> *Du bonheur que le ciel nous destine en partage?*
> Of the happiness which heaven designs us at parting?
> *Cet objet consolant nous occupe toujours,* 405
> That comforting object possesses us always,
> *Et repand des douceurs sur nos plus tristes jours.*
> And sheds sweetnesses on our saddest days.

I cannot, without melancholy and pity, see that hope, which is so firmly grounded, so strongly supported, and so highly to be valued; that hope, for which we owe such ardent and frequent acknowledgments to the goodness of our Creator, rank'd among airy visions, and wild chimeras, which are indebted for their influence and existence to nothing but our pride and our inattention.[3]

> *Notre ame en ses desirs inquiete, egaree,*
> Our soul in her desires restless, wandering,
> *Par les liens du corps tristement resserree,*
> By the tyes of the body sadly bound up,
> *Dans un doux avenir se repose, s'etend,*
> In a sweet futurity lulls itself, stretches itself,
> *Et jouit en effet du bonheur qu'elle attend.* 410
> And enjoys in reality the happiness which it expects.

There is nothing in these lines inconsistent with that fatal unconcern, that destructive security, by which souls are be-

---

3. I cannot . . . inattention: "Il est triste de voir l'espérance la plus respectable, & pour laquelle nous devons à Dieu des actions de graces infinies, marcher à la suite d'une liste de chiméres, effets de nôtre orgueil, & de la légéreté de nôtre attention" (p. 215).

tray'd to eternal ruin,[4] by relaxing that vigilance, with which we ought to inspect our own hearts and actions, in order to arrive at a happy immortality. This security is wholly opposite to a certain and well-founded assurance, unless we submit to call in the system of fatality to our assistance. That hypothesis, indeed, makes the virtues and vices of mankind equally parts of the divine plan, equally essential to it, and, by consequence, equally innocent, and exempt from punishment, for the Creator cannot, without injustice, exercise any severity upon one more than upon the other, as they were both equally inevitable, and equally interwoven with the constitution of the universe.

The verses that close this epistle seem written wholly in favour of this system, nor can easily be taken in any other sense.

> *Dans les biens & les maux que le ciel nous dispense*
> In the good things and the ill which heaven on us bestows
> *Reconnois sa bonte, sa juste providence.*
> Acknowledge its goodness, its just providence.
> *Nos vices, nos defauts, l'orgueil, la vanite,*
> Our vices, our frailties, pride, vanity,
> *Tournent souvent au bien de la societe.*
> Turn often to the good of the community.
> *Cet amour naturel qu'on ressent pour soi-meme,* 415
> That natural *love* which a man feels for himself,
> *N'est-il pas un present de la bonte supreme?*
> Is it not a gift of the supreme goodness?
> *Par les divers besoins que l'homme eprouve en lui,*
> By the various wants which man finds in himself,
> *Il mesure, prevoit, soulage ceux d'autrui.*
> He measures, foresees, relieves those of another.
> *Adore donc le ciel, supporte ta foiblesse,*
> Adore then heaven, support thy frailty,

---

4. fatal unconcern ... ruin: "à la sécurité, qui fait périr les ames" (p. 215).

SECOND EPISTLE

Et jusqu'en ta folie admire sa sagesse.   420
And even in thy folly admire its wisdom.

I think I have already sufficiently explained how far vice contributes, in my opinion, to the good of society.

God is, beyond controversy, the author of our self-love. Our sense of his benefits, our thanksgivings,[5] and even our dread of his judgments, if we refuse to obey his holy laws, have no other foundation but a regard for our own interest; a regard, which, if rightly pursued, would recal us to our duty whenever we deviate from it; for whenever we prefer our own will to the will of God, we disappoint our own interest.[6]

To adore God, and to be satisfied with his gifts, is the chief of all duties, the general source from which all piety must be derived;[7] but *to admire his wisdom in our follies,* is a very strong antithesis.* The follies of mankind are not to be imputed to him as their cause, nor is his wisdom display'd, or at all concern'd, in them. With regard to our follies, the instances of his wisdom are the bounds which he has set to their pernicious influence, by which he prevents those dreadful effects, and that fatal confusion, that might be naturally apprehended from them.[8]

> *Till then, *Opinion* gilds with varying rays
> Those painted clouds that beautify our days;
> Each want of happiness by Hope supply'd,
> And each vacuity of sense by Pride:
> These build as fast as knowledge can destroy:
> In folly's cup still laughs the bubble, *joy;*
> One prospect lost, another still we gain;
> And not a vanity is given in vain;
> Even mean *Self-Love* becomes by force divine,
> The scale to measure others wants by thine.
> See! and confess, one comfort still must rise,
> 'Tis this, tho' *Man's a fool,* yet *God is wise.*[9]

---

5. SJ omits "& la sincérité de nos actions de graces" (p. 217).

6. we disappoint . . . interest: "nous péchons contre nous-mêmes" (p. 217).

7. the general source . . . derived: "source de tous les autres" (p. 217).

8. nor is his wisdom . . . them: "Ce n'est point en elles que nous admirons une sagesse, qui n'y a aucune part; nous l'admirons dans les barriéres qu'elle y oppose, pour empêcher qu'elles ne produisent tout le mal qui en devroit naturellement naître" (p. 217).

9. Lines 283–94 (265–76).

COMMENTARY ON THE THIRD EPISTLE

When I first began to read the poem of the Abbe Du Resnel, I obliged myself to attend to it as to a book from which I proposed to receive advantage, and intended, at the same time, to enable others to make the same use of it. With this design, I have examined the particular expressions, that I might satisfy myself about their true meaning. This epistle, in which the social duties of man are laid down, ought to awaken me to double attention.

> *Revien, il en est tems, de ton erreur profonde;*
> Return, it is time, from thy profound error;
> *Apprens, homme borne, que le maitre du monde,*
> Learn, bounded man, that the master of the world,
> *Sans jamais s'ecarter de son premier dessein,*
> Without ever deviating from his first design,
> *Par differens moyens tend a la meme fin.*
> By different means tends to the same end.
> *Au milieu des transports de l'ardente jeunesse,* 5
> Amidst the transports of boiling youth,
> *Dans l'orgueil fastueux qu'inspire la richesse,*
> In the stately pride that wealth inspires,
> *Dans le sein du bonheur ou de l'adversite,*
> In the bosom of prosperity or of adversity,
> *Sois frappe, nuit & jour, de cette verite.*
> Be deeply affected night and day, with this truth.
> *Considere le monde; il est, aux yeux du sage,*
> Consider the world; it is, in the eyes of a wise man,
> *De la societe la plus parfaite image;* 10
> Of society the most perfect resemblance;
> *Voi ces chaines d'amour, ces liens prepares*
> See those chains of love, those bands provided
> *Pour reunir entre eux*[1] *des etres separes.*

---

1. Crousaz has "entr'eux" (p. 219).

To combine among themselves beings separated.
Au premier mouvement que recoit la matiere,
At the first motion that matter receives,
Voi du sein du chaos eclater la lumiere;
See from the bosom of the chaos sparkle forth light;
Chaque atome ebranle courir pour s'embrasser,   15
Each trembling atom run into embraces,
S'attirer tour a tour, s'unir, s'entrelasser.
To attract in its turn, to unite, to twine.
L'univers est forme; la puissance infinie
The universe is formed; the infinite power
Repand dans la nature un principe de vie;
Diffuses in nature a principle of life;
Les etres, animes par ce souffle divin,
Beings, animated by this divine breath,
Se portent de concert vers une meme fin.   20
Tend in concert towards one self-same end.
Sans jamais s'ecarter de la loi qui les presse,
Without ever swerving from the law that impells them,
Pour le bien general chacun d'eux s'interesse.
For the general good each of them concerns itself.
Tu vois les vegetaux devenir l'aliment
Thou seest the vegetables become the food
Des etres que le ciel doua de sentiment;
Of beings which heaven hath endow'd with sensation;
Mais ceux-ci par leur mort changent-ils de nature?   25
But do these by their death change nature?
Ils vont aux vegetaux servir de nourriture.
They go to serve for nourishment to vegetables.
Il n'est rien de durable, & tout etre a son tour,
There is nothing lasting, and each being hath its turn,
Sort du neant, y rentre, & reparoit au jour.
Comes from nothing, returns thereto, and appears anew in sight.
Rien n'est independant, mais toutes les parties

> Nothing is independent, but all the parts
> *Se rapportant au tout, au tout sont assorties.* 30
> Having relation to the whole, to the whole are suited.
> *L'ame de l'univers, leur force & leur soutien,*
> The soul of the universe, their strength and their support,
> *Entr'elles les unit par un meme lien.*
> Unites them together by the same bond.
> *L'homme prete a la brute un secours salutaire,*
> Man lends to the brute a preserving succour,
> *Et la brute a son tour a l'homme est necessaire.*
> And the brute in his turn to man is necessary.
> *Tout donne, tout reçoit, ici bas du secours;* 35
> All give, all receive, here below assistance;
> *Et le foible & le fort l'un a l'autre ont recours.*
> And the weak and the strong each to other have recourse.
> *Cette chaine se suit; repons, ou finit-elle?*
> This chain holds on; answer, where ends it?
> *Qui peut t'en informer? La puissance immortelle.*
> Who can inform thee? The power immortal.

I decline, in this second examination, to repeat any of the remarks which I have made in the former.[2]

The great Governor of the Universe never loses sight of his design, but causes every thing to contribute to one great end. The revolution of the heavenly bodies is constant and regular: that perpetual succession of changes, that subsist in these lower regions, has no effect at so great a distance; and those starts and deviations from the common order of things, which happen about us, and often fill us with astonishment,[3] are not without their uses. All the terrestrial bodies arrive, by different ways, at the same end, at ends which produce the same effect. And with regard to men, whom their Creator has made

---

2. See *Examination*, pp. 137 ff.
3. constant . . . astonishment: "constant; Les variétés qui environnent la Terre n'influent point si haut, & les inégalités qui nous environnent, & qui quelquefois nous étonnent" (p. 220).

free and intelligent agents, there is one eternal rule irrevocably establish'd: every man's lot will correspond with his own choice, so that he may be justly termed the author of his own destiny. Every good that they possess is the free gift of God, who owed them nothing; and the evils they suffer are only to be imputed to that wickedness, by which they have brought them upon themselves.

Mr Pope has given full play to his imagination, in order to discover and describe a conformity between the system of the universe and human society; and of the mutual benevolence, which ought to be found among men, and extend its influence from the whole body to each particular member. On this subject he has lavish'd all his ornaments and embellishments;[4] he has call'd attraction to his assistance, and retained it in his service as long as he wanted it; but has not taken any notice of the power by which bodies are repell'd one from the other, tho' of equal use in the constitution of nature. But poets, when they form comparisons, content themselves with the beauty of their images, without giving themselves any trouble about philosophical exactness: this is their privilege, and if they originally held it by usurpation, they now enjoy it at least by prescription, and seem to desire no other right.[5]

A *principle of life* diffused thro' the whole system of nature, and *the breath of God,* are magnificent[6] expressions, of which, if any man desires an explication, I shall not undertake to give him satisfaction. These terms may be abused to the same ill purposes as that of the *soul of the world,* of which I have already given my sentiments in the *Examen.*[7]

The poets sometimes endeavour to raise our admiration by astonishing us with incredibilities, and sometimes condescend to admit the lowest prejudices into their writings, as Mr

---

4. On this subject . . . embellishments: "afin d'embellir son sujet" (p. 221).

5. and seem . . . right: "& cela leur suffit" (p. 221).

6. magnificent: "pompeux" (p. 221). Boyer defines "Pompeux" as "pompous, stately, glorious, magnificent, lofty."

7. See *Examination,* p. 105. Crousaz speaks of "la cause universelle" and "l'ame de toute la nature" (p. 97) rather than "l'*Ame de l'Univers*" (p. 221).

Pope has done, in affirming, That every *being rises originally from nothing, falls into it again, and then re-appears.* The vulgar think every thing annihilated that disappears; but the atoms, the primitive elements, the *stamina*[8] of bodies, are still preserved; and those particles which had contributed to form a cabbage, after having been united with other bodies in the flesh of an animal, are separated again, and, in another dress and appearance, become part of some other plant of a different species.[9]

The comparison may be reduced to these few words: it were to be wish'd, that the invariable regularity with which all inanimate beings fulfil the ends of their creation, without being conscious of them, were imitated by mankind; they would perform their duty from knowledge, not by the blind impulse of destiny; and would have the honour of determining themselves to that which is right.[1]

Where the chain of beings ends, or how far it holds on, is, as we are told, unknown: I, for my part, must be content that it should be so, for I do not understand the expression.[2]

> *Homme presompteux! quelle erreur te seduit?*
> Presumptuous man! what error misleads thee?
> *Crois-tu que pour toi seul l'univers soit produit?*   40
> Believest thou that for thee alone the universe is
>   produced?

---

8. SJ's translation of "Racines" (p. 222). *Stamina*: "The first principles of any thing" (sense 1 in *Dictionary*). On 10 October 1779 Boswell read to SJ a letter from Hugh Blair stating that Lord Bathurst told him that *The Essay on Man* "was originally composed by Lord Bolingbroke in prose, and that Mr. Pope did no more than put it into verse." SJ responded that "Pope may have had from Bolingbroke the philosophick *stamina* of his Essay" but "we are sure that the poetical imagery, which makes a great part of the poem, was Pope's own" (*Life*, III.402–03). Boyer defines "Racine" in a figurative sense as "(Principe, commencement d'une chose) root, principle, beginning."

9. are separated . . . species: "se dissout & contribue à la formation d'une plante, où il reparoit sous d'autres envelopes" (p. 222).

1. they would perform . . . right: "ils s'acquiteroient, chacun de ce qu'il doit, avec connoissance de cause, & se procureroient l'honneur de s'y déterminer" (p. 222).

2. Where . . . expression: "*Où finit la chaine des Etres?* Je n'entens pas cette Question, comment pourrois-je y répondre?" (p. 222).

This reflection has been made in prose, the grounds of it already examined, and the equivocation and ambiguity of the expression laid open.

Dieu n'a-t-il travaille que pour ta nourriture,
Hath God work'd only for thy sustenance,
Pour ton amusement, ton bien, ou ta parure?
For thy amusement, thy riches, or thy finery?
Pour soulager ta faim, la main qui, dans les champs,
To relieve thy hunger, the hand which, in the fields,
Engraisse des agneaux les troupeaux bondissans,
Fattens of lambs the frisking flocks,
Leur donne comme a toi les besoins de la vie,   45
Gives them as well as to thee the necessaries of life,
Et de gason pour eux embellit la prairie.
And with the green turf for them hath beautify'd the meadow.
Crois-tu que pour toi seul formant de doux concerts,
Thinkest thou that for thee alone forming sweet harmony,
Le tendre rossignol fait retentir les airs?
The tender nightingale makes resound the air?
Il cede aux doux transports de l'ardeur qui le presse,
He gives way to the sweet transports of the passion which urges him,
Il chante ses plaisirs, il chante sa tendresse.   50
He sings his pleasures, he sings his loves.
Ce superbe coursier qui, docile a ta voix,
That proud courser which, docile to thy voice,
Marche pompeusement sous un riche harnois,
Marches pompously under rich trappings,
Est sensible aux beautes qu'il tient de la nature,
Is sensible of the beauties that he possesses from nature,
Et partage avec toi l'orgueil de sa parure.
And shares with thee the pride of his finery.

A poet thinks that his matter lies entirely at his mercy; he either creates it, or at least exhibits it in whatever form he is most inclined; and has here given the horse as much pride as he thought convenient for his purpose. These prosopopoeias please in verse much more than in prose.

> *Crois-tu que pour toi seul tant de grains differens* 55
> Thinkest thou that for thee alone so many different grains
> *Couvrent de leurs tresors la surface des champs?*
> Cover with their treasures the surface of the fields?
> *Les oiseaux avant toi revendiquent leur proie,*
> The birds before thee demand their prey,
> *Et jouissent des dons que le ciel leur envoie.*
> And enjoy the gifts which heaven sends them.
> *Est-ce encor pour toi seul qu'en la riche saison*
> Is it again for thee alone that in the rich season
> *Les rayons du soleil font jaunir la moisson?* 60
> The rays of the sun make yellow the harvest?
> *Pour prix de ces travaux ta main reconnoissante*
> For the price of his labours thy grateful hand
> *En distribue au boeuf une part abondante.*
> Of it distributes to the ox a plentiful share.
> *Mais combien d'animaux rebelles a tes loix,*
> But how many animals rebellious to thy laws,
> *Qui dedaignant le joug habitent dans les bois!*
> Which disdaining the yoke dwell in the woods!
> *Arbitres de leur sort, sans travail & sans peine,* 65
> Arbiters of their fate, without labour and without pains,
> *Ils vivent malgre toi des fruits de ton domaine.*
> They live in spight of thee on the fruits of thy demesne.
> *La nature, attentive a leurs justes besoins,*
> Nature, attentive to their just wants,
> *Entre tous ses enfans a partage ses soins.*
> Among all her children hath divided her care.

The word *nature,* a word of an obscure and doubtful signification, used in various senses, and on different occasions, somewhat contributes to soften the shocking exaggeration, by which the adorable Author of the Universe is described looking with equal regard on every rank of beings, setting man and beast upon the level, and *dividing his care* amongst them as a parent among *his children.*

> *Un roi dans les hyvers s'arme de la fourrure,*
> A king in the winter defends himself with the furr,
> *Qu'a l'ours contre le froid a donne la nature.* 70
> Which to the bear against the cold nature hath given.
> *Tandis que pour lui seul l'homme croit tout forme,*
> While for himself alone man believes every thing made,
> *Et que du createur il se croit seul aime,*
> And that of the creator he believes himself alone beloved,
> *"Voyez a me servir combien l'homme s'empresse"*
> "See to serve me how man busies himself"
> *(Dit un vil animal, qu'avec soin l'on engraisse,)*
> (Says a contemptible animal, which with care we fatten,)
> *"L'homme est fait pour moi seul." Il ne peut penetrer* 75
> "Man is made for me alone." He cannot penetrate
> *Que l'homme ne le sert que pour le devorer.*
> That man serves him only to feed on him.
> *Que pensez-vous de l'homme, est-il plus raisonnable,*
> What think you of man, is he more reasonable,
> *Et ne tombe-t-il pas dans une erreur semblable,*
> And does he not fall into a like error,
> *Lors qu'a ses seuls besoins croyant tout destine,*
> When for his sole use believing every thing ordained,
> *Il ne voit pas qu'au tout il est subordonne?* 80
> He sees not that to every thing he is subordinate?

THIRD EPISTLE   203

Mr Pope has here endued his goose[3] with the gifts of reason and speech; and sets her, thus dignified and exalted, on a level with man.

> *Aux etres sans raison le ciel, par indulgence,*
> From beings without reason heaven, by indulgence,
> *De leur derniere fin cache la connoissance.*
> Of their last end conceals the knowledge.*

This favour is not indulged to mankind, but confined to the brute creation. The beasts alone enjoy the happy privilege of exemption from terrors, that would disturb their quiet, and interrupt their pleasures. But the Creator shews himself a kind and impartial[4] father, in making all his children equally his care; and has therefore furnish'd man with a remedy against this natural fear: this remedy, as Mr Pope informs us, is the happy quality of amusing himself[5] with chimeras, satisfying himself with uncertainties, and arming himself against painful apprehensions, by idle fancies that divert him from them.[6]

> *L'homme sait, il est vrai, qu'il est ne pour mourir;*
> Man knows, it is true, that he is born to die;
> *Mais lors qu'a son esprit cet arret vient s'offrir,*
> But when to his mind that sentence becomes
>   present,
> *D'un avenir heureux son ame possedee*   85
> With a happy futurity his soul taken up

*In this place the translator has, with great fidelity and judgment, entirely omitted a paragraph of twenty-two verses, from the fifty-third to the seventy-fourth.[7]

---

3. Crousaz, quoting Du Resnel (l. 74), has *"un vil animal"* (p. 225). Pope's lines are,

> While man exclaims, "See all things for my use!"
> "See man for mine!" replies a pamper'd goose. (45–46)

4. kind and impartial: "bon" (p. 226).
5. amusing himself: "se repaître" (p. 226). Boyer defines "Se repaître" as "to feed one's self with vain hopes."
6. and arming . . . them: "& de s'armer de distractions" (p. 226).
7. Lines 49–70 (53–74).

Joint un espoir flatteur[8] *a cette affreuse idee.*
Joins a flattering *hope* to that fearful idea.
Un nuage eternel lui derobant le jour,
An eternal cloud from him hiding the day,
Ou la mort doit venir l'enlever sans retour,
When death must come to carry him off without return,
Cet objet menaçant est d'autant moins terrible,
That threatening object is by so much the less terrible,
Qu'eloigne de ses yeux il est presque invisible. 90
As being remote from his eyes it is almost invisible.
De concert avec nous, habile a se cacher,
In good understanding with us, dextrous to conceal itself,
Il approche toujours, sans patroitre[9] *approcher.*
It approaches continually, without seeming to approach.
Miracle! qui du ciel signale la puissance.
Miracle! which of heaven signalizes the power.
Sans cette illusion le seul etre qui pense,
Without this illusion the only being which thinks,
Sachant que tous ses pas le menent a la mort, 95
Knowing that all his steps lead him to death,
Pourroit-il sans horreur envisager son sort?
Could he without horror look his destiny in the face?

I have already offered my sentiments upon the methods used by the goodness of our Creator, according to this author's system, to exempt man from that solicitude which the thoughts of death must naturally cause. Error, illusion, amusements, flattering imaginations, are the great miracles, which Mr Pope alledges to prove the care of our great Cre-

---

8. Crousaz wrongly has "flateur" (p. 226).

9. Crousaz correctly has "paroître" (p. 226).

ator.¹ As for those which are mention'd in the holy writings, and which tend wholly² to establish the truth, he has not let a single word escape him, that insinuates his belief of them.

He seems to write with these three ends in his view. *First*, to set man free from the duty of gratitude, arising from the opinion that God has given him privileges infinitely above other animals, by representing that notion as a mere chimera. *Secondly*, to oppose revelation, and to lead us, by pretty trains of reasoning, into notions inconsistent with it: and, *thirdly*, to prove that revelation is of no use, since error and illusion may produce the same effect, and afford us the tranquillity and peace of mind,³ which we search for in its doctrines.

> *Le Dieu dont le pouvoir sur les etres preside,*
> God whose power over beings presides,
> *Soit que le seul instinct, ou la raison les guide,*
> Whether instinct alone, or reason guides them,
> *A pris un tendre soin de partager entre eux*⁴
> Hath taken a tender care of dividing among them
> *Ce qui pouvoit les rendre aussi parfaits qu'heureux.* 100
> That which might render them perfect as well as happy.
> *Il leur donne un attrait, une regle certaine,*
> He gives them an attractive, a certain rule,
> *Dont l'insensible effort au bonheur les entraine,*
> Whose insensible effort to happiness them draws,
> *Et les porte toujours a remplir leur destin,*
> And them carries always to fulfil their appointment,
> *Soit par reflexion, soit meme sans dessein.*
> Be it by reflection, be it even without design.
> *Si, par l'heureux secours d'une main invisible,* 105
> If, by the happy assistance of a hand invisible,

---

1. Error . . . Creator: "L'erreur, l'illusion, la distraction, les pensées flateuses, voilà les Miracles que Mr. POPE nous donne en preuve des soins de Dieu" (p. 227).

2. tend wholly: "tendent uniquement" (p. 227).

3. tranquillity . . . mind: "repos d'esprit" (p. 227).

4. Crousaz has "entre'eux" (p. 228).

La brute dans l'instinct trouve un guide infaillible.
The brute in instinct finds a guide infallible.
Qu'a-t-elle a desirer? Voudrois-tu qu'un docteur
What hath he to desire? Wouldest thou that a doctor
Lui dictat des leçons, devint son conducteur?
To him dictate lessons, become his leader?
La raison est pour l'homme un serviteur habile,
Reason is for man a skilful servant,
Mais un serviteur froid, paresseux, indocile;   110
But a servant cold, lazy, untoward;
Il le faut appeller dans les pressans besoins,
She must be call'd for on pressing occasions,
Pour forcer sa lenteur a nous donner ses soins.
To compel her slowness to afford us her care.
L'instinct sans cesse agit, presse, avertit, excite,
Instinct without ceasing acts, presses, warns, excites,
Et pour se presenter n'attend pas qu'on l'invite;
And to offer herself expects not that one invite her;
Il ne manque jamais, il est pour tous les tems;   115
She never fails, she is for all seasons;
La raison ne nous sert que dans quelques instans.
Reason serves us only in some moments.
L'instinct sans hesiter, prompt, docile & fidelle,
Instinct without faltering, ready, docil and faithful,
Va droit au but marque par la cause eternelle:
Goes strait to the mark designed by the eternal cause:
De ce but la raison libre de s'ecarter,
From that mark reason free to wander,
Sort de l'ordre prescrit, ose lui resister.   120
Goes out of the order prescribed, dares resist it.
En vain de la raison tu vantes l'excellence,
In vain of reason thou boastest the excellency,
Doit-elle sur l'instinct avoir la preference?
Ought she over instinct to have the preference?
Entre ces facultes quelle comparaison!
Between these faculties what comparison!
Dieu dirige l'instinct, & l'homme la raison.
God directs instinct, and man reason.

THIRD EPISTLE 207

Here we find the brute creation, by the tender care of the common Father, placed in a state of no less perfection than man; so that a nature, susceptible of religion and sense of the kindness of God, and the reverence due to him, does not at all contribute to the perfection of created beings.[5]

The brutes, furnish'd with instinct,

> *To Bliss——by that direction tend,*
> *And find the Means proportion'd to the End.*[6]

Reason is far from being a guide equally infallible:

> *Reason, however able, cool at best,*
> *Cares not for Service, or but serves when press'd;*
> *Stays till we call, and then not always near;*
> *But honest Instinct comes a Voluntier:*
> *This, too, serves always, Reason never long;*
> *One must go right, the other may go wrong.*[7]

Thus we see man degraded from his superiority, and find very far from true what was so lately asserted, that

> *——Nature's Children all divide her Care.*[8]

Mr Pope seems extremely pleased with his useful and important notion of the inferiority of reason to instinct: he dwells long upon it, and concludes with this happy couplet:

> *——Reason raise o'er Instinct as you can;*
> *In this 'tis God directs, in that 'tis Man.*

If, therefore, we take his word, instinct is not only superior, but superior to an infinite degree.[9]

---

5. so that a nature . . . beings: "d'où il suit qu'une nature susceptible des sentimens de Religion, ne le rend point plus parfait que les bêtes" (p. 229).

6. SJ adds the introductory phrase and substitutes ll. 81–82 (85–86) of Pope for Crousaz's quotations of l. 106 of Du Resnel (p. 229). The first line omits "alike" and the second line should read "their end."

7. SJ substitutes ll. 85–88 (89–94) and 93–94 (97–98) for Crousaz's paraphrase from ll. 110, 116–19 of Du Resnel (p. 229). The third line should read "often near," and "Voluntier" should read "volunteer."

8. SJ substitutes the greater part of l. 43 of Pope for Crousaz's paraphrase of ll. 67–68 of Du Resnel (p. 229).

9. Mr Pope . . . degree: "Mr. POPE

But it is plain, that this antithesis is a great exaggeration, and only put into poetry to dazzle and confound;[1] for it had been shorter to have said, that *God regulates the actions of the brute by his* immediate *direction, without the intervention of instinct.*

There are objects, which, in brute animals, neither excite pleasing nor painful ideas, that neither raise desire nor aversion. There are others which make impressions that produce desire, such desire as determines them to approach them; and others, that raise dislike, and make them retire from them. These impressions, with their effects, must be uniform, regular, and certain, because those creatures have no reason to correct, animate, or restrain their desires, or to awake them from perfect indifference.[2] But the supreme Creator has formed man capable of reasoning, of acting in pursuance of his own choice, and of procuring no less than infinite happiness, if he will undergo the labour of reasoning justly, and of chusing right.

> *Sans jamais les tromper, quelle lumiere sure*   125
> Without ever deceiving them, what sure light
> *Apprend aux animaux a trouver leur pature,*
> Teacheth animals to find their food,
> *A choisir le remede, a laisser le poison;*
> To chuse physick, to forbear poison;

Several animals are destroy'd by poison;[3] pigeons and fish are made drunk, and by that means taken. Is the infallibility of instinct in these particular instances less certain?

---

ne peut se lasser de nous répéter cette importante leçon. *Quelle comparison,* dit-il, *entre ces facultés! Dieu dirige l'instinct, & la Raison dirige l'homme.* La distance est donc infinie, si on veut l'en croire" (pp. 229–30). SJ substitutes most of ll. 97–98 of Pope for Crousaz's paraphrase of ll. 123–24 of Du Resnel.

1. to dazzle and confound: "pour éblouïr" (p. 230). SJ adds the italics below.

2. or restrain . . . indifference: "ni modérer leurs desirs & leurs aversions, ni changer leur indifférence" (p. 230).

3. Several animals . . . poison: "On empoisonne les animaux nuisibles" (p. 231).

> *A changer de demeure en changeant de saison,*
> To change abode at changing season,
> *A predire le vent, les frimats & l'orage;*
> To foretel wind, frost and tempest;

Men that have been wounded, often perceive any impending change of weather, by aches in the healed part. Storks and swallows may feel prickings or uneasiness,[4] that may instigate them to take their flight, and leave a climate that makes painful impressions upon their organs, for one that favours them with more agreeable sensations.

> *A resister aux flots qui battent le rivage;*   130
> To resist the waves which beat on the shore;
> *A former en commun de solides travaux,*
> To frame in common solid works,
> *Pour etablir en paix leur sejour dans les eaux?*
> In order to establish in peace their habitation in the waters?
> *Sans regle & sans compas qui montre a l'araignee*
> Without rule and without compass who shews the spider
> *A tracer avec art une toile alignee?*
> To draw with art a web by line?
> *Moivre, par le secours de divers instrumens,*   135
> *Moivre,* by the help of various instruments,
> *Met-il plus de justesse & plus[5] d'ordre dans ses plans?*
> Does he lay more of exactness and more of order in his plans?
> *Qui montre tous les ans a la prudente grue[6]*
> Who shews every year the sagacious stork
> *A chercher dans l'hyver une terre inconnue?*
> To search in the winter a land unknown?
> *Qui preside au conseil, ou l'on fixe le jour*
> Who presides at council, where they fix the day

---

4. uneasiness: "chatouillemens" (p. 231).

5. SJ adds "plus."

6. "Grue" is a crane, a bird that migrates to Africa in the winter.

> *Et l'instant du depart, & celui du retour?* 140
> And the moment of departure, and that of return?

Beavers and other animals suffer themselves to be taken and destroy'd by very coarse and artless stratagems, and by traps, which, with a very little reason, they might escape, and would have escaped long ago.

An animal that has only one idea, can only act according to it; and as its organs are constituted only in order to pursue[q] that one, it has not the power of trying to form any other.[7] The productions of human contrivance admit of variety, and in proportion as a man applies himself with more or less attention, he draws plans with more or less exactness, and executes them with greater or less success.[8]

Mr Pope seems to have a strong inclination to the marvellous and the hyperbolical; and, to gratify his darling passion, imagines and supposes not only a day but a moment fixed for the departure and return of the flight of storks.[9] When a man has once arrived at the privilege of supposing what he pleases, he easily raises[1] the admiration of those readers that are so obliging as to adopt his notions.

> *Le moyen d'etre heureux, sans sortir de soi-meme,*
> The means to be happy, without going out of itself,
> *Chaque etre l'a recu de la bonte supreme.*
> Every being hath received of the supreme goodness.
> *Mais le bonheur du tout etant le grand objet,*
> But the happiness of all being the great object,
> *Que Dieu s'est propose dans tout ce qu'il a fait,*

---

q. pursue *om.*

---

7. its organs . . . other: "sa machine uniquement construite pour la suivre est incapable de faire l'essai d'une autre" (p. 232).

8. The productions . . . success: "L'homme varie ses ouvrages, & suivant qu'il applique plus ou moins son attention, il forme des plans plus exacts, & il les exécute plus heureusement & avec moins de distraction" (p. 232).

9. Mr Pope . . . storks: "Mr. POPE a un grand goût pour les exagérations, voilà pourquoi il s'imagine & se donne la liberté de supposer un jour, & un instant même, fixe, pour le départ & le retour" (pp. 232–33).

1. he easily raises: "s'empare aisément" (p. 233).

> Which God proposed to himself in all that which he
>   hath made,
> *Du besoin mutuel le concours necessaire* 145
> Of necessity mutual the unavoidable concurrence
> *D'un bonheur reciproque est la source ordinaire.*
> Of happiness reciprocal is the ordinary source.
> *Cet ordre unit entr'eux tous les etres divers,*
> That order unites among themselves all the various
>   beings,
> *Destines a peupler cet immense univers.*
> Appointed to people this immense universe.

This last period begins and ends with hyperboles. Animals, as they cannot live without food, are compell'd to procure it, and consequently are in want of something *without,* something not compris'd in their own natures.[2] And those that cannot live without being shelter'd from the impressions of the weather,[3] are no less necessitated to make use of external assistance.

There is nothing in the world more paradoxical, or advanced with less appearance of probability, than the notion of a mutual relation and dependance between the wild beasts of the woods,[4] and the fishes of the sea; between the inhabitants of our earth, and those of Venus and of Jupiter.

> *La nature y produit, par sa flamme feconde,*
> Nature there produces, by its generating flame,
> *L'esprit vivisiant qui conserve le monde.* 150
> The quickening spirit which maintains the world.

These are words of a lofty sound, but of which I do not understand the meaning; one of Spinosa's disciples would more easily comprehend[5] it.

---

2. "and consequently . . . natures" is an SJ addition.

3. impressions of the weather: "impressions de l'air" (p. 233). *Impression:* "Effect of an attack" (sense 6 in *Dictionary*).

4. or advanced . . . woods: "& moins fondé qu'une dépendance mutuelle entre les animaux qui se nourrissent dans les bois" (pp. 233–34).

5. comprehend: "adopteroit" (p. 234).

If this author writes with an ill design, he takes little care to disguise it;[6] if his sentiments be agreeable to those of other Christians, or not widely different from them, can he not foresee the bad uses that may be made of almost every line of his poem? Or, if he does see them, is he entirely indolent and unconcerned?[7]

> *L'attrait est general, l'homme, les animaux*
> The attraction is general, man, animals
> *Qui vivent dans les bois, dans les airs, dans les eaux,*
> Which live in the woods, in the air, in the waters,
> *Commencent par s'aimer d'une ardeur naturelle:*
> Begin by loving themselves with a natural passion:
> *Mais bien-tot cette ardeur devenant mutuelle,*
> But soon that passion becoming mutual,
> *Chaque sexe pour l'autre eprouve un feu commun,*   155
> Each sex for the other experiences a common flame,
> *Qui les reunissant des deux n'en forme qu'un.*
> Which them reuniting of two makes but one.
> *De ce second amour un autre prend la place:*
> Of that second love another takes the place:
> *Ils transmettent leur sang, ils s'aiment dans leur race.*
> They transmit their blood, they love themselves in their offspring.
> *Les betes, les oiseaux, par cet amour pousses,*
> The beasts, the birds, by that love pushed on,
> *A servir leurs petits se montrent empresses;*   160
> To serve their young shew themselves forward;
> *La mere les nourrit, & plein de vigilance*
> The dam them nourishes, and full of watchfulness
> *Le pere prend sur lui le soin de leur defense.*
> The sire takes upon himself the care of their defence.
> *Sont-ils devenus grands, ces nourrissons si chers,*
> Are they grown great, these fosterlings so dear,
> *Ils courent habiter les bois, les champs, les airs;*
> They go off to inhabit the woods, the fields, the air;

---

6. he takes . . . disguise it: "il jouë gros jeu" (p. 234).

7. is he . . . unconcerned: "ne s'en fait-il aucune peine?" (p. 234).

> *L'instinct s'arrete alors, le pere, ni la mere* 165
> Instinct stops then, the sire, nor the dam
> *Ne reconnoissent plus cette troupe etrangere;*
> No more own that strange crew;
> *Si-tot qu'a leurs petits leurs soins sont superflus,*
> As soon as to their young their cares are unnecessary,
> *Les noeuds qui les lioient pour toujours sont rompus,*
> The bands which ty'd them for ever are broken.
> *Mais des tristes humains les maux & la foiblesse,*
> But of sorrowful mankind the ills and the weakness,
> *Une enfance sans force, une infirme vieillesse,* 170
> An infancy without strength, an infirm old age,
> *Leurs raports mutuels, leurs differens besoins,*
> Their mutual relations, their different needs,
> *Demandent plus d'egards, exigent plus de soins;*
> Demand more regards, require more cares;
> *Ces soins multiplies augmentent la tendresse;*
> Those cares multiply'd increase tenderness;
> *L'un a l'autre a l'envi se lie & s'interesse.*
> One to another with emulation binds and engages himself.

These are truths about which there is no disagreement, and of which this elegant account cannot but be read with pleasure. These are passages which relieve the attention, and charm the mind of a good man, who cannot but wish at the same time that he could be equally delighted with every other part of the composition.[8]

> *La raison & le tems nous montrent chaque jour* 175
> Reason and time shew us every day
> *A resserrer encor les noeuds de cet amour.*
> To tie yet closer the knots of that affection.
> *Si le panchant au mal d'un cote nous incline,*
> If the bent to evil on one side us inclines,

---

8. elegant account ... composition: "On en lit la description avec plaisir, & l'on n'y recontre rien qui offense. Un honnête homme respire dans ces endroits, & souhaiteroit de savoir également bon gré au Poëte, dans tous les autres" (pp. 235–36).

De l'autre la raison au bien nous determine.
On the other reason to good us determines.

I am glad to find reason re-established in her rights, her authority, and her honours. Mr Pope, at length, consents to acknowledge, that man is capable of doing well or ill. He allows, that his inclinations give him a tendency to ill: a man who resolves to act rationally, is to consider the probable effects of such passions, and divert his attention from them to better views.

But, upon this head of reason, it is not easy to clear Mr Pope from the charge of inconsistency. But is it not the established prerogative of poets to contradict themselves? Big with unbounded designs, they treat of every subject, and are hurried by the enthusiasm of poetry beyond the limits of just reason.[9] Nor do they want the examples of the greatest masters of their art, to plead in their excuse. Homer has given us, in very pompous lines, a description of the habitations of unhappy[1] souls, and has informed us of the great difference between the happiness of living and the misery of being dead.

The modest and pious Virgil rises, in one of his pastorals, to the most sublime theology, and, in another, sinks into loose and obscene ideas.

Horace, that great master of the art of poetry, treats of morality with much juster notions than the Stoicks, and seems to write from his heart; but, in other places, appears a very gross Epicurean, a mere sensualist.[2]

> *L'interet, seconde par les reflexions,*
> Interest, assisted by reflections,
> *Fait naitre les vertus du sein des passions.*   180
> Brings forth the virtues from the womb of the
>   passions.

---

9. Big . . . reason: "Ils veulent parler de tout, leur feu les emporte" (p. 236).
1. unhappy: "bienheureuses" (p. 237). Crousaz is referring to *Odyssey*, IV.561, the Elysian plain, the abode of happy souls, whereas SJ seems to be referring to *Odyssey*, XI, the book of the dead, particularly in the exchange of views between Odysseus and Achilles.
2. SJ adds "a mere sensualist."

That is, the passions are corrected, restrained, and first inclined towards virtue by a sense of interest. But from these prospects, which first excite their attention, men rise to more pure desires, and more exalted views;[3] which, when they have once found the value of them, they never forsake.

> *Des besoins satisfaits nait la reconnoissance;*
> From wants supply'd grows gratitude;
> *A l'amour naturel se joint la bienveillance;*[4]
> To natural affection is join'd benevolence;
> *Ces tendres sentimens, gardes au fond du coeur,*
> Those tender sentiments, preserv'd at bottom of the heart,
> *Des peres aux enfans transmettent leur douceur.*
> From fathers to children transmit their sweetness.
> *A peine ces derniers en prennent l'habitude,*   185
> Hardly do these last of it take the habit,
> *Que deja leurs parens, dans la decrepitude,*
> When now their parents, in decrepitness,
> *Viennent leur demander, foibles & languissans,*
> Come to demand of them, feeble and languishing,
> *Les soins qu'ils ont pris d'eux dans leurs plus jeunes ans.*
> The care which they had taken of them in their younger years.
> *Nous rappellons alors le tems de notre enfance;*
> We recal then the time of our infancy;
> *L'esprit dans l'avenir porte sa prevoyance,*   190
> The mind into futurity carries its prospect,
> *Et le fils a son pere accorde des secours,*
> And the son to his father affords the assistances,
> *Qu'il attend pour lui-meme a la fin de ses jours.*
> Which he expects for himself at the end of his days.
> *Les services recus, joints a ceux qu'on espere,*
> The services received, added to those which we hope,

---

3. men . . . views: "on passe à des vûës plus pures" (p. 237).
4. Crousaz wrongly has "bienveuillance" (p. 237); Du Resnel has "bienveillance" (l. 182).

> *Sont ainsi des humains le lien ordinaire;*
> Are thus of mankind the ordinary tie;
> *Et de tous ces motifs le melange divers* 195
> And of all these motives the different combination
> *Les porte a concourir au bien de l'univers.*
> Impells them to concur for the good of the universe.

Here again we have a confused notion of the universe, which recurs without necessity, and which the imagination adopts[5] by mere habit.

> *Croyez-vous que sorti des mains de la nature,*
> Think ye that come out of the hands of nature,
> *L'homme marchant sans frein, erroit a l'avanture?*
> Man marching without curb, wander'd at adventure?
> *Dieu meme en cet etat etoit son conducteur,*
> God himself in that state was his guide,
> *Eclairoit son esprit & dirigeoit son coeur;* 200
> Enlightned his mind, and governed his heart;
> *L'amour-propre regnoit, mais soumis & tranquille;*
> Self-love reigned, but humble and quiet;
> *Du bonheur mutuel il etoit le mobile.*
> Of mutual happiness it was the moving cause.
> *Sans le secours des arts par l'orgueil inventes,*
> Without the help of arts by pride invented,
> *La nature etaloit ses naives beautes.*
> Nature display'd its native beauties.
> *Avec les animaux l'homme d'intelligence* 205
> With the brutes man in correspondence
> *A l'ombre des forets vivoit en assurance;*
> In the shade of the forest lived in security;
> *On ne le voyoit point ensanglanter sa main,*
> He was never seen to imbrue in blood his hand,
> *Pour defendre son corps du froid ou de la faim.*
> That he might defend his body from cold or from hunger.

---

5. adopts: "aime à s'y livrer" (p. 238).

La terre sans travaux, sans soins & sans culture,
The earth without labour, without care and without culture,
Leur donnoit meme lit & meme nourriture. 210
Them afforded the same bed and the same food.
L'homme & les animaux reunissant leurs voix
Man and beasts uniting their voices
Pour louer leur auteur, s'assembloient dans les bois;
To praise their creator, assembled in the woods;
Ces bois etoient leur temple; un culte sanguinaire
These woods were their temple; a bloody worship
N'en deshonoroit point l'auguste sanctuaire.
Never dishonour'd the magnificent sanctuary.
L'or au sein de la terre, ignore des mortels, 215
Gold in the bosom of the earth, unknown by mortals,
N'eclatoit point alors jusques sur les autels;
Glitter'd not then even upon the altars;
Sans faste, sans eclat, le pretre irreprochable
Without pride, without pomp, the priest unblameable
Par ses seules vertus s'y montroit respectable.
For his virtues alone there appeared venerable.
Le ciel gouvernoit tout en maitre universel,
Heaven govern'd all as universal master,
Et par tout signaloit son amour paternel. 220
And every where signalized its paternal love.
L'homme sur la nature exercoit son empire,
Man over nature exercis'd his sway,
Pour y maintenir l'ordre, & non pour le detruire.
To establish order therein, and not to destroy it.

In the first and eighth verses of this paragraph, we meet with the word *nature*, which we must necessarily take in two senses very different from each other, unless we allow matter to be the only original of man. It were to be wish'd, that a word of so uncertain an import were less in fashion than it is. This term, apply'd to things so very different, is subject to more cavils and misconstructions, as it sometimes gives a writer an occasion to represent the creation, or work of nature, as a person, or active being.⁶

I shall not repeat the remarks that I have already made upon the imagination of this writer from ver. 205 to 215. He speaks of what passed in the earliest ages of the world no less positively than an eye-witness: but what he tells us is much less credible, consider'd merely in itself, than the account which Moses hath given us.

By this new relation of a religion common to man and beast, it is insinuated, that, in those happy times, man was restrained by no other laws, nor practised any other duties than the brute creation.⁷

They are allowed by Mr Pope to have been directed by God: if they were directed by means of a revelation, whence comes it to pass that there are now no traces of it remaining? Or if that which we receive be authentick and genuine, why is it treated by this author with so much contempt?⁸ If God guided mankind by the light of reason, is it not in a high degree criminal to debase that sacred light below the instinct of the brutes? But Mr Pope does not give himself the trouble to review his notions, or to make that connection between them which he is fond of supposing between the parts of the universe: for when he adds that it was

———*Man's Prerogative to rule, but spare,*⁹

he evidently represents *man* as the king of the creation, and it was necessary that he should be so, that he might keep the brutes in order and just subordination.*

---

*I cannot but stop to take notice of the great inequality between the original of this paragraph and the French ͬ version, tho' I hope the reader prevents my remarks

---

6. as it sometimes . . . being: "qu'elle donne lieu à personifier l'Ouvrage" (p. 240).

7. By this new . . . creation: "Cette Religion, commune aux animaux brutes & aux hommes, nous insinuë que, dans ces heureux tems, les hommes n'en avoient pas plus que des bêtes" (p. 240).

8. Or if . . . contempt: "que Mr. POPE regarde avec tant de mépris, ce qui nous en reste" (p. 240).

9. SJ substitutes most of l. 160 (161) of Pope for Crousaz's quotation of ll. 221–22 of Du Resnel (p. 241).

O! combien different, & de gouts & de moeurs,
Oh! how different, both in taste and in manners,
L'homme degenera de ses premiers auteurs!
Hath man degenerated from his first ancestors!
Il remplit de terreur les airs, les mers, & la terre;   225
He has filled with terror the air, the seas, and the earth;
Aux foibles animaux il declara la guerre.
To weak animals he hath declared war.
Tantot leur meurtrier & tantot leur tombeau,
Now their murderer, and then their tomb,
Il se couvrit les yeux d'un coupable bandeau;
He has cover'd his eyes with a guilty veil;
Aux cris de la nature il devint insensible;
To the cries of nature he is become insensible;
Le sang n'effraya plus son courage inflexible;   230

---

by comparing them, which is the only method of doing justice both to the author and translator.[1]

r. French *om.*

---

[1]. IV. Nor think, in NATURE's STATE they blindly trod;
The state of Nature was the reign of God:
Self-love and Social at her birth began,
Union the bond of all things, and of Man.
Pride then was not; nor Arts, that Pride to aid;
Man walk'd with beast, joint tenant of the shade;
The same his table, and the same his bed;
No murder cloath'd him, and no murder fed.
In the same temple, the resounding wood,
All vocal beings hymn'd their equal God:
The shrine with gore unstain'd, with gold undrest,
Unbrib'd, unbloody, stood the blameless priest:
Heav'n's attribute was Universal Care,
And Man's prerogative to rule, but spare.
Ah! how unlike the man of times to come!
Of half that live the butcher and the tomb;
Who, foe to Nature, hears the gen'ral groan,
Murders their species, and betrays his own.
But just disease to luxury succeeds,
And ev'ry death its own avenger breeds;
The Fury-passions from that blood began,
And turn'd on Man a fiercer savage, Man. (147-68; 148-69)

Blood has no more dismay'd his undaunted
  courage;
Cruel aux animaux, injuste pour les siens,
Cruel to brutes, unjust towards his kind,
Avec son innocence il perdit tous ses biens.
With his innocence he has lost all his blessings.

In my former *Examen* I have spoken of the right of man to take away the lives of other animals, which, however, does not extend to unnecessary cruelty. I have treated likewise of sacrifices.[2]

De ce luxe effrene *l'affreuse tyrannie*
Of that *unbridled* luxury the horrid tyranny
Par un juste retour fut aussi-tot punie.
By a just recompense was soon punished.
La fievre, la douleur, une foule de maux   235
The fever, pain, a crowd of ills
Sortirent a l'envi du sang des animaux.
Burst forth thronging[3] from the blood of animals.
De ce sang etranger la fougue impetueuse
Of that strange blood the violent transport
Mit dans les passions une ardeur furieuse.
Begot in the passions an unruly heat.

That diseases arise from a moderate use of animal food, is not easily made to[s] appear; men bring them upon themselves by intemperance.

Et, malgre ses remords,[4] *dans le crime affermi*
And, spite of his remorse, harden'd in crimes
L'homme trouva dans l'homme un farouche ennemi.   240
Man has found in man a fierce enemy.

s. to *om.*

---

2. See *Examination*, pp. 144–45, 151.

3. SJ seems to be paraphrasing Pope's "The Fury-passions from that blood began" (167; 168), rather than just translating "à l'envie du," meaning "with a desire for, or as a result of the thirst for."

To Throng: "To croud; to come in tumultuous multitudes" (*Dictionary*).

4. Crousaz wrongly has "remors" (p. 242); Du Resnel has "remords" (l. 239).

THIRD EPISTLE

Is this remorse, by which men are witheld from a confirmed state of wickedness, contrary to reason? Mr Pope will tell us, hereafter, that it is contrary to reason to suppose the Supreme Being otherwise than supremely good.*

> *La nature indignee alors se fit entendre;*
> Nature indignant then made herself be heard;
> *"Va, malheureux mortel, va," lui dit-elle, "apprendre,*
> "Go, wretched mortal, go," says she to him, "to learn,
> *Des plus vils animaux, l'industrie & les soins*
> From the vilest animals, the industry and the cares
> *Qu'exigent ta foiblesse & tes divers besoins.*
> Which thy weakness and thy various necessities require.
> *Va parcourir les bois; que les oiseaux t'instruisent,*   245
> Go search the woods; let the birds instruct thee,
> *Et te montrent les fruits que les buissons produisent.*
> And shew thee the fruits which the bushes produce.
> *Observe dans les champs les pas des animaux,*
> Observe in the fields the steps of animals,
> *Leur instinct t'apprendra l'art de guerir tes maux.*
> Their instinct will teach thee the art to cure thy ills.
> *Voudrois-tu des saisons braver l'intemperie?*
> Would'st thou of the seasons defy the intemperature?
> *De l'abeille en sa ruche imite l'industrie.*   250
> Of the bee in her hive imitate the industry.
> *Que la taupe t'aprenne a labourer les champs;*
> Let the mole teach thee to till the fields;
> *Que l'exemple du ver forme des tisserans.*
> Let the example of a worm train up weavers.
> *Vois-tu le nautilus sans rame, sans boussole,*
> Seest thou the nautilus without oar, without compass,
> *Sur le vaste ocean conduire sa gondole?*
> On the vast ocean steer his boat?
> *Qu'il te montre a voguer sur l'humide element,*   255
> Let him shew thee to row upon the wat'ry element,
> *A maitriser les flots, a profiter du vent.*

---

*This remorse is only mentioned by the translator.

To conquer the waves, to take advantage of the wind.
Ici les animaux, par des regles certaines,
Here animals, by certain rules,
Construisent avec art des cites souterraines;
Erect with art subterranean cities;
La batissant en l'air, sur des arbres flottans,
There building in the air, upon waving trees,
Ils sçavent se parer des injures du tems. 260
They know to ward off the injuries of the season.
De leurs societes les differentes formes
Of their societies the different forms
Toujours a leurs besoins te paroitront conformes,
Always to their necessities will appear to thee adapted,
T'apprendront, mais trop tard, quelles heureuses loix
Will teach thee, tho' too late, what happy laws
Font la felicite des peuples & des rois.
Make the felicity of nations and kings.
Tu vois de la fourmi la sage republique; 265
Thou seest of the pismire the wise republick;
L'abeille offre a tes yeux un etat monarchique:
The bee offers to thine eyes a monarchical state:
Compare leur genie & leur gouvernment;
Compare their genius and their government;
L'une pour le public toujours en mouvement,
The one for the publick always in motion,
Enrichissant les siens, elle-meme enrichie,
Enriching her own, herself enriched,
Possede l'art d'unir l'ordre avec l'anarchie; 270
Possesses the art of uniting order with anarchy;
L'autre, quoique soumise aux volontes d'un roi,
The other, though subject to the will of a king,
N'en est pas moins heureuse & moins libre chez soi;
Is no less happy or less free at home;
Contente dans le fond de sa chere cellule,
Content in the depth of her beloved cell,
Elle jouit en paix des biens qu'elle accumule.
She enjoys in peace the good things which she heaps up.
Grave dans ton esprit les immuables loix, 275

Engrave in thy mind the immutable laws,
Qui mettent a couvert leur etat & leurs droits;
Which set in security their estate and their rights;
Loix, qui de la nature ont les sceaux respectables,
Laws, which of nature have the venerable seals,
Loix que l'arret du ciel rendit irrevocables.
Laws which the ordinance of heaven hath made irrevocable.
Ta frivole raison, pour regler les humains,
Thy trifling reason, to regulate mankind,
En vain multiplira ses decrets incertains,   280
In vain will multiply its *dubious* statutes,
En vain contre la fraude armera la justice,
In vain against fraud will arm justice,
Tu verras sous son nom triompher la malice;
Thou wilt see under its name malice triumphant;
Et victime des loix & de son defenseur
And the victim of the laws and of his own advocate
Le pauvre succomber sous le riche oppresseur.
The poor man to sink under the rich oppressor.
Va, cependant, mortel, sans loix, sans regles sures,   285
Go, notwithstanding, mortal, without laws, without sure rules,
Va soumettre a ton joug toutes les creatures;
Go subject to thy yoke all the creatures;
Et que le plus habile, attirant tout a lui,
And let the most accomplish'd, engaging all to himself,
Commande a ses egaux, & leur serve d'appui;
Command over his equals, and serve them for a defence;
Que sachant adoucir leurs moeurs encor sauvages,
Let him who knows to soften their yet savage manners,
En leur portant des arts les divins advantages,[5]   290

---

5. Crousaz correctly has "avantages" (p. 245).

> By bringing among them of arts the divine
>   accomplishments,
> *Il soit, par les bienfaits que repand sa bonte,*
> Let him be, for the benefits which his goodness
>   dispenses,
> *Obei comme un roi, comme un Dieu respecte."*
> Obey'd as a king, as a God reverenced."

Are we by the *voice of nature* to understand in this place the voice of its author? Had man, whose *prerogative* extended thro' the whole creation,[6] hitherto been so void of reason as not to have discovered any way of supplying such pressing necessities? If by *nature* he means here only the objects that surround us, when nature in this sense is said to speak, it is by the assistance of the voice of man, as on this occasion she has made use of Mr Pope's, and her precepts are nothing more than the reflections that rise at the sight of those objects, by which man instructs himself.

Upon the insufficiency of these pretended instructions, which we receive from the brute creation, I have already made my observations, and shewn upon what weak foundations the author raised this romantic structure.[7]

> *Laws wise as Nature, and as fix'd as Fate,*

are doubtless excellent instructions, but they do not secure the *monarchy of bees*[8] from a great number of accidents. They

---

6. Had man . . . creation: "Mais jusqu'ici l'*Homme qui avoit exercé, sous Dieu, son empire sur la nature* créée" (p. 245).

7. and shewn . . . structure: "& sur le peu de fondement de cette Harangue Romanesque" (p. 245).

8. *Laws . . . bees:* "Des Loix irrévocables ne mettent point à couvert la République des Abeilles (pp. 245–46). SJ substitutes l. 190 (191) of Pope. "République" can be used figuratively in French to mean an association of animals living together. Monarchy is an interesting substitution by SJ. It may simply reflect the commonplace notion that since beehives have queens, they are monarchies. Crousaz, in an ambiguous passage below, seems to suggest that man learned the monarchial form of government from the bee (322). The change may also reflect SJ's reading of Bernard Mandeville's *Fable of the Bees:* "I read Mandeville forty, or, I believe, fifty years ago," SJ observed on 15 April 1778. "He did not puzzle me; he opened my views into real life very much" (*Life*, III.292). See also ll. 265 ff. above.

do not preserve their provisions without putting to death, with the most unpitying cruelty, the most laborious of those inhabitants that assisted in collecting them: so that nothing can be more unreasonable than for them to harangue upon the insufficiency of human laws to protect one part of mankind from the oppression of the other.

> *Par ces mots la nature excita l'industrie,*
> By these words nature excited industry,
> *Et de l'homme feroce enchaina la furie.*
> And of fierce man chained up the fury.
> *On vit, de toutes parts, s'elever des cites,*   295
> There were seen, on all sides, cities arise,
> *Et les mortels s'unir par des societes.*
> And mortals join themselves in societies.

Such an oration as the foregoing, and the effects here supposed to be produced by it, would make no disagreeable scene in an opera.[9]

> *D'un etat commençant la police nouvelle*
> Of a rising state the new policy
> *Aux peuples ses voisins sert bien-tot de modelle;*
> To people its neighbours serves quickly for a model;
> *Et tous deux a l'envi*[1] *s'augmentant chaque jour,*
> And both striving in growth every day,
> *Ils s'unissent entr'eux par crainte ou par amour.*   300
> They united together thro' fear or thro' love.
> *L'un offre-t-il aux yeux l'agreable, & l'utile?*
> Does one offer to sight the agreeable, and the useful?
> *Le soleil y rend-il la terre plus fertile?*

---

9. Such an oration . . . opera: "On pourroit voir sur un Théatre d'*Opera*, le promt effet d'un Discours si bien composé" (p. 246).

1. Here "à l'envie" is used in the older sense of "with emulation" (p. 246). *To Strive:* "To vie; to be comparable to; to emulate; to contend in excellence" (sense 3 in *Dictionary*).

Does the sun there render the earth more fruitful?
L'autre est-il arrosé de paisibles ruisseaux?
Is another water'd with gentle streams?
Voit-on dans ses vallons abonder les troupeaux?
Do you see in its valleys abound flocks?
Chacun d'eux, attiré par cette douce amorce,   305
Each of them, allured by that pleasing bait,
Contre l'etat voisin veut employer la force.
Against the neighbouring state, resolves to employ force.
Le jour de la raison leur défile[2] les yeux,
The light of reason uncloses their eyes,
Et bannit de leur coeur ces transports odieux.
And banishes from their heart those malicious passions.

Reason might[3] formerly produce the same consequences as we see it produce in our time. When I read Mr Pope's discourses upon reason, I cannot help thinking that I am looking at the sky in those variable days of the spring, in which the sun is one moment hidden by the clouds, and another shining out in full brightness.

Ce qu'ils alloient ravir par la force des armes
What they went about to ravish by force of arms
Ils l'obtiennent bien-tot sans combat, sans allarmes.   310
They obtain soon without fighting, without alarms.
D'un commerce reglé les retours assures
Of a regulated commerce the sure returns
Leur apportent chez eux ces biens si desires.
Bring home to them those commodities so desired.
L'interet satisfait, la paix est retablie;
Interest satisfy'd, peace is re-established;
Chacun a son voisin de plus en plus se lie.

---

2. Crousaz wrongly has "défille" (p. 247).   3. Reason might: "La Raison a pu" (p. 247).

Each to his neighbour more and more ties himself.
Dans ces jours, ou regnoient les moeurs, la bonne foi,   315
In those days, when morals reigned, plain dealing,
Ou la pure nature, etoit l'unique loi;
Or pure nature, was the sole law;
Ou le coeur s'exprimant sans art, & sans contrainte,
When the heart expressing itself without art, and without constraint,
Decouvroit son amour & sans honte & sans feinte;
Discover'd its love without shame and without disguise;
Dans ces jours fortunes l'union & la paix
In those fortunate times union and peace
Avoient pour les humains d'invincibles attraits.   320
Had for mankind invincible attractives.
Les villes, les etats prirent ainsi naissance.
Cities, states thus took birth.
Arbitre de son sort, & dans l'independance,
Disposer of his fortune, and independent,
L'homme ignoroit encor ce pouvoir redoute,
Man knew not yet that formidable power,
Qui dans les mains d'un seul place l'autorite.
Which in the hands of one alone places authority.
Mais bien-tot ce pouvoir devenant necessaire,   325
But soon that power becoming necessary,
On chercha dans un roi moins un maitre qu'un pere.
They sought in a king less a master than a father.
Un mortel genereux, par ses soins, sa valeur,
Did a generous mortal, by his cares, his valour,
Du public, qu'il aimoit, faisoit-il le bonheur?
Of the public, which he loved, procure the happiness?
Admiroit-on en lui les qualities aimables
Did they admire in him the amiable qualities
Qui rendent aux enfans les peres respectables?   330
Which render to children fathers venerable?
Il commandoit sur tous, il leur donnoit la loi,
He commanded over all, he gave them law,

Et le pere du peuple en devenoit le roy.
And the father of the people became their king.

Mr Pope in these lines attempts to give an account of the original of good and happy governments,[4] and succeeds in his design; for his poetical vein makes him equal to any thing. He takes the liberty of supposing[5] such facts as are most agreeable to his scheme.

Jusqu'a ce tems fatal, seul reconnu pour maitre,
Till that fatal period, alone acknowledg'd for master,
Tout patriarche etoit le monarque, le pretre,
Every patriarch was monarch, priest,
Le pere de l'etat qui se formoit sous lui;   335
Father of the state which was formed under him;
Ses peuples apres Dieu n'avoient point d'autre appui;
His people under God had no other support;
Ses yeux etoient leurs loix, sa bouche leur oracle;
His eyes were their laws, his mouth their oracle;
Jamais ses volontes ne trouverent d'obstacle.
Never did his will find resistance.
De leur bonheur commun il devint l'instrument;
Of their common welfare he became the instrument;
Du sillon etonne sortit leur aliment;   340
From the wond'ring furrow he drew forth their food;
Il leur porta les arts, leur apprit a reduire
He brought them arts, taught them to reduce
Le feu, l'air & les eaux aux loix de leur empire;
Fire, air and waters under the laws of their empire;
Fit tomber a leurs pieds les habitans des airs,
Made to tumble at their feet the inhabitants of the air,

---

4. good . . . governments: "Gouvernemens heureux" (p. 248).

5. He takes . . . supposing: "il suppose" (p. 248).

Et tira les poissons de l'abime des mers.
And drew the fishes from the abyss of the seas.

This paragraph is not to be considered as a continuation of the account comprised in the foregoing lines. This would be a great error in chronology; regal authority was not succeeded by patriarchal, but patriarchal by regal.*

Perhaps also men were not so generally or so firmly established as Mr Pope pleases himself in supposing. The sons of the same father are often observed to incline each to his different humour; private interest often outweighs the publick good, and men every day prosecute it by the breach of those laws to which they have consented. Children, as well as older persons, find it easy to believe what they wish to be true, and prevail upon themselves to believe that the Supreme Being will never take an account of their irregularities, or punish them tho' they persevere in disobedience.

The original of arts is ascrib'd in this paragraph, not, as before, to the example of the beasts, but to the instructions of the patriarchs, who have taught their posterity to hunt and fish.

> *Lorsqu'enfin, abbatu sous le poids des annees,*   345
> When at length, drooping under the weight of
>   years,
> *Il s'eteint, & finit ses longues destinees,*

---

*This is one of the criticisms for which there is no foundation, either in the original or translation; for nothing is advanc'd in either, but that, before kings became necessary, each father was the legislator of his own family.⁶

---

6. Thus States were form'd; the name of King unknown,
'Till common int'rest plac'd the sway in one.
'Twas VIRTUE ONLY (or in arts or arms,
Diffusing blessings, or averting harms)
The same which in a Sire the Sons obey'd,
A Prince the Father of a People made.
VI. 'Till then, by Nature crown'd, each Patriarch sate,
King, priest, and parent of his growing state;
On him, their second Providence, they hung,
Their law his eye, their oracle his tongue. (209–18; 210–19)

He deceases, and finishes his tedious fate,
Cet homme, comme un Dieu si long-tems honore,
This man, as a God so long time honoured,
Comme un foible mortel par les siens est pleure.
As a frail mortal by his people is lamented.
Jaloux d'en conserver les traits, & la figure,
Fond to preserve his lineaments, and shape,
Leur zele industrieux inventa la peinture. 350
Their industrious zeal invented painting.
Leurs neveux, attentifs a ces hommes fameux,
Their posterity, mindful of those famous men,
Qui par le droit du sang avoient regne sur eux,
Who by right of blood had reigned over them,
Trouvent-ils dans leur suite un grand, un premier pere;
Find out in their succession one great, one first father;
Leur aveugle respect l'adore & le revere.
Their blind respect him adores and him reverences.

According to Mr Pope, the descendants of a patriarch, equally astonished and afflicted at his death, invented painting to perpetuate his memory; then, gazing on his picture, they by degrees imagine that he is present; they address their discourse to him, invoke his assistance, and at last receive him for their divinity.*

*To comment on a translation is a very adventurous task: the invention of painting, ascribed to the piety of the posterity of the first patriarchs, is an addition by the translator. But Mr Crousaz has notoriously misinterpreted the translation itself, in which there is no mention of divine honours paid to the picture or to the person represented. Men are said, by the English poet, to have been awaken'd, by the death of the patriarch, to reflections upon his original, and to have advanced upwards from father to father, that is, from cause to cause, till their enquiries terminated in one original father, one first, independent, uncreated cause. This account is so clear, that nothing but extreme carelessness could have mistaken it.[7]

---

7. Pope's lines are,

'Till drooping, sick'ning, dying, they began
Whom they rever'd as God to mourn as Man:
Then, looking up from sire to sire, explor'd
One great first father, and that first ador'd. (223–26; 224–27)

By all this I am confirmed in my opinion, that there is a wide difference between history and poetry. The earliest funeral monuments were nothing more than plain columns; painting was the invention of later ages.

Mr Pope in the following verses recollects, that an antient tradition, supported by reason, had taught men to acknowledge the great Creator, who had given being to the universe, for the Master and Governor of it, and that this retarded the progress of idolatry.

> *Cependant la raison venant leur retracer* 355
> Nevertheless reason coming to remind them
> *Que la terre & les cieux avoient du commencer,*
> That the earth and the heavens must have had a beginning,
> *Ce principe certain, conserve d'age en age,*
> That certain principle, preserv'd from age to age,
> *Apprit a distinguer l'ouvrier de l'ouvrage;*
> Taught to distinguish the worker from the work;
> *Mais un seul ouvrier, sans egal, sans adjoint:*
> But one sole worker, without equal, without assistant:
> *En admettre plus d'un, c'est n'en admettre point.* 360
> To admit more than one, is to admit none at all.
> *Avant que l'esprit faux, rebelle a la lumiere,*
> Before false wit, rebel to the light,
> *De ce dogme constant eut franchi la barriere,*
> Of that fixed article had leap'd the barrier,
> *L'homme usoit des presens dont le ciel est l'auteur,*
> Man used the gifts of which heaven is the author,
> *Sans jamais y trouver un piege seducteur.*
> Without ever finding in them a deceitful snare.
> *Loin de regarder Dieu comme un maitre severe,* 365
> Far from regarding God as a severe master,
> *Il le voyoit toujours sous l'image d'un pere;*
> He viewed him always under the image of a father;
> *L'amour de ses devoirs etoit sa seule loi,*
> The love of his duty was his sole law,

Et par ce seul amour il lui marquoit sa foi.
And by that love alone he measured out his faith.
Le droit divin etoit le droit de la nature;
Right divine was the right of nature;
Il presentoit a tous une lumiere pure. 370
It offered to all a pure light.
De l'etre souverain ils n'aprehendoient rien;
Of the sovereign being they stood in no fear;
Ils ne voyoient en lui que le souverain bien.
They regarded him only as the sovereign good.
Ces deux puissans ressorts, la foi, la politique,
Those two potent springs, faith, policy,
Rouloient egalement sur un principe unique;
Rolled equally on one sole principle;
Elles avoient pour but, d'unir dans notre coeur 375
They had for end, to unite in our heart
A l'amour des humains l'amour du createur.
With the love of mankind the love of the creator.

In this manner men ought to live, and in this manner good men undoubtedly lived. The bad made probably a party by themselves, and, that they might be out of the way of molestation, conveyed themselves to other habitations, and left their censurers to talk without condescending to hear them, or giving themselves any concern about their admonitions.

Quel barbare mortel a des ames esclaves,
What barbarous mortal to souls enslaved,
A des peuples captifs dans de dures entraves
To nations captive in hard shackles
Enseigna le premier, malgre l'ordre commun,
Taught first, in spite of the common order,
Que tous en general n'etoient faits que pour un? 380
That all in general were made but for one?
Enorme opinion! exception cruelle
Enormous opinion! cruel exception
Aux points les plus precis de la loi naturelle!
To points the most express of the law of nature!
Tu renverses le monde, aneantis les loix,

> Thou invertest the world, annihilatest laws,
> *Enfantes les tyrans, & degrades les rois.*
> Bringest forth tyrants, and degradest kings.*

There are few men who do not indulge their own particular humours, of which there is so great a variety, that it is impossible that all men should be satisfied. Subjects are for this reason uneasy in their minds, and discontented with their condition; in time they inquire into the cause of their own disquiet, and begin to suspect their governors, at first without daring to tell their sentiments; at length they venture to speak out, and, if they find others of their mind, make no scruple of censuring them openly. Proud and envious tempers take advantage of these dispositions, join in the complaints of oppression and restraint, and set the charms of liberty in the strongest light; and when they have once engaged their adherents by these arts to an insurrection, leave them no other happiness than that of being the blind instruments of their master's will, in whom they expected a protector and deliverer.[8]

> *De la fureur aveugle a l'injustice unie,*   385
> Of blind rage with injustice united,
> *Dans le trouble & l'horreur, naquit la tyrannie.*
> In trouble and horror was born tyranny.
> *Bien-tot, pour affermir sa domination,*
> Soon after to establish her empire,
> *Avec elle parut la superstition;*
> With her appeared superstition;
> *La cruelle, employant son zele fanatique,*
> Cruel she, making use of her fanatic zeal,

---

*The last line of this passage I cannot understand; how can kings be degraded by the supposition that whole nations were made for them?[9]

---

8. their master's will ... deliver: "les volontés de leur nouveau Maître, en qui ils comptoient de trouver un Libérateur" (p. 253).

9. Pope's lines are,

> Who first taught souls enslav'd, and realms undone,
> Th' enormous faith of many made for one;
> That proud exception to all Nature's laws,
> T'invert the world, and counter-work its Cause? (241–44; 242–45)

S'etendit a l'abri du pouvoir despotique. 390
Spread under the shelter of despotic power.

Pride insinuates itself into the hearts of those who serve at the altar, with no less ease than into those of other men, and is not less encouraged and supported by self-love. These persons look upon themselves as distinguished from the rest of the world, and imagine that they have a right to the veneration of mankind on account of their relation to the divinity. Such notions as these incline them to lend their assistance to the support of arbitrary power, with a prospect of being supported by it. And the more to gain the people, they recommend such a religion as suits their taste and their temper, a religion ceremonious, and full of exterior solemnity, but not severely strict with regard to moral duties. The divinity is served, like a grandee, with pomp and show, and great regularity of external worship. Such prejudices as these brought in idolatry as their natural consequence. Great men require such a respect as may keep their inferiors at a distance, and govern them by the intervention of inferior officers. It was anciently, and still continues to be, too much the custom of mankind to judge of the Deity by themselves. Ignorance of nature made them conceive intelligences, each of which had his peculiar province allotted him.[1] They did not stop here. The universe is an assemblage, a collection consisting of a multitude of different parts. It contains men of warlike and peaceable dispositions, men of sanguinary and fiery, as well as of compassionate[2] and moderate tempers: all these mixtures were proper, that the whole might be compleat, and that the Creator might behold in his work a variety more proportion'd to the extent of his power. They fancied that each class of men, as distinguished by their various inclinations, had a peculiar deity presiding over them. To this notion

---

1. which had . . . allotted him: "qui présidoient sur chacune de ses merveilles" (p. 255).

2. compassionate: "voluptueux" (p. 255). It is difficult to account for this uncharacteristic blunder in translation by SJ. Perhaps there was a momentary confusion of "de voluptueux" with "de bonne volonté" or "bienveillant."

did Mars and Bellona, Bacchus and Venus, owe their worship and their adorers. There was no danger that the worship of the gods, established upon this principle, could ever fall to the ground; in such a variety of tempers every man had his patron, his favourite deity, and justified all his conduct by the example of his darling god;[3] as his god was unanswerably vindicated by the notion of a destiny, to which every being was inevitably subject. Such is the philosophy and the divinity of a corrupted heart. The original and progress of idolatry, of which I have here discovered[4] the interior causes in the inclinations of the heart of man, are describ'd in the following lines.

> *Erigea lachement les conquerans en dieux,*
> Erected basely conquerors into gods,
> *Et courba leurs sujets sous un joug odieux.*
> And bow'd their subjects under a hateful yoke.
> *Elle les asservit aux plus folles chimeres,*
> She them subjected to the most foolish chimeras,
> *Fabriqua de ses mains des dieux imaginaires,*
> Framed with her own hands imaginary gods,
> *Dieux foibles, dieux changeans, injustes, emportes,*   395
> Gods weak, gods fickle, unjust, hasty,
> *Jouets des passions, amis des voluptes;*
> The sports of passions, friends of pleasures;
> *Formes par les tyrans, ils en eurent les vices,*
> Made by tyrants, they took their vices,
> *Et de leurs noirs forfaits devinrent les complices.*
> And of their black crimes became the accomplices.

A man made a god is a wild paradox, but, astonishing and incredible as it appears, there is no room for doubting of it.[5]

---

3. To this notion . . . god: "De là un *Mars,* une *Bellone,* un *Bacchus,* une *Venus,* &c. Le Culte des Dieux ne pouvoit tomber. Dans la variété des inclinations des hommes, chacun avoit son Patron, & chacun trouvoit sa justification dans ce que son Dieu faisoit" (pp. 255–56).

4. I have . . . discovered: "je viens de découvrir" (p. 256).

5. a wild . . . it: "un Paradoxe étonnant; mais tout incroyable qu'il paroisse, on n'en sauroit douter" (p. 256).

236   A COMMENTARY

History, both sacred and profane, gives us too many examples of this madness. These deifications were countenanced by the system of subaltern divinities: conquerors, from considering themselves as the favourites of the gods, began in time to think themselves their associates. The conquer'd nations, whatever reasons they might have to hate their new masters, yet, for the sake of avoiding evils which they thought greater, carried their submission so far, as to pretend to believe of their conquerors what they were very far from thinking in reality, and consented that their children should be brought up in those salutary notions, upon which their ease and prosperity so much depended.⁶ Upon these principles, the love of quiet, and regard to interest, Mohametanism has established itself.

> *L'amour-propre effrene voulut tout envahir;*
> Self-love unbridled would all usurp;
> *Du juste & de l'injuste habile a se servir,*   400
> Of just and unjust prompt to serve itself,
> *Il soumit ses egaux a des loix arbitraires,*
> It subjected its equals to arbitrary laws,
> *Fit valoir pour lui seul des droits imaginaires,*
> Made the most use for itself alone of rights
>   imaginary,
> *S'empara des honneurs, des biens & des plaisirs,*
> Laid hold on honours, wealth and pleasures,
> *Et se crut tout permis pour flater ses desirs.*
> And thought itself allow'd every thing to flatter
>   its desires.

The mind of man is formed for a felicity infinitely superior to all the satisfactions which this world can afford; but, instead of searching after untasted happiness, men imagine⁷ that, by adding one enjoyment to another, they shall arrive at length at perfect happiness. When a man has once fixed his

---

6. in those salutary notions . . . depended: "dans des erreurs qui faisoient leur sureté" (p. 257).

7. untasted happiness, men imagine: "d'un nouveau genre, il espére" (pp. 257–58).

chief satisfaction in the pleasure of seeing himself master of others, there is no sort of tyranny which he does not think himself at liberty to exercise.[8] This is the fatal prejudice, in which flatterers make it their practice to confirm those whom it is the interest of mankind to awaken from it. The confusions of anarchy, and the calamities of civil wars, have given occasion to some men, not very scrupulous in their morals or religion, to exhaust their abilities in reducing tyranny to a system, and supporting arbitrary power with a shew of reason.[9]

> *Mais ce meme amour-propre est la premiere cause* 405
> But this very self-love is the chief cause
> *Des digues qu'a son cours la politique oppose.*
> Of the restraints which to its course government opposes.
> *Si l'objet, que je cherche avec empressement,*
> If the object, which I seek with eagerness,
> *Les autres comme moi l'aiment uniquement,*
> Others as well as I love entirely,
> *D'un bien dont cent rivaux veulent la jouissance,*
> Of a good whereof a hundred rivals wish the enjoyment,
> *Je voudrois vainement flater mon esperance;* 410
> I should vainly flatter my hope;
> *Des prieres, des pleurs, un impuissant courroux,*
> Prayers, tears, an impotent anger,
> *Pourront-ils me sauver de leurs efforts jaloux?*
> Will they be able to save me from their jealous efforts?
> *Au defaut de la force une coupable adresse,*
> In default of strength a culpable dexterity,
> *Pour enlever mes biens, emploira la finesse.*
> To rob me of my goods, will make use of cunning.
> *Ainsi la raison veut que, pour ma surete,* 415

---

8. When a man . . . exercise: "s'il le cherche dans le plaisir de se voir Maître des autres, il n'y a rien qu'il ne se permette sur eux" (p. 258).

9. to exhaust . . . reason: "d'employer toute la fécondité de leur génie, à donner une forme de Systéme à l'autorité sans bornes des Monarques" (p. 258).

Therefore reason wills that, for my security,
Je souffre que la loi gene ma liberte.
I suffer that the law shou'd restrain my liberty.

It is to no purpose to decry reason; we must have recourse to it at last, as the only source of our happiness.

> *L'interet est egal, alors chacun conspire*
> The interest is equal, then each agrees
> *A garder de conert ce que chacun desire.*
> To guard in concert what each desires.
> *Pour leur propre avantage a la vertu forces*
> For their own advantage to virtue forced
> *Les rois, meme les rois, furent interesses*   420
> Kings, even kings, were engaged
> *A regner par douceur, & non par violence,*
> To rule by gentleness, and not by violence,
> *A regler les desirs de l'avide puissance;*
> To regulate the desires of greedy power;
> *Et l'amour propre fit un habile trafic*
> And self-love set up a cunning traffick
> *Du bien particulier contre le bien public.*
> Of private good against public good.

There is a great deal of artifice in this commerce; it were to be wished that it were carried on with less cunning, and more honesty. This is a commerce in which every man endeavours to be a gainer, and for that end cheats as much as he can. The *general good* is the pretended motive, but *private good* the real incentive. He gratifies himself most, who most skilfully conceals his real views.

If I am prevailed on by my interest to promise another not to oppose him, I shall keep my word as long as my interest determines me to fidelity, and if our circumstances are such that there is no danger of being convicted of a breach of promise, I shall have no regard to any thing but my own convenience. But if I sincerely love God as I ought, in the highest degree; if I consider it as one of the duties of that unbounded gratitude which I owe to him, to love mankind as his work, as creatures of the same order with myself, honour'd by their Creator with the same regard, and equally called by his grace to acknowledge him as their father; if, under a sense of God's perpetual presence and inspection, I look upon every man as my brother,[1] I shall be very far from making my duty a sacrifice to my advantage, for I shall consider it as my great interest to love them sincerely, and to do them all the good in my power.

> *Alors le ciel forma des hommes magnanimes,* 425
> Then heaven form'd men of great souls,
> *Poetes, orateurs, philosophes sublimes;*
> Poets, orators, sublime philosophers;
> *Les uns pleins de respect pour la divinite,*
> Some full of veneration for the divinity,
> *Les autres par amour de la societe,*
> Others through love of the community,
> *Trouverent cette foi, cette morale pure,*
> Found out that faith, that pure moral,
> *Que leurs premiers auteurs tenoient de la nature.* 430
> Which their first authors held from nature.
> *Ils marcherent au feu de son ancien flambeau,*
> They walked by the light of its ancient torch,
> *Trop sages pour vouloir en chercher un nouveau;*
> Too wise to desire to seek a new;
> *Cherchant du createur a retablir l'ouvrage,*
> Endeavouring of the creator to restore the work,
> *Ils tracerent l'ombre au defaut de l'image.*
> They drew the shadow instead of the image.

> '*Twas* THEN *one studious Head*, &c.[2]

It is no easy matter to guess what period of time Mr Pope intends to mark out by *then;* was it after that age in which

---

1. equally called . . . brother: "appellés à la même grace d'être ses enfans; si sous ses yeux, qui voyent tout, je les aime comme mes freres" (p. 260).

2. SJ adds part of l. 283 (284) of Pope which should read "the studious head." Crousaz refers to "Alors" at the beginning of l. 425 of Du Resnel (p. 261).

*Ev'n Kings learn'd Justice and Benevolence?*³

But the establishment of societies is more ancient, and is ascribed both by poets and historians, to those extraordinary persons that appeared according to our author, after self-love had been circumscribed within its proper limits.⁴

In verse 430 (287 of the original) the word *nature* occurs again.⁵ Mr Pope seems either to be in pain, or out of countenance, at the mention of God in express terms, and rather chuses to veil his thought in dark and ambiguous language.

Was this *nature* from whom the ancients received their morality the corporeal world? Or rather revelation and inspiration from above? Did it consist in clear ideas, and consequences evidently resulting from them? Or is this name to be given to the first inclinations of animal nature?

The men of whom Mr Pope speaks,⁶ were too wise not to wish for new light. The want of it was obvious to the great Socrates. The insufficiency of natural light is evident by experience, and those who profess to desire no other give every day new proofs of it. They would be ashamed to make tryal of the direction given them by our blessed Saviour:⁷ *He who shall desire to do the will of him who hath sent me, shall know whether I teach men on his behalf, or only speak to them of my own head.* John vii. 16, 17.

> *On dut a leurs avis ces salutaires loix,*   435
> We owe to their counsel those wholesome laws,
> *Qui reglent le devoir des sujets & des rois;*
> Which regulate the duty of subjects and of kings;
> *Ils leur apprirent l'art d'user leur puissance,*

---

3. SJ substitutes l. 280 (281) of Pope for Crousaz's quotation from ll. 420, 422 of Du Resnel (p. 261).

4. to those extraordinary . . . limits: "attribuent la naissance des Etats & la formation des Sociétés Politiques, à ces Hommes extraordinaires qui parurent, si l'on en croit Mr. POPE, après qu'on fut venu à bout d'assigner des bornes à l'Amour propre" (p. 261).

5. The Faith and Moral, Nature gave before (286; 287).

6. The men . . . speaks: "Les Hommes dont Mr. POPE fait ici l'éloge" (p. 262).

7. our blessed Saviour: "JESUS-CHRIST." SJ provides the citation (p. 262), but translates the French rather than quoting the Authorized Version.

They taught these the art of using their power,
Et sans trop de rigueur, & sans trop d'indolence;
Both without too much rigour, and without too much indolence;
Malgre l'ordre inegal & des biens & des rangs,
Notwithstanding the unequal disposition both of wealth and of places,
Ils lierent entr'eux les petits & les grands.   440
They united among themselves the little and the great.
Un seul est opprime; des rapports infaillibles
An individual is oppressed; the relation inviolable
Rendent a son malheur tous les autres sensibles.
Renders of his misfortune all the others sensible.
D'un desordre apparent vint un ordre reel;
From seeming disorder came real order;
Des divers interets le choc continuel
Of different interests the continual jarring
Produisit de soi-meme un concert agreable,   445
Produced from itself an agreeable harmony,
Et l'etat prit enfin une forme durable.
And the state took at length a lasting form.
Tel est de l'univers l'harmonieux accord,
Such is of the universe the harmonious accord,
Ou, par leur union, par leur commun effort,
Where, by their union, by their joint effort,
Dans un ordre constant, les differentes causes
In a constant order, different causes
Aux desseins du tres-haut ramenent toutes choses.   450
To the purposes of the most high bring all things.
Sans pouvoir se soustraire a ses pressantes loix,
Without power to retreat from his coercive laws,
Homme, anges, animaux, maitres, esclaves, rois.
Man, angels, animals, masters, servants, kings,
Courent au meme but d'une vitesse egale,
Tend to the same point with swiftness equal,
Et servent de concert a la fin generale.
And help in concert towards the general end.

To pretend that all created beings tend to the same end with equal swiftness, is to confound physicks and morality. These notions, which recur very often in this author, may be abused to a very enormous end. For if there be a mutual influence and dependance[8] between the different parts of the universe, if a man be only moved in consequence of some operation of external agents, if no single part acts or suffers any thing but what contributes to the advantage of the whole, every man who interests himself in the general good must, at the close of every day, however spent,[9] review all his actions with satisfaction, because he has done nothing which has not promoted the general interest of the universe, or which the perfection of the whole, or the connection of its parts, did not make necessary.

> *Que les speculatifs recherchent follement*   455
> Let the theorists inquire foolishly
> *Quel plan est le meilleur pour le gouvernment;*
> What plan is the best for government;
> *Tel qu'il soit le meilleur, c'est le plus equitable,*
> Whatever be the best, it is the justest,
> *Et dont le bien public est l'objet immutable.*
> And that of which the common weal is the
>   immutable object.

Yet in what did these celebrated men, these gifts of heaven, upon whom Mr Pope has congratulated the world, and whose praises he has just been writing, employ their abilities more than in establishing maxims, by the exact observation of which, sovereigns might govern with less fatigue, and subjects live in more security and quiet, and feel less pain from the necessity of obeying.[1]

> *Laissons les faux zeles, dans leur prevention,*
> Let us leave false zealots, in their prejudice,

---

8. influence and dependance: "influent" (p. 263).
9. SJ adds "however spent."

1. In Crousaz this paragraph ends with a question mark (p. 264).

THIRD EPISTLE   243

>   *Parler aveuglement de la religion:*   460
>   To talk blindly of religion:
>   *Tout ce qui contredit cette fin principale,*
>   Whatever contradicts that principal end,
>   *Que Dieu se proposa pour sa loi generale,*
>   Which God proposed to himself for his general law,
>   *Porte visiblement l'empreint[2] de l'erreur;*
>   Carries visibly the stamp of error;
>   *Mais la religion qui, corrigeant le coeur,*
>   But the religion which, mending the heart,
>   *Seule procure a l'homme un bonheur veritable,*   465
>   Alone procures to man a true felicity,
>   *Ayant Dieu pour auteur, est seule respectable.*
>   Having God for author, is only to be regarded.

Mr Pope succeeds no better in his divinity than his philosophy: he advanced in other places assertions utterly inconsistent with that religion which he now affirms to be the only one that is worthy of God. The religion of the earliest ages, which was the purest, was the common religion of man and beast. Was this the school where we and our fellow-students, the other animals, learned our morality, and kindled in ourselves the love of goodness? Was it here that this author learned to advance that *creatures have nothing to apprehend from the Supreme Being;* to break down the restraints of fear, so necessary to the greatest part of mankind, and to put an end to the necessity of vigilance and self-examination, which is superfluous as well as troublesome? Since *man, beast and angel, servant, lord and king, tend to one point, and one center;*[3] since all our vices, our crimes, our pride, and our vanity, all tend to the same end, and since all is right. Take all this away from religion, what is there left to convince us that our duties are of indispensable obligation?[4] The bad

---

2. Crousaz correctly has "l'empreinte" (p. 265).

3. Since *man, beast ... center:* "*Hommes, Anges, Animaux, courons au même but, avec la même vitesse*" (265). This is a rare example in SJ's writings of an incomplete sentence.

4. indispensable obligation: "d'une observation indispensable" (p. 266).

consequences[5] of such passages as these are discovered by the elegant translator, who has therefore soften'd the expression more than once.

> *L'homme, ainsi que la vigne, a besoin de support;*
> Man, just as the vine, hath need of support;
> *Il lui faut des liens, pour le rendre plus fort.*
> He must have bands, to make him stronger.

Fear is one of those restraints by which men are hindered[6] from deviating so often from the end of their being, as they would do if they were left entirely at liberty, and dared to say to themselves every night, *All that has been done to-day was right.*

> *Comme ces feux du ciel, ces planetes brillantes,*
> As those lights of heaven, those shining planets,
> *Qui roulent sur leur axe en leurs marches constantes,*   470
> Which roll upon their axis in their constant marches,
> *Du meme mouvement, qui subsiste toujours,*
> With the same motion, which always subsists,
> *Vont autour du soleil continuer leurs cours,*[6a]
> Go on round the sun to continue their courses,
> *Quoi qu'opposes entr'eux, cependant compatibles,*
> Though opposite to one another, yet consistent,
> *L'homme eprouve en son coeur deux mouvemens divers,*   475
> Man finds in his heart two different motions,
> *Dont l'un tend a lui-meme, & l'autre a l'univers.*
> Of which one tends to himself, and the other to the universe.

It would be, in my opinion, a juster notion to suppose two motives of action implanted in man, the love of himself, and the love of God. He is by the one capable of gratitude and of happiness, and rises by the means of the other to the source

---

5. The bad consequences: "les inconvéniens" (p. 266).

6. by which men are hindered: "qui sert puissamment à le retenir" (p. 266).

6a. The following line (473) is omitted: Ainsi par des rapports reels, mais insensibles (p. 205).

of virtue and felicity. This self-love is never extinguished: but when he attends to the nature of God, to the gifts he has received from him, and the gratitude which he owes for them, he is ravish'd with the thought, carried away, and wholly engrossed by admiration; he forgets his own passions, views, and pursuits,[7] to devote himself entirely to the service of God. This devotion so just, and so well grounded,[8] is not long without its reward, but soon produces happiness.[9] At this accession of felicity his gratitude is doubled, and his piety gains new strength. Thus by these two motives he experiences in the present life the first dawn of that perfect felicity which in a future state he shall enjoy without interruption.

> *Par l'ordre merveilleux qui regne en ses parties,*
> By the wonderful order which reigns in its parts,
> *Qui pour la meme fin les tient assujetties,*
> Which to the same end keeps them subordinate,
> *L'amour propre & l'amour de la societe,*
> Self-love and love of the community,
> *Tous deux de meme espece, ont meme utilite.* 480
> Both of the same kind, have the same use.

The idea of an universe, formed with a mutual dependance of one part upon another, in the manner of a machine, which only he who formed and regulated it has power to disconcert, has something grand and magnificent; it is confused indeed,[1] but does not strike the imagination less forcibly. It is, upon the whole, a fine subject for poetry, and therefore Mr Pope very frequently returns to it.

But this idea, adopted in its full extent, will lead us to very destructive consequences;[2] for if, by the immutable order of things, my motions have an influence upon the whole universe, the whole universe must unite its influence to act upon

---

7. his own passions ... pursuits: "soi-même" (p. 267).

8. well grounded: "si dû" (p. 267).

9. but soon produces happiness: "sa félicité en est la suite infaillible" (p. 267).

1. which only ... indeed: "que celui qui en a rangé l'ordre a seul le pouvoir de démonter, présente une grande idée, confuse à la vérité" (p. 268).

2. will lead ... consequences: "on pourroit faire un très grand abus" (p. 268).

me, and necessitate my motions and determinations. Here then is an end of morality; every thing that comes to pass, comes to pass by physical necessity. Whatever I do, good or bad, however I may seem to act by choice, is inevitably determin'd by a chain of causes not to be broken; and therefore I may justly look upon myself as out of the reach of reproach or punishment.[3] This is the pleasing consequence by which men have been allur'd to adopt the most incredible system that was ever formed.

---

3. reproach or punishment: "tout reproche & de toute punition" (pp. 268–69).

COMMENTARY ON THE FOURTH EPISTLE

O bonheur, le mobile & la fin de tout etre!
O happiness, the first mover and the end of all beings!
Sous quel nom aux humains te ferai-je connoitre?
Under what name to mankind shall I make thee known?
Tranquillite, douceur, plaisir, contentement,
Tranquillity, ease, pleasure, contentment,
Charmant je ne sai quoi, qu'un secret sentiment,
Charming I know not what, which a secret sentiment,
Qu'un soupir eternel incessamment appelle; 5
Which an eternal sigh incessantly invokes;
Toi! dont l'espoir flateur, dans leur course mortelle,
Thou! whose flattering hope, in their mortal course,
Endurcit les humains contre les coups du sort,
Hardens mankind against the strokes of fate,
Qui leur fais sans palir envisager la mort;
Who makest them without turning pale to look death in the face;
Objet fixe & changeant dont les fous & les sages
Object fixt and changing, of which the fools and the wise
Se forment tour a tour de confuses images, 10
Form to themselves successively confused notions,
Qui toujours pres de nous trompes notre desir,
Which always near to us bilkest our desire,
Et fuis dans le moment ou l'on te croit saisir;
And flyest in the moment when we think to seize thee;
Plante! qui dans les cieux as pris ton origine,
Plant! which in the heavens hast taken thy root,
Si portee ici-bas par une main divine
If brought here below by a hand divine
Tu juges des mortels dignes de t'elever, 15
Thou judgst mortals worthy to nurse thee,
Di-nous en quel climat ils peuvent te trouver.

Tell us in what climate they may find thee.
Est-ce aux rayons trompeurs d'une cour opulente
Is it in the deceitful rays of a wealthy court
Qu'on voit s'epanouir ta beaute ravissante?
That we see blooming thy ravishing beauty?
Sors-tu des lieux profonds, qui derobent aux yeux
Risest thou from deep places, which cover from the eyes
De l'or, du diamant les tresors precieux? 20
Of gold, of diamonds the precious treasures?
Peut-on, dans les transports d'une savante yvresse,
Can we, in the raptures of learned drunkenness,
Te trouver sur les bords qu'arrose le Permesse?
Find thee on the banks water'd by the Permessus?
Ou doit-on te chercher a l'ombre des lauriers,
Or must we seek thee under the shade of laurels,
Que la gloire promet aux travaux des guerriers?
Which glory promises to the labours of warriors?
Quels sont les champs heureux ou tu te plais a naitre? 25
Which are the happy fields where thou art pleas'd to grow?
Quels sont les tristes lieux ou tu crains de paroitre?
Which are the dismal places where thou dread'st to appear?
Quand pour te voir fleurir nous travaillons en vain,
When to see thee flourish we labour in vain,
Accusons la culture, & non pas le terrain.
Let us blame the culture, and not the soil.
Le plus affreux sejour, le lieu le plus-tranquille,
The most frightful abode, the seat most peaceful,
Au bonheur tour a tour peuvent servir d'azile. 30
To happiness in their turn may afford a sanctuary.
Ou l'on ne doit jamais le voir & le gouter,
Either we are never to see it and taste it,
Ou par tout sur nos pas il doit se presenter.
Or every where in our way it must offer itself.
L'or, ce grand seducteur, sur lui n'a point d'empire,
Gold, that great seducer, over it hath no command,

FOURTH EPISTLE   249

> *Le merite lui plait, & la vertu l'attire;*
> Merit pleaseth it, and virtue attracts it;
> *S'il dedaigne des rois la fastueuse cour,*   35
> If it disdains of kings the stately court,
> *Il a chez toi, milord,*[4] *etabli son sejour.*
> It has with you, my lord, established its residence.

To deplore with so much elegance and wit the misery of man who languishes after happiness, the great and constant scope of all his endeavours,[t] without even knowing where to search for it; to lament such evils with so free and so fruitful an imagination, the poet must certainly have a mind very much at ease, which he has doubtless obtained by living with his lord and friend.[5]

But is this true happiness? Is this the place whither we must all go to search for it? Mr Pope talks in another strain, and tells us that

> *'Tis no where to be found, or every where.*[6]

Happiness then, this happiness which we all so passionately pant after, is at no great distance from me;[7] this kind assurance revives my hopes, but unhappily my hopes last but for a moment, and are soon succeeded by new perplexities; I am in the hands of a poet, who does with me just what he pleases, and who, after having led me almost[u] to the seat of happiness, shuts up all the avenues that lead to it.

> *Ask of the Learn'd the Way, the Learn'd are blind,*
> *This bids to serve, and that to shun Mankind;*
> *Some place the Bliss in Action, some in Ease,*

---

t. en-|vours   u. lamost

---

4. Crousaz has "Mylord" (p. 270).

5. to lament . . . friend: "pour déplorer de si grands maux avec tant d'esprit, d'élégance, & une imagination si libre, si riche, si féconde, il faut avoir l'esprit bien content, & se trouver fort à son aise. D'où lui vient ce rare bonheur? C'est qu'il a *établi son séjour* chez son Lord & son ami" (p. 271).

6. SJ substitutes l. 16 of Pope for Crousaz's quotations from ll. 31 and 32 of Du Resnel (p. 271).

7. Happiness then, this . . . me: "Il est donc près de moi" (p. 271).

Those call it Pleasure, and Contentment these:
Who thus define it, say they more or less
Than this, that Happiness is Happiness?
One grants his Pleasure is but Rest from Pain;
One doubts of all; one owns ev'n Virtue vain.
Take Nature's Path, and mad Opinion's leave,
All States can reach it, and all Heads conceive.[8]

Au solide bonheur quel chemin peut conduire?
To solid happiness what path can lead?
Philosophes fameux, daignez nous en instruire.
Ye famous philosophers, condescend to instruct us
  in it.
Mais vous ne debitez, que songes incertains.
But ye utter no more than idle dreams.
L'un veut que je me livre a servir les humains;   40
One would have me give myself to serve mankind;
L'autre veut qu'en secret une vie inutile
Another would have it that in private a life useless
Me rende, sans emplois, satisfait & tranquille;
May render me, without business, satisfied and calm;
Celui-ci moins sense me repond vaguement,
This less judicious answers me loosely,
Qu'il place le bonheur dans le contentement;
That he places happiness in contentment;
Celui-la, du plaisir esclave volontaire,   45
That other, of pleasure the voluntary slave,
Le croit pour le bonheur un secours necessaire;
Thinks it to happiness a necessary help;
Un autre, condamnant jusqu'au moindre desir,
Another, condemning ev'n the least desire,
Croit qu'un[9] *vivant sans peine on vit avec plaisir.*

---

8. SJ adds ll. 19–28 of Pope. This passage was extensively revised for the Pope and Warburton collected edition of 1743. See the Twickenham Edition, p. 130.

9. Crousaz correctly has "qu'en" (p. 272).

> Believes that in living without pain he lives without pleasure.
> *Honteux egarement! trop aveugle ignorance!*
> Shameful mistake! too blind ignorance!
> *Jamais du vrai bonheur ils n'ont connu l'essence.* 50
> Never of true happiness have they known the nature.
> *D'autres doutent de tout, & par un fier dedain*
> Others doubt of all, and by a proud disdain
> *Refusent de chercher un bonheur incertain.*
> Refuse to seek an uncertain happiness.
> *De ces guides trompeurs fuyez la route obscure,*
> Of these deceitful guides fly ye the dark road,
> *Et suivez constamment les pas des¹ la nature.*
> And follow constantly the steps of nature.

I may, perhaps, be told on this occasion that I complain of Mr Pope without reason, and that he shuts up all the avenues but one, to prevent my choice of the wrong. But I cannot help renewing my complaints: he seems, indeed, to shew me that single true way, but in effect leaves me still ignorant of it. He points out a wide road at a great distance, which, when I enter it, divides into many different paths.

> *Take Nature's Path*——²

Once more what is the meaning of the term NATURE? Is *nature* the Author of the Universe? How shall I know his voice? Is it the visible³ work of that author? But among the multitude of objects that press upon my senses, what choice shall I make? Or what rules must I follow? Am I to take *reason* for my guide? She, according to our author, has been already consulted by the philosophers to no purpose. Shall I give myself up to *animal nature*? One is often put to pain by this conduct. Thus surrounded with uncertainties, what have I to do but go

---

1. Crousaz correctly has "de" (p. 272).
2. SJ substitutes l. 29a (27a) of Pope for Crousaz's quotation of l. 54 of Du Resnel (p. 273).
3. visible: "même" (p. 273).

on at random? And he that directs me to take *nature's path,* only advises me *to sail passively down the stream of fatality.*⁴

Shall I not too rashly expose myself to the character of a paradoxical writer,⁵ if I affirm, that the reason why men do not attain to the knowledge of true happiness is, that they make too much haste to search after it. This enquiry supposes another, which ought to precede it. Of this notion I am convinced of the truth, and if others are inclined to attain the same conviction, let them form the idea of a man newly sent forth out of the hands of his Creator, with all the powers of his mind in full strength. "I am here," says he, "one of the number of beings; this existence I have but lately received; I now think, perceive, and find in myself a perpetual succession of perceptions, and see myself surrounded by an immense assemblage of wonders." *If he should then add,* "Since I am placed here, it is my business to make the most of life, and to turn every thing about me to the greatest advantage, to keep my thoughts constantly intent upon my own interest, and consider every thing with a view to my own satisfaction," would not these resolutions appear too precipitately form'd? Would he not think more justly thus: "I am not the author of my own existence; a few moments ago I had no being; and so far am I from having given being to myself, that I am at a great distance from the true knowledge of my own nature. How can I better begin my life than by studying myself, and endeavouring[v] to know what this being is that I have now received, and what I owe to him who conferred it on me. Wherever I turn my eyes⁶ I see instances of wisdom and goodness that ravish and charm me? The wonderful relations between me and every thing about me convince me that the common Creator

v. en-|vouring

---

4. *to sail . . . fatality:* "*marcher constamment sur les traces de la Fatalité*" (p. 273). Here SJ changes Crousaz's metaphor to a favorite of his own. Cf. especially *The Vanity of Human Wishes,* l. 346.

5. *Shall . . . writer:* "Ne me hazarderai-je point trop, & ne craindrai-je point d'avancer un sentiment qui paroitra trop paradoxe" (p. 273).

6. *Wherever . . . eyes:* "Mais dès les premiers coups d'oeil" (p. 275).

FOURTH EPISTLE

formed us all. Thou universe! that in all thy parts settest his wisdom, his power, his greatness, and his incomprehensible and unutterable goodness so conspicuously before my eyes! What art thou but the temple of his glory? Wilt thou hide him from my sight for ever? Shall I be allowed to adore and to love him, to pay him my thanksgivings, and devote myself to his service? May I be permitted to hope that he will inform me of the end for which I was created, and of the duties which he requires from me? That he will honour me with his commands, and grant me the infinite happiness of obeying him? This is the hope that makes me rejoice at the existence which I enjoy; and if this happiness be denied me, that life, which I exulted in so lately, will become a burthen."

Let us now suppose that while our new-created man is revolving such thoughts as these, and passing successively from a state of the darkest ignorance to some degree of knowledge, from strong desire to faint hope, and from those hopes to fears that depress and overwhelm him, he is accosted on a sudden by a being like himself, who, seeing perturbation and inquietude in his look and gesture, inquires the reason,[7] and being told it, returns this answer: "I have myself passed through the same perplexities and agitations of mind,[8] and am sent to you by Divine Providence, that I may communicate to you those favours which I have received. You are my brother, and we have both the same father, one common Creator: him we are permitted to love and adore; and lest the infinite distance between him and thee should affright, or at least discourage, thee from daring[9] to approach him, he is pleased to receive this love and adoration as homage due to his nature, and to be himself the reward of that zeal which you feel to obey him. Your most active diligence, and your most fervent acknowledgments, can add nothing to his felicity: he

---

7. who, seeing . . . reason: "qui, à son air, le reconnoit très agité, & lui en demande la cause" (p. 276).

8. same perplexities . . . mind: "mêmes agitations" (p. 276).

9. daring: "ôte" (p. 277). SJ seems to have confused "ôter" with "oser."

contains not only all perfection, but all happiness in himself. But your benevolence to mankind, and the kindnesses they shall receive from you, will be accounted by his infinite goodness as actions performed for his service; you are therefore to look upon other men, as they are his children, to be your brothers."

This kind friend, having discover'd to him all these truths, continues to confirm them, by all the arguments which natural reason suggests, and which revelation compleats.

The perplexities of this new man are soon changed to raptures and transports,[1] and he perceives, in a very different manner than before, how great happiness it is to have received the gift of life.[2] He does not, indeed, see God with his corporeal eyes, but he doubts no more of his presence than if he was perpetually visible.[3] He feels his presence in his inward faculties, and is convinced that God alone excites in him those motions of heart which no language can express, to which no other felicity bears any proportion, and which therefore can proceed only from God the fountain of happiness.[4]

All that he has is the gift of God, even the power of devoting himself to his service. This devotion is accepted by God, who sheweth his approbation by recompences worthy of infinite beneficence. These favours redouble his gratitude, and his increase of gratitude procures him new favours. — Let not these be looked upon as empty notions, or the dreams of enthusiasm; he that has never known this reciprocation of grace and gratitude is yet unacquainted with all real happiness.[5]

---

1. raptures and transports: "ravissemens" (p. 277).

2. to have ... life: "d'avoir reçû la vie" (p. 278).

3. than if ... visible: "que s'il le voyoit" (p. 278).

4. God ... happiness: "Dieu seul peut naître des sentimens, dont rien n'approche, qu'aucune expression ne peut représenter, & qui par là portent incontestablement le caratére de leur adorable Auteur" (p. 278).

5. Let not ... happiness: "Qui n'a pas éprouvé ces retours, ignore encore ce que c'est que Félicité" (p. 278). The dash which sets off this passage does not appear in the original. In fact, SJ adds "Let not these ... dreams of enthusiasm."

Nor is this all: these transports of mind influence the corporeal senses. The creation is beheld with new pleasure by him that thinks, while he looks upon it, "This is the work of my Creator, which is with the utmost justice the subject of my admiration; since the plan was conceived by infinite wisdom, and executed by almighty power. Even he himself looks with pleasure on these beings, which are the work of his own creation, and formed in pursuance of his own idea." He then resigns up himself to admiration, and contemplates the universe with a sense of pleasure, far more quick and penetrating than that of those cold spectators who are distracted with the low cares and pleasures of life.[6] The pleasing images, which mutually strike the mind from the action of different objects upon the senses, become much more pleasing, and derive almost an infinite value from the thought that they are the gifts of his eternal master the God whom he adores.

When his mind is thus enlarged by looking on the magnificence of nature as his own possession, and by contemplating the gifts which he has received from his Creator, he considers all the superfluities of life as too worthless and contemptible to claim any part either of his time, or of that wealth, which he can employ in the relief and assistance of his brethren, who are equally with himself the care of their common Father.[7]

As he is the work and image of the Eternal Being, he loves himself, and endeavours after the perfection of his own nature. He now knows in what the perfection of man consists, and looks with contempt and detestation upon every being that tends to corrupt or debase him.

To such truths as these we may justly apply that judicious line of Manilius,

---

6. contemplates the universe . . . life: "il la lui livre avec une tout autre vivacité, que celle avec laquelle le contemple l'esprit dissipé des hommes du monde" (p. 279).

7. When his mind . . . Father: "Enrichi à la vûë de tant de grandeurs, & satisfait par le sentiment de tant de présens, le superflu lui paroit trop petit pour y destiner ni une partie du tems, ni une partie des revenus qu'il est en pouvoir de consacrer à l'utilité des hommes ses freres, les objets de l'attention de son Dieu" (p. 279).

Ornari Res ipsa negat, contenta doceri.[7a]

This great subject stands not in need of borrow'd ornaments, it affects the mind by its own importance, and to raise attention wants only to be mention'd.[8]

All that Mr Pope will say in the following pages with truth and reason is comprised in these principles, and all that does not flow naturally from them, is mere empty sound, a vapour that will vanish of itself.[9]

One more argument which seems, in my opinion, equally satisfying to the reason and passions, and which may convince us that we are born to derive our happiness, from the reflections of which I have here exhibited a specimen, is, that all other pleasures lose their power to delight by their continuation, and we still require variety to preserve ourselves from weariness and disgust. This happiness grows every day greater, these transports stronger as they are more frequent, nor does the pleasure of piety pall by repetition.[1]

> *Oui, sur tous les esprits, & sur tous les etats,*   55
> Yes, on all minds, and on all conditions,
> *Le bonheur fait briller ses solides appas.*
> Happiness makes to shine its solid charms.
> *Au gre de nos desirs il s'offre de lui-meme,*
> To the bent of our desires it offers itself of its own accord,
> *Et dedaigne toujours ce qui tend a l'extreme?*[2]
> And disdains still what tends to the extreme?
> *Qui possede un sens droit, qui possede un bon coeur,*

7a. The subject of itself precludes adornment, content but to be taught (Manilius, *Astronomica* 3.39).

8. This great subject . . . mention'd: "*Ce grand sujet se refuse aux ornemens; il n'a pas besoin de secours & d'emprunt pour briller; il tire sa force de lui-même; & pour la faire sentir, il suffit de la présenter*" (p. 280).

9. is comprised . . . itself: "se trouvera enté sur ces principes, & ce qui n'en découlera pas, est une écume, qui s'évanouïra d'elle-même" (p. 280). SJ translates "enté sur" ("grafted on") as "comprised in" and "écume" ("foam" or "froth") as "vapour."

1. This happiness . . . repetition: "au lieu que ceux-ci deviennent d'autant plus vifs qu'ils sont plus fréquens; on n'y sauroit trop revenir" (p. 281).

2. Crousaz correctly has a semicolon (p. 281).

He who has a right sense, who has a good heart,
A dans son propre fonds la source du bonheur. 60
Hath in his own fund the source of happiness.
Chacun se plaint du ciel, & follement l'accuse
Every one complains of heaven, and foolishly charges it
De prodiguer a l'un ce qu'a l'autre il refuse;
With lavishing on one what to another it refuses;
La raison est pour tous, & ce riche present
Reason is for all, and this noble gift
Est pour les rendre heureux un moyen suffisant.
Is to make them happy a means sufficient.

Mr Pope is reduced once more to the necessity of restoring reason to her just claims.

Mortels, je le repete, une loi generale 65
Mortals, I repeat it, a general law
Determine toujours la cause principale.
Determines still the principal cause.
Vous voulez que sez[3] *soins ne s'attachent qu'a vous;*
You will that its cares should be devoted only to yourselves;
Elle veut le bonheur non d'un seul, mais de tous.
It wills the happiness not of one alone, but of all.
Dans les dons differens que le ciel distribue,
In the various gifts which heaven distributes,
Sa profonde sagesse a ce principe en vue; 70
Its profound wisdom hath this principle in view;
Tout bien particulier que nous verse sa main
Every particular blessing which his hand pours down on us
Sert au bien general de tout le genre humain.
Conduces to the general good of all the human kind.
"Pourquoi, me direz-vous, le bonheur des mortels
"Why will ye tell me, the happiness of mortals

---

3. Crousaz has "ses" (p. 281).

> *Etant l'unique objet des decrets eternels,*
> Being the entire object of the eternal decrees,
> *Pourquoi dans tous les biens un inegal partage* 75
> Why is there in all the good things an unequal division?
> *Pourquoi ne pas donner a tous meme advantage?"*[4]
> Why is there not given to all the same advantage?"
> *L'ordre, cet inflexible & grand legislateur,*
> Order, that inflexible and great lawgiver,
> *Qui des decrets du ciel est le premier autheur,*
> Who of the decrees of heaven is the first author,
> *L'ordre veut que les uns brillent par sagesse,*[5]
> Order wills that some be conspicuous for wisdom,

Order and the *first author of these laws* are harsh expressions,[6] of which Mr Pope in other passages censures the temerity.

> *Les autres par le rang, ceux-ci par la richesse,* 80
> Others for rank, these for riches,
> *Ceux-la par leurs talens; tandis qu'abandonnes*
> Those for their talents; while destitute
> *Sans aucuns de ces dons la plupart semblent nes.*
> Without any of these gifts the most part seem born.
> *Quiconque du bonheur connoitra la nature,*
> Whosoever of happiness will know the nature,
> *Et bravera des sens l'agreable imposture,*
> And will defy of the senses the pleasing imposture,
> *Ne pensera jamais qu'il ne puisse etre heureux* 85
> Will never think that he cannot be happy
> *Sans le fragile appui de ces biens dangereux.*
> Without the frail support of these dangerous goods.
> *De l'etre souverain l'eternelle sagesse*
> Of the sovereign being the eternal wisdom
> *Pour tous egalement agit & s'interesse,*

---

4. Crousaz correctly has "avantage" (p. 282).

5. Crousaz correctly has "la sagesse" (p. 282).

6. are harsh expressions: "présente des expressions dures, & des idées hardies" (p. 282).

>   For all equally acts and is concerned,
>   *Et de ses dons divers le partage inegal*
>   And of its various gifts the unequal distribution
>   *Devient le fondement du bonheur general.* 90
>   Becomes the foundation of the general happiness.
>   *C'est par ce seul motif qu'elle le fait dependre*
>   It is for this only reason that it makes it depend
>   *Des secours mutuels que nous devons nous rendre;*
>   On the mutual assistance which we ought to
>   render to one another;
>   *Et chacun, attache par ce secret lien,*
>   And every one, ty'd by this secret bond,
>   *Fait le bonheur commun en travaillant au sien.*
>   Makes the common happiness in working out
>   his own.

According to the principles that I have laid down, the happiness of man arises from his adherence to his duty, which duty directs him to dedicate his endeavours to the general good. To endeavour after the good of others, only because he shall by that conduct promote his own private advantage, is to change the true motives of action; but this change does not destroy the order of society.

The abilities of men are very different, but every man has reason to account himself happy, who, by applying his talents to a proper use, of whatever nature or degree they are, secures to himself the approbation of his Almighty Master, who has made the distribution according to his own choice, with which every one ought therefore to be satisfied.

>   *Ce melange etonnant qui regne en la nature,* 95
>   That surprizing medley which reigns in nature,
>   *Des monts & des vallons l'inegale structure,*
>   Of hills and of valleys the unequal structure,
>   *Et du chaud & du froid les contrastes divers,*
>   And of heat and of cold the different contrasts,
>   *Ne concourent ils pas au bien de l'univers?*
>   Do they not concur to the good of the universe?
>   *Des differens etats la trompeuse apparence*

Of different states the fallacious appearance
Ne met dans le bonheur aucune différence. 100
Sets not in happiness any difference.
Il ne change jamais, il est le meme, en soi,
It never changes, it is the same, as to itself,
Dans le plus vil sujet, & dans le plus grand roy.
In the meanest subject, and in the greatest king.
Lorsque de l'eternel la sagesse infini
When of th' eternal the infinite wisdom
Soufla sur les mortels un principe de vie,[7]
Breathed on mortals a principle of life,
Il mit en meme tems, dans le fonds de leur coeur, 105
He placed at the same time, in the bottom of their heart,
Un principe secret d'ou coule le bonheur.
A secret principle whence flows happiness.

*Heav'n breaths through every Member of the whole
One common Blessing as one common Soul,*[8]

is a manner of speaking scarcely clear enough on so great and important a subject.[9]

Mais que distribuant les biens de la fortune,
But if, in bestowing the goods of fortune,
Il en forme pour tous une masse commune,
He of them formed for all a common heap,
De cette egalite naitroient mille debats;
From that equality would arise a thousand contests;
L'homme seroit en proie a d'eternels combats. 110
Man would be a prey to eternal conflicts.
S'il est vrai qu'au bonheur tout mortel peut pretendre,

---

7. Crousaz has "Roi," and "infinie" and "Souffla" (p. 284).

8. SJ substitutes ll. 61–62 (59–60) for Crousaz's paraphrase of ll. 101ff. of Du Resnel (p. 284). SJ in the *Dictionary* and Nathan Bailey before him give "breathe" as the verb.

9. is a manner . . . subject: "ne présentent pas des idées assez nettes & assez instructives pour un sujet si intéressant" (p. 284).

FOURTH EPISTLE

> If it be true that to happiness every mortal may pretend,
> *Et que d'un juste choix le ciel l'ait fait dependre,*
> And that on a just choice heaven hath made it to depend,
> *L'aura-t-il donc place dans des biens superflus,*
> Would he then have placed it in superfluous goods,
> *Plutot duz[1] au hazard qu'a nos propre vertus?*
> Oftener owing to chance than to our own proper virtues?
> *A ses adorateurs la fortune propice*   115
> To her adorers fortune propitious
> *Dispense ses presens au gre de son caprice;*
> Bestows her gifts after her capricious humour;
> *Selon qu'elle est facile, ou rebelle a leurs voeux*
> According as she is condescending or averse to their wishes
> *Le vulgaire les nomme heureux ou malheureux.*
> The vulgar them calls happy or unhappy.
> *Laissons-le s'eblouir d'une fausse apparence:*
> Let us leave it to be dazzled with a false appearance:

The *gifts of fortune*[2] is an expression almost authorised by prescription in poetry, but not to be allowed in a treatise designed for instruction.

> *Le ciel les rend egaux dans sa juste balance.*   120
> Heaven makes them even in its just balance.
> *Vouz[3] verrez les premiers par la crainte agites,*
> You will see the first by fear disquieted,
> *Tandis que les seconds par l'espoir sont flattes.*
> Whilst the second by hope are soothed.
> *Les biens, les maux presens, que le ciel leur envoie,*
> The good things, the evil gifts, which heaven sends them,

---

1. Crousaz correctly has "dûs" and later in the same line "propres" (p. 284).

2. SJ substitutes this phrase for Crousaz's paraphrase of ll. 115–16 of Du Resnel, p. 285). Pope's lines are,

But Fortune's gifts if each alike possest,
And each were equal, must not all contest? (63–64; 61–62)

3. Crousaz has "Vous" (p. 285).

> *Ne font point des mortels la tristesse ou la joie;*
> Cause not at all of mortals the sorrow or the joy;
> *Mais le crainte, ou l'espoir, qu'ils ont de l'avenir,* 125
> But the fear, or the hope, which they have of the future,
> *Font toujours en secret leur peine ou leur plaisir.*
> Cause ever in secret their pain or their pleasure.

By what means is the *just balance of heaven* made *equal?*[4] Is it not because all men, by performing with equal care the duties of their station, may equally hope for the approbation of God? No, says this writer, it is because men are harrassed with fears in proportion to their elevation, and amused with hopes in a state of poverty and distress.[5] But experience will not inform us that these are certain consequences. Men are too much influenced by their natural temper, whether elate or timorous.[6] A man may be good, and therefore happy, either in high or low rank: nor does God, to make the happiness of mankind equal, fill the heart of one with idle fears, and of the other with chimerical hopes.

> *O! quelle est votre erreur, vils enfans de la terre!*
> Oh! what is your error, base children of the earth!
> *Osez jusques aux cieux porter encor la guerre;*
> Ye dare even against heav'n to carry on still a war;
> *Allez, &, par des monts sur des monts entasses,*
> Go, and, by mountains on mountains piled,

---

4. By what means . . . equal?: "Comment est-ce que *le Ciel rend égaux, ceux que le Vulgaire appelle heureux ou malheureux?*" (p. 285). Pope's lines are,

> Fortune her gifts may variously dispose,
> And these be happy call'd, unhappy those;
> But Heav'n's just balance equal will appear,
> While those are plac'd in Hope, and these in Fear:
> Not present good or ill, the joy or curse,
> But future views of better, or of worse. (67–72; 65–70)

5. state of . . . distress: "abbaissement" (pp. 285–86).

6. Men are . . . timorous: "L'humeur influë pour beaucoup sur cette inégalité" (p. 286). This sentence is largely an embellishment by SJ.

FOURTH EPISTLE

Retracez des geans les projets insenses.   130
Draw afresh of the gyants the senseless plans.
Mais d'un bras immortel la foudre vengeresse
But of an immortal arm the avenging thunderbolt
De vos honteux efforts confondra la foiblesse;
Of your shameful attempts will confound the weakness;
Votre rebellion, vos projets, votre orgueil,
Your rebellion, your projects, your pride,
Sous ces rochers brulans vous ouvrent un cercueil.
Under these burning rocks open you a grave.

Here is magnificence of diction, and poetical grandeur, but the words convey no ideas, unless we reduce them to common sense; they then imply only that pride in proportion as it is more insolent, and forgets its own nature too much, deserves to be punished. This punishment supposed just, implies a freedom of action, and a power in man of determining himself to be good or ill. What conduct is punishable *if whatever is, is right,* and the inevitable consequence of an invariable concatenation. For it is to no purpose to banish the ideas of nature to make way for a system that will in spite of our caution be perpetually breaking in upon us.[7]

Sachez que tous les biens, dont la nature sage   135
Know that all the blessings, whereof wise nature
En nous donnant le jour nous procure l'usage,
In giving us the light, procures us the use,
Le charme seducteur, dont s'enyvrent les sens,
The seducing charm, with which the senses are inebriated,
Les plaisirs de l'esprit en encor[8] plus ravissans,
The pleasures of the mind still more ravishing,

---

7. *if whatever is . . . upon us:* "si tout ce qu'on fait est bien, & l'effet d'un arrangement merveilleux auquel il est impossible de rien changer? On a beau chasser à coup de Systême des sentimens naturels, on ne sauroit empêcher que de tems en tems ils ne reviennent" (p. 287).

8. Crousaz has "l'esprit encor" (p. 287).

I own this great and adorable[9] Author of Nature to be the cause of those rational pleasures which deserve to be preferred beyond comparison to those of sense, which only engage us by our own faults, and owe their power over us to a vicious indulgence.

> *Ces biens, qui du bonheur portent le caractere,*
> Those blessings, which of happiness bear the character,
> *Sont la sante, la paix, le simple necessaire.* 140
> Are health, peace, mere necessaries.
> *Lors que sur la nature on regle ses besoins,*
> When by nature a man regulates his wants,
> *Combien s'epargne-t-on de travaux & de soins!*
> How much does he save of pains and of cares!
> *Cherche a suivre en tous points la sage temperance,*
> Seek to follow in all points wise temperance,
> *Un corps robuste & sain en est la recompense.*
> A body robust and sound of it is the recompence.
> *Pour vous, O paix du coeur, digne fille des cieux* 145
> As for thee, O peace of heart, worthy daughter of heaven
> *Vous etes du bonheur le gage precieux.*
> Thou art of happiness the precious pledge.

Peace is that happiness, and by the infinite goodness of God is the certain consequence of true devotion.

> *La fortune, en suivant un aveugle caprice,*
> Fortune, in following a blind caprice,
> *Aux bons comme aux mechans peut se montrer propice;*
> To the good as well as to the wicked may shew herself propitious;
> *Mais en vain de ses dons nous sommes possesseurs,*
> But in vain of her gifts we are possessors,
> *S'ils ne sont merites; ils n'ont plus de douceurs.* 150

---

9. great and adorable: "très sage" (p. 287).

FOURTH EPISTLE

If they are not deserved; they have no more sweetness.

There are multitudes who live without concern about deserving the fortune they enjoy. There are those[w] whose riches are not acquired either by good or bad methods, but received from their ancestors; these are more vain of their wealth in proportion as it has descended to them through a longer line; and as for those that have raised themselves the mere *sons of fortune,* they are surrounded with too many flatterers to have time for reflection upon the arts by which their possessions were acquired.[1]

> *Comparez deux rivaux, dans leur poursuite ardente;*
> Compare two rivals, in their ardent pursuit;
> *Des biens & des honneurs ils ont la meme attente;*
> Of wealth and of honours they have the same expectation;
> *L'un veut y parvenir a force de vertus,*
> The one would arrive thereat by force of virtue,
> *L'autre par des forfaits; Qui des deux risque plus?*
> The other by crimes; Which of the two risks more?

An unshaken virtue on one side, and uninterrupted wickedness on the other, are extremes too much opposed to each other. There is a kind of middle conduct sometimes rising into virtue, and sometimes sinking into wickedness, tho' not flagrant or enormous, which often acquires what are called the gifts of fortune, calmly incurring any great hazards, or awakening the mind, by any horrid guilt, to remorse and reflection. A man of this character goes calmly on, and contracts an habitual carelessness and security.[2]

---

w. those *om.*

---

1. There are multitudes ... acquired: "C'est dequoi le grand nombre ne se met point en peine. Celui qui se trouve riche par une Succession, de Pere en Fils, plus loin elle remonte, plus il en est vain, & la Cour qu'un Enfant de la Fortune se voit, ne lui laisse pas le tems de se rappeller par quelles voies il a amassé ses biens" (pp. 288–89).

2. An unshaken virtue ... security: "Progrès en vertus d'un côté, crimes & forfaits d'un autre, sont des extrémités trop opposées. Une conduite équivoque, qui laisse voir de la vertu de tems en

> *Contemplez, par le sort, la vertue³ poursuivie,*   155
> Contemplate, by fate, virtue persecuted,
> *Aux plus funestes coups sans relache asservie.*
> To the most deadly strokes without intermission subjected.
> *Voyez regner le vice au gre de ses desirs,*
> See vice reigning at the humour of its wishes,
> *Triomphant dans le sein des biens & des plaisirs;*
> Triumphant in the midst of wealth and pleasures;
> *Qui des deux est pour vous un objet respectable?*
> Which of the two is in your account an object to be regarded?
> *Qui des deux, dites-moi, vous paroit miserable?*   160
> Which of the two, tell me, seems to you to be pity'd?

To whom does he address these interrogatories?ˣ To those whose character I have drawn in the comment following v. 50?ʸ They indeed will have sentiments very much of the same kind. But ask the opinion of young libertines, such as are to be met with in the army and great cities, and such as are described by Mr Du Pin in the 12th chapter of his *Instruction to a Son*. This laughing generation will not be on your side. They are insufficiently convinced that they are the great masters of right reason, and are determined not to grow dotards before old age has taken away their senses.[4]

> *Ces biens & ces plaisirs, ou vains ou dangereux,*
> That wealth and those pleasures, whether vain or dangerous,

---

x. interrogato-|gatories   y. 50.

---

tems, & se permet aussi des écarts fréquens, mais modérés, conduit souvent à ce qu'on appelle *Fortune;* elle y conduit sans risque, & forme à l'habitude de ne se faire aucun reproche" (p. 289). The second sentence in this paragraph of SJ's translation is unclear and seems to require a "without." Perhaps it should read "without incurring any great hazards, or awakening the mind" or "calmly incurring any great hazards, without awakening the mind."

3. Crousaz correctly has "vertu" (p. 289).

4. They are insufficiently . . . senses: "Ils croyent le bon sens renfermé chez eux, & n'ont garde de radoter avant que l'âge l'ait affoibli" (p. 290).

> *Qui flatent bassement l'orgueil du vice heureux,*
> Which flatter basely the pride of prosperous vice,
> *Ou la vertue[5] les fuit, redoutant leur surprise,*
> Either virtue flies them, dreading their surprize,
> *Ou sa noble fierte les hait & les meprise.*
> Or its noble haughtiness hates them and despises them.
> *Ce mepris, cette haine, empoisonne les biens*   165
> That contempt, that hatred, poisons the blessings
> *Dont jouit un mechant par d'indignes moyens;*
> Which a wicked man enjoys by unworthy means;
> *Il manque a son bonheur de ne pouvoir pretendre*
> There wants to his happiness the power of pretending
> *Aux respects que les bons refusent de lui rendre.*
> To the respect which good men refuse to pay him.

A man dazzled by fashionable notions, who sees nothing but the bright side of things, and enjoys pleasure without any solicitude about its consequences,[6] is in very little concern at wanting the esteem of men who value themselves upon their virtue. Their disregard appears to him only the effect of stupidity, or ill-breeding, and he makes no scruple of returning their contempt with interest.

> *Funeste egarement! trop aveugles mortels,*
> Fatal mistake! too blind mortals,
> *Que vous connoissez mal les decrets eternels!*   170
> How ill do you understand the eternal decrees!
> *La vertu, selon vous, n'est qu'un triste advantage;*[7]
> Virtue, according to you, is but a melancholy advantage;
> *Selon vous le malheur en est tout l'apanage;*
> According to you misfortune is all its dowery;

---

5. Crousaz correctly has "vertu" (p. 290).

6. A man dazzled . . . consequences: "Un homme ébloui par les idées du monde, un homme qui ne voit que charmes dans les plaisirs" (p. 290).

7. Crousaz correctly has "avantage" (p. 291).

Tandis qu'en ses projets le vice fortune
While in its undertakings vice fortunate
A jouir du bonheur vous paroit destine,
To enjoy happiness seems to you designed,
Qui sait se renfermer dans de justes limites, 175
Who knows to confine himself within just bounds,
Toujours soumis aux loix que le ciel a prescrites,
Always submissive to the laws which heaven hath prescribed,
Attentif a regler son esprit & son coeur,
Mindful to regulate his mind and his heart,
Et dans le vrai chemin qui conduit au bonheur.
Is in the true way which leads to happiness.

These lines are compleatly beautiful and fill'd with ideas entirely just,[8] but these ideas will never become realities without religion.

Voi Turenne arrete dans sa noble carriere,
See Turenne stopt in his illustrious course,
Par un coup foudroyant couche sur la poussiere; 180
By a thundering stroke laid in the dust;
Voi son digne rival, ce coeur plein d'equite,
See his worthy rival, that heart full of justice,
Dans l'horreur du tombeau Barwick[9] precipite;
Into the horrors of the grave Berwick precipitated;
Voi Sidney, voi Falkland, si fiers dans les alarmes,[1]
See Sidney, see Falkland, so stout in arms,
Tout couverts de leur sang, nous demander des larmes.[2]
All cover'd with their blood, demand our tears.
Parle est-ce la virtu[3] *qui termine leur sort,* 185
Say is it virtue that determines their fate,
Ou le noble mepris qu'ils ont fait de la mort?

---

8. These lines . . . just: "Les Vers qu'on vient de lire sont parfaitement beaux; Je conviens encore qu'il présentent de très belles idées" (p. 291).
9. Crousaz has "BARWIK" (p. 291).
1. Crousaz has "allarmes" (p. 291).
2. Crousaz has "armes" (p. 292); Du Resnel has "larmes" (l. 184).
3. Crousaz has "vertu" (p. 292).

> Or the brave contempt which they had conceiv'd of
>   death?
> *Cher Digby! digne objet des pleurs de la[4] patrie,*
> Dear Digby! worthy object of the tears of thy country,
> *Est-ce donc la vertu qui t'arrache a la vie?*
> Is it then virtue that tears thee from life?
> *Des traits les plus brillans apres t'avoir orne,*
> With strokes the most shining after having adorned
>   thee,
> *Comme une jeune fleur t'a-t-elle moissonne?*   190
> As an opening flower hath it cropt thee?

If these heroes, whose names Mr Pope and his translator have transmitted to futurity,[5] were so situated, that their *contempt of life* was a virtue, it cannot, in my opinion, be denied, that their death, which was the consequence of that contempt, was the consequence of their virtue.

> *Si la vertu du fils hata ses destinees,*
> If the virtue of the son hasten'd his fate,
> *Pourquoi, comble d'honneurs, & surcharge d'annes,*[6]
> Wherefore, loaden with honours, and burden'd with
>   years,
> *Le pere jouit-il d'un destin glorieux?*
> Doth the father enjoy a glorious destiny?
> *Lorsqu'aux champs de Marseille un air contagieux*
> When into the fields of Marseilles a contagious air
> *Portoit l'affreuse mort sur ses rapides ailes,*   195
> Brought dreadful death on its rapid wings,

---

4. Crousaz has "ta" (p. 292).

5. have transmitted to futurity: "ont voulu faire vivre les noms" (p. 292). Pope's "heroes" are Lucius Cary, second viscount Falkland; Henri de la Tour d' Auvergne, vicomte de Turenne; Sir Philip Sidney; the Hon. Robert Digby, second son of William, fifth baron Digby; and Belsunce, bishop of Marseille (ll. 93–110). Du Resnel adds James Fitzjames, duke of Berwick, natural son of James II, who entered the service of Louis XIV and rose to the rank of Maréchal de France. For SJ's interest in the duke of Berwick, and his involvement in a 1779 edition of the *Mémoires*, see *Life*, III.286, 522.

6. Crousaz correctly has "d'années" (p. 292).

> *Pourquoi toujours en bute a ses fleches mortelles*
> Why always as a mark to its mortal shafts
> *Un prelat s'exposant, pour sauver son troupeau,*
> A prelate exposing himself, to save his flock,
> *Marche-t-il sur les morts sans descendre au tombeau?*
> Walked over the dead without descending to the grave?
> *Pourquoi le juste ciel, dans cette courte vie,*
> Why does just heaven, in this short life,
> *Qui par tant d'accidens nous est souvent ravie,* 200
> Which by so many accidents is often snatch'd from us,
> *Aux pauvres, comme a moi, preparant des secours,*
> To the poor, as well as me, providing succour,
> *D'une mere que j'aime epargne-t-il[7] les jours?*
> Of a mother whom I love spare the life?

The notions which we have been establishing as the true foundation of solid happiness, do not allow us to look upon the length or shortness of life as any certain mark of the favour or anger of our Creator. It was not proper that Providence should give in this life such visible marks of its decisions; the short life of a beloved person would have made those inconsolable to whom he was endeared by lawful ties of nature or affection. Nor was it agreeable to the design of God that men should be forced to virtue by such evident and sensible motives, as would, in some measure, have taken away the power of choice, and consequently all the value of voluntary obedience.[8]

In these lines[9] Mr Pope shews that there is an entire difference between natural and moral evil, and I am persuaded that some passages of this kind have been so agreeable to the

---

7. Crousaz has "épargne-t-il" (p. 293); Du Resnel has "épargne-t'il" (l. 202).

8. Nor was it . . . obedience: "il ne convenoit pas non plus que les hommes fussent comme forcés à se déterminer à la vertu, par des motifs si grossiers, & qui en auroient obscurci tout le prix" (p. 293).

9. In these lines: "Dans les vers qu'on va lire" (p. 293).

FOURTH EPISTLE

Abbe Du Resnel, that they engaged him to translate the whole work, and made him esteem it fit to be laid before so great a friend to religion as the first prince of the blood.[1]

Qu'est-ce qu'un mal physique? Un changement contraire
What is a physical evil? A change contrary
Au loix de la nature en son cours ordinaire.
To the laws of nature in an ordinary course.
Qu'est-ce qu'un mal moral? Un triste egarement 205
What is a moral evil? A sad deviation
De notre volonte, qui change a tout moment.
Of our will, which changes at every moment.
Dieu, seul auteur du bien, en formant toute chose,
God, the sole author of good, in forming all things,
Du desordre & du mal ne peut etre cause;[2]
Of disorder and of evil cannot be the cause;
Sa sagesse immutable,[3] *en formant l'univers,*
His immutable wisdom, in forming the universe,
Laisse un mouvement libre a ses etrez[4] *divers.* 210
Leaves a principle of motion free to its different beings.
L'homme voit dans le mal une flateuse amorce,
Man sees in evil an alluring bait,
L'admettant dans son sein il en accroit la force.
Receiving it into his bosom he increases its strength.
Lors qu'un fils en naissant apporte un mal cache,
When a son at his birth brings a latent disease,
Fruit honteux des plaisirs d'un pere debauche,
The shameful fruit of the pleasures of a debauched father,
Vous en blamez le ciel; blamez donc sa justice, 215
You for it blame heaven; blame then its justice,
Lors qu'il permet qu' Abel, le juste Abel perisse.

---

1. prince of the blood: "Prince du Sang de France" (p. 294).
2. Crousaz has "la cause" (p. 294).
3. Crousaz correctly has "immuable" (p. 294).
4. Crousaz correctly has "êtres" (p. 294).

When it suffers that Abel, the righteous Abel should perish.

Ne pensez pas que Dieu, comme un timide roy,
Think not that God, like a timorous king,
Changeant a votre gre sa primitive loi,
Changing at your humour his primitive law,
Pour quelques favoris, qu'il adopte & qu'il aime,
For some favourites, whom he adopts and whom he loves,
De ce vaste univers derange le systeme.   220
Of this vast universe disorders the system.
Quoi! pour ceder aux cris d'un sage infortune,
What! to yield to the cries of an unfortunate sage,
D'un tourbillon de feu par tout environne,
With a whirling fire on all sides encompass'd,
L'impetueux Ethna rappellant son tonnerre,
Shall raging Aetna recalling its thunder,
Le renfermera-t-il dans le sein de la terre?
Close it up in the bowels of the earth?
Bethel, lors que l'hyver tu te sens oppresse,   225
Bethel, when in winter thou feelest thyself opprest,
Cedant a tes vertus le ciel sera force
Giving way to thy virtues shall heaven be forced
De fixer des saisons l'inconstance ordinaire,
To settle of seasons the usual inconstancy,
Pour rendre en ta faveur l'air doux & salutaire?
To render for thy sake the air sweet and wholesome?
Suspendra-t il[5] dans l'air un rocher ebranle
Shall it suspend in the air a tottering rock
Parce que sous son poids tu peux etre accable?[6]   230
Because that under its weight thou mayest be crushed?

There is not in this world any necessary connection between morality and the course of natural things, either with

---

5. Crousaz has "Suspendra-t-il" (p. 295); Du Resnel has "Suspendra-t'il" (l. 229).

6. In Crousaz ll. 231–36 of Du Resnel follow this line (p. 295).

FOURTH EPISTLE

respect to good or ill. Moral actions depend upon the free will of man, but physical events fall out by a chain of necessary consequences, which it is nevertheless in the power of the first, or Supreme Cause, to alter or suspend; but this power is rarely exerted. We ought to be thankful for the good that results from this established order, and to be resigned under the evils.

> *Ira-t-il revoquer la loi qui determine*
> Shall he go to repeal the law which determines
> *Chaque corps a tomber du cote qu'il incline?*
> Every body to fall on the side to which it leans?
> *Faudra-t-il d'un vieux temple, abaisse*[7] *par les ans,*
> Must it of an old church, sunk with years,
> *Raffermir tout a coup les pillers*[8] *chancellans;*
> Stay on a sudden the reeling pillars;
> *Attendre que Chartres*[9] *y porte un front coupable?*   235
> To wait till Chartres there carry a guilty front?
> *Et qu'en ce meme instant une voute l'accable.*
> And at that very instant a vault overwhelming him.
> *Que si vous condamnez, dans vos injustes voeux,*
> But if you condemn, in your unreasonable wishes,
> *L'arrangement d'un monde ou le crime est heureux,*
> The regulation of a world where villainy is happy,
> *Suivons pour un moment votre aveugle manie,*
> Let us follow for a moment your blind madness,
> *Mettons dans l'univers plus d'ordre & d'harmonie.*   240
> Let us set in the universe more of order and of harmony.
> *J'en conviens avec vous, des hommes verteux*
> I in it agree with you, virtuous men
> *Meritent le projet que nous formons pour eux.*
> Deserve the scheme which we design for them.

The question asked in these verses seems to be, whether the Almighty could not have formed a world where happiness

---

7. Crousaz has "affaissé" (p. 295).
8. Crousaz has "piliers" (p. 295); Du Resnel has "pilliers" (l. 234).
9. Crousaz has "Charters" (p. 295).

should have been the consequence of virtue?[1] And this, if I understand it right, is in our poet's answer. "Well, suppose a nation only consisting of just men, where will you find them, or how will you make your choice?" Thus he eludes instead of answering the question, which is not whether it be possible to fill a little kingdom with good men, but whether it was not in the power of the Almighty to have filled the whole world with them. This is the important and affecting question; the other is of no use.

> *De justes seulement composons un empire.*
> Of the just only let us form an empire.
> *Mais dans le fond des coeurs Dieu seul a droit de[z] lire;[2]*
> But in the bottom of hearts God alone hath a privilege to read;
> *He! quel autre qu'un dieu pourra nous reveler*   245
> Alas! what other being than a god will be able to discover to us
> *Ces justes que vos soins pretendent rassembler?*
> Those just whom your diligence means to get together?
> *L'un croit voir dans Calvin un organe celeste;*
> One thinks he sees in Calvin a heavenly instrument;
> *Comme un monstre infernal un autre le deteste.*
> As an infernal monster another detests him.
> *Ce qui pour une secte est une verite*
> That which with one sect is a truth
> *Comme un dogme trompeur par l'autre est rejette.*   250
> As a false doctrine by another is rejected.
> *De divers prejuges nos ames possedees*
> With various prejudices our minds possessed
> *Sur les memes sujets ont diverses idees.*
> About the same subjects have different notions.

z. le

---

1. whether the Almighty . . . virtue: "s'il n'auroit pas été plus digne du Tout-Puissant, de former un Monde où la félicité marchat de pair avec la vertu" (p. 296).

2. Crousaz has "de lire" (p. 297).

> *Ce qui fait mon plaisir deviendroit ton tourment;*
> What causes my pleasure would become thy torment;
> *Le prix de ma vertu seroit ton chatiment.*
> The reward of my virtue would be thy punishment.
> *Les plus sages toujours ne pensent pas de meme;* 255
> The wisest do not always think alike;
> *Seroient-ils donc heureux par un meme systeme?*
> Could they then be happy by a like system?
> *Que chacun des mortels en ait un different,*
> Let each mortal have a different one,
> *On verroit bientot naitre un desordre plus grand.*
> We should soon see arise a greater disorder.

Mr Pope here expatiates to show the difficulty of such a choice, but he does not make it appear that God could not easily have peopled a world with such inhabitants; and when it is demanded why he has not done it, if it be true that, from the first impulse that put the universe in motion, all events have had their rise from an establish'd chain of causes, which no created being had power to break or to change, there is no answer in any degree satisfactory to be imagin'd; but we must content ourselves with thinking that as variety was to be the beauty of the universe, an apparent mixture of order and irregularity was necessary, and that the lustre of virtue becomes more amiable and conspicuous by the blackness and deformity of vice.[3] But that vice is not to be avoided by those that are guilty of it, unable as they are to form their own determinations, and free only in appearance; nor can it be conceived that they can be punished with justice, or that they will suffer for what was not chosen but necessary.[4] Such are the sentiments of those philosophers who are at present in fashion. But this shift will by no means clear them from their difficulties; for it may always be asked, Whence it comes to pass that

---

3. that the lustre ... vice: "que la laideur du vice y relevat l'éclat de la vertu" (p. 298).

4. nor can it ... necessary: "ils n'en seront point punis, & ne le pourroient être sans injustice" (p. 298).

wicked men suffer from their vices in this life, and that the good are often prejudiced by those crimes to which they do not contribute?

But when it is acknowledged that the Supreme Being, a being infinitely wise and good, has given his creatures the gift of freewill, that they may procure to themselves the infinite happiness of loving and obeying him, it is easy to comprehend that the transgressions of those who are only miserable by their own fault, by the bad use of that liberty which it was in their power to have employed to better purposes, ought not to provoke God to withdraw from those who persevere in the duties that he has allotted them, that glory and happiness which his bounty has conferr'd upon them.

The trouble and confusion which vice brings into the world, afford those who devote themselves to the service of God, an opportunity of honouring him by the virtue of resignation, and a patient expectation of that happiness with which a future state will recompense their sufferings; a virtue which could not exist if the moral world were without irregularity. Not that God ordained crimes for the sake of producing this virtue, but such is his goodness, that even wickedness has this good effect. In this leaf[5] Mr Pope may justly say,

> *Tout est bien comme il l'est; l'arrangement du monde*
> All is right as it is; the order of the world
> *Prouve de l'Eternel la sagesse profonde.*   260
> Proves of the Eternal[a] the profound wisdom.

It was better that the world should be inhabited by free agents, than by beings whose actions should flow from inevitable necessity, and whose determinations should arise from external causes.[6] The disorders which men occasion by abus-

---

a. eternel

---

5. leaf: "sens" (p. 300). *Leaf:* "A part of a book, containing two leaves" (sense 2 in *Dictionary*). Here SJ is using it to mean "context."

6. and whose determinations . . . causes: "dans l'impuissance où ils seroient de se déterminer" (p. 300).

ing their liberty will cease, and their effects[7] will extend only to those by whom they were produced.

We may observe farther, that Mr Pope's notion of peace,[8] without an uniformity of sentiments, is carried too far. Men are bound to social duties,[9] notwithstanding their different opinions. For my part, I am very grateful for the regard and friendship of persons whose sentiments by no means agree with mine, and never think of the goodness with which they excuse that contrariety, without the warmest affection. I had not always the sentiments which I have at present, and flatter myself that I have changed some opinions for the better, and am very sensible of my obligations to those who have contributed to that change, in which, if they had not had some regard for me, they would not have interested themselves; nor had their endeavours been of any effect, had I had any abhorrence of my instructors. The practical duties of religion, and even the speculative truths in which we agree, ought to unite us for our mutual advantage, and to produce in us esteem and tenderness for each other.[1]

To propose to make a man a better Christian by inciting him to severity against those who differ with him, is to propose to improve him in Christianity by persuading him to abandon it: for what does he less than abandon religion, who renounces that charity and benevolence which is its grand characteristick?[2]

A man who has no views beyond his own immediate gratifications, whose prevailing passion is the desire of surpassing his competitors, and setting his own reputation above theirs,

---

7. their effects: "leurs tristes & justes effets" (p. 300). This is a rare occasion when SJ eschews a doublet.

8. Mr. Pope's . . . peace: "l'idée que Mr. POPE se fait de l'impossibilité de vivre en paix" (p. 300).

9. Men . . . duties: "Il ne tiendroit qu'aux hommes de vivre en concorde & de s'aimer" (p. 300).

1. The practical duties . . . other: "De quelle efficace ne doivent pas être pour nous lier & pour nous engager à un mutuel & charitable support, à nous estimer les uns les autres, & à nous rendre justice, la probité, la douceur, en un mot, la bonne vie & les vérités même de spéculation dont nous convenons?" (p. 301).

2. charity . . . characteristick: "charité est le caractére le plus essentiel" (p. 302).

can hardly preserve his breast from the infection of envy; and ignorance is far preferable to knowledge bought at that price: for however he may imagine himself enlightened, his conduct and his artifices will shew, that his mind is clouded with false notions.³

Upon this subject the succeeding passages brighten upon us, and reason and Christianity after some time take place.

> *A Cesar criminel ce monde abandonne,*
> To guilty Cesar this world left,
> *Aux verteux⁴ Titus ne fut-il pas donne?*
> To virtuous Titus was it not given?
> *Qui fut le plus heureux? l'un dont l'ame hautaine*
> Who was the happier? the one whose haughty soul
> *Fit gemir dans les fers la libertie⁵ Romaine;*
> Made to mourn in chains the Roman liberty;
> *Ou l'autre dont les voeux n'etoient point satisfaits,*   265
> Or the other whose wishes were never satisfied,
> *S'il ne marquoit ses jours par autant de bienfaits?*
> If he did not distinguish his days by as many acts of beneficence?

This is a question which cannot be decided. Perhaps Caesar had all the satisfaction which can arise from the gratification of the ruling passion, as he had subdu'd all rivals, and saw all his attempts attended with success. Perhaps Titus, tender as he was of human kind, might feel no small pain from the oppressions and cruelty that he must frequently observe.⁶

Long life, or an untimely death, are no proofs of either the virtue or the wickedness of those who enjoy the one, or are snatch'd away by the other. Providence makes use of men as they offer themselves for carrying on its purposes. Caesar did

---

3. that his mind . . . notions: "qu'on est encore plongé dans d'épaisses & d'honteuses ténébres" (p. 302).

4. Crousaz correctly has "vertueux" (p. 302).

5. Crousaz has "liberté" (p. 302).

6. might feel . . . observe: "eût beaucoup à souffrir d'y voir régner tant de brutalité" (p. 303).

not deserve long life after having slaughtered thousands and ten thousands,[7] and Providence with great justice snatch'd him early away from the enjoyment of his usurpations. With regard to Titus the Romans did not deserve long an example which they did not imitate.

> *La vertu, direz vous, froidement admiree,*
> Virtue, you will say, coldly admired,
> *A la triste indigence est quelquefois livree,*
> To sorrowful indigence is sometimes abandoned,
> *Et le vice orgueilleux jouit du superflu.*
> And haughty vice enjoys superfluity.
> *Quoi! l'abondance est-elle un prix de la vertu?* 270
> What! is plenty the reward of virtue?
> *C'est le prix du travail; les soins, la vigilance*
> It is the reward of labour; care, vigilance
> *Doivent meme aux mechans procurer l'abondance;*
> Must even to the wicked procure plenty;
> *C'est bien la meriter que d'affronter les mers,*
> It is richly to deserve it to outbrave the seas,
> *Ou pour l'avidite tant d'ecueils sont couverts.*
> Where for greediness so many rocks are covered.
> *Le sage est quelquefois ami de l'indolence,* 275
> The wise man is sometimes a friend of indolence,
> *Et d'un oeil dedaigneux regarde l'opulence;*
> And with a disdainful eye looks on wealth;
> *Le seul contentement est l'object*[8] *de ses voeux.*
> Contentment alone is the object of his wishes.

The author appears, at the first view, rather to evade, than answer the question which is frequently produced by the distresses of the good; but an attentive reader may collect from him a satisfactory answer.

A man is not to expect that he shall obtain what he does not endeavour after; we must steer towards that point at which

---

7. thousands and ten thousands: "un million de personnes" (p. 303).

8. Crousaz correctly has "objet" (p. 304).

we wish to arrive. A man[9] whose chief attention is employ'd upon his duty, and whose care is to omit no opportunity of practising it, is less solicitous to acquire wealth, if he has it not, than to use it, if Providence has conferred it on him, to good purposes. The good archibishop of Cambray managed his revenue in such a manner as to owe nothing, and to have nothing to spare. The bishop[1] of Salisbury maintained and taught in his house a number of young divines. These are not the arts by which riches are acquired.

There may likewise be often solid virtue, and unshaken integrity, without great abilities or quick discernment; good men are often very unable to conduct their affairs, and of very little sagacity in points of interest.[2]

But upon the whole, if we except those whom severity of temper, and want of compliance with the temper of others, buries in solitude, and involves in misery,[3] it is very seldom that the distresses of good men are not observ'd by others, and relieved as far as the necessities of life require.

If Providence were to exert extraordinary powers, and work miracles for the assistance of good men under misfortunes, and for the recompense of their virtues[4] according to their exact merit, we should be incited to our duty by motives too sensual, instead of that satisfaction which devotion inspires, and that sense of the approbation of the Supreme Being, which affords a far nobler enjoyment, to be tasted in its high-

---

9. A man . . . A man: "Dans ce monde, on n'arrive point à un but que l'on ne se propose pas. Un homme vertueux" (p. 304).

1. nothing to spare. The bishop: "non plus aucune épargne au bout de l'an. Le pieux Evêque" (p. 304). The archbishop of Cambray was François de Salignac de la Mothe Fénelon, whose *Télémaque* (1699) SJ thought "pretty well" (*Life*, V.311). The bishop of Salisbury was Gilbert Burnet.

2. There may likewise . . . interest:

"D'ailleurs on peut avoir un grand fonds de probité, sans posséder tous les talens d'un homme d'esprit; On voit des gens de bien d'une grande simplicité dans les affaires d'intérêt" (p. 305).

3. But upon . . . misery: "Enfin à l'exception de ceux que l'esprit d'intolérance réduit à la misére" (p. 305).

4. If providence . . . virtues: "Si la Providence, suivant son pouvoir, mettoit en oeuvre des voies extraordinaires, pour ne laisser pas la vertu sans les récompenses extérieures" (p. 305).

FOURTH EPISTLE

est degree only by those who are persecuted for their adherence to a good cause.

Should a good man look upon the goods of fortune, as they are called, as the proper recompense of virtue; should he allow himself to make them the chief objects of his desire and affection; these desires, like other passions favoured and indulged, would for ever increase upon him; and as they could never find adequate and compleat gratifications, would never suffer him to arrive at happiness and content.[5]

> *Mais donnons-lui du bien, le croirez-vous heureux?*
> But let us give him wealth, will you believe *him* happy?
> *Non sans doute, il lui faut la sante, la puissance;*
> No doubtless, he must have health, power;
> *C'est la de ses vertus la juste recompense.*   280
> It is but of his virtues the just reward.
> *Ajoutons, j'y consens, & puissance & sante;*
> Let us add, I agree to it, both power and health;
> *Qu'il ait ce qui peut plaire a la cupidite.*
> Let him have whatever can please desire.
> "*Pourquoi, me direz-vous, lui donner des limites?*
> "Wherefore, you will tell me, do you set him bounds?
> *Aux dons qu'il doit pretendre en est-il de prescrites?*[6]
> In the gifts to which he may pretend is he one to be
>   prescribed?
> *Voulez-vous que d'un autre il recoive la loi?*   285
> Would you that from another he receive law?
> *Pour prix de ses vertus je pretens qu'il soit roi.*"
> As a reward of his virtues I demand that he be a king."

---

5. these desires . . . content: "ces desirs croitroient dans son coeur, comme ils font dans celui de tous les hommes, & par leurs vivacités toûjours croissantes, l'empêcheroient de parvenir jamais à une plénitude de satisfactions" (p. 306).

6. This is an extremely awkward line. Pope's lines are,

> But grant him Riches, your
>   demand is o'er?
> "No—shall the good want Health,
>   the good want Pow'r?"
> Add Health and Pow'r, and ev'ry
>   earthly thing;
> "Why bounded Pow'r? why
>   private? why no king?" (157–60;
>   155–58)

What follows will appear upon the first view very much exaggerated, and the author will be charged with having indulged his poetical imagination too much: yet he is not the first that has believed of the infernal beings, that their pride and self-love have transported them so far, that they have look'd with envy upon the superiority of their Creator; and, as disagreeable truths are naturally rejected, have persuaded themselves to doubt of the justice of his claim to boundless authority, and to impute their existence to some other original.

> *Mais pourquoi de ses droits restraindre l'etendu*
> But wherefore of his rights do you limit the extent
> *Aux biens exterieurs, qui brillent a la vue?*
> To external riches, which glitter to the sight?
> *Demandez qu'il soit dieu, demandez qu'a ses yeux*
> Insist that he be a god, insist that to his eyes
> *La terre offre l'eclat & les plaisirs des cieux.*   290
> Earth should offer the splendor and pleasures of heaven.
> *De desirs en desirs, votre aveugle manie*
> By wishes upon wishes, your blind madness
> *Epuiseroit de Dieu la puissance infinie.*
> Would exhaust of God the infinite power.
> *Pourroit-elle jamais rassasier un coeur*
> Could omnipotence ever satisfy a mind
> *Qui dans ce qu'il n'a pas veut chercher le bonheur?*
> Which searcheth after happiness in things out of its possession?

It is impossible to read the following lines too often, and much would these great poets merit of mankind, if they would more frequently employ their abilities upon this subject, which they need be under no apprehensions of exhausting.

> *Le calme d'un coeur pur, les delices d'une ame*   295
> The tranquility of a pure heart, the pleasures of a soul
> *Qu'aucun trouble n'emeut, qu'aucun desir n'enflamme,*
> Which no calamity disturbs, which no desire inflames,

> *Bonheur que l'univers ne sauroit procurer,*
> A happiness which the world cannot furnish,
> *Que tout l'effort humain ne sauroit alterer,*
> Which no human effort can change,
> *Bonheur qui dans nos seuls doit prendre sa naissance,*
> A happiness which in ourselves alone must take its rise,
> *Voila de la vertu la digne recompense!* 300
> Behold here the worthy recompense of virtue!

The true Christian is not without passions or desires,[7] but his passions are subjected to exact regulations, and his desires after sensual objects are easily gratified, and always resigned to the dispositions of Providence.

> *Voulez-vous qu'en un char, fait pour la vanite,*
> Would you that in a coach, made for vanity,
> *De superbes coursiers trainent l'humilite?*
> Drawn by proud steeds humility should ride?
> *Qu'a conserver nos droits la justice occupee*
> That justice employ'd in preserving our rights
> *Porte du conquerant la criminelle epee?*
> Should bear the conqueror's avenging sword?
> *Et que la verite, simple dans sa candeur,* 305
> And that truth, plain in her snowy robe,[8]
> *Se pare de la pourpre, & marche avec splendeur?*
> Should deck herself with purple, and walk in pomp?
> *Que l'amour genereux, qui defend la patrie,*[9]
> That publick spirit, the protectress of her country,
> *Prenant le sceptre en main se change en tyrannie?*
> Should take its sceptre, and become its tyrant?
> *De ces dons la vertu connoissant le danger,*
> Virtue aware of the danger of these gifts,
> *Ou les fuit, ou du moins gemit de s'en charger.* 310

---

7. passions or desires: "desirs" (p. 308).

8. SJ's "snowy robe" for "candeur" is his own embellishment.

9. SJ's "publick spirit" is not a translation but is taken directly from Pope: "Or Public Spirit its great cure, a Crown" (172; 170).

Either shuns them, or at least laments under their load.
Tel, qui dans son printems etoit plein de sagesse,
Thus, the man who in his youth was full of wisdom,
Gate par la fortune, a terni sa vieillesse.
Undone by fortune, hath blemish'd his old age.

From these general views of things, with which the reader is dazzled and amused, the poet descends to a more particular inspection.[1]

Commencons par l'attrait, qui sur le coeur humain
To begin with an attractive, which over the heart of man
A pris plus que tout autre un pouvoir souverain.
Has more command than any other sovereign power.
La richesse jamais n'eut un droit legitime   315
Riches never had a just right
De gagner notre amour, d'attirer notre estime.
To win our love, to attract our esteem.
Des parlemens entiers, a la honte des loix,
Whole parliaments, to the disgrace of laws,
Ont quelquefois vendu leur criminelle voix;
Have sometimes sold their guilty votes;
Mais l'estime & l'amour, libres dans leurs suffrages,
But esteem and love, free in their suffrages,
A la seul vertu presentent des hommages.   320
To virtue alone offer homage.
Ce mortel vertueux, dont le coeur & l'esprit
The virtuous man, whose heart and spirit
Le font cherir des siens autant qu'il les cherit,
Render him as much the darling as the lover of his kind,
Qui porte en un corps sain une ame encore plus saine,

---

1. From . . . inspection: "De ces généralités, très frapantes pourtant, Mr. POPE descend à des détails" (p. 308).

FOURTH EPISTLE

> Who carries in a sound body a still sounder soul,
> *Le croirez vous l'objet de la celeste haine,*
> Will you believe him the object of the divine hatred,
> *Parce qu'au necessaire etroitement borne* 325
> Because confin'd within the narrow limits of necessaries
> *A d'amples revenus il n'est point destine?*
> He was not born to large possessions?

After having shewn the falsehood of the common notions about riches,[2] he proceeds to the false notions which are conceived of honour.

> *Et la honte & l'honneur sont dans les mains des hommes;*
> Shame and honour are in mens power;
> *Il ne dependent point de la place ou nous sommes.*
> They depend not at all on the station wherein we are placed.
> *Le ciel en divers rangs voulut nous etablir;*
> Heaven has been pleased to settle us in different degrees of life;
> *Le veritable honneur est de les bien remplir.* 330
> True honour is to discharge the duties incumbent on them.
> *La fortune, a juger par la seule apparence,*
> Fortune, if we judge by outward appearance,
> *Entre tous les mortels met quelque difference.*
> Between all men makes some difference.
> *L'un dans un riche habit nous montre sa fierte;*
> One shews his pride in a rich dress;
> *L'autre sous des lambeaux cache sa vanite.*
> Another under rags hides his vanity.
> *Couvert d'un tablier l'artisan se pavane,* 335
> The artificer struts behind an apron,

---

2. After . . . riches: "Après avoir combatu & démontré l'erreur des préjugés si communs" (p. 309).

Le pretre s'applaudit dans sa longue soutane,
The priest hugs himself in his long cassock,
Un moine de son froc se couvre gravement,
A monk gravely wraps himself in his gown,
La couronne est d'un roi le superbe ornement.
The crown is a king's stately ornament.
Quoi, s'ecrira quelqu'un, le froc & la couronne!
What, will one cry, a gown and a crown!
Rien n'est plus different. Mon discours vous etonne; 340
Things cannot differ more. My discourse surprises you;
Apprenez qu'a mes yeux, les vices, les vertus,
Know ye that to my view, vice and virtue,
Le sage & l'insense, different encor plus.
The wise man and the fool, differ yet more.
Que d'un lache artisan imitant la bassesse,
By an unworthy imitation of the lazy mechanic,
Le pretre comme lui se plonge dans l'yvresse;
Let the priest like him plunge himself in debauchery;
Qu'a l'exemple d'un moine un monarque indolent 345
After the monk's example let the indolent monarch
N'aporte a ses conseils qu'un esprit nonchalant,
Carry with him into council his regardless temper,
Et le pretre & le roi n'ont rien de respectable;
Both the priest and the king deserve not the least reverence;
C'est un vil artisan, un moine meprisable.
The first is a base mechanic, the other a pitiful monk.
Par le merite seul on peut etre eleve;
By merit alone is a person raised;
Tout est bas & rampant quand on en est prive. 350
All is mean and servile when devoid of that.
L'etat le plus abject, comme le rang supreme,
A condition the most abject, a station the most exalted,
Sont les dehors de l'homme, & non pas l'homme meme.
Are the externals of a man, and not the man himself.

Les rois, & plus souvent les maitresses des rois,
Kings, or, what oftner happens, their whores,
Te pourront illustrer sans raison, ni sans choix.
May make thee illustrious for no reason, and with no discernment.
Du sang de tes ayeux tu vantes la noblesse; 355
Thou boastest of the noble blood of thy ancestors;
Je veux qu'il ait coule de Lucrece en Lucrece;
I grant it to have flow'd from Lucretia to Lucretia;
Mais ne m'etale point leurs titres fastueux,
But do not display to me their arrogant titles,
Il faut me les montrer constamment vertueux,
Shew me them walking successively in the paths of virtue,
Dignes par leurs travaux de vivre dans l'histoire;
Worthy for their labours to live in history;
Si tu veux sans rougir te parer de leur gloire. 360
If thou wilt without blushing deck thyself with their reputation.
S'ils ont vecu sans moeurs, sans courage, & sans foy,
If they have lived without morals, without fortitude, or honesty,
Le nom qu'ils t'ont laisse ne parle plus pour toi.
The name they have left thee no longer pleads for thee.
Vainement leur noblesse, ou ton orgueil se fonde,
In vain their nobility, on which thy pride is founded,
Remonteroit; au tems du naufrage du monde,
Would trace itself upwards to the time of the deluge,
Ce nom qu'ils ont terni, bien loin de t'illustrer, 365
That name which they have spotted, far from honouring,
Aux yeux de la raison doit te deshonorer.
Before the face of reason serves to disgrace thee.
D'un coeur ignoble & bas rien n'eface les taches.
Of a base and ignoble spirit nothing wipes out the stains.
Rien ne peut anoblir ni des sots ni des laches;
Nothing can enoble sots or cowards;

> *Et fussent-ils issus du premier des Talbots,*[3]
> Tho' they were descended from the first of the
>   Talbots,
> *Je ne respecte point des laches ni des sots.* 370
> I owe no respect to cowards or sots.

Honour is the property of all conditions, of subjects as well as kings; but *greatness* is the privilege of men distinguish'd either by real or imputed superiority of genius.

> *Contemplons la grandeur, d'ou prend-elle naissance?*
> Look we on greatness, whence does it take its rise?
> *Qui la fait eclater? la valeur, la prudence.*
> What makes it shine? valour, wisdom.
> *Politiques profonds, rapides conquerans,*
> Profound politicians, rapid conquerors,
> *L'univers ebloui vous place aux premiers rangs;*
> The dazzled world places you in the first class of
>   mankind;
> *Que, pour en mieux juger, la raison nous eclaire.* 375
> But let reason teach us to form a better judgment.
> *Les guerriers sont marques au meme caractere,*
> Warriours pass under one character,
> *Depuis ce furieux de carnage altere,*
> From that madman stained with blood,
> *Du beau titre de Grand par la Grece honore,*
> By Greece honour'd with the fine title of Great,
> *Jusqu'a ce roi du Nord, dont la valeur extreme*
> To that northern king, whose excess of valour
> *Ne fut pas moins funeste aux autres qu'a lui-meme.*[b][4] 380
> Was no less fatal to others than himself.

b. luimeme

---

3. Pope's lines are,

> What can ennoble sots, or slaves,
>   or cowards?
> Alas! not all the blood of all the
>   HOWARDS. (215–16; 213–14)

Du Resnel has substituted "Talbots" for Pope's "Howards," presumably to rhyme with "sots." The Talbots, an ancient English family, trace their descent and surname from the Norman conquerors of England, and at this time are the earls of Shrewsbury.

4. Crousaz has "lui-même" (p. 312). The "northern king" is Charles XII of Sweden, in whom SJ had a special inter-

I have already observed,* that the translator uses less freedom of language than the original. It is possible to preserve truth and decency at the same time; and when we speak of men in high rank, and particularly of crown'd heads, this restraint is certainly proper.

> *Un heros cherche a vaincre, & ne peut s'en lasser*
> A hero aims at victory, and can never be tired
> *Tant qu'il lui reste encore un peuple a terrasser.*
> While there remains a nation for him to subdue.
> *Un heros sur ses pas ne tourne point la tete,*
> A hero on his steps never turns his head,
> *Il court rapidement de conquete en conquete,*
> He hurries on from conquest to conquest,
> *Et sans cesse de sang arrose les lauriers,* 385
> And with fresh blood still waters his laurels,
> *Seul & frivole objet de ses travaux guerriers.*
> The sole and trifling object of his warlike toils.
> *Voila le conquerant! Quel est le politique?*
> See there the conquerer! What is the politician?
> *Un mortel circonspect, dont tout l'esprit s'applique*
> A circumspect mortal, whose whole study is bent
> *A lire dans nos coeurs par ses tours captieux*
> To pry into our hearts by his subtle artifices
> *Sans que jamais le sien se devoile a nos yeux.* 390
> Without ever discovering his own to our view.
> *Il cherche a nous tromper. Nommerons nous sagesse*
> He seeks to deceive us. Shall we call wisdom
> *Un art qui n'est fonde que sur notre foiblesse?*
> An art which is only founded on our weakness?
> *Mais enfin j'y consens; que des succes heureux*
> Well but I allow, that a series of success
> *Les conduisent au but ou tendent tous leurs voeux;*

---

*That observation is already examined. See the beginning of the first essay.[5]

est. See *The Vanity of Human Wishes*, ll. 191–222. As early as 10 August 1742 SJ contemplated writing a play about him. See *Letters*, I.28.

5. See p. 38.

May conduct them to the scope to which all their wishes tend;
Que l'un nous asservisse, & l'autre nous abuse,   395
That one enslaves us, and the other imposes on us,
L'un par la force ouverte, & l'autre par la ruse.
The first by open force, the other by cunning.
L'artifice pervers, l'homicide valeur,
Can industry misapply'd, murdering valour,
Seroient-ils, selon vous, les sources de l'honneur?
Become, in your opinion, the fountains of honour?
Non; celui qui ne prend que la vertu pour guide,
No; he who takes virtue for his only guide,
Qui s'eleve aux honneurs dont il n'est point avide;   400
Who ascends to honours of which he is not ambitious;
Celui qui sans gemir, dans l'exil, dans les fers,
He who without complaining, in exile, in chains,
Conserve sa grandeur au milieu des revers,
Maintains his greatness in the midst of changes,
Soit que par ses vertus aime de sa patrie,
Whether for his virtues beloved of his country,
Sage comme Antonin il desarme l'envie;
Like the wise Antoninus, he disarms envy;
Soit que persecute par un injuste sort,   405
Or whether persecuted by an unjust sentence,
Ferme comme Socrate, il recoive la mort,
Compos'd like Socrates, he meets death,
Celui-la seul est grand, & digne qu'on l'admire.
He is the only great man, and worthy of admiration.

False honour, with which men suffer themselves to be dazzled and captivated, is a mere external advantage,[6] independent of themselves, which, as it adds nothing to their real value, can add nothing to the esteem which they have a right to demand.

---

6. suffer . . . advantage: "se laissent éblouïr, se réduit à un extérieur" (p. 313).

That which is generally supposed to constitute grandeur, is so far from raising them to any real superiority above others, that it hinders them not from being mean and contemptible, slaves to false appearances, and, by their injustice and rapacity, the object of detestation.[7]

Yet these titles, worthles as they are, men determine to obtain, and feast upon the imagination of immortality, an immortality of which they will not be conscious, or will be conscious only to their misery. True and desirable immortality is the reward only of virtue, and that chimera, which ambition has substituted in its place, is well shown by our author to be an idle sound.[8]

> *Cette immortalite que notre orgueil desire,*
> That immortality which our pride covets,
> *Que par tant de travaux nous voulons acheter,*
> Which we would purchase by so many toils,
> *N'est qu'une illusion, qui doit peu nous flater.* 410
> Is but a fancy, which ought not to flatter us.
> *Le tems de notre vie est le tems de la gloire;*
> The time of our life is the season for glory;
> *Celle que vous voulez retrouver dans l'histoire*
> That which you desire to find in history
> *N'est qu'un frivole amas d'eloges superflus,*
> Is but a trifling collection of superfluous panegyric,
> *Un vain concert de voix, que vous n'entendrez plus.*
> A vain concert of voices, which you will hear no more.
> *Milord,[9] quand le destin bornant votre carriere* 415
> My lord, when fate that bounds your race
> *Viendra, malgre nos voeux, vous ravir la lumiere,*
> Shall come, in spite of our prayers, to deprive you of light,

---

7. slaves . . . detestation: "jouets des illusions, & souvent injustes & odieux" (p. 314).

8. Yet these titles . . . sound: "Cependant on se résout à mériter ces noms flétrissans. On abandonne le mérite réel, qui seroit accompagné d'une solide récompense, & on est à se repaitre d'une immortalité dont on n'aura aucun sentiment, car la véritable est le fruit du mérite. Mr. POPE fait vivement sentir le néant de la chimérique, qu'on substitue à la véritable" (p. 314).

9. Crousaz has "Mylord" (p. 314).

Que vous servira-t-il qu'un suffrage incertain
What will avail you as unsettled approbation
Se partage entre vous & l'orateur Romain?
In suspense between you and the Roman orator?
Du bruit doux & flateur, qu'on nomme renomme,[1]
With a smooth and flattering report, which men call renown,
Notre ombre chez les morts peut-elle etre charmee? 420
Will our ghost among the dead be charmed?
Ce plaisir se termine a voir autour de nous
That pleasure goes no farther than to see around us
Des amis satisfaits, ou des rivaux jaloux.
Our friends contented, or our rivals jealous.
Le reste des humains confusement admire
The rest of mankind indiscriminately admire
Cesar qui ne vit plus, Eugene qui respire,
Ceasar who lives no more, and Eugene who breaths,
Sans distinguer les lieux, ni le tems, ni le nom, 425
Without distinguishing places, times, or names,
L'un traversant le Rhin, l'autre le Rubicon.
One passing the Rhine, the other the Rubicon.
Tel est le triste sort du plus ferme courage.
Such is the melancholy fate of the most resolute valour.
Les talens de l'esprit ont-ils plus advantage?[2]
The endowments of the mind have they more advantage?
Les honneurs passagers d'un sterile laurier
The transitory honours of a barren laurel
Sont le prix du savant ainsi que du guerrier. 430
Are the reward of the learned as well as of the warrior.[3]

The beauties that cannot but be observed between verse 295 and 430, the pleasure which the reader indulges in read-

---

1. Crousaz has "renommée" (p. 315).
2. Crousaz has "d'avantage" (p. 315).
3. These lines should be read in conjunction with SJ's *The Vanity of Human Wishes.*

FOURTH EPISTLE 293

ing them, and self-approbation that arises from the indulgence of it, will be found by every man, that examines the motions of his own heart, to arise from that supposition which common sense, neither instructed, nor perverted, teaches every man[4] to form, that he is a free agent, master of his own determinations, and placed in the capacity of recommending himself to his Creator, and becoming more or less worthy of reward, as he shall make his duty more or less the rule of his choice.[5]

These admirable lines exhort us, in the strongest manner, to make a wise choice; to enter into the ways that may lead us to virtue and true honour, and to avoid those paths that carry us away to vice, ignominy, and contempt:[6] but if men should act in direct opposition to these salutary rules, if they should abandon themselves to passions directly contrary to their duty, how would they be blameable, or yet worthy of punishment, if it be true that their bodies are only parts of the great machine, and dependent on the motions of the universe; if all the impulses they receive or communicate proceed from a train of causes not to be interrupted; and, to carry the notion yet farther, if THE FIRST and RULING CAUSE has determined from the beginning to create and unite to these corporeal machines, substances that should will and think exactly according to these particular notions and passions?

How great is the difference between the notion of happiness, which Mr Pope here lays before us, as the consequence of virtue, and the just recompense of so good a choice, from the passage in his second essay,[7] in which, to prove that hap-

---

4. common sense ... every man: "le sens commun améne tous les hommes" (p. 315).

5. and placed ... his choice: "& qu'ils se rendent estimables & dignes de récompense, à proportion qu'ils veulent choisir ce qu'ils doivent" (p. 315).

6. These admirable ... contempt: "Dans ces vers si beaux, on nous donne des leçons, on nous exhorte à faire d'heureux choix, à entrer & à persévérer dans des routes qui nous rendent respectables & aimables, & à nous éloigner de celles qui nous rendroient odieux & méprisables" (pp. 315–16).

7. from the passage ... essay: "dans ces derniers vers, & la description qu'il en fait dans sa deuxiéme Epitre" (pp. 316–17).

294   A COMMENTARY

piness is equally distributed, he supposes that the Supreme Cause supplies the want of talents, by bestowing on those to whom he has denied them proportionable degrees of error and of pride! He that dwells with a proper attention upon the foregoing lines of this essay,[8] cannot but lament that in the second should be found notions so directly opposite, and that an ecclesiastic should be constrain'd, by an exact adherence to his original, to copy notions so contrary to truth.[9]

> *Un mortel vertueux, un mortel vraiment sage,*
> A virtuous man, a man truly wise,
> *De la main du tres haut est le plus noble ouvrage;*
> Is the most noble work of the hand of the most high;
> *Et le seul dont le nom justement respecte*
> And the only one whose name with just respect
> *Soit digne de passer a la posterite.*
> Is worthy to be transmitted to posterity.
> *Cet intime plaisir, qui nait de l'innocence,*   435
> That inward pleasure, which flows from innocence,
> *Que la vertu produit, qui fait sa recompense,*
> Which virtue produces, which is its reward,
> *N'est-il pas plus touchant que ces airs redoubles*
> Is not this more affecting than those repeated blasts of huzzahs
> *Qu'exhale la faveur des peuples assembles?*
> Puff'd on thee from the favour of the crowd?
> *Quel seroit ton bonheur, lors que la renommee*
> What would be thy happiness, when fame
> *D'un encens imposteur t'offriroit la fumee,*   440
> Shall offer thee the smoke of flattering incense,
> *Si ton coeur, dementant ses eloges pompeux,*
> If thy heart, in defiance of her pompous elogies,[1]

---

8. essay: "Epitre IV" (p. 317).

9. and that . . . truth: "& on est encore plus mortifié, que la nécessité d'une fidéle traduction ait déterminé un illustre Abbé à retracer ces idées d'après son Original" (p. 317).

1. Used interchangeably with "eulogies" in the eighteenth century. In the *Dictionary* SJ has "Elogy. *n.s.* [*eloge,* French] Praise; panegyrick," with the first two of three illustrative quotations using "elogies." He also has "eulogy,"

FOURTH EPISTLE

T'accabloit en secret de reproches honteux?
Should load[c] thee in secret with shameful reproaches?
Marcellus est rempli d'une plus vive joie,
Marcellus is fill'd with a more lively joy,
Dans cet illustre exil, ou le tyran l'envoie,
In that illustrious exile, whither the tyrant sends him,
Que Cesar triomphant, en voyant a ses pies 445
Than Caesar triumphant, in seeing at his feet
Le peuple, & le senat ramper humilies.
The people, and the senate creeping lowly.
Les funestes auteurs d'une trahison noire,
The mischievous[2] plotters of black treason,
D'un parricide affreux, sont places dans l'histoire;
Of horrid parricide, are recorded in history;
Quels noms sont plus connus, plus souvent repetes?
What names are more known, oftener repeated?
Mais plus ils sont fameux, plus ils sont detestes. 450
But the more famous they are, the more they are detested.

I have made in my *Examen* some little remarks, which I will not repeat.[3]

There are men, who, if they can please themselves, give themselves no pain about the praise or reproach of their contemporaries, and yet less do they consider what will be the sentiments of posterity, to which they have no relation. Their ruling passion is a brutal self-love, others suffer by their cruelty; but they gratify their own pride by making their power felt, and their severity dreaded.[4] If therefore we suppose the universe to be governed by a being equally powerful and

---

c. lead

---

from the Greek, defining it as "Praise; encomium; panegyrick." Boyer defines "Eloge" as "Elogy, praise, encomium, commendation, panegyrick."

2. SJ's "mischievous" for "funestes" ("fatal, deadly") is something of an understatement (p. 318).

3. See *Examination*, pp. 199 ff.

4. Their ruling passion . . . dreaded: "Leur passion dominante est la *Brutalité*. Les autres gémissent sous son poids; mais pour eux, ils se plaisent à leur faire sentir le joug" (p. 318).

just, he must decree rewards and punishments in a future state.

Mr Pope then proceeds to examine the value of *superior parts,* considered without regard to the right use of them, and the satisfaction that arises from the consciousness of having employ'd such blessings to the end for which they were bestowed.

> *Les sublimes talens furent votre partage;*
> Sublime talents fell to your share;
> *Apprenez-nous, milord, quel en est l'avantage,*
> Let us learn, my lord, what is their advantage,
> *Qu'apportent-ils a l'homme? Un triste desespoir.*
> What do they procure to a man? Melancholy despair.
> *Il voit que plus il sait, plus il reste a savoir.*
> He sees that the more he knows, the more there
>   remains to be known.
> *Ils eclairent[5] nos yeux sur les defauts des autres,*   455
> They clear up our eyes to the faults of others,
> *Et nous font ressentir plus vivement les notres.*
> And make us more feelingly sensible of our own.
> *Occupe nuit & jour dans les premiers emplois,*
> Busy'd night and day in the highest employments,
> *Un esprit transendant en soutient tout le poids:*
> An extraordinary genius sustains all their weight:
> *Si l'amour des beaux arts le conduit au Parnasse,*
> If the love of the belles lettres conduct him to
>   Parnassus,
> *Quel juge y trouve-t-il pour y regler sa place?*   460
> What judge finds he there to appoint him his due
>   place?
> *En bute au traits malins d'un rival envieux,*
> As a butt to the spiteful arrows of an envious rival,
> *Plus il acquiert d'eclat, plus il blesse ses yeux.*
> The more lustre he acquires, the more he hurts his
>   own eyes.

---

5. Here SJ has confused "éclairer" and "éclaircir."

Let us imagine⁶ a man that has received an immense sum from the bounty of his prince, shutting it up in a chest, and hiding it with the utmost industry from the sight of mankind: let us suppose another shewing it them at a distance to raise envy and admiration, but making no other use of it. The first is a just representation of a learned man, who confines his knowledge to his own study; and the second, of one that communicates his ideas with unwillingness and malignity, that envies mankind the learning which he dispenses, and would carefully conceal the discoveries that he has made, did not his vanity prompt him to publish them.⁷ There are others that display all their learning, and yet endeavour to persuade the world that they know much more than they communicate.

Let us, in contrast with these vain and malevolent students, consider the character of a man, who, without affection or hypocrisy,⁸ devotes to the honour of God those abilities with which he has endowed him, and that knowledge with which he has enlightened him;⁹ and applying all his learning to its proper end, endeavours with all the zeal of benevolence to instruct others, whom he considers as his brethren, and equally the sons of the Universal Father.

Many, 'tis true, will be ungrateful for his good intentions, and their own improvement; but still he does his duty in attempting their advantage, nor do opposition or perverseness discourage his endeavours. The favours of Providence itself are often bestowed without excitingᵈ gratitude, and some-

---

d. exciting,

---

6. Let us imagine: "Je me figure" (p. 319).

7. let us suppose . . . them: "Un autre les étale, mais c'est de loin; Il n'en fait même voir qu'une partie, & n'en permet pas l'usage. C'est l'emblême d'un Savant qui ne fait part de ses lumiéres qu'à regret, qui envie même aux autres le peu qu'il leur en communique, & qu'il ne répandroit point, s'il n'étoit forcé par sa vanité à faire connoître, par quelque preuve, qu'il est habile homme" (p. 320). Here SJ alters the sequence of Crousaz's sentences.

8. without . . . hypocrisy: "dans la sincérité de son coeur" (p. 320).

9. knowledge . . . enlightened him: "de toutes les lumiéres qu'il en a tiré" (p. 320).

times upon those who deny its superintendence, or censure its impartiality; and how weak must he be that can expect more regard than is paid to heaven![1]

> *Veut-il, d'un plus beau zele animant son courage,*
> Would he, with a most excellent zeal animating his courage,
> *De l'etat en danger prevenir le naufrage,*
> Of the state in danger prevent the shipwreck,
> *Loin de le seconder dans ses nobles transports,* 465
> Far from being seconded in his noble transports,
> *Ou l'on blame, ou l'on craint ses genereux efforts.*
> Either he is blamed, or his generous efforts are suspected.

A statesman, if he be wise, and a Christian, will have the same views with the scholar, and alike devote his attainments to the publick good.

> *O funeste bonheur! triste preeminence!*
> O fatal happiness! sad preheminence!
> *Que donnent aux mortels l'esprit & la science!*
> Which wit and learning bestow on mortals!
> *Trop sages pour gouter ces frivoles plaisirs,*
> Too wise to relish those trifling pleasures,
> *Qui du foible vulgaire amusent les desirs,* 470
> Which of the weak vulgar amuse the wishes,
> *D'un cote la raison, & de l'autre envie,*[2]
> On one side reason, on the other envy,
> *Les privent tour a tour des douceurs de la vie.*
> Rob them by turns of the comforts of life.

A wise man has a more certain method of eluding envy than that of despising it; his consciousness of the divine ap-

---

1. The favours . . . heaven: "Veut-il que les hommes ayent plus d'égard pour lui que pour la divine Providence, aux bienfaits de laquelle un si grand nombre de personnes font si peu d'attention, & d'autres portent l'audace jusqu'à s'en plaindre, ou à refuser de la croire?" (p. 321).

2. Crousaz correctly has "l'envie" (p. 321).

probation, the smile of that Being which it is his chief and only ardent desire to please, exempts him from any concern at the weak attacks of human malice. If any short emotion be raised, his reason, enlightened by piety, immediately confirms his virtue, and restores his tranquillity.

> *Parcourons d'un coup d'oeil les differens objets,*
> Let us run over with a glance the different objects,
> *Ou se portent nos voeux, ou tendent nos projets;*
> Whither our wishes carry us, whither our projects tend;
> *D'abord, reduisons les a leur juste mesure,*   475
> First, let us reduce them to their just measure,
> *Et pesons le bonheur, que chacun d'eux procure.*
> And let us weigh the happiness, which each of them yields.
> *Toujours l'un prend sur l'autre, & souvent le detruit;*
> Still one encroaches on the other, and often destroys it;
> *La peine les precede, & le degout les suit.*
> Pain goes before, and satiety follows them.
> *A quelle prix*[3] *leur douceur nous est-elle donnee!*
> How dearly does he pay for their sweetness!
> *De combien d'amertume est-elle empoisonnee!*   480
> With how much bitterness is it allayed!
> *Si de leur faux eclat tes yeux sont fascines,*
> If with their false lustre thy eyes are bewitched,
> *Voi donc a quel mortels ces biens sont destines:*
> See then to what kind of mortals these good things are allotted:
> *Voudrois-tu te changer contre ces ames basses,*
> Wouldst thou change with those base spirits,
> *Sur qui le sort se plait a repandre*[4] *ses graces?*[5]
> On whom fortune is pleased to bestow her favours?
> *Si l'eclat d'un ruban, vaine gloire d'honneur,*   485

---

3. Crousaz correctly has "quel prix" (p. 322).

4. Crousaz has "réprendre" (p. 322); Du Resnel has "répandre" (l. 484). SJ either consulted Du Resnel here or rightly emended the text as "répandre" which means "to pour, to distribute" and "reprendre" means "to get back, to resume."

5. Crousaz has "ces graces" (p. 322).

If the lustre of a ribband, the vain glory of honour,
En flatant ton orgueil, te paroit un bonheur,
By flattering thy pride, tricks thee up an happiness,
Voi si cet ornement donne un air de noblesse
See if that ornament gives an air of nobleness
Au chevalier S——s, a milord In——sse.[6]
To Sir—— S——s, to my lord In——sse.
L'or seroit-il objet de tes desirs jaloux?
Were gold the object of thy jealous wishes?
Jette les yeux sur L——e,[e][7] *& sur son triste epoux.*   490
Cast thy eyes on L——e,[f] and his melancholy wife.
De briller par l'esprit aurois-tu la manie?
To shine in parts wouldst thou madly wish?
Rapelle-toi Bacon, ce sublime genie,
Call to mind Bacon, that sublime genius,
Cet homme si profond, si grand dans ses ecrits,
That man so profound, so noble in his writings,
Devient par sa conduite un objet de mepris.
Become by his conduct an object of contempt.
De l'immortalite si le desir te touche,   495
If the desire of immortality affects thee,
Si tu veux que ton nom passe de bouche en bouche,
If thou wouldst have thy name pass from mouth to mouth,
Songe que de Cromwel le nom & les forfaits
Consider that Cromwel's name and crimes
Devenus immortels ne periront jamais.
Become immortal will never perish.
De ces differens biens si le riche assemblage
If the rich union of those different blessings
Du solide bonheur te presente l'image,   500
Presents thee with the image of solid happiness,

e. L—E   f. L—E

---

6. Crousaz's line reads, "Au Chevalier SANDERS, à Mylord INVERNESSE (l. 488, p. 323).

7. Crousaz has "LISE" (l. 490, p. 323).

Pren de leur faussete l'histoire pour garand;
Take history for witness of their imposture;
Vois y l'homme d'etat, & le riche, & le grand,
See there the man of quality, the rich, and the great,
Et les guerriers fameux, conduits par l'apparence,
And the famous warriors, who were led by show,
De ces fragiles biens pleurer l'insuffisance.
Lament the insufficiency of these frail enjoyments.

That man to whom God grants the wisdom and happiness of making the maxims of which I have been proving the necessity, (v. 54.) the unvaried rule of his conduct, and the perpetual foundation of his peace; the man whose employment it is to hear and obey the call of God, will pass his days without any danger of being the sport of those passions, which are here so elegantly described.[8]

Qu'un courtisan sans foi, par son art imposteur, 505
Let a courtier without faith, by his cozening arts,
D'un maitre qu'il trahit ait su gagner le coeur;
Know how to gain the heart of a master whom he betrays;
Crois-tu qu'il soit heureux, quand l'intrigue & la ruse
Dost thou think him happy, when intrigue and cunning
Sont les honteux appuis d'un rang dont il abuse?
Are the shameful supports of a place which he abuses?
Dans sa propre grandeur il trouve son tourment,
In his own greatness he finds his torment,
Quand la honte & la fraude en sont le fondement. 510
When villainy and fraud are its foundation.

There are some men so entirely possessed by ambition, that they never stop in their career, long enough to exam-

---

8. and the perpetual . . . described: "& le fondement inébranlable & perpétuel de sa félicité, vivra très éloigné de devenir le jouet des agitations, donc on vient de lire une très élégante peinture" (pp. 323–24).

ine[9] whether the advantages they attain are worth more or less than the labour of the acquisition.

> *Ainsi des vils roseaux d'une rive fangeuse*
> Thus from vile reeds of muddy shores
> *On vit jadis sortir Venise l'orgueilleuse.*
> Was seen of old proud Venice to arise.
> *Voi parmi les heros, voi, malgre leur splendeur,*
> See among the heroes, see, notwithstanding their splendor,
> *Marcher d'un pas egal le crime & la grandeur.*
> Guilt and greatness walking side by side.
> *En vain de ce beau nom le vulgaire le nomme;*   515
> In vain the vulgar call him by that fine name;
> *Ce qui fait le heros degrade souvent l'homme.*
> What makes the hero oft degrades the man.
> *Dans le plus grand eclat de leurs exploits guerriers,*
> In the greatest lustre of their warlike atchievements,
> *Regarde-les couverts d'equivoques lauriers;*
> Behold them cover'd with false laurels;
> *Lauriers, toujours le fruit d'une ardeur sanguinaire,*
> Laurels, always the product of a sanguinary fire,
> *Et quelquefois le prix d'un trafic mercenaire.*   520
> And sometimes the purchase of a mercenary traffick.
> *Contemple-les enfin epuises de travaux,*
> Behold them at last worn out with toils,
> *Ou perdus de mollesse, & consumes de maux;*
> Or undone with luxury, and wasted with diseases;
> *On ne voit plus en eux que d'illustres coupables;*
> You regard them as no other than illustrious criminals;
> *Dans leurs propres palais devenus meprisables,*
> In their own palaces grown contemptible,

---

9. that they . . . examine: "qu'elle ne leur laisse pas le tems nécessaire pour décider" (p. 324).

> *Ils trainent sans honneur le reste de leurs jours.* 525
> They linger out the remainder of their days in dishonour.
> *La mort vient-elle enfin en terminer le cours?*
> Comes death at length to finish their course?
> *Une femme hautaine, un heritier avide,*
> An imperious wife, a greedy heir,
> *Se font de leur trepas une douceur perfide;*
> Reap the sweet fruits of treason over their grave;
> *Et, loin de soulager leurs mortelles langueurs,*
> And, far from lending support under declining nature,
> *Du sort qui les accable augmentent les rigueurs.* 530
> Augment the horrors of the fate that overwhelms them.
> *Helas! par leur midi que ta vue emblouie*[1]
> Alas! let not thy sight dazzled with their noon
> *Ne te seduise pas sur le jour de leur vie;*
> Betray thy judgment on the day of their life;
> *De leur matin obscur, de leur soir tenebreux,*
> Of their louring morn, of their gloomy evening,
> *Rappelle a ton esprit les momens malheureux.*
> Recall to thy mind the unhappy moments.
> *Eh! que restera-t-il de tant de renommee,* 535
> Ah! what will remain of all this fame,
> *Qu'un souvenir confus, qu'une vaine fumee,*
> But a confused remembrance, an empty smoak,
> *Ou leur gloire & leur crime egalement traces,*
> Where their glory and their guilt equally marked,
> *L'un par l'autre seront tour a tour effaces?*
> Shall be by one another in turns effaced?

This picture has so much the marks of an original, that it may be readily conceived to have been copied from the life. Whether any of the features are aggravated by the passions

---

1. Crousaz correctly has "éblouie" (p. 325).

of the painter, it is not my business to decide; that kindness will soften, and ill-will heighten a deformity, is without dispute:[2] but I cannot forbear to observe, that the life and spirit of the version deserve our admiration, as the translator could be animated only with his natural fire, not agitated by personal motives.

> *Appren, foible mortel, (& qu'a cette science*
> Learn, weak mortal, (and by this science
> *Se borne, s'il se peut, toute ta connoissance)*   540
> Be bounded, if possible, all thy knowledge)
> *Appren, donc, qu'il n'est point ici bas de bonheur,*
> Learn, then, that there is no happiness here below,
> *Si la vertu ne regle & l'esprit & le coeur.*
> If virtue does not regulate the passions and heart.
> *La vertu fait trouver le seul point immuable;*
> Virtue can discover the only fixed point;
> *Elle rend le bonheur aussi parfait que stable;*
> She renders happiness perfect as well as lasting;
> *Des traits de la fortune elle brave l'effort;*   545
> Of the bolts of fortune she defies the shock;
> *Et nous met au dessus des caprices du sort.*
> And sets us above the caprice of fate.
> *Sans flatter notre esprit d'une vaine esperance,*
> Without flattering our mind with vain hopes,
> *Elle donne a chacun sa juste recompense.*
> She gives to every one his just reward.
> *Soit que sa main recoive ou verse des bienfaits,*
> Whether her hand receives or bestows benefits,
> *Son plaisir est egal, ses voeux sont satisfaits.*   550
> Her pleasure is equal, her wishes are satisfied.

An instance, that may easily be understood, will sufficiently demonstrate that an equality of wealth and estate could not long subsist in the world. Let us suppose a small number

---

2. Whether any . . . dispute: "La Passion prête quelquefois de la beauté à un objet pour lequel on est prévenu; une passion contraire aura aussi un effet opposé; c'est sur quoi je ne décide pas" (pp. 325–26).

of families obliged by persecution to fix their residence in a desart island. All the members of this new community, united by their religion, their virtue, and their sufferings, love each other with the utmost tenderness:[3] in a short time[4] they clear and cultivate their island, and make it a commodious habitation; the stronger assist the weaker, and they that have more than their necessities demand, bestow their superfluities upon those that have less: such would be the state of this new colony for some time after their settlement; but this fervour of affection would in time abate, and this amiable friendship be disturbed: their numbers would perpetually increase, and new families be formed;[5] after a few generations, sloth, ill-nature, and interest would intrude, and envy and malice would soon put an end to this peaceable equality.

Many are the accidents to which families owe their distresses or decay. In some the infirmities of age hinder the father from conducting his affairs; in others, the bad conduct of the chief involves the rest in poverty: some are impoverish'd by sickness: an estate is sometimes lost in the hands of orphans, and sometimes is sub-divided into so many portions for numerous descendants, that no single person has sufficient for his support. Others not only receive large inheritances from their ancestors, but increase them by strength and application. Thus, while some are hourly gaining what others lose, either by their faults or misfortunes, an equality of condition cannot be maintained; and if it could, it would deprive us of all opportunity to exercise either the virtue of liberality, or that of resignation.[6]

As a man is empower'd to give, or obliged to receive, he has an opportunity of practising two great virtues. An ungenerous man,[7] that desires to engross all he has for his own use,

---

3. All the members . . . tenderness: "Tous ceux qui les composent s'aiment tendrement, unis par le puissant lien d'une Religion sincére" (p. 327).

4. SJ adds "in a short time."

5. such would be the state . . . families be formed: "C'est ce qui ne manque pas d'arriver au commencement. Mais les familles se multiplient, & le nombre des Habitans croit d'année en année" (p. 327).

6. SJ omits Crousaz's introduction and repetition of the quotation of ll. 548–50 of Du Resnel (p. 328).

7. An ungenerous man: "Un mauvais coeur" (p. 328).

never gives without reluctance; and he whose vanity makes a state of inferiority uneasy to him, cannot without pain receive those favours which his circumstances require; however he may appear grateful, and submissive, in reality he envies his benefactor, and feels nothing within but discontent. But a good man, enriched by the bounty of his Maker, knows that his wealth was bestowed for no other purpose than to be diffused, and delights in concurring with the designs of Providence;[8] nor if, by a change of his circumstances, gratitude and humility become the duties of his life, is he less ready to obey the call. In one state he will give without haughtiness, in the other ask without dejection:[9] when he bestows he will appear to receive the obligation he confers, and when his necessities reduce him to receive, he will observe the affluence of others, perhaps, with more satisfaction than the possessors enjoy; for a wise man is cautious of giving himself over to the contemplations of his own prosperity, but indulges, without restraint, the satisfactions which are afforded him by partaking of that of others. To know how to give, and how to receive, is of great use; and, however difficult to the envious and ill-natur'd, is very easy to the benevolent and good.[1]

> *En proie a la douleur, seule dans sa retraite,*
> A prey to grief, alone in her retreat,
> *Elle goute toujours une douceur secrete;*
> She always tastes a secret sweetness;
> *Le vice en ressent moins au milieu des plaisirs,*
> Vice relishes less in the midst of pleasures,
> *Qui sans remplir son coeur irritent ses desirs.*
> Which without satisfying her inclination provoke her longings.
> *Du plus affreux objet, du lieu le plus sauvage,* 555

---

8. But a good man . . . Providence: "Mais un homme de bien, qui sait pourquoi il a reçû, aime à se répandre en distributions" (p. 329).

9. in the other . . . dejection: "l'autre n'est point importun dans ses demandes" (p. 329).

1. To know how . . . good: "Savoir donner & savoir accepter, sont deux sciences différentes, mais l'une & l'autre d'un grand prix. Le vice en rend l'exercise bien difficile; la vertu le rend très aisé" (p. 329).

> From the most dismal object, from the most desart place,
> *La vertu sans effort tire quelque avantage;*
> Virtue without labour draws some advantage;
> *Sans jamais se lasser, toujours en mouvement;*
> Without ever being tired, always in motion;
> *Toujours prete, sans trouble, a tout evenement.*
> Always ready, without disturbance, for every event.
> *Que ses rivaux jaloux tombent dans la disgrace,*
> Let her jealous rivals fall into disgrace,
> *Qu'un revers imprevu confonde leur audace;* 560
> Let an unforeseen accident confound their confidence;
> *Qu'ils montent par le crime au comble des honneurs;*
> Let them mount by crimes to the height of honour;
> *Elle voit du meme oeil leur gloire & leurs malheurs.*
> She sees with an indifferent eye their glory and their misfortunes.
> *Soumise au loix du ciel, & jamais empressee*
> Submissive to the laws of heaven, and never busied
> *A former de projets une chaine insensee,*
> In forming a mad chain of projects,
> *Elle etouffe ou bannit tous desirs superflus;* 565
> She suppresses or banishes all superfluous desires;
> *Les siens sont satisfaits aussi-tot que concus.*
> Her own (wishes) are satisfied as soon as conceived.
> *Tel est le vray bonheur; la divine sagesse*
> Such is true happiness; the divine wisdom
> *En a fait aux humains une egale largesse:*
> Hath made of it to mankind an equal distribution:
> *Il est le seul sensible aux plus grossiers esprits,*
> It is the only one perceptible to the grossest understandings,
> *Le seul dont tous les coeurs puissent sentir le prix.* 570
> The only one whose worth every heart can feel.

This truth, which is hinted to us by reason, is confirmed by revelation, and proved by experience. This happiness is not the prerogative of deep reasoners, or capacities exalted above the common level;[2] for it often happens, that such men, endeavouring to rise still higher than nature intended, and aiming at reputation for discoveries out of the reach of vulgar minds, fall into errors, in which none but the subtle, and the inquisitive, could possibly have been entangled, and adhere with inflexible obstinacy to notions wholly opposite to the plainest truths, and most fundamental doctrines of religion.

> *Bonheur que les mechans, pauvres dans l'opulence,*
> A happiness which the wicked, poor amidst abundance,
> *Et, malgre leur savoir, plonges dans l'ignorance,*
> And, in spite of their learning, sunk in ignorance,
> *Recherchent nuit & jour sans pouvoir l'acquerir,*
> Search after night and day without being able to attain it,
> *Tandis que de lui-meme aux bons il vient s'offrir.*
> While of its own accord to the good it presents itself.
> *A l'homme vertueux l'esperance fidele* 575
> For the virtuous man hope assured
> *Fait briller pour lui seul sa lumiere immortelle,*
> Kindles up for him alone its immortal light,
> *Jusqu'a cet heureux jour, ou l'ardeur de la foi*
> Unto that happy day, when the fervour of faith
> *La remplisse, l'absorbe, & la confonde en soi;*
> Compleats, absorbs, and[g] blends it in itself;
> *Jour heureux, ou de Dieu notre ame penetree*
> Happy day, when with the Divinity our soul penetrated
> *Sera du vrai plaisir pour toujours enyvree!* 580
> Shall be with true pleasure for ever satiated!

I wrote my remarks on this poem as I read it,[3] and I have the satisfaction to find, as I proceed in it, that I have been

g. land

---

2. "or capacities . . . level" is an SJ addition.

3. SJ omits "de Mr. Du Resnel" (p. 331).

too hasty in producing my illustrations: so clear and so bright is the light in which the poetical translator has placed those, which the prose version exhibited with greater obscurity![4] I find here the sacred terms of *faith, hope,* and *charity;* but so introduced, that I find it not easy to know whence they came, or to annex to them, as they now stand, the ideas which they generally produce.

> *La nature nous porte, en ces terrestres lieux,*
> Nature leads us, in these terrestrial mansions,
> *A rechercher les biens qui s'offrent a nos yeux;*
> To court those good things which offer themselves
>   to our sight;
> *Tandis que de la foi les arrets infaillibles*
> Whilst of faith the dictates infallible
> *Nous montrent le bonheur dans des biens invisibles.*
> Shew us happiness in blessings invisible.

The word *nature* is here evidently intended to mean the passions[5] of a soul united to the body; passions which faith teaches us to subdue.[6] So that we have now, at length, recourse to REVELATION, which teaches to consider the natural, in opposition to the spiritual man; or the man that has no other ideas than what his senses suggest, that has no view beyond the gratification of his appetites, and the pleasures of the present life, to him that knows by experience the assistance of the divine grace, and that happiness which arises from devotion to his Creator.

> *Les animaux, guides par l'attrait de leurs sens,*   585
> The brutes, guided by the allurement of their
>   senses,

---

4. so clear . . . obscurity: "tant il m'a paru que l'illustre Abbé mettoit dans un beau & grand jour des vérités beaucoup moins précisément énoncées dans la Traduction en Prose" (p. 331).

5. passions: "panchans" (p. 332). In the *Dictionary* under "Anger," sense 3, SJ quotes Isaac Watts: "The word *passion* signifies the receiving any action in a large philosophical sense; in a more limited philosophical sense, it signifies any of the affections of human nature; as love, fear, joy, sorrow: but the common people confine it only to anger."

6. faith . . . subdue: "La Foi l'éléve au dessus" (p. 332).

> *Bornent tous leurs desirs aux seuls besoins presens;*
> Confine all their desires to present necessities only;
> *Mais l'homme, que le ciel doua d'intelligence,*
> But man, whom heaven hath endow'd with understanding,
> *S'etend dans l'avenir aide par l'esperance.*
> Reaches into futurity assisted by hope.

Man is here once more re-instated in his privileges, and exalted as far above the brute creation, as the heavens are above the earth. How widely doth this passage differ from some which are found in the three former essays![7] But this is perhaps not sufficient to remove the prejudices of corrupt minds, which the former assertions had contributed to strengthen. The ideas of virtue are here elegantly explained, but stand unsupported with such arguments, as might resolve the doubts that have been already raised. The poet, after having amused[8] us with such a description of the tranquillity, and pleasing ideas of the savage Indian, as might almost incline us to envy his condition, now exerts all the power of his fancy to exhibit a view of the virtuous man, whom he represents as worthy of the highest regard, and as entitled to boundless rewards: a delightful idea, a pleasing prospect, and exalted hopes;[9] but how well grounded he does not tell us, but leaves us still to doubt on about man's superiority to brutes.

> *La nature & la foi, par l'appas du bonheur,*
> Nature and faith, by the attractive of happiness,
> *Tournent a la vertu les desirs de son coeur,* 590
> Turn towards virtue the desires of his heart,
> *Redressent doucement sa pente tortueuse,*
> Rectify gently his inclination perverse,

---

7. in the three former essays: "dans la premiére, & dans une partie des deux suivantes" (p. 333).

8. after having amused: "Après avoir étalé" (p. 333).

9. whom he represents . . . hopes: "on lui promet de grandes récompenses; mais c'est un portrait, c'est une belle idée; ce sont de magnifiques espérances" (p. 334).

FOURTH EPISTLE 311

> *Brisent des passions la fougue impetueuse,*
> Break of the passions the tide impetuous,
> *Et le portant sans cesse a tendre vers le bien,*
> And inducing him continually to tend towards good,
> *Dans le bonheur d'autrui lui font trouver le sien.*
> In the happiness of others make him find his own.
> *Ainsi donc l'amour propre est rendu sociable;* 595
> Thus then self-love is rendered social;
> *Aux yeux meme du ciel il devient agreable;*
> In the sight of heaven itself it becomes agreeable;
> *Par lui l'homme se rend doux, bienfaisant, humain,*
> By it man is made gentle, beneficent, humane,
> *Et ne sauroit s'aimer qu'il n'aime son prochain.*
> And knows not to love himself but in loving his neighbour.

Man is conscious of his existence, and delighted with it: he inquires after the Author of so great a blessing,[1] to return his acknowledgments, to receive his commands, and to make them the rule of his life: finding his search not vain, and his wishes granted, he feels new ardours of gratitude, and is more zealous to obey: this zeal is rewarded, and his gratitude still increases. God furnishes him with proper objects for the exercise of his gratitude, and teaches him to regard other men as his brethren, and to love them as he loves himself. As the love of himself prompts him to acquire what is convenient for him, and to preserve his acquisitions, so his love of others inclines him to endeavour the increase of their happiness: he has a like sense of their advantage and his own, and the affection[2] he has for them and for himself are so connected in his mind, that he forgets to distinguish them.

---

1. the Author . . . blessing: "Créateur" (p. 334).

2. As the love . . . affection: SJ eschews a series of questions posed by Crousaz: "Pourquoi prend-il plaisir à sentir ses propres biens? Pourquoi prend-il plaisir à les conserver & à les augmenter? C'est qu'il s'aime. De même, pourquoi prend-il plaisir à voir ses freres heureux? Pourquoi prend-il plaisir à y contribuer? C'est qu'il les aime. L'affection" (p. 335).

> *Des nobles sentimens, dont ton ame est pourvue,*
> Of the noble sentiments, with which thy mind
>   is furnished,
> *Est-ce trop, selon toi, resserrer l'etendue?* 600
> Is it too hard, in thy opinion, to confine the
>   extent?
> *Jusqu'a*[h] *tes ennemis, par de plus grands efforts,*
> Even to thy enemies, by the greatest efforts,
> *Porte de ton amour les genereux transports;*
> Extend of thy love the generous transports;
> *Sur celle de ton Dieu regle ta bien-veillance;*
> By that of thy God regulate thy benevolence;

Of this conclusion we see the reasonableness and the necessity, but do not so easily concur with the following exhortation:

> *Que ton coeur s'interesse a tout etre qui pense,*
> Let thy heart interest itself for ev'ry being that
>   thinks,
> *A tout etre qui vit, a ces mondes divers,* 605
> For ev'ry being that lives, in those various worlds,
> *Qui forment, avec toi, cet immense univers.*
> Which makes up, with thee, this immense universe.

It is not without some struggles that we prevail upon ourselves to love our enemies, and the grace of God is necessary to raise us to an affectionate and warm concern for them. But as for the rest of the universe, and all those immense spaces which we gaze at from afar, or which are expanded at an immense distance beyond our view,[3] we do not feel for their inhabitants any emotions of aversion, or any tendencies to love. And indeed while we are encompassed more nearly with so great a number of objects that demand our attention and re-

h. Jusq'a

---

3. and all . . . view: "& de tous les Etres vivans qui les habitent, de ce que l'on ne voit pas" (p. 336).

gard, it would be at least a very unnecessary, perhaps an unreasonable solicitude, to encourage any sentiments of tenderness for the inhabitants of Jupiter, or to send up wishes for the prosperity of the planetary nations.[4]

Would it not be an extraordinary conversation, if a minister should ask one of those whom he was instructing in religion, *What tenderness do you feel for the inhabitants of Saturn?* Might he not answer properly, *I never once thought of them*,[5] *there are men sufficient to engross my affection, and employ my benevolence.* And would not the teacher make himself compleatly ridiculous, if he should proceed to admonish him in terms like these, viz. *How little, poor-narrow-thoughted wretch, art thou acquainted with the extent of Christian charity! Learn to raise thy affection yet higher than the orb of Saturn, and diffuse it to the utmost bounds of the creation.*[6] Such hyperboles as these prove that the writer does not well consider what he is saying; a negligence, which often steals upon a writer that has no farther views than to dazzle the imagination of his reader.[7]

I acknowledge that a man devoted to God, and elevated to raptures with admiration at the view of his amazing works, may sometimes wish that he could communicate, even to inanimate beings, his sentiments and his voice,[8] that they might all unite with him in paying their thanksgiving to their common Creator, whose glory they display with so much magnificence, without[i] being conscious of the hand that formed them.

---

i. with

---

4. or to send . . . nations: "& pour ceux des Planétes, qui peuvent environner toutes les Etoiles fixes" (pp. 336-37).

5. Might he . . . them: "Ne mériteroit-il pas qu'on lui répondît: 'Je n'y ai jamais pensé, pas seulement en rêve'" (p. 337).

6. *How little . . . creation:* "O misérable! que vous connoissez peu l'étenduë de la Charité Chrétienne! Apprenez à l'élever infiniment au delà de Saturne" (p. 337).

7. a negligence . . . reader: "c'est ce qui arrive ordinairement, quand on n'a en vuë que de briller" (p. 337).

8. at the view . . . voice: "à la vuë attentive de ses ouvrages uniquement corporels, voudroit être en état de leur prêter sa voix & ses sentimens" (p. 337). SJ's description of God's works as "amazing" is a long way from Crousaz's "solely material" or "uniquely physical."

I own too, that a soul filled with piety, and informed of the existence of those happy beings that are without number employ'd in the praises of their Creator, with raptures which we cannot yet conceive, may dwell with delight upon their excellence and happiness. He may rejoice at their superior bliss, and tho' he feels himself yet unworthy to be admitted to bear his part in those sacred festivities, hopes to arrive at length to the same perfection, and those hopes enable him to rise towards it. But the regard and reverence with which he considers those exalted beings, are very different from that goodwill and kindness which he feels for his brethren on earth. With such compassion and love the angels may, perhaps, look down upon us; but we cannot reflect upon them without far different emotions.[9]

This chimerical diffusion of benevolence can exist only upon the absurd supposition of a totality, or complex system,[1] of which all the parts are so constantly dependent upon each other, that no one can be displaced, or interrupted in its motion, or suffer any alteration in its manner of action, without bringing confusion upon the whole, and consequently upon us, who are an essential part of it: thus[j] interest will extend our kindness as wide as motion and existence are diffused. Yet we are without any apprehensions of such irregularities;[2] for the machine of the universe, with the various particles that contribute to it, are so formed and regulated, that no power less than that of God can produce the least alteration; and that infinite perfection, which determined him to create this work in that state, which of all others was alone worthy

j. But *errata*

9. He may rejoice . . . emotions: "elle sent combien elle est éloignée de mériter de se voir reçuë dans leurs divins concerts; elle l'espére pourtant, ses desirs s'y élévent; mais ce ne sont pas là des élévations de charité pour ces glorieuses Intelligences. C'est à nous à être les objets de la leur, & non pas à elles à être les objets de la nôtre" (p. 338).

1. This chimerical . . . system: "Cette prétenduë & chimérique affection ne peut avoir de fondement que dans le chimérique systême d'une Totalité" (p. 338).

2. Yet we . . . irregularities: "Mais vivons en repos sur ce sujet" (p. 339).

FOURTH EPISTLE 315

of his wisdom, will determine him likewise to preserve it entire and unchanged, since every variation must diminish its excellence, which is already such, that it cannot be imagined greater without absurdity.

The consequences of this hypothesis extend far. The credit of miracles, or deviations from the natural order of things, falls immediately; for nothing that has been, could have been[k] otherwise, or could possibly not have been. Such is the foundation of the grand paradox, so often repeated, and strongly recommended, *Whatever is, is right;*[3] it was necessary to the perfection of the universe, that every thing should be as it really is.

The universe would be a work less worthy of its Author, if there were neither atheism nor superstition to be found in it; it would be defective without persecution and idolatry, nor could the tyrant, the poisoner, and the assassin be reformed without destroying part of the beauty of the creation.[4] When, therefore, one of these ornaments of nature[5] should be asked, *How many have died this month by his ponyard,* or another, *How many have tasted his powder to their destruction,* the asserter of this happy hypothesis might answer, upon hearing the number,[6] *I congratulate you upon your good actions, which may be likewise a rational ground of satisfaction to yourselves. Whatever you have done was right. This may be proved without difficulty: you have done it,* And whatever is, is right. *The universe had been less perfect, if what has happened had either not happened at all, or happened in any other manner;* the grand machine, of which the motions are irresistible, and the effects certain, was so consti-

k. heen

---

3. SJ substitutes Pope (I.294 and IV.394) for Crousaz's *"Tout ce qui existe est Bien"* (p. 340). In the next paragraph he substitutes the line for Crousaz's quotation of Silhouette" (pp. 25, 111).

4. The universe ... creation: "L'Univers ne seroit pas un ouvrage assez digne de Dieu, s'il n'y avoit pas des Athées, des Superstitieux, des Persécuteurs, des Tyrans, des Idolâtres, des Assassins, des Empoisonneurs" (p. 340).

5. ornaments of nature: "braves gens" (p. 340).

6. the asserter ... number: "l'un en nommeroit dix, & l'autre quinze. Un homme zêlé pour le Système, auroit lieu de leur répliquer" (p. 340).

tuted from the beginning, as to produce those actions in you which you have now been performing.

> *De l'amour propre en nous l'impetueuse flamme*
> Of self-love in us the vehement flame
> *Anime a la vertue les puissances de l'ame.*
> Animates to virtue the powers of the soul.

When self-love is predominant and unrestrained,[7] the effects of it are uncertain, but for the most part prejudicial to society; for it suffers the man who is enslaved by it, to regard nothing but his own advantage, it incites him to exert his utmost force; to gratify his desires;[8] and unhappy is that man, who, without strength to conquer him, shall have spirit to oppose him. On the contrary, the more a man studies the good of others, the less he considers his own interest, and while he is attentive to serve the public, suffers his own affairs to pass less regarded. The impetuous nature of self-love is therefore only maintained here, to give dignity to the following comparison.

> *Comme on voit une pierre, en tombant dans les eaux,*
> As you see a stone, in falling into the water,
> *Y former a l'instant des circles*[9] *inegaux,*   610
> There make at that instant circles unequal,
> *Qui croissant, par degres, de distance en distance,*
> Which increasing, by degrees, distance after distance,
> *A mille autres bientot donnent encor naissance;*
> To a thousand others soon again give rise;
> *De meme l'amour propre, agissant sur le coeur,*
> Even so self-love, working in the heart,
> *Fait cherir le parent, l'ami, le serviteur;*
> Endears the kinsman, the friend, the servant;

---

7. When self-love . . . unrestrained: "Dès que l'amour propre est impétueux" (p. 341).

8. for it suffers . . . desires: "Un amour propre véhément rapporte tout à soi, il se livre à ses desirs, & tout ce qu'il se trouve de puissance, il le met en oeuvre pour les faire remplir" (p. 341).

9. Crousaz correctly has "cercles" (p. 341).

FOURTH EPISTLE

> *Apres eux la patrie attire sa tendresse;* 615
> Next to them his country draws his affections;
> *A tout le genre humain enfin il s'interesse,*
> For all mankind at last he is concerned,
> *Et suivant de son coeur les premiers mouvemens,*
> And following of his heart the first propensities,
> *Il en repand par tout les vifs epanchemens.*
> He diffuses all around the lively overflowings.

These circles are formed in a regular succession, and extend but to a small compass; as they are multiplied they rise less, and soon sink to a level with the rest of the water. These circumstances make the comparison just. Our sensibility, activity, and strength, are confined to narrow limits, and as our love is diffused to a great number of objects, its motions are more languid, and less perceptible. If a father has twelve sons whom he loves equally, and to whose interests he has an equal regard, no sooner does one of these fall dangerously sick, than the father's whole solicitude is engrossed by him, and he is treated with a degree of tenderness which he never found before. The rest do not in reality lose the affection of their father, but his thoughts are at that time so contracted by the present danger, that he does not attend to his affection for them, or dwell upon any sentiments of love that arise in his mind.[1]

> *Plus l'homme vertueux devient sensible & tendre,*
> The more a virtuous man becomes sensible and tender,
> *Plus il sent son bonheur s'aggrandir & s'etendre;* 620
> The more does he feel his happiness spread and increase;

We are born to love one another, and the more any man indulges his benevolence, the more sensibly he perceives the

---

1. than the father's . . . mind: "son attention ne s'occupe que de lui; ce n'est pas que les autres lui soient indifférens; mais dans cette circonstance, il ne se donne pas le tems de sentir à quel point il les affectionne" (pp. 342–43). This is a particularly good example of SJ's tendency to expand the meaning.

happiness of loving; the more he practises his duty, the more agreeable does his duty grow.

> *Et quand son feu s'enpure,*[2] *& devient charite,*
> And when his fire is purified, and becomes charity,
> *Il met enfin le comble a la felicite.*
> He puts at last the finishing stroke to happiness.

The meaning of these two lines is not extremely clear, but this is the sense in which I understand them. In proportion as our self-love becomes more pure, that is, as we have less need to make use of private considerations to incite us to love others, as we love them, with less attention to our own interest, and less regard to the return of kindness that may be expected from those who receive proofs of our regard; as the bare consideration that they are our brethren, the sons of the same father, and the works of God, is sufficient to influence us to love and esteem them, the more certainly do we love them as we ought, and that love so purified acquires the name of charity, and becomes a virtue of the first rank.[3] With such affection as this, do we love those objects which are really dear to us.

At the conclusion, Mr Pope, that he may deserve, in every respect, the character of a great poet, addresses his patron in the same manner which the ancients used to call upon the muse; and it may be asserted, without flattery, that he has improved upon his originals. He confesses himself indebted to the just discernment, extensive knowledge, and boundless invention of his noble friend, for all the beauties of his poem; and in a few lines gives us a succinct account of the science of poetry, which, if it is read with Horace's long letter to the Pisoes will will not suffer by the comparison.[4]

---

2. Crousaz correctly has "s'épure" (p. 343).

3. the more certainly . . . rank: "plus il est vrai que nous les aimons effectivement; & cette affection, ainsi pure, & ainsi dégagée de vuës intéressées, porte le nom de *Charité*" (p. 344).

4. Pope's concluding lines are also partly suggested by Horace's *Satires*, I.10.1–19. Du Resnel's translation of these lines is, at this point, reasonably accurate. The letter to the Pisos is the *Ars Poetica*.

FOURTH EPISTLE

Arbitre de mes chants, mon genie, & mon maitre,
Judge of my song, my genius, and my master,
Seconde les transports que toi-meme a fait naitre;
Assist the raptures which thyself hast raised;
Tandis qu'en liberte variant mes accens   625
While with freedom changing my notes
Je m'eleve tantot, & tantot je descens;
I soar sometimes, and sometimes stoop;
Que ma muse de l'homme expose la noblesse,
That my muse of man may set forth the dignity,
Ou decouvre au grand jour le fond de sa bassesse;
Or displays in full light his lowest pitch of meanness;
Qu'anime par le feu de tes doctes lecons
That quicken'd by the fire of thy learned instructions
Je prenne, comme toi, tous les airs, tous les tons;   630
I may comprehend, like thee, all forms, all sounds;
Que selon le sujet, par un sage contraste,
That according to the subject, by a judicious contrast,
Je tombe sans bassesse, & m'eleve sans faste:
I may sink without meanness, and soar without ostentation:
Que je puisse, imitant ton stile ingenieux,
That I may, in imitation of thy ingenious stile,
Passer du grave au doux, du vif au serieux,
Pass from grave to pleasing, from lively to severe,
Dans les traits les plus forts eviter la rudesse,   635
In strokes the boldest to avoid harshness,
Dans le plus grand essor conserver la justesse,
In the loftiest flight to preserve correctness,
Et donner de la grace a mes raissonnemens,[5]
And to add grace to my arguments,
Sans affoiblir leur poids par de vains ornemens.

---

5. Crousaz has "raisonnemens" (p. 345).

Without weakening their force by vain embellishments.

Mr Pope, to omit nothing that the rules of poetry require, or which the examples of those who are allowed the greatest masters of that art had recommended to the imitation of posterity, expatiates upon the pleasing hopes of transmitting his patron's name, and his own to immortality, but he expresses these sentiments with more delicacy and address than his predecessors.[6]

> *O! tandis que ton nom recueillant notre hommage,*
> Oh! while thy name, collecting our homage,
> *Sur le courant du tems passera d'age en age,*   640
> Down the current of time shall pass from age to age,
> *Di-moi, puis-je esperer que mon frele vaisseau*
> Tell me, can I hope that my frail vessel
> *Accompagne de loin un triomphe si beau;*
> Shall accompany at distance a triumph so fair;
> *Qu'avec toi partageant le vent qui te seconde,*
> That with thee partaking the gale that thee favours,
> *Mon nom avec le tien vole un jour dans le monde?*
> My name with thine shall fly one day through the world?

Mr Pope writes like a poet, and a poet of the first class. But every man has his inadvertencies, and Mr Pope, while he wrote this passage, forgot the judicious precepts he had been laying down, and the censures which he had so justly cast upon that vain desire of an useless immortality.[7]

This is not the only inconsistency to be found in these essays,[8] and I know some who, from the author's disagreement with himself, have conjectured, that he did not com-

---

6. but he expresses . . . predecessors: "Mais il le fait avec plus de détour & de modestie qu'eux." (p. 345).

7. Mr Pope, while . . . immortality: "Mr. POPE paroit avoir oublié les leçons qu'il donne si judicieusement sur cette soif d'une vaine immortalité, dans le Vers 408. & les suivans" (p. 346). See p. 291 above.

8. these essays: "ces quatre Epitres" (p. 346).

pose these poems in a regular series of study, but that having written several fragments of poetry, each finished in its kind; such as the parallel of reason and instinct, the ill-grounded vanity of mankind,[9] the contrast of religion and superstition, the original of communities, and several paragraphs upon the passions and self-love, he digested them into these four essays,[1] as they are said to have anciently collected the rhapsodies of Homer.

> *Lorsqu'enfin les heros, les ministres, les rois,* 645
> When at last heroes, ministers, kings,
> *De l'implacable mort auront subi les loix,*
> Of implacable death shall have submitted to the laws,
> *Que les fils rougiront, informes que leurs peres,*
> How the sons will blush, when told that their fathers,
> *Jaloux de ton eclat, furent tes adversaires!*
> Jealous of thy glory, were thy enemies!

Mr Pope does not seem to flatter himself with the improvements which posterity will make by his precepts, and particularly by that grand and philosophical conclusion, on which he dwells with so much pleasure, *Whatever is, is right;* for if the *sons shall blush that their fathers were the foes*[2] *of* Lord Bolingbrooke, they must be so far from believing that *whatever is, is right,* that with regard to the opposition made by their fathers to his designs, they must be convinced that *many things are wrong.*

> *Percans*[3] *de l'avenir les* voiles *tenebreux,*
> Penetrating of futurity, the dark *veil,*
> *Ces vers apprendont-ils*[4] *a nos derniers neveux,* 650
> These verses will inform our latest posterity,

---

9. SJ omits "un autre sur les *Prérogatives* de la Nature humaine" (p. 346).

1. essays: "Lettres" (p. 346).

2. SJ substitutes Pope (I.294 and IV.394) for Crousaz's quotation and paraphrase of Silhouette (pp. 25, lll). He also substitutes a paraphrase of IV.388 (378) for a paraphrase of ll. 647–48 of Du Resnel (p. 347).

3. Crousaz correctly has "Perçant" (p. 347).

4. Crousaz correctly has "apprendront-ils" (p. 347).

Que, m'ouvrant les tresors de la philosophie,
That, opening to me the treasures of philosophy,
Tu fus et le soutien & l'honneur de ma vie:
Thou wast both the support and ornament of my life:
Qu'encourage par toi, je cherchai dans mes chants
That animated by thee, I have sought in my song
Non le charme des sons, mais la beaute du sens;
Not the charm of sounds, but the beauty of sense;
Que j'osai negliger les peintures *brillantes,* 655
That I have dared to neglect glittering *expressions,*
Pour presentir[5] *au coeur des* verites *touchantes;*
To offer to the heart affecting *truths;*

Mr Pope[6] thinks too modestly of his poetry, and I believe he is indebted to the power of that engaging art, to the charms of his music, and the brightness of his colouring, for having been able to dazzle or affect any other readers[7] than such as were already prejudiced in favour of his hypothesis, an hypothesis that recommends itself to regard by flattering the inclination so prevalent in most men, to live without constraint, without remorse, and without apprehension of future punishment.

Let him say in plain terms without the blaze of description, or the allurements of verse, that men, however they may exult upon their superiority to the brute creation, received far less benefits from their boasted reason than were bestowed by instinct on other animals; that they had never known how to build without being instructed by the mole, or to sail without the example of the nautilus, that they owed the art of weaving to the spider, the laws of republicks to the ant, and the monarchical form of government to the bee.[8]

---

5. Crousaz correctly has "présenter" (p. 347).
6. Mr. Pope: "Pour le coup Mr. POPE" (p. 347).
7. I believe...readers: "je doute que, sans tout le secours de l'Art, le charme des sens, & ses peintures brillantes, il eût ébloui d'autres Lecteurs" (p. 348).
8. Let him say . . . bee: "S'il avoit dit tout simplement, l'Homme est un Animal bien orgueilleux de se croire plus que les Bêtes; sa Raison le sert-elle

FOURTH EPISTLE 323

Let him declare, that the religion of men, while they lived under the direction of God, was the same with that of beasts, that the first adorations of the Divine Being were paid jointly by men and beasts in the desarts.⁹ To conclude, let the philosophy and divinity of Mr Pope be proposed in a plain summary, without embellishments, and it will appear whether such positions as he has here laid down, will obtain credit by their own evidence, and it will be more easy to examine whether some secret passions, and latent ill principles,¹ are not the chief motives of the desire that any man feels to find them true.

> *Qu'eteignant de l'erreur le vulgaire flambeau,*
> That extinguishing of error the vulgar torch,
> *Je fis sur les mortels briller un* jour *nouveau;*
> I caused on mortals to shine a new *light;*

These opinions, which he terms a false mirror,² appear to me the most valuable truths, by which the conduct of the truly knowing is regulated, and upon which the hopes of the good are founded. What he terms the light of nature, is a gloomy glimmer, which affords no certain direction. That his principles are without proof, and, if they are disintangled from equivocations, without consequence, we have not only asserted, but often proved, as well in the foregoing *Examen* as in this attempt.

> *Que de l'*orgueil *humain confondant l'imposture,*
> That of human *pride* confuting the imposture,

---

aussi bien que l'Instinct sert ceux qui ne connoissent pas la Raison? Sans les instructions qu'il a reçû des Araignées, des Taupes, des Fourmis, des Castors, des Abeilles, du petit poisson Nautilus, y auroit-il jamais eu parmi les hommes de Tisserans & de Laboureurs? auroient-ils jamais pensé à faire des maisons, ni à construire des bateaux? & l'idée leur seroit-elle jamais venuë, ni de République, ni de Monarche?" (p. 348).

9. desarts: "forêts" (p. 349).

1. some secret . . . principles: "des principes & des panchans secrets peu louables" (p. 349).

2. SJ substitutes the image from l. 393 of Pope for Crousaz's "*le flambeau du Vulgaire,*" paraphrasing l. 657 of Du Resnel (p. 349).

> *J'appris que tout est bien dans toute la nature,* 660
> I have taught that all is right throughout all nature,

But what can be more agreeable to the pride of man, than to be told that he is under no restraint, that the reproaches of his conscience are chimerical anxieties, that there is no punishment to be feared, and that whatever he has done *is right*.

> *Que de nos passions, les prompts elancemens*
> That of our passions the sudden sallies
> *Pretent a la raison d'utiles instrumens;*
> Lend to reason useful instruments;
> *Que l'amour-propre,*[3] *loin d'etre meprisable,*
> That self-love, far from being contemptible,
> *Fait le bonheur de l'homme, & le rend sociable;*
> Makes the happiness of man, and renders him social;

An attempt has been already made to explain the nature, and show the necessity of self-love, and to distinguish the good from the bad use of it, without ambiguity or perplexity.

> *Qu'il ne peut ici bas etre vraiment heureux,* 665
> That he cannot here below be truly happy,
> *Si la seule vertu n'est l'objet de ses voeux;*
> If *virtue* alone be not the object of his desires;

To free the idea of virtue from the exaggerations of Stoicism, has been likewise endeavoured. The source of true virtue has been laid open and it has been proved that it is not to be accounted a moral excellence, but merely a physical effect, unless we allow in man not only the faculty of receiving different determinations, which is only a kind of *passive* liberty, but also an *active* liberty, or power of determining himself.[4]

> *Et que, pour un mortel, la* science *supreme*
> And that, for a mortal, the highest *knowledge*
> *Et enfin de savoir se connoitre soi-meme.*
> Is in short to learn to know himself.

---

3. Crousaz has "l'amour propre au fond" (p. 350).

4. power ... himself: "un pouvoir de se déterminer lui-même" (p. 351).

He that studies that important science, the knowledge of himself, under the direction of Mr Pope, will, at the end of his enquiries, find his mind clouded with uncertainty, and perplexed with contradictions, he will have few clear ideas to contemplate, and yet less evidence to support his opinions. If it be true that he has in reality adopted the system to which he seems too much inclined, his ideas of human nature are directly opposite to those that are discovered to us by that Light which most deserves to be reverenced and followed.

FINIS.

A LETTER TO MR CROUSAZ.

Sir,

I have been reading[5] your second examen in your friend's hands, and am astonished at the efforts that you make to free Mr Pope from the suspicion of favouring the fatalists;[6] a sincere account of the reasons of this conduct will be considered as a great favour, by, Sir,
    Your, &c.

The ANSWER.

Sir,

My intention is to give you the satisfaction that you desire, without any artifice or disguise.[7]

When I take an impartial survey of the Leibnitzian system, without any regard to the celebrated name of its author, from which all the prejudice that can affect my enquiries must proceed; for I never had the least reason for personal malevolence to his character:[8] the more attentively I dwell upon it, the more inconsistent does it appear, not only with revealed truths, but with those that seem most confirmed by the evidence of reason, and the more plainly do I discover how weakly it is supported by argument and proof:[9] so that, in consequence of my own observations,[1] I always de-

---

5. Sir, I . . . reading: "*Je viens, Monsieur, de lire*" (p. 352).

6. and am astonished . . . fatalists: "*Je m'étonne que vous vous donniez tant de mouvemens, &, si je l'ose dire, tant d'entorses, pour dégager* Mr. POPE *du soupçon de* Fatalisme" (p. 352).

7. Sir, My intention . . . disguise: "Je vai, *Monsieur,* vous satisfaire en toute sincérité" (p. 352).

8. When I take . . . character: "Lorsque, mettant à part la réputation de Mr. *Leibnits,* j'examine son Systême d'un esprit dégagé de toute prévention, car je n'en eus jamais la moindre ombre contre lui" (p. 352).

9. the more inconsistent . . . proof: "plus je le trouve incompatible avec la Révélation, destituté en lui-même de preuves évidentes, & en contradiction avec ce que la Raison me paroit établir avec le plus d'évidence" (pp. 352–53).

1. observations: "sentimens" (p. 353).

cline charging any man with adhering to so absurd and pernicious an hypothesis,[2] who does not in plain terms profess that he adopts it.

Some of these profound theologians I have met with,[3] who have declared expressly, that God will not inflict any punishment in a future state,[4] because no being can suffer for its actions without injustice. And others that profess this system, however they may disguise their sentiments, prove, by their conduct, that they are in very little apprehension of retributions to come, and live with great security in a course of debauchery and drunkenness, and practise any artifice, without scruple, by which they can impose on the credulity, or encroach upon the property of others.[5]

There are some slow capacities that are satisfied with sounds, and embrace opinions dressed up in plausible language,[6] without seeing the dreadful consequences that flow necessarily from them. Some of these are even stupid enough to celebrate the justice of Providence, for adding new followers to their sect, and fortifying their opinion with new vindicators, when they ought rather to blush at their associates, and abandon the system, when they see it only supported by libertines, the meanest, and the worst part of mankind.[7]

Many of these give themselves very little trouble to examine the foundations of a system, the absurdity of which they cannot but perceive; they have a nearer way to security, and lull themselves in their negligence, by knowing in general, that some men of the first character[8] have set them at full liberty, and freed them from the fetters of moral obligations,

---

2. absurd . . . hypothesis: "ce Système" (p. 353). This is a remarkable example of slanting by SJ, consistent with his view of Leibnitz: "Leibnitz was as paltry a fellow as I know" (*Life*, V.287).

3. Some of these . . . with: "Entre ceux-là" (p. 353).

4. SJ adds "in a future state."

5. and live . . . others: "yvrognes, impurs, menteurs, de mauvaise foi, & disposant hardiment de ce dont il ne leur étoit pas permis de rien distraire" (p. 353).

6. There are . . . language: "Il est des esprites pesans, qui se payent de mots" (p. 353).

7. fortifying their opinion . . . mankind: "lorsqu'ils devroient s'en faire une honte, parce que ce sont des Libertins" (p. 354).

8. some men . . . character: "des Savans de réputation" (p. 354).

by proving that there is nothing to be feared in another life. These men, so learned, and so inquisitive, compose the main body of the present fatalists.[9]

It seems now not improper to acquaint you with the principal reasons,[1] that hold me at the greatest distance from this opinion: some of them you have read already, and of the others I shall give you only a short summary, having a design of enlarging on this question, in a new edition of my *Treatise on the Mind of Man,* to which I intend to make large additions.

In the first place it seems a very improper, if not a criminal degree of rashness, for understandings, limited like ours, to determine, That of all the plans of the creation that could be formed by infinite knowledge, one only appeared so compleat, that the Divine Being was, by his own attributes, laid under the necessity of chusing it. Whatever degree of perfection we assign to a system of created and independent beings, this perfection must have its limits, and fall below the supreme excellence, the excellence of the Divine Being, the only being absolutely infinite. Now that of several systems, each excellent indeed, but not strictly perfect, there may not be more than one, of which the excellence, considered in general, may be equal to the excellence of any other, is a supposition, of which we cannot have evidence sufficient to make it the foundation of a system, a system not only unheard of till now, but entangled with such great and terrifying difficulties.

In the second place, who shall convince us, that of two plans of an universe, that which is inhabited by beings invested with powers to deliberate, and freedom to chuse, is not more perfect than that which is only a receptacle of passive creatures, free only in appearance, acted upon irresistibly by superior powers, and unable to regulate their own motions. But I shall not repeat, upon this occasion, what I have already said on this subject.

Thirdly, by this the doctrines of natural philosophy are entirely destroyed, for it is agreed by the writers of that science,

---

9. These men . . . fatalists: "ceux-ci font le gros du cortége" (p. 354).

1. the principal reasons: "quelques-unes des raisons principales" (p. 354).

that to give a rational explication of natural appearances, it must first be made appear, that the effects bear a just proportion to the causes to which they are assigned.

That nothing can deviate more widely from this principle, than the hypothesis which we are now examining, I shall prove by one instance: there is in letters, or marks, differently combined, no inherent, or physical power of signifying words, but their force depends wholly upon custom, and an arbitrary choice to which mankind has agreed.

Yet, according to this system, a machine not directed by any power of intelligence, and entirely unconscious of its own motions, shall, upon the pronounciation of these words, *Take this* Greek, *and translate it into* Latin, *and you shall receive a guinea a page*,[2] immediately, without understanding the import of those words, have its parts so disposed, that it shall call for pens, ink, and paper,[3] and, from the impression made upon its eyes by the Greek, of which impression it has no perception, writes Latin characters, which having no natural relation to the Greek, express the same things, and represent exactly the same ideas. This instance will press upon the mind more strongly, if it be carried on through the booksellers,[4] the purchasers, the machines that read, and that write remarks.

Such is the constitution of the universal machine, that subordinate machines, called human bodies,[5] after several encampments and battles, in which they have, without knowing why, cut the throats of each other, in pursuance of some orders, of which they have no idea, shall be disposed to lie without action; during which time, some other human machines hold a congress, and after some preliminaries, entirely uncomprehended by any of the negociators, come to the principal question, and, after some debates, utterly unintelligible to the disputants, one machine receives several millions, which he carries off without being sensible of it; and

---

2. *a guinea a page:* "*un Ducat par feuille*" (p. 357).

3. pens, ink, and paper: "papier blanc, de l'encre, des plumes, des canifs pour les tailler" (p. 357).

4. This instance . . . booksellers: "Suivez cela jusques aux Libraires" (p. 357).

5. human bodies: "Corps humain, placées sur la Terre" (p. 357).

then the machines of war march out of the cities which they had taken possession of, and others return to their habitations, without knowing, on either side, what they are leaving, or whither they are coming.

And that this universal machine may want nothing that can contribute to its perfection, the Great Creator has chosen, or, to speak in the language of this wonderful philosophy, was determined by his own immutable nature,[6] to chuse one out of an innumerable number of possible beings, a being capable of thinking, and to make him *me;* with regard to this being it was decreed, that from the birth of this corporeal machine with which he was associated, a series of sentiments should be inevitably produced in him, in exact conformity with the motions of my corporeal machine, and the impressions which should be made upon it, of which sentiments he should imagine himself to be invested with the direction. Another substance is doom'd in the same manner to receive its determinations from your body, and to a third is assigned another mode of thinking, to be produced with equal certainty by like causes.[7] Thus the motions of our bodies have been determined from the beginning of the world, and we act by a constant impulse, of which we are not conscious, and which we cannot resist while our souls are exposed by their relation to our bodies to a continual train of chimeras and delusions.[8]

But this is not all that may be urged against the perfection of the Leibnitzian universe. One machine is impelled, by the great series of causes, to commit murder, its parts are disposed, and its springs set to produce this particular effect: another mixes a bowl of poison, in consequence of the same over-ruling direction,[9] and when, by the motions of other machines acting in concurrence with some parts of the uni-

---

6. or, to speak . . . nature: "ou plutôt est déterminé inévitablement par ses souvéraines perfections" (p. 358).

7. a third . . . causes: "Une troisiéme seroit assignée à penser conformément à une autre &c." (p. 359).

8. a continual . . . delusions: "une suite éternelle d'illusions" (p. 359).

9. But this . . . direction: "Ce n'est pas tout; une machine est inévitablement déterminée à assassiner, & montée pour produire ces effets; une autre, pour empoisonner" (p. 359).

verse, it shall come to pass that the one shall be broken on the wheel, and the other burned at a stake, though they will neither know the sentence, nor feel the punishment, they will vent the most dreadful outcries of impatience and despair,[1] which yet have no meaning with regard to those that utter them. But these two substances, chosen from all eternity out of an infinite number of beings, that might possibly have been formed to accompany those bodies, would suffer horrid tortures, without having deserved them; for how could beings incapable of directing their own motions, and unable to break the chain of sentiments following each other by a physical necessity, offend a just master, or expose themselves to his vengeance.[2]

Let us now withdraw our attention from these horrid consequences,[3] and direct it to absurdities of another kind, absurdities that may rather excite mirth than indignation; for such they are, and in such numbers, that upon a moment's reflection they crowd themselves upon us.

The corporeal machine of Mr Resnel is so formed, and his hand, without the direction of his mind, so impelled by the influences of the universe, that it has written a poem, which, by a series of irresistible and invariable causes, has been laid before my eyes;[4] but those eyes have never seen it yet. However, the thinking substance, which I call *myself*, has been so properly selected, that an inevitable train of ideas, perceptions, and inclinations, have produced in it the very same sentiments, sounds, and characters, that had before arisen in the mind of that great poet, though I was never able to write a verse.

---

1. though they will . . . despair: "à la vérité elles n'en sauroient rien, & n'en sentiroient rien, cependant elles feroient des cris desesperés" (p. 360).

2. "offend . . . vengeance" is an SJ addition. He also turns the sentence into a question.

3. consequences: "réflexions" (p. 360).

4. The corporeal machine . . . eyes: "La machine corporelle de Mr. l'Abbé DU RESNEL a été déterminée par sa construction & par celle de l'Univers; & la main de cette machine, sans savoir ce qu'elle faisoit, & sans être dirigée par l'ame de cet élégant Auteur, aura tracé des Vers que l'enchainure des événemens aura amené sous mes yeux, c'est-à-dire sous les yeux de ma machine" (pp. 360–61).

If I was at Paris, and should in passing over the Pont Neuf hear certain machines sing ballads,[5] if the song made any impression upon me, I should, by the same series of causes, be made a wretched poet, and an unsufferable fidler.[6] At the opera, the case would be alter'd, I should immediately rise up a poet and musician of the first class, without being indebted to the actors for my new accomplishments; for whatever impressions they may make upon my eyes and ears, they could have, according to this admirable system,[7] no effect upon my thinking part. At the French theatre I should shed tears, and have the sentiments of Voltaire. At the Italian I should burst into laughter,[8] and form such scenes as would suit the character of Harlequin. At the academy I should receive not the least instruction from my learned associates, but should imagine myself indebted to their conversation for those ideas that would have arisen in my mind without their assistance. And, to conclude, when, by the great chain of causes, I have been introduced to the conversation of the first persons in the world, I should, by such a succession of ideas as would then be produced in me, find myself exalted to a degree of genius and elevation, of which I never believed myself capable, but unfortunately this illumination would be withdrawn at the instant in which I took my leave.

Is this the universe, the perfect system which the omniscience of God was necessitated to make choice of out of an infinite number of other schemes? Is the continual motion of unintelligent machines, are the perpetual dreams of beings that falsely imagine themselves vested with freedom, the noblest exertions of infinite power?[9]

But a great mathematician, a man of extensive learning, a fruitful imagination, a ready comprehension, and attention

---

5. ballads: "vers" (p. 361).
6. unsufferable fidler: "très chétif Musicien" (p. 361).
7. according to ... system: "suivant le Systême" (p. 362).
8. I should ... laughter: "je rirois" (p. 362).
9. Is the continual ... power: "Jeu perpétuel de machines qui ne savent ce qu'elles font! & illusions continuelles de Substances qui pensent, & qui s'imaginent faire ce qu'elles ne font pas!" (pp. 362–63).

not easily to be depressed or diverted, animated by an ambition of distinguishing himself by novelties, and eclipsing the rest of mankind, persuaded himself that he had clear notions of an inexplicable system, and that he was able to support it against weaker abilities. These hopes made his new system, his favourite idea, and nothing has engrossed so much of his endeavours as its establishment and vindication: disciples were found proud enough to adopt it,[1] and their heads were filled with innumerable terms and evasions, to be made use of in defending it against the dangerous attacks of right reason. This herd of slavish adherents were soon joined by the loose and the prophane, who came over to this pleasing system in such multitudes, that of the assemblies of these philosophers, we may truly say, *castra deserat qui volet esse pius;* let him that would preserve his morals avoid their conversation.[2]

The laws of logick allow any supposition, however absurd or inconsistent[3] to be made, for the sake of consequences that may promote the confirmation of truth. Let us make use, for once, of this privilege, and suppose a wise man to be empowered by God to give existence to beings yet uncreated, and allowed to use this power according to his own choice; would he confine himself to the creation of machines, which should move for ever, in consequence of the first impulse impressed upon them? Would he next summon into being substances capable of ideas, perceptions, and desires, that should rise in a determinate succession, in a manner agreeable to the motions of the bodies with which they are connected; and which, during the whole continuance of their existence, should falsely imagine that they received impressions from the body, though all their perceptions were produced by other causes, and that they directed its motions, upon which, in reality, they had no influence: no wise man

---

1. These hopes . . . adopt it: "C'a été son enfant chéri. Des Disciples se sont vendus à la gloire de l'adopter" (p. 363).

2. This herd . . . conversation: "A des esprits serviles se sont joints des esprits libertins. Il s'en trouve par tout; & la maxime, '*Deserat castra qui volet esse pius,*' s'étend plus loin que les armées" (p. 363). The Latin says, "whoever wants to be good, let him quit the camp."

3. however absurd or inconsistent: "contradictoires même" (p. 363).

surely would be the author of perpetual ignorance and error; and yet men have been found capable of asserting, that such are the beings which the infinite perfection of the Deity necessarily determines him to create. So far can the mind of man, however, assisted by learning and study, wander from the truth, when vanity, and a wild desire of superiority, have provoked God to withdraw his direction, and to resign him to be led away by his own presumption.[4]

For what use those machines that are generally called human bodies are intended, the Leibnitzian system no where informs us.[5] To exist without consciousness, is no advantage or happiness to them; they are therefore not made for their own sakes, nor do they, as these philosophers teach, make any impressions on the thinking part; nor, to conclude, do they, according to this system, receive any from it.

Nor does the argument end here; for if we suppose the thinking substance to have been created without the body, and to have existed apart from it, the same succession of ideas and desires had nevertheless been produced in it:[6] so that there is no method by which it can be evident to me, that there are any corporeal beings, or any thinking substances, except myself; for all my ideas arise originally within my own imagination, without the assistance of any outward objects, and were continued by an endless series of successive illusions.[7]

We may proceed farther, and demonstrate from the fundamental principles of this philosophy, that we are without any characteristick of truth or certainty. It has been hitherto universally allowed, that we are certain of the truth of a proposition, when we are forced to admit it as soon as we understand

---

4. So far can . . . presumption: "Jusques où l'esprit humain ne porte-t-il pas ses égaremens, dès que, par sa vanité, & par sa passion dominante de se distinguer, il s'est rendu digne que Dieu l'abandonne à sa présomption?" (p. 365).

5. SJ adds "the Leibnitzian system no where informs us."

6. for if we . . . it: "Quand cette substance qui pense, que j'appelle *moi*, seroit le seul ouvrage du Créateur, ses idées, ses sentimens, ses volontés se succéderoient l'une à l'autre, tout comme il leur arrive de se succéder" (p. 365).

7. by an endless . . . illusions: "par une suite inévitable d'*illusions*, & d'*imaginations*" (p. 366).

it, and have no power to suspend our belief, when we attend to it. The machine of a Leibnitzian is inevitably confined to think and speak in this particular manner, and the substance united to that machine lies under a necessity of thinking what the corporeal part pronounces in words, or exhibits on paper. And since I oppose his system, and oppose it with the utmost sincerity, these philosophers will surely favour me with admitting, that all my parts are so constituted, as necessarily determine me to speak and write in this manner, without knowing what I speak or write, and at the same time think as I do, and to believe that I voluntarily, and by choice, form in my mouth the sounds that I utter, and direct my pen to produce the lines and characters which it delineates. Both they and I must inevitably think as we do,[8] nor is it in my power to entertain their notions, or in theirs to embrace mine. We are determined by invincible necessity to differ in opinion, and to believe ourselves in the right, and our opponent mistaken.

The machine of a philosopher advances, without knowing it, some propositions which it has no conception of; which are received by the machine of a divine with exclamations so vehement and loud,[9] that the hearers are inclined to believe it very much offended, tho' it never knew what was meant by offence. The two machines proceed to reciprocal reproaches, and severe censures. Each of these machines is accompanied with a thinking substance, of which one believes itself to be revealing wonders, and enlightening the world; the other imagines itself to be detecting imposture, and confuting impiety.[1]

Among those machines that engage the side of the philosopher, there is one inevitably determined by its own construction, and the co-operating constitution of the universe, to assert, that the Supreme and Eternal Wisdom[2] produced the machine at a particular predestined point of time, that it

---

8. as we do: "tout différemment" (p. 367).

9. vehement and loud: "très fortement" (p. 367).

1. one believes . . . impiety: "l'une croit dicter des merveilles, & l'autre réfuter des impiétés" (p. 367).

2. Supreme and Eternal Wisdom: "Sagesse éternelle" (p. 368).

might hold among philosophers the same rank that a young prince of conspicuous qualities will one day hold among kings.*

But what account can be given of the transmigration of the philosopher, and its causes? To this question, however curious and unexpected, an answer may easily be made. Though it is not in any degree the property of a machine, which is only determined to write and speak, and to write and speak in a particular manner.

While I was employed in writing this letter, I have more than once called to mind two occurrences which have a close connection with this subject.

I was once acquainted with a man of great reputation for learning, piety, and strict life, whose predominant passion was to form systems, which he contrived with such a regular concatenation, that if you granted him his first principles, you could not deny the justness of his conclusions, or the succession of his consequences.[3] He had some relating to natural philosophy, drawn from the writings of Moses; some upon the several dispensations of nature, law and grace, and some upon the conversion of a sinner; but I shall only make you acquainted with his favourite hypothesis. God was, according to him, the only being truly real, all others being no more than mere appearances, like the circles of fire which are made by turning about a lighted brand. His assertion was founded upon this passage, viz. *Surely every man walketh in a vain show.* Psalm xxxix. 6.[4]

There was then no cause, except the first, and from that he therefore supposed all the actions of created beings, as well vices as virtues, to proceed; and when it was objected to

---

*This passage probably alludes to some panegyrical parallel drawn between Leibnitz and some prince by one of his followers.

---

3. whose predominant . . . consequences: "qui avoit un grand goût pour les Systêmes, & qui mettoit entre leurs parties beaucoup de liaison, de sorte qu'on les trouvoit assez assorties, dès qu'on lui en avoit accordé les fondemens" (pp. 368–69).

4. SJ does not translate the French but takes it from the Authorized Version and provides the citation.

his hypothesis by asking him whether, as vice had only the appearance of guilt, he believed that it would be punished. Without doubt, answered he, and very consistently with my system, for as we exist but in appearance, we can only in appearance commit crimes, or be punished for them.

Thus when a man's head is once possessed by a darling system,[5] he imagines all objections eluded by a nice distinction, and never perceives that every attempt to clear himself from difficulties, entangles him more closely.

This philosopher had still a conscience easily touched, and more than once I have seen him with tears and lamentations reproach himself for some miscarriages of which he had been guilty. *I could never,* says he, *either pardon myself, or receive any comfort, if I had myself been the author of those actions which I condemn; but when I ascend to the original cause, my sorrows are at an end, and I say with great tranquillity,* I LAY MY HAND UPON MY MOUTH, FOR THOU HAST DONE IT.

Of this system, wild as it was, he was a zealous vindicator,[6] and imagined he could support it by more than 300 passages of the Holy Scriptures yet, as I before said,[7] I always observed him to be a man of conscience and probity, so hard is it to efface, by chimerical speculations, sentiments founded in our natures, and written on our hearts, and by means of these principles yet unextinguished, it pleased God to recall him from all his errors,[8] of which there appear no trace in any single page of his numerous writings.

I was likewise acquainted with a young man of great learning for his age, who had joined to a fine taste and bright imagination, discretion, modesty, and every other virtue. Good-nature constituted his character, and to that all his errors and perplexities are to be ascribed, for the pain which he felt from

---

5. a darling system; "un Systême" (p. 370).

6. Of this system ... vindicator: "Ce Savant avoit beaucoup écrit sur ce Systême, en faveur duquel il étoit extrémement prévenu" (pp. 370–71).

7. as I before said: "comme je viens de le dire" (p. 371).

8. to recall him ... errors: "de revenir avant sa mort de tous ses égaremens" (p. 371).

the opinion that men would suffer eternal damnation, made him employ all his speculations in search of some train of thought by which he might be set free from imaginations so terrible, not on his own account, but that of others, and to this end he studied a long time without communicating to any either his doubts or his conclusions. At length he fell into an opinion, that nothing is in reality criminal, but that God has thought fit to interdict some actions, and enforce the prohibition with threatenings of eternal punishment, that those whom he suffers to commit them, may have a quicker sense of their felicity after having been alarmed with apprehensions of misery.

Many would have been corrupted in their morals, and made irregular in their conduct by such an opinion; but this man did not suffer his hypothesis to have any effect upon his conduct, to relax the severity of his life, or vitiate the purity of his mind; but the struggles which his understanding, naturally sound and clear, necessarily underwent in his endeavours to confirm himself in his new system, and habituate himself to such wild ideas, at length disordered his head, and soon after, young as he was, he sunk into dotage and stupidity.[9]

It is to the last degree dangerous for a man to confine all his imagination to his own breast, to be wholly buried within himself, and to revolve a set of odd ideas in his mind without communicating them, till by long meditation they have gained possession of his attention, and are become predominant. He is, perhaps, at first convinced of their absurdity, at least knows them to be very uncertain, but by slow degrees he loses his conviction, thinks them every day less chimerical, and at length resigns himself up wholly to them.[1] So some-

---

9. dotage and stupidity: "l'imbécilité" (p. 372).

1. It is . . . to them: "Il est extrémement dangereux de se renfermer uniquement en soi-même, & de rouler seul, dans son esprit, de certaines idées extraordinaires, jusques à ce qu'elles se soient emparées de l'attention, au point de devenir dominantes. Peu à peu on cesse de s'en défier, & à la fin on s'y rend entiérement" (p. 372).

times at the end of a dream which has made a strong impression upon our minds, we wake, and for some moments believe it real.

Perhaps the fool of Athens, by amusing himself with building what the English call castles in the air,[2] and accustoming himself to fancy as he walked upon the key, that everything which he saw there was his own, familiarized his mind so long to that notion, that at length it overbore his knowledge, and was believed by himself to be true.

So there was a hatter who by constantly reading the newsletters, and giving himself up to the infatuating amusement of forming schemes, at length imagined himself a king.—— Thus chemists have dwelt so long on the philosopher's stone, that they have at length bequeathed it to their heirs.——Thus likewise it is that young ladies have had their imaginations disordered by reading romances; and the history of the celebrated knight of La Mancha, may inform us how much a good understanding may be impaired by an incessant attention to the books of chivalry. Discourse with him upon many occasions, and he expressed himself very judiciously, but even upon indifferent subjects was less rational, as his mind was more intent upon his system.[3]

The sceptics make themselves appear fools by giving themselves up to the pleasure of contradiction, and by seeking perpetually for subterfuges to avoid the necessity of admitting any certainty.

Misera mens hominum quo te fata sepissime trahunt. Unhappy mind of man! whither art thou hurried by destiny?

Should any man accost me with such language as this, I should very readily answer, "Far be it from me to subject the Supreme Being to the dominion of destiny, nor may I ever

---

2. what the English . . . air: "ce que nous appellons des *Châteaux en Espagne*" (p. 373).

3. and the history . . . system: "Et voila à quoi l'Histoire des Chevaliers Errans à amené un Don-Quichotte, qui, dans diverses circonstances, s'énonçoit très sensément, mais lequel aussi, hors de là, s'égaroit d'autant plus qu'il demeuroit plus attaché à sa supposition" (p. 373).

have the impiety and insolence to imagine in the Eternal Creator, infinitely pure, holy and happy, such determinations as produce all the effects of destiny, our vices, and by means of our vices, our miseries."

Our hard fate, the cruel destiny that we complain of, is nothing more than our appetites and inclinations which we indulge and gratify, instead of making use of our power to resist them, and which, as we resolve to continue that indulgence, incite us to search every where for systems that may set us free from the apprehensions of punishment. When the mind is thus secretly prejudiced and disposed, a genius eager of shining and being distinguished from the crowd, easily invents, and as easily establishes an hypothesis which boasts at once two alluring but fatal advantages, as it encourages every gratification of the appetite by removing the restraints of religion, and flatters the pride of man by an appearance of great elevation, profundity and extent.[4]

---

4. Our hard fate . . . extent: "Nôtre malheureuse Destinée, ce sont nos convoitises qui la font, lors qu'au lieu de leur résister, comme nous en avons la puissance, nous nous abandonnons à leurs desirs, & afin de vivre à nôtre gré, nous nous tournons de tous côtés, pour nous persuader que nous n'avons rien à craindre. Dans ces dispositions intérieures, il ne faut plus qu'un Esprit avide de briller, en se distinguant des autres, pour imaginer & pour donner crédit à une Hypothése, qui aura tout à la fois deux grands, mais funestes avantages, l'un de flater la sensualité en éloignant la barriére de la crainte, l'autre de flater l'orgueil par des apparences de l'élévation la plus sublime" (pp. 374–75).

THE ABBE DU RESNEL'S *PREFACE* TO HIS TRANSLATIONS OF MR POPE'S *ESSAY ON MAN* AND *ESSAY ON CRITICISM*. CONTAINING, OBSERVATIONS UPON THE ENGLISH AND FRENCH POETRY, AND THE DIFFERENT TASTES OF THE TWO NATIONS.

The taste of the present age seems to be confined to romances, stories and novels, nor does the polite part of the world appear sensible of any other merit either in men or books, than the quality of diverting; a quality so much in esteem, that authors are afraid of professing any thing beyond it, and think excuses and vindications necessary when they attempt to profit or instruct.[5] It required therefore no small degree of courage to present the public at one time with two performances, of which the first is filled with profound truths and severe morality, entirely opposite to those trifling and licentious systems[6] which some authors of late times labour to support, and the other contains principles of criticism, and precepts of taste wholly irreconcileable with that which is daily encroaching upon us, insensibly getting possession both of our authors and readers.

I published, in 1730, a poetical translation of Mr Pope's *Essay on Criticism,* a production which had done him more

---

5. The taste . . . instruct: "Il semble que le goût pour les Romans, les Historiettes, les Contes & semblables Ouvrages soit presque devenu le goût général de notre siécle. Le mérite d'être amusant est non seulement aujourd'hui le grand mérite des hommes, mais encore celui des Ouvrages qui ont cours parmi ce qu'on appelle le Monde poli. Nos Auteurs n'oseroient presqu'avouer qu'ils se proposent d'être utiles, & se croyent obligés de faire sérieusement des excuses au Public, lorsqu'ils travaillent à l'instruire" (p. i).

6. profound truths . . . systems: "des vérités profondes & sévéres, combat directement cette Morale frivole & voluptueuse" (p. ii).

honour than any other, and the only piece, except the *Essay on Man*, which he has published without being attacked by the criticks of his own country.*

I have now in my hand about twenty pamphlets written against that great poet, without the least regard to *decency*, and with all the virulence that envy of superior abilities can produce in a narrow mind; yet even in these the *Essay on Criticism* is never mentioned, but with commendations, and the same respect which is paid in France to Boileau's *Art of Poetry*.

The only reason for which this poem can be properly termed an essay is, that the author has not formed his plan with all the regularity of method which it might have admitted; but this omission must be allowed to be more pardonable in him than in Aristotle and Horace, because a compleat treatise is not promised. Such a piece well deserved, in my opinion, to be translated into our language; and the favourable reception which my version has found, encourages me to believe, that I have not wholly miscarried in my attempt, and that my performance is, in some measure, what I intended.

But as the faculties of the understanding constitute no more than half of the man, and, if not associated with rectitude of mind, have often no other effect than that of making him more abject and despicable;[7] I thought it not improper to add to the *Essay on Criticism* the *Essay on Man*, another of Mr Pope's productions, which is regarded by the English as one of the most beautiful poems in their language; being, by

*The *Essay on Criticism* was animadverted upon by Mr. Dennis, with great fury and malice, and has been denied by others, who could not but allow its excellence to be Mr. Pope's; but not to have heard of these censures and calumnies is very pardonable in a foreigner, since, there are perhaps not many, even of our own countrymen, better acquainted with them.[8]

---

7. But as the faculties . . . despicable: "Mais comme les qualités de l'esprit ne sont, pour ainsi dire, que la moitié de l'homme, qu'elles ne servent même souvent qu'à le dégrader, si elles ne sont jointes aux qualités du coeur" (pp. iii–iv).

8. John Dennis, *Reflections, Critical and Satyrical, Upon A Late Rhapsody, Call'd,* *An Essay Upon Criticism* (1711). "The pamphlet is such as rage might be expected to dictate," SJ observes in the "Life of Pope," where the attack is discussed in some detail. See *Lives*, III.95–98 (pars. 34–42). For other attacks on the poem, see J. V. Guerinot, *Pamphlet Attacks on Alexander Pope, 1711–1744* (1969).

the persuasions of many persons, whose virtue and capacity gave them a claim to respect and distinction, prevailed upon to engage in a second task of the same kind, however laborious and unpleasing, in hopes that these two poems published together, might contribute at the same time to rectify the taste and the inclinations, to improve the genius, and reform the conduct of great numbers,[9] who want either leisure or learning to go regularly through the studies of morality and polite literature.

From the *Essay on Criticism*[1] the reader will learn to know the tendency of his own genius, to comprehend the endless diversity that is to be found in the minds of men, and to remark the original causes of our errors and false opinions; he will there be shewn the sources from which he must draw precepts for forming his judgment,[2] and will learn what are the true and valuable beauties of a writer of genius, what caution a reader is to use, that he may not confound excellencies with faults, and what are the qualities that constitute not only a good critic, but a good author.

In the *Essay on Man* he will meet with all that metaphysics teach, with any great degree of certainty, relating to the knowledge of ourselves, and all the necessary rules which morality lays down for the practice of our duty to God and man.[3]

Poetry and metaphysics, say the authors of *The Memoirs of Trevoux*,[4]* are generally considered as two kinds of writing in-

---

*June, 1736.
1. *Man*

---

9. by the persuasions . . . numbers: "Des personnes aussi distinguées par leur esprit, que respectables par leur vertu, m'ont engagé à surmonter les dégoûts d'un semblable travail, & m'ont fait espérer que ces deux Ouvrages ainsi réunis, ne seroient pas inutiles pour former l'esprit & le coeur, le goût & les moeurs d'une infinité de gens" (p. iv).
1. *Essay on Criticism:* "l'*Essai sur la Critique*" (p. iv). SJ has *Essay on Man*.

2. judgment: "goût" (p. v). Boyer defines "Goût" in a figurative sense as "(discernement, finesse du jugement) taste, palate, discerning faculty, judgment, parts, skill."
3. This paragraph is part of the previous paragraph in the French.
4. By adding "say the authors of *The Memoirs of Trevoux*" to the text and shortening the footnote, SJ obscures the fact that the reference is to Silhouette's prose

consistent with each other; nor is that opinion without some foundation in experience. The extasies and flights of the poet, and the nicety and cool argumentation of the abstracted reasoner, are not easily united. This conjunction has not been attempted by many writers; and of those few that have endeavoured it, yet fewer have succeeded. To form such a design, and execute it in such a manner, as to attain the applause of all true judges, was an honour reserved in these later ages for Mr Pope.[5]

He begins with an examination of the nature of man, according to the light of unassisted reason, and shews, in the *first epistle,* that reason represents man as created to inhabit this world; and that from this notion of his state considered together with our ideas of the wisdom and goodness of the Supreme Being, we may conclude, that he has all the perfections suitable to his present state, and to the relation which he bears both to his fellow-creatures here, and to the other parts of the universe; that as we do not see this relation in its whole extent, we cannot discover what degree of wisdom God has exerted in the formation of the human species; but we know in the general, that man is a finite being, and therefore cannot reasonably be surprised at the weakness and imperfection both of his mind and body.

In the *second* he discovers, that the goodness and wisdom of God are conspicuous even in those miseries and infirmities which are so numerous in our present condition, and which are sometimes useful and advantageous;[6] that the passions

---

translation. Du Resnel's footnote says, "Mémoires de Trévoux. Extrait de la Traduction de l'Essai sur l'Homme, par M. D. S. mois de Juin 1736" (p. v). The entire paragraph is in quotation marks in the French. *Journal* or *Mémoires de Trévoux,* a critical and literary miscellany, published from 1701 to 1755 by the Jesuits of Trévoux, the former capital of Dombes, to combat the influence of the Jansenists and the philosophes.

5. The extasies . . . Pope: "L'entou-siasme de la premiere & ses écarts ne peuvent que très-difficilement s'allier avec le flegme & la précision de la seconde. Peu de génies ont été assez hardis pour essayer cet accord, & moins encore ont eu la gloire d'y réussir. Il étoit réservé dans ces derniers tems à M. Pope plus qu'à tout autre de s'ouvrir cette carriere, & de la parcourir avec l'applaudissement des vrais Connoisseurs" (p. vi).

6. In the *second* . . . advantageous:

are good in themselves, and that by using them well or ill, we produce as well private as publick happiness or calamities. That the notion embraced by man, *that all is made for him,* is the original of his mistakes, and of his unreasonable complaints against Providence, it being certain that he is made for the whole, not the whole for him.

The *third epistle* teaches man, that it is vain to endeavour after an happiness unconnected with that of others; and that he neither can nor ought to be happy, but as he contributes to the reciprocal communication of happiness established between all the different parts of the universe, which is the great object of the Creator's regard.[7] This disposition for happiness can be produced only by virtue, and therefore as men improve in virtue, they advance in felicity.[8]

But the author does not confine himself to inspire his readers with that justice, benevolence, and rectitude of mind which constitutes an honest man, but raises their thoughts, by a just gradation from natural and moral virtues, to the perfection which mere nature cannot attain.[9] Though Christianity presupposes moral honesty, there is nevertheless a great distance from one to the other; faith only can bring to perfection those virtues which reason can only sketch out: he therefore shews, in the *fourth epistle,* that whoever would attain to the utmost happiness which his present condition admits, and assure himself of eternal felicity in a future state, must elevate his mind, above the doctrines of mere reason, apply himself to the precepts of religion, and found his happiness, upon a steady faith, an unshaken hope, and a glowing charity.

"(Epitre deuxiéme.) La sagesse & la bonté de Dieu éclatent jusque dans les miséres & dans les foiblesses, qui sont le partage de l'Homme, elles tournent même quelquefois à son avantage" (p. vii).

7. reciprocal communication . . . regard: "bonheur réciproque de tout le Genre humain, & même de tout l'Univers; bonheur qui est le principal & le grand objet du Créateur" (p. viii).

8. and therefore . . . felicity: "& à mesure qu'elle se forme dans leur coeur, ils avancent dans l'unique voie qui conduit au bonheur" (p. viii).

9. rectitude of mind . . . attain: "de droite raison qui constitue l'honnête Homme. Par les vertus morales & naturelles, il les conduit de dégrés en dégrés jusqu'à la connoissance des vertus surnaturelles" (p. viii).

This is a short view of the general plan of the poem, which has no other tendency than to inflame us with an ardent love[1] both of God and man, to raise in us an exalted idea of the great Creator, and enforce an implicit submission to his will. I am therefore surprised that some readers of this translation, after having owned, that in some places they could not understand it, should pretend to discover in it a lurking poison, and charge it with the absurdities of Spinosa's system. An accusation so ill-grounded does not deserve that any time should be spent in confuting it, as it has obtained credit only among very few, and these either unable to form a true judgment of the question, or misled by a desire to discover in Mr Pope those notions which they have themselves unhappily adopted.[2] I shall therefore forbear to engage in so needless a controversy, and refer it to the *Journal des Scavans*,* the *Memoires de Trevoux*,† and the *Observations upon Modern Writings*, Vol. IV. Letter 47.[3] The character of Mr Pope is a sufficient vindication, and ought to secure his work from such odious suspicions. He has always openly professed the Catholick religion, in which he was born and educated, in a country where so much is lost by dissenting from the established religion, that every man who adheres to any other communion, gives a sufficient testimony of his sincerity.[4] Those enemies which his merit has raised in his own country, are so far from doubting his principles, that they reproach him with them in their

---

*April, 1736.
†June, 1736.

---

1. inflame us . . . love: "inspirer une grande idée" (p. ix).

2. only among . . . adopted: "sur un petit nombre de personnes peu instruites, ou assez à plaindre pour souhaiter d'y trouver leurs propres sentimens" (p. x).

3. SJ has introduced part of Du Resnel's footnote into the text: "Voyez le Journal des Sçavans, mois d'Avril 1736. Mémoires de Trévoux, mois de Juin même année. Observations sur les Ecrits Modernes, Tome IV. Lettre 47" (p. x). When SJ met George III in February 1767, he told the king that the *Journal des Savans* "was formerly well done, and gave some account of the persons who began it, and carried it on for some years" (*Life*, II.39).

4. that every man . . . sincerity: "ce qu'il en coute à ceux qui se déclarent contre la Religion dominante, est un sûr garand de l'intime persuasion de leur coeur" (p. xi).

libels, and pretend, however ridiculously, that his popery affects his compositions and deprives them of that daring freedom of thought⁵ which they regard as the very soul of poetry.

Strict justice however requires, that in reading the following poem, we never suffer ourselves to forget the title, and that we always remember that we are not promised a compleat body or system, but a mere *essay,* and that this is only *the general map of man.*⁶*

It was not his design to give us a collection of all that might be said on so extensive a subject, but only to lay down the general principles upon which morality is founded. It is always to be remembered that he writes not in the character of a divine, but of a philosopher, a philosopher professing Christianity, who, by making the proper use of the light of reason, disposes the mind to admit the brighter illuminations of faith, and ends at the very point at which the divine is to begin.

I therefore cannot but flatter myself that I have done some service to the publick, by translating this work, which is of a particular kind, too short to frighten away indolence by its bulk, and yet large enough to instruct and improve,⁷ written with too much truth and judgment to shock the reader with unheard of singularities, and yet so disposed and contrived as to recommend the most common maxims and known truths, by an air of novelty, too much embellished to appear tedious or jejune, and yet so just and solid as to engage the attention rather by the strength of argument, and importance of precept, than by the glare of expression, and variety of images.⁸

---

* *Vide* Pref.

---

5. daring freedom of thought: "hardiesse & cette liberté d'esprit" (p. xi). Boyer gives one definition of "Hardiesse" as "(*ou* liberté) à parler, boldness or freedom of speech."

6. This note, added by SJ, refers to "The Design" prefaced to the poem by Pope (p. 8). SJ substitutes Pope's "and that this is only *the general map of man*" for Du Resnel's French translation of the first sentence of Pope's final paragraph. Neither Du Resnel nor Silhouette include Pope's "The Design" in their translations.

7. to instruct and improve: "instruire" (p. xii).

8. tedious or jejune . . . images: "sec ou ennuyeux, mais en même tems assez solide pour attacher encore plus par le fond des choses, & par la suite

It is with poetry, says Mr de Fenelon,* *as with architecture, the necessary parts must be made ornamental, but every ornament which serves no other purpose than that of embellishment is to be rejected as superfluous.* This precept Mr Pope seems always to have had before him; he was determined to write in verse rather than prose only by the desire of expressing himself with greater closeness; and it is well known that precepts⁹ written in verse have this farther advantage, that they strike with more force upon the mind, and fix themselves more ᵐ deeply in the memory.

Lord Roscommon¹ in his essay upon translated poetry, affirms, that to succeed in a translation, we must single out some writer whose taste and sentiments resemble our own.

> ———*Chuse an Author as you chuse a Friend,*
> *United by this sympathetic Bond,*
> *You grow familiar, intimate and fond,*
> *Your Thoughts, your Words, your Stiles, your Tastes agree,*
> *No longer his Interpreter, but he.*²

*Lettre a l'Academie Francoise.
m. mor

---

du raisonnement, que par les graces de l'expression, ou par la variété des images" (p. xiii).

9. precepts: "les maximes & les préceptes" (p. xiii).

1. SJ omits a footnote: "Je suis obligé d'avertir que dans la première Edition de ma Traduction de l'Essai sur la Critique qui parut en 1730, j'ai fait usage de cette pensée, & des deux passages de M. de Roscomon, qu'on trouve ici cités" (p. xiv).

2. Du Resnel paraphrases these lines from Roscommon's *An Essay on Translated Verse* in French and gives the English lines in a footnote. SJ omits the paraphrase. The fourth line reads correctly in Du Resnel, "your souls agree" (p. xiv) rather than "your Tastes agree." SJ may be quoting from memory since the first edition (1684), the second edition (1685), and *Poems by the Earl of Roscommon* (1717) have "souls." In his "Life of Roscommon," SJ describes the *Essay* as his "great work" but dismisses his principles of translation as rather obvious and not very useful (*Lives*, I.235–37, pars. 25–27). SJ may have owned a copy of Charles Gildon's *The Laws of Poetry, as Laid Down by the Duke of Buckinghamshire, the Earl of Roscommon, and by the Lord Landsdowne, Explained and Illustrated* (1721), which has comments on the *Essay* and is mentioned in the "Life of Roscommon" (*Lives*, I.237, par. 28). See Donald Greene, *Samuel Johnson's Library: An Annotated Guide* (1975), p. 61. He certainly owned a copy of the first volume of *The Works of the Most Celebrated Minor Poets* (1749), which contains Roscommon's works. See J. D. Fleeman *A Preliminary Handlist of Copies of Books Associated with Dr. Samuel Johnson* (1984), no. 213.

DU RESNEL PREFACE

Gladly should I persuade myself that my choice of this work was produced by the similitude of my own sentiments to those of my author; but who would dare to attempt a translation of him, if such a resemblance was necessary to his success?

That poetry can only be translated into verse, is agreed, I think, by all the learned, except Madam Dacier, whose interest in the question makes her judgment of no great weight; and experience, without authority, is a sufficient proof of the justness of that opinion, which I shall the less labour to support here, because a man of the first character, who has shewn the present generation, what those learned magistrates were that appeared in the time of the revival of learning, has in a work lately published,* proved both by unanswerable arguments, and by his own example, that nothing but poetry can give any representation of the genius and manner of a poet. As this is true of poetry in general, it is in my opinion more eminently true of the English poetry. The writers of that nation make use, even in prose, of such daring sentiments, and strong expressions, as our poetry scarcely ventures to admit, or is able to copy, without losing some part of their force. How then shall we, without grasping all the advantages, and taking all the liberties which verse is allowed, be able to give any idea of their *poetry*, which rises very far above the prose even of that language.

The English is allowed, by all who understand it, to be the most concise language in the world; and this quality it is in which the writers of that country place its beauty, and for which they prefer it to the French, a language which Lord Roscommon, who is acknowledged to have held the first rank among their critics, allows to be copious, florid, pleasing to the ear, and to have more softness than the English; but defies us to produce a single instance of equal strength, closeness and energy.[3] A thought, says he, which we comprehend in a

---

*President Bouhier's poetical translation of Petronius on the Civil War.

---

3. but defies . . . energy: "mais en récompense il défie qu'on lui montre jamais dans aucuns de nos Ouvrages cette force & cette énergie Angloise, qui en peu de mots comprend tant de choses" (p. xvii).

single line, diffused by a French author, would glitter through whole pages.*

In reading this production of Mr Pope, it is not easy to forbear thinking that he had the honour of the English brevity in view, which he has preserved so tenaciously, that some have accused him of cramping his stile, by crouding it too closely.[4] I know not indeed any writer either of the former or later ages that can enter into competition with him, for the prize of conciseness, or has said so much in so few words; but then it must be owned that he sometimes presumes too much upon the penetration of his readers, for which reason some pas-

*I know not what edition of Roscommon has fallen into the hands of Mr Du Resnel, or whence it proceeds, that the quotation which he has subjoined in his margin, differs from those copies which I have seen.[5] The passage, as he has published it, is this:

> 'Tis copious, florid, pleasing to your Ear,
> With Softness, more, perhaps, than ours can bear.
> But who did ever in French Authors, &c.

Which in all the editions that I have read, stands thus:

> 'Tis courtly, florid, and abounds in Words
> Of softer Sound than ours perhaps affords.

How much more poetical and correct this reading is, requires no proof, nor is the difference only in elegance but in truth. The genuine reading only admits that the French language is *courtly*, a quality which cannot be denied to a speech consisting wholly of hyperbole: the passage, as cited by Du Resnel, asserts it to be copious, an excellence for which even their own writers have never ventured to commend it.

---

4. In reading . . . closely: "On diroit que M. Pope ait affecté de soutenir la gloire de sa Nation sur ce point. Je ne dissimulerai pas même, qu'il est accusé d'avoir voulu la porter un peu trop loin" (pp. xvii–xviii).

5. Du Resnel is quoting the lines from Roscommon's *An Essay on Translated Verse* essentially as they appear in the 1684 first edition (p. 4). Substantial revisions were made for the 1685 second edition (p. 4) and it was this edition that continued to be reprinted. See, for example, *Poems by the Earl of Roscommon* (1717), p. 9. Du Resnel's note says,

"'Tis Copious florid, pleasing to your ear,
With softeness more perhaps than ours can bear,
But Who did euer in French authors see
The comprehensive Inglish energy?
The Weighty bullion of one sterling line
Drawn to Franchwire, woud through whole page[s] shine.
Roscom. ibid."

sages in these epistles resemble the first rough draughts of a great master; they are struck out with a strength and spirit that charm the judicious, but escape the observation of common eyes. Those touches which the critic looks upon with admiration, appear rude and artless to the unskilful, who are inclined to imagine that there are not really in those sketches the beauties which more knowing spectators discover and applaud.[6] If in these poems there appear some expressions that may be cut off, either as superfluities or repetitions, there is not, even in those considered by themselves, a single word unnecessary. There is a distinction to be made between exact closeness of expression, which our critics will not deny the English, and exact regularity of thought, which they will not so easily allow them.

This brevity was, in my opinion, to be most successfully imitated by a close stile, not weakened by scrupulous regard to connection, or a rigid adherence to the niceties of construction.[7] I would not willingly have made use in my version of any other liberties than such as the author himself must have taken, had he attempted a French translation of his own work; but I was, by the unanimous opinion of all those whom I have consulted on this occasion, and among them of several Englishmen compleatly skilled in both languages, obliged to follow a different method. The French are not satisfied with sentiments, however beautiful, unless they are methodically disposed,[8] method being the characteristic that distinguishes our performances from those of our neighbours, and almost the only excellence which they agree to allow us. That Mr Pope did not think himself confined to a regular plan in writing his *Essay on Criticism* I have already observed. I have there-

---

6. who are inclined . . . applaud: "ils ne peuvent s'empêcher de croire que les Curieux ne voyent dans ces esquisses beaucoup au-delà de ce qui y est réellement" (p. xviii).

7. This brevity . . . construction: "Quoiqu'il en soit, la Poësie dont le tour est plus pressé, plus indépendant des liaisons; & moins asservi aux contraintes de la construction, m'a paru seule capable de répondre en quelque sorte à cette briéveté" (p. xix).

8. The French . . . disposed: "Quelques belles que soient les choses, nous y voulons absolument de l'ordre" (p. xx).

fore, by a necessary compliance with our taste, divided it into five cantos;[9] nor have I only in this particular deviated from the original, but have changed the place of some sentiments, which seemed too far distant from each other, and have connected some passages which appeared independent of the main work.

The *Essay on Man* is in reality more methodically drawn up, tho' the order of its parts is not very easily discovered by those who are accustomed to the exact regularity of our treatises in prose. But every one knows that poetry could not admit of divisions, definitions, proofs, objections, and solutions, without losing its spirit, languishing into prose, and being entirely deprived of that freedom and wildness that constitute its character.[1] But tho' a poet may, without censure, pass from one thought to another, without leading the reader through a regular transition, yet he is to take care that his thoughts have, tho' not a verbal, an intellectual connection, and that they follow one another in such a train as corresponds with the natural order of things.[2] And therefore whenever Mr Pope appeared to have neglected to follow this rule, I have chosen to conform to the taste of our nation, without regarding whether strangers will call it weakness or accuracy, or being at all solicitous about the censure usually thrown upon us, that we are babes that cannot take a single step without being led. But it was not in my power to reduce these poems to such a method as a Frenchman expects, without forsaking the province of a translator, and modelling them afresh; it is, however, not so much the manner in which the English range[3] their notions that has made several considerable alterations necessary, as that in which they form them.[4]

---

9. five cantos: "quatre Chants" (p. xx).

1. of divisions . . . character: "de divisions, de preuves, d'objections & de réponses. Cet assujétissement la feroit languir, lui ôteroit sa vivacité, & sur tout cet air de liberté qui caractérise les Poëtes" (p. xxi).

2. and that they follow . . . things: "& par l'enchaînement des matieres" (p. xxi).

3. range: "expriment & arrangent" (p. xxii).

4. as that . . . form them: "que la diversité qui se trouve entre leur façon

Whatever is foreign, says Aristotle,[5] raises admiration, and whatever raises admiration gives pleasure; a remark, which, tho' perhaps generally true, is not applicable to us, who are accused of endeavouring by a national prejudice, which we call the love of elegance,[6] to reduce every thing to our own notions; and certain it is, that a foreign air is so far from a recommendation to our favour, that we are strongly prepossessed to its disadvantage. As in this particular we resign ourselves up rather to inclination than to reason, these impressions can only be effaced by time and custom; reformers,[7] that proceed but slowly, and act generally in a manner that we ourselves scarcely perceive.

Since the last peace we have begun to be more acquainted with the English, and most who desire to be thought either men of taste or learning, think themselves obliged to study their language. We are now no longer strangers to the great writers of that nation, from whom some of our authors if they could be suspected of understanding them, might be reasonably imagined to have learned the use of some very extraordinary words, as well as the art of distinguishing between the several passions and inclinations of the mind,[8] where scarcely any difference is to be found, and the practice of expressing these subtilties in a metaphysical cant, not more intelligible than that of the schools. But this kind of conformity is of too late a commencement to prove that we are naturally disposed to a similarity of notions; and it is matter of wonder that these two nations, so near to each other by situation, should be so remote in their tastes and ideas. We approach more nearly to the Italians, tho' neither they, nor the English, are without something in their writings which appears to us extremely odd and singular; but their singularities or oddnesses are different; and this difference it may not be improper to ex-

---

de concevoir les choses & la nôtre" (p. xxii).

5. SJ omits "dans sa Rhétorique" (p. xxii).

6. elegance: "bon goût" (p. xxii).

7. reformers [i.e., time and custom]: "Mais l'un & l'autre" (p. xxiii).

8. the art . . . mind: "à rafiner sur les sentimens du coeur" (p. xxiii).

plain,⁹ that the reader may have a more adequate conception of the English writers.

The Italian, transported by his fire, and vigour of imagination, flies off,¹ if I may use that term, in spirit, and presents us with the quintessence of his genius.² The Englishman dives into himself,³ and draws all his conceptions from the depth of his own breast.⁴ The Italian only pleases us by his ingenuity, the Englishman only strikes us by his solidity. The sentiments of the Italian lose their force, those of the Englishman gain new strength by a severe examination; the ideas of the Italian have indeed the grace of novelty, but then they generally appear such as might have been easily struck out.⁵* Those of the Englishman have so much subtilty and are so remote from common life, that it is not easy to conceive how he was led to them.⁶ Both of them fall often into meanness and puer-

---

*The Abbe, in this comparison, whether by design or not, ascribes to the Italians, perhaps the highest perfection of writing; such thoughts as are at once new and easy, which, tho' the reader confesses that they never occurred to him before, he yet imagines must have cost but little labour. This is not the character which other critics give of those authors.

---

9. tho' neither they . . . explain: "Les uns & les autres ont à la vérité, par rapport à nous, quelque chose de très singulier dans leur façon de penser; mais avec de grandes différences qu'il n'est pas inutile de remarquer" (p. xxiv).

1. flies off: "s'évapore" (p. xxiv).

2. the quintessence of his genius: "la fleur de son esprit" (p. xxiv).

3. dives into himself: "rentre en lui-même" (p. xxiv).

4. the depth of his own breast: "la profondeur de son génie" (p. xxiv).

5. such as might . . . struck out: "qu'on auroit pû les imaginer aisément" (p. xxv). SJ's observation in the footnote that he finds the "new and easy" to be "perhaps the highest perfection of writing" anticipates his definition of "wit" in the "Life of Cowley": "Wit which is at once natural and new, that which though not obvious is, upon its first production, acknowledged to be just" (*Lives*, I.20, par. 55). His comments in the "Life of Pope" on the *Rape of the Lock*, give the fullest treatment of this important principle: "In this work are exhibited in a very high degree the two most engaging powers of an author: new things are made familiar, and familiar things are made new. A race of aerial people never heard of before is presented to us in a manner so clear and easy" (*Lives*, III.233, par. 338). See Jean H. Hagstrum, *Samuel Johnson's Literary Criticism* (1952), pp. 156–60.

6. Those of the Englishman . . . them: "Celles des Anglois ont je ne sçai quoi de si extraordinaire & de si abstrait, qu'on a peine à comprendre comment elles ont pû se présenter à leur esprit" (p. xxv).

ility; but the Italian seems to fall into them by negligence and levity,[7] and the Englishman to run into them upon reflection, and with design.[8] The Italian cannot refrain from throwing some comic and ludicrous ideas into his most serious writings; the Englishman even in his amusements of gaiety and merriment, retains an air of thoughtfulness and gravity;[9] the Italian dazzles the reader at first, but when, upon a closer inspection, offers him nothing but false metal, and empty glitter; the Englishman comes always with true gold in his hand, but it is gold just taken from the mine unrefined, clouded and debased with extraneous mixtures. The Italian diverts and gladdens the imagination, but rarely affords any instruction; to instruct is the grand design of the Englishman, a design in which he seldom fails of success; but then he so much wearies and harrasses the mind, that when the reader rises from his book, he leaves the company of an austere and dogmatical scholar, who wearies and depresses him at the same time that he raises his admiration.

Such is, in my opinion, the difference and the resemblance between the two nations in stile and conception.[1] It is enough, if the picture which I have drawn, has the features of the greatest part of their writers; nor have those particular authors, who have risen above the general rate of their countrymen, in that case, any reason to complain of injustice. As all other writers have not a just pretence to the excellencies allowed them, so all are not to be charged with the defects imputed to them: such general draughts have always many exceptions, and with this precaution I intreat the reader to peruse what I am obliged to say farther of the differences between the English taste and ours, by the necessity which I discovered of varying from my author in several places.

They love even in the least performances to leave room for

---

7. negligence and levity: "légereté" (p. xxv).

8. reflection, and with design: "réflexion" (p. xxv).

9. the Englishman . . . gravity: "L'Anglois au contraire conserve toujours un certain air rêveur & sérieux jusques dans son comique" (p. xxv).

1. stile and conception: "matiere d'esprit" (p. xxvi).

reflection, and imagine that they give the reader pleasure, by leaving always something to be discovered by himself. We demand that every thing be clear without the labour of enquiry, and that our eagerness be not opposed by any difficulties. They imitate nature with great happiness, but, like the Flemish painters, they have not much delicacy in their choice, but a true picture, whatsoever it represents, gains their applause. We are rigid exactors of delicacy and discrimination, and how skilfully soever the pencil may be handled,[2] if the subject has not grandeur and dignity, quarrel with the performer. They bestow more attention upon the subject than upon the expression, and expect, that, if their ideas are explained with perspicuity and energy, the reader should be satisfied. By us beauty of stile is often confounded with beauty of sentiment, and we attend more to the turn of the thought, than to the thought itself, and almost always think that low, coarse, and despicable, which they consider as easy, simple, and familiar.[3] They allow that we speak and write well, but say, at the same time, that we know not how to think; and for our part, we object, that their thoughts are so strained, farfetched, and subtle, that instead of enlightening, they only perplex. They will not grant us any of the qualities that constitute a poet, and make no scruple of asserting,[4] in plain terms, that we cannot

---

2. We are rigid . . . handled: "nous y souhaitons du choix, & malgré la finesse & la correction du pinceau" (pp. xxvii–xxviii).

3. SJ omits a footnote: "C'est le sentiment du célébre Waller, dont j'aurai occasion de parler ailleurs. Il n'en exceptoit que Corneille, comme on le peut voir dans une Lettre de S. Evremond au même Corneille. Et en général, si les Anglois lisent & pillent même souvent Racine, Moliere, la Fontaine, Regnier, Despréaux, &c. il est certain qu'ils les regardent plûtôt comme de grands Ecrivains, que comme de grands Poëtes" (p. xxviii). Edmund Waller, who spent some eight years in exile in France during the period of the Civil Wars, translated the first act of Corneille's *Pompée* into English.

4. SJ omits a footnote: "Nos Compatriotes, dit le C. de Bolimbroke, écrivant au sieur Prior, sont aussi mauvais Politiques, que les François sont mauvais Poëtes. *Report of the committee appointed for, &c.* pag. 339" (p. xxix). SJ had a strong antipathy to Bolingbroke. When Bolingbroke's *Works* were issued posthumously by David Mallett in 1754, SJ called him a "scoundrel and a coward" and, when asked by Charles Burney if he had read William Warburton's book against Bolingbroke's philosophy, he commented: "No, Sir; I have never

pretend to them. We admit that they have fire, but so gloomy, that it emits more smoke than flame; we allow that they have a strong imagination, but such as has more of the dreams and chimeras of melancholy,[5] than the flights and follies[6] of the fruitful and happy genius. That their stile is bold, and its elevation quite enthusiastic, we do not deny; but we say of them in the words of Petronius, *Plus poetice quam humane locutus est.*[7] They write more like poets than like men, and what is said by the Duke of Buckingham, of poets in general, we think more particularly applicable to them.

For ten inspir'd, ten thousand are possest.[8]

Sir W. Temple in his essays, calls England the country of the *spleen;* and Mr Addison, *Spec.* 419, confesses, that the *English are naturally fanciful, and disposed by that gloominess and melancholy of temper, which is so frequent among them, to many wild notions and visions to which others are not so liable.*[9] This produces, in

---

read Bolingbroke's impiety, and therefore am not interested about its confutation" (*Life,* I.268, 330). See also the negative comments, for example, in his "Life of Pope" (III.193, pars. 250–52; 205–06, par. 272) and "Life of Mallet" (III.407, par. 18).

5. dreams ... melancholy: "noires rêveries d'un mélancolique" (p. xxix).

6. flights and follies: "vives saillies" (p. xxix).

7. SJ provides the translation of Petronius. Both Du Resnel and SJ have "plus" for the usual "saepius." Petronius is talking to the poet Eumolpus, who has been pelted with stones during his recitation: "saepius poetice quam humane locutus es": "you have talked more often like a poet than like a man" (*Satyricon,* 90).

8. Du Resnel has *"Pour un seul inspiré, dix seront possédés"* in the text with the English in a footnote, identifying the source as *An Essay upon Poetry.* The line, however, is not from the Duke of Buckingham's *An Essay upon Poetry* (1682) but from the Earl of Roscommon's *An Essay on Translated Verse.* It appears on p. 19 of both the first and second editions. The confusion may have arisen because the works were published together. See *Poems by the Earl of Roscommon. To which is added, An Essay on Poetry, By the Earl of Mulgrave, now Duke of Buckingham* . . . (1717), p. 39.

9. Du Resnel paraphrases this passage in the text and gives the English in a footnote. SJ inserts the footnote into the text. It should read: "For the *English* are naturally Fanciful, and very often disposed by that Gloominess and Melancholly of Temper, which is so frequent in our Nation, to many wild Notions and Visions, to which others are not so liable." *The Spectator,* ed. Donald F. Bond, 5 vols. (Oxford, 1965), III.572. Du Resnel has *"la Région de la Rate"* and Sir William Temple in "Of Poetry" says it is "the Region of the Spleen." See *Works* (1731), I.248. SJ told Boswell that

the opinion of that great genius, their inclination to allegorical fictions; and why may we not ascribe to this the multitude of comparisons which they croud into their compositions of every kind, just indeed, but produced with too much labour of the invention? The Frenchman lively and eager, can bear nothing that puts any stop to his career, but condemns every thing as trifling and impertinent, that retards his attainment of the object he pursues. The English, in whom, to an extensive genius and profound knowledge is joined a wonderful facility of invention, cannot confine themselves to severe accuracy, but sometimes venture beyond rules or bounds, and maintain that no poet is to own any other master than Apollo, which, in plain terms is his own fancy. We who think it more shameful to miss our way, than to take a guide, submit ourselves willingly to the conduct of the ancients; and as we allow that we ourselves are obliged to the observation of rules, are not easily persuaded, that any nation can claim a just exemption from them.

What justice or what exaggerations there are in these mutual objections, is not my province to decide, and yet less will I undertake to settle the balance between the excellencies which we pretend to above our neighbours, and those by which they claim a superiority to us. Perhaps no man is so much emancipated from the power of custom, and the prejudices of education, as to engage in this task, without hazard.[1] But though the English should prove, that our authors are rather timorous than prudent,[2] that what we censure as temerity, is only boldness, that what we term licentiousness is only a noble contempt of restraint,[3] and that the scrupulous nicety with which we avoid all common ideas and expressions

---

Temple was one of the writers on whom he formed his style (*Life*, I.218–19).

1. to engage ... hazard: "pour oser le faire" (p. xxxii).

2. prudent: "la sagesse & la circonspection" (p. xxxii).

3. only a noble . . . restraint: "ce qui mérite le nom de généreuse liberté" (p. xxxiii). *Generous:* "*adj.* [*generosus*, Latin; *genereux*, French] Not of mean birth; of good extraction" (sense 1 in *Dictionary*). Boyer defines "Généreux" as "generous, noble."

proceeds only from a false delicacy, and instead of embellishing enervate our productions; yet will our authors, however satisfied of the truth of these positions, continue to believe that rules are still to be observed to a certain degree, and that without a blind compliance with them, where they are defective, are to be kept inviolable where they are just.[4] If it be at all allowable to flatter men in their weaknesses, it must be when the intention of it is to cure them, and to lure them to right reason. Our language does not want force and energy,[5] but ourselves, who know not how to make the true use of it, as appears from the nervous stile, and masculine air, the daring felicity, the strong and sprightly periods, and that vigour of sentiment, which foreigners admire in Montaigne, la Bruyer and more eminently in Bossuet.[6] However, tho' the disgust and particular aversions of a sick man be merely the effect of weakness, yet as he cannot conquer them while his distemper continues, it would be folly and cruelty to treat them with entire disregard, but much more would he be blameable, who, by too easy a compliance, should contribute to the continuance of them.

Mr Pope, from whom I borrowed this reflection, will be so generous as to pardon the use which I have made of it in my own vindication even against himself. With regard to this translation, if I have even taken away from the dignity of his sentiments, it has been only that I might reduce them to the level of our capacities; if I have sometimes ventured to substi-

---

4. yet will our authors . . . just: "nos Ecrivains n'en conclueront jamais qu'il leur soit permis de blesser ouvertement les Loix qu'ils trouvent établies. C'est à eux de s'y conformer jusqu'à un certain point, & de conserver ce qu'elles peuvent avoir de bon, sans chercher à plaire par ce qu'elles ont de défectueux" (p. xxxiii).

5. force and energy: "force" (p. xxxiii).

6. more eminently in Bossuet: "sur tout dans feu M. Bossuet Evêque de Meaux, le prouvent invinciblement" (p. xxxiv). Since SJ gives "eminently" for "dans feu" (warmly), perhaps he is indulging in a little punning. Jacques Bénigne Bossuet was a prelate (Bishop of Condom in 1669, Meaux in 1681) and *not* a cardinal (therefore never "son éminence"), but his sermon, "Sur l'éminente dignité des pauvres dans l'Eglise," was well known. Though SJ is reported to have said "nobody reads him," Boswell disagreed (*Life*, V.311 and n.3).

tute the plain and natural[7] expression, instead of metaphors, with which he elevates his poetry, and to suppress some of his images and comparisons, I here declare, that it is not so much, because my own judgment disapproves them, as because I found it impossible to reconcile them to the taste of common readers.

One instance which I shall give, seems to deserve the more regard on account of the consequences that may be drawn from it, of which great use may be made in an attempt to ridicule those critics, who, after fruitless endeavours to make themselves authors, fall without mercy upon the reputation of those who have succeeded better.[8] Mr Pope, in his *Essay on Criticism,* uses this comparison:

> *So modern 'Pothecaries taught the Art,*
> *By Doctors Bills, to play the Doctor's Part;*
> *Bold in the Practice of mistaken Rules,*
> *Prescribe, apply, and call their Masters Fools.*[9]

This image with which the English are pleased, shocks every Frenchman to whom I have mentioned it. It may be remarked that the word *apothecary*[1] is the same, except the termination, in both languages, and therefore no reason can be given why it may not be used in both with equal dignity or propriety; or why certain unpleasing ideas annexed in common conception to that profession, may not as well be revived by the mention of it, in one country as another. We can therefore only ascribe this difference to the opposite character of the two nations, of which one regards every thing that is of use in common life, as indifferent at least, if not elevated, provided

---

7. plain and natural: "naturellement" (p. xxxv).

8. to ridicule . . . better: "dans le dessein de jetter plus de ridicule sur certains Critiques qui déchirent impitoyablement les Poëtes, après avoir travaillé sans succès à le devenir" (p. xxxv).

9. Du Resnel paraphrases this passage (ll. 108–11) in the text and gives the English, with a few small variants, in a footnote. Several points raised by Du Resnel in the following discussion of poetic diction are treated by SJ in *Rambler* 168. See also his comments in the "Life of Dryden," *Lives,* 1.420 (pars. 219–21).

1. SJ omits "est tiré du Grec, comme notre mot François Apothicaire" (p. xxxvi).

it have nothing contrary to our natural ideas;[2] and the other habitually considers every phrase appropriated to those actions or employments which do not belong to persons of high rank, as low and despicable.[3]

It is for this reason alone, if I may be permitted to say it, that Homer, without losing any part of his grandeur, was at liberty to descend to such particular descriptions as would make any other poet ridiculous. In his days, as in those of the patriarchs, kings and princes killed their beasts for their own table, dressed their dinners for themselves, and harnessed their own horses to their chariots. Their sons kept their flocks, and their daughters wash'd their linnen with their own hands, and drew water at the common fountains. The terms in which these actions were expressed, and the names of the instruments used for those purposes, had then no meanness of sound, because they participated in some degree of the dignity of the person that made use of them, but among us, the low rank of those that practise the mechanical arts, inclines us insensibly to affix ideas of contempt to every sound appropriated to them. Nor are we at all to wonder that men of literature do not affix the same ideas to the words of the same import in the learned languages, since they are so far from hearing them in the mouths of the lowest of the people in shops and streets, that they find them only in books of great antiquity, and habitually reverenced. We may observe farther, that in the ancient languages these words were more harmonious and sonorous, than in the modern. But this could only add to the flow and cadence of the stile, and could produce no constant or lasting effect;[4] for, tho' a melodious line may impose upon the ear, yet the fallacy is quickly detected; and how agreeable soever a language may be, it is a vain attempt

---

2. of which one . . . ideas: "dont l'une regarde comme noble, ou du moins comme indifférent tout ce qui entre dans le commerce de la vie, dès qu'il a quelque utilité, & qu'il n'a rien de contraire aux premieres impressions de la nature" (pp. xxxvi–xxxvii).

3. low and despicable: "basse" (p. xxxvii).

4. But this could . . . effect: "mais cet avantage ne peut servir qu'à rendre le stile plus doux, ou plus nombreux" (p. xxxix).

of some of the critics to persuade us that it^n can, by its^o music, exalt meanness, or give graces to deformity.⁵

Thus it evidently appears, that it is not the fault of our language, but our own weakness; or if we might be admitted as judges in our own cause, 'tis the delicacy of our taste, and the elevation of our genius,⁶ that deprives all our polished writings of a multitude of subjects, that supplied the ancients with such a variety of affecting passages and which give us pleasure in the compositions of most of our neighbours.

Every nation concludes, that the way of writing practised among themselves, is the least exceptionable,⁷ and gives often the same reasons for their esteem, that are urged by others, for their contempt of it. All have, when they are vigorously attacked, at least one answer to make, which seems sufficient to repress the most resolute critic, *that those who censure do not understand them.* Thus the Abbe Fontanini, a man not more valuable even for his great learning, than for the exactness of his taste, instead of admitting the censure of Father Bohours, upon the Italian authors,* maintains, that he only condemns them, because he did not understand them,⁸ and makes no scruple to say, no foreigner is capable of judging, because he has been educated in a high notion of the productions of his

n. they *errata*   o. their *errata*
*Maniere de bien penser.⁹

---

5. that it can . . . deformity: "qu'elle donne jamais par elle-même de l'agrément & de la noblesse aux plus petites choses" (p. xxxix).

6. but our own . . . genius: "mais plûtôt la nôtre; ou, si les Etrangers veulent nous en croire sur notre parole, l'élévation & la délicatesse de notre génie" (p. xxxix).

7. Every nation . . . exceptionable: "Chaque Nation se croit en possession de la meilleure maniere d'écrire" (p. xl).

8. SJ omits a footnote containing a quotation from Giusto Fontanini, archbishop of Ancyra: "Ogni forastiere non é atto a giudicar degli altri stranieri, perche egli é nudrito dell'altera opinione delle cose proprie, e del conto leggierissimo delle altrui. *Lettera sulla eloquenza Italiana*" (p. xl).

9. This is the only instance where SJ indicates the wording of the French. Du Resnel has correctly "Bouhours" (p. xl), a reference to Dominique Bouhours, a French Jesuit grammarian, classicist, and critic whose *La Manière de bien penser dans les ouvrages de l'esprit* (1687), a critical dialogue, attacks obscurity, inflated language, and exaggeration, most notably in Italian and Spanish writers.

own country, and has but an imperfect knowledge of those of another.*

That this principle is true to a certain degree, cannot be denied, but if it be unjust in us to pass a judgment upon foreigners, of whom, being at a distance from them, we have but little knowledge, are we not equally unqualified to decide upon the merit of our own writers on account of our too near acquaintance? When we are too far from an object we see it but confusedly, and seldom otherwise than in part; if we are near it, it ingrosses our sight, and hides every thing else from us, with which we might compare it.[1] How shall a proper medium be assigned, where we may determine between foreigners and ourselves, without danger of erring, by knowing too little of one, and too much of the other?[2]

The same pride that blinds particular men, operates likewise upon whole nations. Every man thinks himself obliged to support his honour, and becomes a party in the question, by the secret influence of a persuasion that his native country excells all others. This he seriously believes, and the prejudice becomes too strong to be distinguished from reason.[3] 'Tis to little purpose that those who differ from us, after having exhausted their arguments, appeal to experience, and demand, that the merit of authors be decided by the pleasure

---

*Fontanini died at Rome, in 1736. He was titular Archbishop of Ancyra.

---

1. ingrosses . . . compare it: "on ne voit que lui; il offusque la vûe, & dès lors on ne peut le comparer avec les autres" (p. xli).

2. where we may . . . other: "où l'on n'ait à craindre aucuns de ces deux inconvéniens, lorsqu'il sera question de juger entre les Etrangers & nous" (p. xli).

3. "Scarce any can hear with impartiality a comparison between the writers of his own and another country; and though it cannot, I think, be charged equally on all nations, that they are blinded with this literary patriotism, yet there are none that do not look upon their authors with the fondness of affinity, and esteem them as well for the place of their birth, as for their knowledge or their wit. There is, therefore, seldom much respect due to comparative criticism, when the competitors are of different countries, unless the judge is of a nation equally indifferent to both. The Italians could not for a long time believe, that there was any learning beyond the mountains; and the French seem generally persuaded, that there are no wits or reasoners equal to their own" (*Rambler* 93, par. 7; iv.132).

which they give; for opinion[4] in time becomes nature, and what others cannot read without weariness in our authors, we peruse with pleasure, because we desire nothing better. Thus, when we love any thing, it is past controversy, that we think it amiable, but to determine that it is therefore amiable in reality, would be to decide with very little regard to reason or experience.

Since therefore no man can be admitted to judge his own cause, of whatever kind it be, and questions of taste are such as may betray us to impose upon ourselves, more easily than any other, where shall we find an arbitrator disinterested enough to decide between reason and self-love? Nothing is in its nature less fixed, or certain than taste, how far it proceeds upon necessary principles, and where it begins to depend upon arbitrary precepts, the most penetrating eye cannot exactly discover; and that the most celebrated critics of every age have determined in direct opposition to each other, is well known. Cicero, whose judgment will not be disputed, recommends Plautus as the great pattern of genteel raillery, and discovers in him a peculiar delicacy of wit, and an happy genius for a jest.[5] But Horace, who seems to have been master of all the good taste of Augustus's court declares, without any hesitation, that the old Romans were too good natur'd, if not stupid, in commending his low mirth.[6] Hegesias remark'd,[7]

---

4. appeal to experience . . . opinion: "en appellent au sentiment; l'opinion" (p. xlii).

5. genteel raillery . . . jest: "la fine plaisanterie, & lui trouve une délicatesse particuliere pour les rencontres ingénieuses" (p. xliii–xliv). SJ omits a footnote: "Duplex est jocandi genus . . . alterum elegans, urbanum, ingeniosum, facetum, quo genere Plautus noster refertus est. *Cic. Off. L. 1.*" (p. xliii).

6. low mirth: "Comique" (p. xliv). SJ omits a footnote:

"At nostri proavi Plautinos &
    numeros, &
Laudavere sales, nimium patienter
    utrumque,
Ne dicam stultè mirati, si modo
    ego & vos
Scimus in urbanum lepido
    seponere dicto.
Horat. Art. Poët." (ll. 270–74)

7. Hegesias remark'd: "Un Ancien avoit dit" (p. xliv). SJ found Hegesias of Magnesia, Greek orator and historian, in the passage from Plutarch's "Life of Alexander" (3) given in n. 9 below.

upon hearing that the Temple of Diana was burned the same night in which Alexander was born, that Diana's habitation might easily be destroyed, while she was gone to the assistance of his mother; an observation recorded by Cicero with applause,[8] but so much disapproved by the judicious Plutarch,[9] that he holds it *frigid* enough to have put out the fire.

Horace, Virgil, Livy, Salust, Tacitus, Cicero, are indeed universally esteemed, the *Iliad* and *Aeneid* are equally approved by the Italian advocates for Tasso, and the English admirers of Milton; but this approbation, however general it may appear at the first view, is well known not to extend to particular parts of those works, tho' the beauty of the whole is uncontested;[1] but while they all agree in that one position, nothing can be more opposite than their opinions upon the stile and sentiments of those great authors. Nor did those who are now the most loudly celebrated, arrive immediately at the height of reputation, where they now stand; their writings struggled for whole centuries, with the bad taste of mankind,[2] and only time produced this general acknowledgment of their merit. Nor is it necessary to prove this from examples of ancient times, the attacks upon the *Gierusalemme Liberata*, by the Italian critics, and the obscurity in which the *Paradise Lost*,[3] now so much admir'd, lay buried for a long time among the English, may clearly demonstrate the weakness of the human mind, and the uncertainty of its judgment.

More needs not surely to be said, after these examples,

---

8. an observation ... applause: "Le même Cicéron, qui rapporte ce mot, (*a*) ajoûte, qu'il le trouve très-juste & très-agréable, *concinnè ut multa Timaeus, &c.*" SJ again omits a footnote: "Qui cum in historia dixisset quâ nocte natus esset Alexander Dianae Ephesiae Templum deflagravisse, adjunxit id minimè esse mirandum, quod Diana cum in partu Olympiadis adesse voluisset, abfuisset domo. *Cic. L. 2. de Nat. Deor.*" (p. xliv).

9. SJ omits a footnote from Plutarch's "Life of Alexander," III.3: "ᾧ γ' Ἡγη-σίας ὁ Μάγνῃς ἐπιπεφώηκεν ἐπιφώνημα κατασβέσαι τὴν πυρκαιὰν ἐκείνην ὑπὸ ψυχρίας δυνάμενον· Vita Alexand." (p. xlv).

1. tho' the beauty ... uncontested: "que sur le tout qui en résulte" (p. xlv).

2. SJ omits "ou l'envie de leurs Contemporains" (p. xlvi).

3. the attacks ... *Paradise Lost:* "les assauts que le Tasse eut à soûtenir de la part des Critiques dans son propre Pays, & l'obscurité où le Poëme de Milton" (p. xlvi).

to prevail upon us to suspend our sentences not only upon those writers, whom nature seems to have placed beyond the bounds of our jurisdiction, but upon our countrymen concerning whom we seem more able to decide. Till therefore some uncommon genius shall arise, whose authority mankind shall so generally agree to allow, that his determinations shall be the last appeal, we can take no method of deciding upon the merit of foreigners, more prudent or just, than that which Quintilian recommends to the moderns with regard to the ancients, *We ought,* says he, *to be cautious, and modest in our criticisms upon such great writers, lest, as has been the fate of many, we censure what we do not understand.*[4] Though we have not ourselves any indisputable right to the first rank in the republick of letters, yet neither have they any better pretensions to superiority,[5] but have, like us, their perfections and defects, and perhaps in the same proportion. Of these we have doubtless a right to tell our opinions, but reflection will teach us to do it with the utmost modesty and diffidence, lest we should condemn or even applaud what we shall appear not to comprehend. And perhaps in such enquiries it may be proper to confine our remarks to the general design and plan of the work, which, depending upon principles established in nature, must, in all places and all ages, be the same, without extending our criticism, to the particular dress or ornaments of the several parts, which being not in themselves reducible to certain rules,[6] may be compared to fashions indifferent in themselves, and only necessary to be observed in those countries where they prevail.

---

4. This is SJ's translation of Quintilian; Du Resnel has the Latin in a footnote: "Modeste tamen & circumspecto judicio de tantis viris pronuntiandum est, ne, quod plerisque accidit, damnent quae non intelligunt" (p. xlvii). Modern texts read "modesto" (*De Institutione Oratoria,* X.1.26). SJ quotes part of the same passage, but wrongly attributes it to Cicero, as his motto for *Adventurer* 58.

5. yet neither ... superiority: "ils sont aussi dans l'impuissance d'en alléguer aucun qui nous force à le leur céder" p. xlvii).

6. which, depending . . . rules: "qui doivent être les mêmes en tout tems & en tout Pays, qu'aux ornemens de chaque partie qui ne sont point fondés sur des principes invariables" (p. xlviii).

As for our own writers, tho' it be allowed that the authority of custom ought not to prevail so far as to oblige them to rack their imaginations, and force their stile[7] for the sake of surprising their readers with new and unexpected epithets, or to fill their writings with antitheses and oppositions, which owe all their beauty to the choice and disposition of the words, tho' they ought yet less to abandon true wit for glittering points, solid sense for sparkling trifles, and instruction for amusement;[8] yet it must be owned that they ought to pay some deference to the taste of the nation, by which they are to be judg'd, but they are under a necessity of conforming to it no farther than that they cannot be accused of too great a deviation from it.

And since, notwithstanding all his reason, man finds himself unhappily constrained often to submit himself to the conduct of prejudice, and can generally make no further use of his wisdom than to chuse of two opinions, neither of which are fully comprehended by him, rather that which is better supported, than that which can show less authority, it must be at last confessed, that nothing is more rational or less servile,[9] than in compliance with the general prejudice of every age and nation to consider the great authors of antiquity, as the only models which we ought to imitate; yet without suffering our veneration to persuade us that there is in every passage of their works, the same strength, and the same beauty. If our gratitude[1] will not allow us to charge them with the least defect,[2] there is yet a way by which we may, in imitation of their

---

7. tho' it be allowed . . . stile: "si le torrent de la coutume ne doit jamais les contraindre à forcer leur stile & leur esprit" (p. xlviii).

8. true wit . . . amusement: "le solide pour le brillant, l'utile pour l'agréable, & le vrai pour le spécieux" (p. xlix).

9. two opinions . . . servile: "les bons & les mauvais, il paroît qu'il n'en est point de plus raisonnable, ni de moins honteux" (p. xlix).

1. If our gratitude: "si par un principe de reconnoissance" (p. l).

2. SJ omits "selon M. de la Motte" and the footnote: "Discours sur la Poësie" (p. l). Although SJ most likely deleted an earlier reference to Bolingbroke because of antipathy to his ideas (p. 358, n. 4), it is not clear why he deleted a reference to Antoine Houdar de La Motte and his work, which was published in 1730.

warmest defenders, preserve their characters, without injuring our own; let us, at the same time that we defend what is disapproved by their adversaries, forbear to copy it.³

If any man, more a Frenchman than a critic, should conceive, that I have not sollicitously enough maintained the honour of my country, I shall reply with Voltaire,⁴ *That the true love of our country consists in being good subjects, and promoting the general happiness, but to contend solely for the reputation of our authors, and to boast of having better poets among us than our neighbours, is rather self-love than patriotism.*

That there is much more to be said upon subjects of so great importance, is easily discovered, especially as questions of this kind admit of such diversity of opinions,⁵ and perhaps I may some time treat of them in greater latitude, but at present I believe, that what I have said is sufficient to qualify the reader to peruse the following poems with advantage, and to justify myself for having transgressed the limits of an exact translation.

That it is generally to be wished, that translators would consider themselves as *having their hands tied,** is not to be denied, and that they would, without any regard to their own particular taste or prejudices, endeavour to exhibit the work as it really is in itself, that they would not so much endeavour to give us pleasure, as to show us what has given pleasure to the nation, for which the original was written. Great would be the

---

*See the Journal *des Scavans*, April, 1736, upon the Silhouette ᵖ version of the *Essay on Man*.
p. Silhouette *om*.

---

3. let us . . . copy it: "qui se gardent bien de les imiter en certaines choses, quoiqu'ils trouvent toujours des raisons ingénieuses pour les justifier de tout ce qu'on leur reproche" (p. l).

4. SJ omits the footnote: "Traduction de son Essai sur le Poëme Epique" (p. li). Voltaire's *Essai sur la poésie épique* was first published in English in 1727 as *An Essay upon the Civil Wars of France, Extracted from Curious Manuscripts. And Also upon the Epick Poetry of the European Nations from Homer down to Milton*. The French "translation" did not appear until 1733. SJ translates the French and does not use the English version, which differs from the French in its emphasis. See R. S. Ridgway, *Voltaire and Sensibility* (1973), p. 120.

5. subjects . . . opinions: "matieres si importantes, & sur lesquelles il est si difficile de fixer les esprits" (p. li).

use of such versions,⁶ as they would not disguise the real manner or character of foreign writers, and would preserve the peculiar and natural air of every author, without concealing even his defects.

That nothing would be more useful or more curious, at least, than such translations as these I readily admit, but must confess, at the same time, that, in my opinion, no such translation can possibly be written, at least of an author like Mr Pope. Expression is the soul of poetry, and there is no representation to be made of a poet, without giving an idea of his expression; even the sentiments will often be lost, which always depend on the language, and of which, if you divest the thoughts of our best French poets, all their force and sublimity will vanish, and nothing will be left but a few well-known, and beaten truths,⁷ which I do not indeed deny, but cannot applaud. The skeleton of a poet will indeed remain, but without any beauty or power to please.⁸

The basis or solid sentiment may very compleatly, says a celebrated critic, be preserved in prose, but it can retain neither the force nor the beauties which arise from the artful disposition of chosen words, nor can any idea be given of the numbers or harmony. A French translation can, in his opinion no more enable us to determine the poetical merit of the Greek or Latin writers, than a graver can give us in a print a compleat view or idea of the genius exerted in painting by Titian or Carache.

What the author of the *Observations upon Modern Writings**
has said of the Greek and Latin poets, he had asserted with

---

*Tom III. Letter 40.⁹
q. 420

---

6. Du Resnel's footnote reads: "Voyez le Journal des Sçavans, sur la Traduction de l'Essai sur l'Homme, par M. D. S. mois d'Avril 1736" (p. lii), making it clear that "the version" is that by Silhouette.

7. well-known, and beaten truths: "vérités triviales" (p. liii).

8. but without . . . please: "mais vous ne me donnez pas le Poëte même" (p. liii).

9. Du Resnel has "Lettre 40" (p. liv). The author was Abbé Pierre François Guyot Desfontaines.

greater reason of the English, whose manner of expression[1] is more distant from ours, than ours from that of the ancients; and therefore what value soever may be justly set upon the translations which Mr D. S. has given of these two poetical works,[2] yet those who are in the same degree masters of the English and French, say, in plain terms, that there is nothing of Mr Pope to be found in them, and that if they sometimes discover the philosopher, the poet is always lost.

I am far from concluding, that my version will enable the reader to judge better of the particular character of Mr Pope's poetry, and am convinced that part of what I have urged against prose translations may be retorted upon those in verse. They may, to a certain degree, preserve the force and fire, the daring spirit and rigorous imagination, that make the original admired, but the particular strokes that mark out and distinguish that force, spirit, and imagination from the same excellencies in any other writer, cannot be expected from a translation, and can only be learned by learning to perfection the original language.

In 1717 came out a poem in five cantos,[3] called *An Essay on Criticism,* in imitation of Mr Pope, but Mr Roboton,[4] the author of it, who was counsellor and privy secretary to the late King of England, has treated the thoughts of his author so much like his own, and given them so compleat a French dress, or rather garnished them so much, according to his own fancy, that it would not be easy for the original writer to know them. It is strange that with such excellent materials, for less cannot be said of Mr Pope's performance, he could

---

1. manner of expression: "façon de penser & de s'exprimer" (p. liv).

2. Du Resnel identifies the works as "l'*Essai sur l'Homme,* & de l'*Essai sur la Critique*" (p. liv). Mr. D. S. is Silhouette, who published prose translations of both works in 1736.

3. SJ omits "imprimé à Londres & à Amsterdam" (p. lv).

4. Du Resnel has "Robeton" (p. lvi); the usual English spelling is Robethon (Jean de). In his "Life of Pope" SJ mentions that the *Essay on Criticism* was translated into French "by Robotham, secretary to the King for Hanover" (*Lives,* III.99, par. 43). Robethon, a Huguenot refugee, came to England c. 1689 and was employed by William III. In 1705 he entered the service of George Lewis, the future George I, and accompanied the king to England in 1715.

frame nothing more accurate or perfect; all the faults which a Frenchman would find in an English poem, he has retained, but almost all the beauties he has lost. *It is impossible,* say the journalists of Trevoux,* *to judge whether this poem was written to shew how a work of the imagination may be written without faults, or to teach the art of criticising such works; he throws out at hazard some observations upon the writers and criticks of all nations, and particularly his own, sometimes indeed not without wit, but always without order or judgment.* Though it cannot be said, that a poetical essay requires the same degree of regularity as a treatise in prose, yet no writer is exempted from the necessity of making his thoughts just, and his reasonings connected. In this respect there may perhaps appear the same difference between my translation and Mr Roboton's, as between his performance and that of Mr Pope.

With regard to my stile, I suppose it is not necessary to inform the reader, that he is not to expect here the pomp and elevation of the epic language, or of those poems of which the diction is adapted to marvellous events, and great actions.⁵ Instruction, not imagery, is the business of the didactic writer, and the excellencies of his stile are simplicity, accuracy, and perspicuity. The poets of this class, if they can claim that title, apply to the reason, not the imagination, and are therefore not at liberty to give full play to the efforts of genius. So generally has this truth been allowed, that Horace has, by many critics, been affirmed to have descended in his epistles from the natural sublimity of his stile to make his precepts more efficacious, and to shew that his instructions were founded on truth, and needed not the assistance of sounding syllables, or magnificence of language.⁶

*August, 1717.

---

5. SJ adds "and great actions."
6. So generally . . . language: "Cette vérité a toujours paru si constante, que les Critiques (*a*) ont prétendu qu'Horace dans ses Epitres, & sur tout dans son Art Poëtique, avoit exprès rabaissé son stile, pour donner plus de poids à ses préceptes, & pour faire voir que ce n'étoit pas sur de grands mots, ni sur des expressions superbes, mais uniquement sur le vrai, qu'il vouloit établir la solidité de ses maximes" (lviii). SJ omits the footnote: "Voyez les jugemens des Sçavans, par M. Baillet à l'article d'Horace."

There are, however, some elegancies and ornaments which didactic poetry may properly admit, tho' its province is always rather that of instructing than entertaining; and even Mr Pope, tho' he teaches with more politeness, insinuation and address, than his predecessors, is nevertheless a teacher, and has consequently something disgusting in his manner. He endeavours not to dissipate the attention by variety, but to contract it to a single point. To impress his precepts with more force, he sometimes traces back his own reasonings, and returns to his first principles.

For the relief of his readers he sometimes roves into digressions, but there are few who are willing to be fatigued for the sake of knowing the satisfaction of repose. Satire contributes much to the pleasure of this kind of performance,[r] but the strokes which are to be found here, will not much gratify the malignity of corrupt hearts, because they are for the most part general, or, if ever pointed at particular persons, directed at such as are not known in our country. Whoever therefore will be his pupil here, must attend only from principles of reason, a kind of attention, which even philosophers can rarely support without some struggles and reluctance.[7]

These poems are therefore by no means accommodated to those who read, rather to lull themselves in tranquillity and indolence, than to enlarge their views and fortify their minds.[8] But those who penetrate farther, who are not afraid of the labour of reflection, and whose judgments are too solid to applaud a book which does not require more than a single reading, will find here no disagreeable employment.

Should any man attempt to run over the maxims of Rochefoucault with equal rapidity as a novel or a history, he would

r. performances

---

7. Whoever therefore ... reluctance: "Il faudra donc se résoudre à l'écouter par raison; mais tout ce qu'on fait de la sorte, coute toujours un peu, même aux Sages" (p. lix).

8. who read ... minds: "qui lisent beaucoup moins pour s'instruire que pour s'entretenir dans une douce oisiveté" (p. lx).

harass himself without advantage, and would find only a croud of maxims[9] that would burthen the mind, without enriching it, unless he allowed himself time to dwell upon them, and to apply them to his own ideas and experience.

To make the translation of the *Essay on Criticism* more compleat, and more useful to young readers desirous of forming a taste, and qualifying themselves to judge upon solid and extensive principles, not only of poetry, but of all the polite arts, I have subjoined to some particular passages,[1] either my own observations, or remarks extracted from authors ancient or modern of greater authority, in which some of Mr Pope's sentiments are more fully explained.[2] Some of the notes I was obliged to insert, merely for the sake of common readers. As to the imitations which I have been careful to remark, I was of opinion that it would be agreeable to observe what passages Mr Pope thought worthy of his choice, and that by pointing them out, I should rather heighten than depress his character. Doctor Atterbury,[3] a wit of the first class, to whose friendship I had the honour of being admitted, often asserted that there never was a good writer who had not the art of transplanting into his own writings the beauties of his predecessors, and that the man who imitated no body, would probably find no imitators.

FINIS.

---

9. a novel . . . maxims: "une Comédie ou des Mémoires Historiques, s'y ennuyeroit immanquablement. Il en est à peu près de même de ces Essais; ce n'est qu'un enchaînement de pensées" (p. lx).

1. SJ omits "insérées au bas de la page" (p. lxi).

2. SJ adds "in which . . . explained."

3. Du Resnel has "un Homme" with a footnote: "Le Docteur Atterbury Evêque de Rochester" (p. lxi). Francis Atterbury, whose sermons SJ considered among the best English sermons for style (*Life*, III.247), was found guilty by the House of Lords in 1723 of strongly Jacobite leanings and banished *sine die*, his bishopric being annulled. It was probably during his exile that Du Resnel met and befriended him.

LETTER TO THE *GENTLEMAN'S MAGAZINE*
ON THE CONTROVERSY
BETWEEN
WARBURTON AND CROUSAZ ON POPE'S
ESSAY ON MAN

EDITOR'S INTRODUCTION

When Johnson came to write his "Life of Pope," he remembered the controversy surrounding the *Essay on Man,* neglecting, unfortunately, to mention any of the roles he played. The charges against the *Essay on Man* brought by Jean Pierre de Crousaz in his *Examen* and *Commentaire* were answered by the Reverend William Warburton, Johnson recalls, who "About this time . . . began to make his appearance in the first ranks of learning"; a growing reputation gained by his controversial works on religion, *The Alliance between Church and State* (1736) and *The Divine Legation of Moses* (first volume, 1737).[1] Warburton, Johnson continues, "undertook without solicitation to rescue Pope from the talons of Crousaz by freeing him from the imputation of favouring fatality or rejecting revelation."[2] His defense began in December 1738 in a letter that appeared in the *History of the Works of the Learned,* and four more letters appeared in January, February, March, and April 1739. These five letters, with the addition of a sixth, were published as *A Vindication of Mr. Pope's Essay on Man, from the Misrepresentations of Mr. Crousaz* on 15 November 1739. A seventh letter was published separately on 13 June 1740, with a final revision incorporating all of the letters, entitled *A Critical and Philosophical Commentary on Mr. Pope's Essay on Man,* published on 10 August 1742.[3] Warburton's "vindication" of the *Essay on Man* from Crousaz's strictures brought him to Pope's attention: "From this time Pope lived in the closest intimacy with his commentator, and amply rewarded his kindness and zeal; for he introduced him to Mr. Murray, by whose interest he became preacher at Lincoln's Inn, and to Mr. Allen, who gave him his niece and his estate, and by consequence a bishoprick."[4]

---

1. "Life of Pope" (*Lives,* III.165, par. 184).
2. *Lives,* III.167, par. 189.
3. See Mack, *Twickenham Pope,* p. xxi, n. 3.
4. *Lives,* III.169, par. 194. Reverend

Here Johnson begins a restrained defense of Crousaz against Warburton, in which in his later account of the controversy in the "Life of Pope," Crousaz comes off considerably better than Warburton—or Pope.[5] Johnson's defense, which appeared in the March and November 1743 issues of the *Gentleman's Magazine*, consists largely of four passages quoted from his own translation of the *Commentaire*, which the reader is asked to accept as proof that Crousaz's "notions are just" and that "his abilities and piety are such as may entitle him to reverence."[6] The first passage, directed by Crousaz at Pope, might well be directed at Warburton, Johnson implies. The second, not surprisingly, happens to be on the ruling passion, a topic of continuing interest and one on which he had already commented.[7] When Johnson turns to Crousaz's comments on the attainment of happiness, he silently omits a lyrical, somewhat enthusiastic, paragraph with which he may not have agreed.[8] The final passage from Crousaz gives the "true sense," Johnson believes, of "Pope's assertion, that *Whatever is, is right.*" The continuation, suggested in the last paragraph of the letter, did not appear.

The first installment of the letter to the *Gentleman's Magazine* fills the final column of a gathering and may have been broken off because the next gathering, containing "Poetical Essays," had already been printed. When the letter was resumed eight months later the reader, and perhaps Johnson, no longer remembered that the stated intention was to medi-

---

George Strahan recollected to Boswell that SJ had told him that George III had observed that Pope made Warburton a bishop. "True, Sir, (said Johnson,) but Warburton did more for Pope; he made him a Christian" (*Life*, II.37, n. 1.).

5. *Lives*, III.164–70, pars. 182–94. In the interval between this essay and the writing of the "Life of Pope" SJ encountered the pugnacious Warburton in connection with their editions of Shakespeare. See *Johnson on Shakespeare*, ed. Arthur Sherbo (Vol. VII, Yale Edition of the Works of Samuel Johnson, 1968), pp. xxxvi–xxxviii; *Life*, I.175–76. See also Fleeman, *Bibliography*, I.93.

6. The four quotations are found on pages 35, 118–19, 59–61, and 84 of the 1739 edition. See pp. 68, 155, 94–95, 120 above.

7. See p. 145 above.

8. The paragraph occurs between those beginning "But let a man study and labour" and "When this is our frame of mind." See p. 95 above.

ate the disagreement between Crousaz and Warburton. The second installment is little more than a series of quotations demonstrating Crousaz's piety and puffing Johnson's translation, undoubtedly the real purpose of the letter. Sir John Hawkins, who first attributed the essay to Johnson, says that Johnson "proceeded no farther than to state the sentiments of Mr. Crousaz respecting the poem, from a seeming conviction that he was discussing an uninteresting question."[9] Thomas Kaminski suggests that "Johnson certainly had no thought of how the piece would look when the two disparate segments would finally be joined in his collected works. He was writing to the moment.... The circumstances, not the nodding of the author, caused the anomalous structure in which a work that began as a formal essay ended as if it were merely another casual letter to Mr. Urban."[1]

Hawkins, after attributing the letter to Johnson in his *Life*, reprinted it in 1787 in the *Works* and the attribution has never been challenged.[2] The text here is that of the *Gentleman's Magazine* for March and November 1743, printed from a copy in the Arizona State University Library.[3] An error of printing in the first installment, noted in an erratum on page 587 of the magazine, has been corrected and reported in the textual notes. The March installment has no title as it appears as a letter to the editor, but the November installment is headed "*Specimens of M. Crousaz's Sentiments from the English Translation of his Commentary on Mr Pope's Essay on Man, continued from p. 152.*" The running head reads "*Sentiments from* M. *Crousaz's Commentary, &c.*" and the entry in the index to volume thirteen reads "*Crousaz* M. Specimens of his Sentiments 587." Since none of these headings suggests a good title, a descriptive title has been supplied by the editor.

---

9. *The Life of Samuel Johnson, LL.D.*, 2d ed. (1787), pp. 70, 351.

1. *The Early Career of Samuel Johnson* (1987), pp. 157–58.

2. IX.364–68.

3. XIII.152, 587–88. The Arizona State University Library copy of the *Gentleman's Magazine* has been compared to copies in the following libraries: British Library, Bodleian, Harvard University, Huntington, Newberry, Yale University, University of Chicago, University of Illinois, University of Iowa, University of Southern California.

MR URBAN,

It would not be found useless in the learned world, if in written controversies as in oral disputations, a moderator could be selected who might in some degree superintend the debate, restrain all needless excursions, repress all personal reflections, and at last recapitulate the arguments on each side, and who though he should not assume the province of deciding the question, might at least exhibit it in its true state.

This reflection arose in my mind upon the consideration of Mr Crousaz's *Commentary* on the *Essay on Man,* and Mr Warburton's answer to it. The importance of the subject, the reputation and abilities of the controvertists, and perhaps the ardour with which each has endeavoured to support his cause, have made an attempt of this kind necessary for the information of the greatest number of Mr Pope's readers.

Among the duties of a moderator, I have mentioned that of recalling the disputants to the subject, and cutting off the excrescences of a debate, which Mr Crousaz will not suffer to be long unemployed, and the repression of personal invectives which have not been very carefully avoided on either part, and are less excusable, because it has not been proved that either the poet, or his commentator wrote with any other design than that of promoting happiness, by cultivating reason and piety.

Mr Warburton has indeed so much depress'd the character of his adversary that before I consider the controversy between them, I think it necessary to exhibit some specimens of Mr Crousaz's sentiments, by which it will probably be shown that he is far from deserving either indignation or contempt;

that his notions are just, though they are sometimes introduced without necessity, and defended when they are not opposed; and that his abilities and piety are such as may entitle him to reverence from those who think his criticisms superfluous.

Page 35. of the English translation he exhibits an observation which every writer ought to impress upon his mind, and which may afford a sufficient apology for his commentary.

a"The more reputation an author is arriv'd at, the more cautious ought he to be, that nothing drops from his pen, from which men of corrupt inclinations may take advantages in opposing religion."[1]

On the notion of a *ruling passion,* he offers this remark.[2]

> Nothing so much hinders men from obtaining a complete victory over their *ruling passion,* as that all the advantages gained in their days of retreat, by just and sober reflections, whether struck out by their own minds, or borrowed from good books, or from the conversation of men of merit, are destroy'd in a few moments by a free intercourse and acquaintance with libertines; and thus the work is always to be begun anew. A gamester resolves to leave off play, by which he finds his health impaired, his family ruin'd, and his passions inflamed; in this resolution he persists a few days, but soon yields to an invitation, which will give his prevailing inclination an opportunity of reviving in all its force. The case is the same with other men; but is reason to be charged with these calamities and follies, or rather the man who refuses to listen to its voice in opposition to impertinent solicitations?"

---

a. On the motion of a *ruling passion* he offers this remark. *om.*

---

1. The March installment ends here.
2. A footnote appears at this point in the text in the *Gentleman's Magazine:* "These words on the *ruling passion,* &c. which were inserted by mistake at p. 152 H, we desire the reader to erase in that place." This sentence, which had introduced the final paragraph of the March installment, beginning, "The more reputation an author," has been erased by the editor.

On the means recommended for the attainment of happiness he observes, that

> the abilities which our Maker has given us, and the internal and external advantages with which he has invested us, are of two very different kinds; those of one kind are bestowed in common upon us and the brute creation, but the other exalt us far above other animals. To disregard any of these gifts would be ingratitude; but to neglect those of greater excellence, to go no farther than the gross satisfactions of sense and the functions of mere animal life, would be a far greater crime. We are formed by our Creator capable of acquiring knowledge, and regulating our conduct by reasonable rules; it is therefore our duty to cultivate our understandings and exalt our virtues. We need but make the experiment to find, that the greatest pleasures will arise from such endeavours.
>
> It is trifling to allege, in opposition to this truth, that knowledge cannot be acquired, nor virtue persued without toil and efforts, and that all efforts produce fatigue. God requires nothing disproportion'd to the powers he has given, and in the exercise of those powers consists the highest satisfaction.
>
> Toil and weariness are the effects of vanity; when a man has formed a design of excelling others in merit, he is disquieted by their advances, and leaves nothing unattempted, that he may step before them; this occasions a thousand unreasonable emotions, which justly bring their punishment along with them.
>
> But let a man study and labour to cultivate and improve his abilities, in the eye of his Maker, and with the prospect of his approbation; let him attentively reflect on the infinite value of that approbation, and the highest encomiums that men can bestow will vanish into nothing at the comparison. When we live in this manner, we find that we live for a great and glorious end.
>
> When this is our frame of mind, we find it no longer

difficult to restrain ourselves in the gratifications of eating and drinking, the most gross enjoyments of sense. We take what is necessary to preserve health and vigour, but are not to give ourselves up to pleasures that weaken the attention, and dull the understanding.

And the true sense of Mr Pope's assertion, that *Whatever is, is right,* and I believe the sense in which it was written is thus explained.

A sacred and adorable order is established in the government of mankind. These are certain and unvaried truths: he that seeks God, and makes it his happiness to live in obedience to him, shall obtain what he endeavours after, in a degree far above his present comprehension. He that turns his back upon his Creator, neglects to obey him, and perseveres in his disobedience, shall obtain no other happiness than he can receive from enjoyments of his own procuring; void of satisfaction, weary of life, wasted by empty cares, and remorses equally harrassing and just, he will experience the certain consequences of his own choice. Thus will *justice* and *goodness* resume their empire, and that order be restored which men have broken.

I am afraid of wearying you or your readers with more quotations, but if you shall inform me that a continuation of my correspondence will be well received, I shall descend to particular passages, show how Mr Pope gave sometimes occasion to mistakes, and how Mr Crousaz was misled by his suspicion of the system of fatality.

I am, Sir, Yours, &c.

REVIEW OF SOAME JENYNS'
A FREE INQUIRY INTO THE NATURE AND ORIGIN OF EVIL. 1757

EDITOR'S INTRODUCTION

Johnson's first contribution to *The Literary Magazine, or, Universal Review* was "To the PUBLIC," the introduction to no. I (published 15 May 1756). His final contribution was his review of Soame Jenyns' *A Free Inquiry into the Nature and Origin of Evil;* the first installment of the review appeared in II, no. XIII (15 April–15 May 1757; published 17 May), the second in II, no. XIV (15 May–15 June; published 17 June), and the third and final installment in II, no. XV (15 June–15 July; published 19 July 1757).

Johnson wrote approximately forty reviews and several essays for the *Literary Magazine*. He also contributed a brief biography, "The Memoirs of the King of Prussia." It is uncertain if he had any role beyond that of contributor. In fact, little is known about the *Literary Magazine*, its printing, publishing, or reception. What is known has been canvassed by Donald D. Eddy.[1] William Faden, who had been printer of the *Rambler,* was probably printer of all twenty-seven issues, the publisher of the first nine issues, and, initially at least, seems to have served as editor. J. Richardson was publisher of the next ten numbers (X–XIX) and John Wilkie the publisher of the last eight. John Newbery, with whom Johnson had extensive business concerns during the period, may have been involved in the venture. That the periodical ceased publication after only twenty-seven issues suggests that it never found an audience and was unable to compete with such formidable rivals as the *Gentleman's Magazine,* the *Monthly Review,* and the *Critical Review.*

Just why Johnson became involved in the *Literary Magazine* may never be fully known; but there are at least two possible reasons: money and a genuine interest in book review-

---

1. *Samuel Johnson, Book Reviewer in the Literary Magazine: or Universal Review,* *1756–1758* (1979), chap. I. See also Fleeman, *Bibliography,* I.685–86.

ing. Whatever sense of relief or satisfaction Johnson had on the publication of his *Dictionary* on 15 April 1755 must have been quickly tempered by the realization that his sanguine expectation of a tidy profit was not to materialize. Sir John Hawkins reports that "Johnson, who was no very accurate accountant, thought that a great part would be coming to him on the conclusion of the work; but upon [the booksellers] producing at a tavern-meeting for the purpose of settling, receipts for sums advanced to him, which were indeed the chief means of his subsistence, it was found, not only that he had eaten his cake, but that the balance of the account was greatly against him." The booksellers, however, "remitted the difference, and consoled him for his disappointment by making his entertainment at the tavern a treat."[2]

Once the shock had subsided, Johnson would have had to apply himself to one or more projects that would enable him to eke out a living.[3] The dilemma of how to make enough money from his writings to support himself was not to ease until the receipt of his pension in 1762. Just how he earned a living between 1755 and 1762 is far from clear, as the works now identified as his would scarce enable him to live. One project Johnson turned to, however, was the *Literary Magazine*.

Johnson's interest in book reviewing was not new; even before the *Dictionary* was published, he had been ruminating on the possibility of establishing a journal to review serious English and European literature. The following undated entry, probably made in late March or early April 1755, appears in his diary:

> *The Annals of Literature, foreign as well as domestick.* Imitate Le Clerck—Bayle—Barbeyrac. Infelicity of Journals in

---

2. Hawkins, *Life*, p. 345–46. See also James H. Sledd and Gwin J. Kolb, *Dr. Johnson's Dictionary* (1955), p. 108, n. 10 for various accounts of this episode.

3. SJ signed a contract with Jacob Tonson on 2 June 1756 but it did not bring him financial security. See J. D. Fleeman, "Johnson's *Shakespeare* (1765), The Progress of a Description" in *Writers, Books, and Trade*, ed. O M Brack, Jr. (1994), pp. 355–65. For other projects during this period, see Fleeman, *Bibliography*, I.657–999, II.1001–40.

England. Works of the Learned. We cannot take in all. Sometimes copy from foreign Journalists. Always tell.[4]

On 25 March 1755 Johnson wrote to Thomas Warton: "I intend in the winter to open a *Bibliotheque*," asking him "to subscribe a sheet a year" and to help persuade his brother to do the same.[5] James Boswell reports that Dr. William Adams, when he visited Johnson one day, "found his parlour floor covered with parcels of foreign and English literary journals." Johnson told him, Adams reported, that "he meant to undertake a Review."[6] The *Bibliotheque* contemplated by Johnson, never materialized, although he did not immediately give up the idea. Thomas Percy wrote to William Shenstone as late as 24 November 1757 that "Mr. Johnson talks of undertaking a kind of Monthly Review upon a New Plan, which shall only extend to the choicest and most valuable Books that are publish'd not in England only but throughout Europe: something like the Acta Eruditorum Leipsiensia, etc."[7] Apparently his reviewing for the *Literary Magazine* did not dampen his enthusiasm for a *Bibliotheque*. In fact, it has been recently suggested, his continuing interest in establishing one indicates that "Johnson looked upon regular reviewing not strictly as a means of earning a living . . . but as a consequential and dignified critical occupation."[8]

Johnson's review of Soame Jenyns' *A Free Inquiry* addresses the problem of evil certainly, but it focuses on issues raised by Pope's *Essay on Man*, which Jenyns follows to a fault. The review continues Johnson's critique of Pope's *Essay on Man* which began with the notes to his translation of Jean-Pierre Crousaz's *Commentaire*, and concludes in the "Life of Pope." Although the passage from the "Life of Pope" is too long to quote in full, it is helpful to remember that it repeats many

---

4. *Diaries, Prayers, and Annals*, ed. E. L. McAdam, Jr., with Donald and Mary Hyde (Vol. I, Yale Edition of the Works of Samuel Johnson, 1958), p. 56.
5. *Letters*, I.101.
6. *Life*, I.284.
7. *The Correspondence of Thomas Percy and William Shenstone*, ed. Cleanth Brooks, Vol. VII of *The Percy Letters*, ed. Cleanth Brooks and A. F. Falconer (1977), p. 2.
8. Brian J. Hanley, *Samuel Johnson as Book Reviewer* (2001), p. 58.

of the observations made in the Jenyns review. Pope, Johnson tells us, and his disciple, Jenyns, are each "proud of his acquisitions, and supposing himself master of great secrets, [is] in haste to teach what he had not learned.... Having exalted himself into the chair of wisdom," Johnson continues, "he tells us much that every man knows, and much that he does not know himself...." After an overview of Pope's argument, Johnson concludes, "Surely a man of no very comprehensive search may venture to say he has heard all this before...."[9]

Critics have frequently observed that this is Johnson's harshest review. The reasons for this harshness are not far to seek. Soame Jenyns (1704–90) was a country squire and man of letters, serving in parliament some forty years and beginning in 1755 as one of the lord commissioners of trade and plantations. He was prominent in political and social circles, with a reputation as a wit, and a proclivity for dandyish dress. In 1748 Robert Dodsley published eighty-seven pages of his poetry in *Collection of Poems. By Several Hands,* including an "Essay on Virtue," indebted to Pope's *Essay on Man,* and adopting the doctrine of plenitude and the chain of being. Then in 1752 Dodsley published Jenyns' first book of poetry, *Poems. By * * * * *.*[1] Johnson had extensive business connections with Dodsley and frequented his shop so there was ample opportunity to read Jenyns' writings, if, in fact, he had not met him.[2] His allusion in the review to the author whose "first diversion commonly begins with an ode or an epistle, then rises perhaps to a political irony, and is at last brought to its height, by a treatise of philosophy," suggests that Johnson was familiar with the outlines of Jenyns' career.

How familiar Johnson may have been with Jenyns and his writings remains open to speculation, but to understand Johnson's unhappiness with Jenyns' work it is scarcely necessary to look past the opening pages:

---

9. *Lives,* III.243 (par. 364), 244 (par. 366). For other discussions by SJ of the problem of evil, see Crousaz above and pp. li–lii and nn. 1, 2.

1. Ronald Rompkey, *Soame Jenyns* (1984), pp. 4–26.
2. See index under "Dodsley" in Fleeman, *Bibliography.*

> I imagin'd it might not be unentertaining ... to put together my sentiments on these important topics [metaphysical, moral, political, and religious subjects], and communicate them ... from time to time as the absence of business, or more agreeable amusements may afford me opportunity. This I propose to do under the general title of an Inquiry into the Nature, and Origin of Evil; an Inquiry, which will comprehend them all, and which, I think, has never been attended to with that diligence it deserves, nor with the success, which might have been hoped for from that little that has been bestow'd upon it.

Later Jenyns observes,

> If God is a good and benevolent Being, what end could he propose from creation, but the propagation of Happiness? And if Happiness is the end of all existence, why are not all creatures that exist happy? The true solution of this important question, so long and vainly searched for by philosophers of all ages, and all countries, I take it at least to be no more than this. . . .[3]

Richard B. Schwartz argues that one reason "behind the vehemence of Johnson's attack is the disparity between the enormity of the subject and the shallowness of Jenyns' treatment of it."[4] Eddy thinks that Johnson was "morally offended by the book and its author" and that he "hoped that if he were severe enough in his review he might counteract the influence of the book and might prevent Jenyns from dabbling again."[5] More recently Brian J. Hanley has argued that the emphasis in the review "falls as much on Jenyns' hubris as it does on the philosophical issues in themselves," going on to add that the review "is important to our understanding of Johnson's outlook on not only authorial self-delusion but the beneficent purposes of all literary activity as well."[6] As Johnson had observed in *Rambler* 93: "There is some ten-

---

3. Jenyns, pp. 1–2, 47–48.
4. Schwartz, *Problem of Evil*, p. 35.
5. Eddy, p. 93.
6. Hanley, pp. 119, 121.

derness due to living writers," except "when they attack . . . those truths which are of importance to the happiness of mankind."[7] Although the moral issues raised by the review are important, too much emphasis can be placed on them, forcing the reader to forget that Johnson, as a young man, was a satirist, influenced by Swift, and that in "the talent of humour there hardly ever was his equal."[8] His satiric and comic thrusts at Jenyns are reminiscent of his earlier attacks on the rivals of the *Gentleman's Magazine*.

Certain things God had shrouded in mystery and hidden from man. Attempting to understand these mysteries man committed the consummate sin of pride. Thinking that one could understand these mysteries was self-delusion and would only disturb man's happiness. Johnson recognized a tendency in himself to try to know more than could be known, and then spoke from his own painful experience. Among his surviving prayers, as early as November 1752, Johnson asks "that I may not lavish away the life which Thou hast given me on useless trifles, nor waste it in vain searches after things which thou hast hidden from me" and near the end of his life, in the course of a prayer for 12 August 1784, he petitions his "Lord," "Maker," and "Protector" that "while it shall please thee to continue me in this world where much is to be done and little to be known, teach me by thy Holy Spirit to withdraw my Mind from unprofitable and dangerous enquiries, from difficulties vainly curious, and doubts impossible to be solved."[9]

Jenyns, no doubt, smarted, at least initially, under the harsh correction he had received from Johnson. In a preface to the 1761 edition of the *Free Inquiry* Jenyns made a feeble defense of his work against "all the senseless misapprehensions, and malicious misconstructions, with which it has been tortured," by simply restating his original arguments. After Johnson's

---

7. *The Rambler*, ed. W. J. Bate and Albrecht B. Strauss (Vol. IV, Yale Edition of the Works of Samuel Johnson, 1969), p. 133 (par. 10).

8. Hawkins, *Life*, p. 281. See also pp. 386–90.

9. *Diaries, Prayers, and Annals*, pp. 48, 383–84.

death a ten-line "Epitaph" by Jenyns appeared in the *Gentleman's Magazine* in May 1786, followed by a sharp response by James Boswell in the *Gentleman's Magazine* for August of the same year. It would be difficult not to concur with Schwartz that the controversy surrounding the epitaph was largely of Boswell's own making to promote himself and his forthcoming *Life*.[1] Jenyns' fame would rest not only on Johnson's review of his *Free Inquiry* but on an epitaph that Boswell would have it believed was a vicious attack and which Jenyns could only have viewed as a jeu d'esprit. A more fitting conclusion to the Johnson-Jenyns affair, one revealing of the true characters of both men, is a memorandum of Johnson's conversation by William Bowles, given to Boswell but not printed by him:

> Soame Jenyns says he to whom I have not been too civil spoke to me with great kindness upon my late sickness & when I came first abroad congratulated me very kindly & and I was pleased with it.[2]

Quotations from *A Free Inquiry* are taken from the 1757 first edition in the British Library. Donald D. Eddy, in his extensive bibliographical examination of copies of the *Literary Magazine*, discovered no variants between copies.[3] The text here is taken from the Herman W. Liebert copy, now in the Beinecke Library, Yale University, reproduced in facsimile by Garland Publishing (1978).

---

1. Schwartz canvasses this entire episode in *Problem of Evil*, appendix I, pp. 89–91.

2. *Life*, 4.524. For a slightly different version of this memorandum, dated 9 November 1787, see *The Correspondence and Other Papers of James Boswell Relating to the Making of the Life of Johnson*, ed. Marshall Waingrow, Boswell Correspondence, Vol. 2; the Yale Editions of the Private Papers of James Boswell (Research Edition), (1969), p. 252.

3. Eddy, pp. 75–76. See also Eddy's "Editorial Note" to the Garland facsimile and Fleeman, *Bibliography*, I.678–90. See also Fleeman, pp. 678–90, whose account is indebted to Eddy.

A FREE INQUIRY INTO THE NATURE AND ORIGIN OF EVIL. IN SIX LETTERS TO———. R. AND J. DODSLEY.

This is a treatise consisting of six letters upon a very difficult and important question, which I am afraid this author's endeavours will not free from the perplexity, which has intangled the speculatists[1] of all ages, and which must always continue while *we see* but *in part.*[2] He calls it a *free*[3] enquiry, and indeed his *freedom*[4] is, I think, greater than his modesty. Though he is far from the contemptible arrogance, or the impious licentiousness[5] of Bolingbroke,[6] yet he decides too easily upon questions out of the reach of human determination, with too little consideration of mortal weakness, and with too much vivacity for the necessary caution.

In the first letter *on evil in general,* he observes, that "it is the solution of this important question, *whence came evil,* alone, that can ascertain the moral characteristic of God, without which there is an end of all distinction between good and

---

1. *Speculatist* does not appear in SJ's *Dictionary,* although he had used it earlier in *Rambler* 14 (par. 5): "The speculatist is only in danger of erroneous reasoning; but the man involved in life, has his own passions, and those of others, to encounter, and is embarrassed with a thousand inconveniences, which confound him with variety of impulse, and either perplex or obstruct his way." The *Dictionary* does include related terms: *speculator* (sense 1) is "one who forms theories," *speculation* (sense 5) is a "mental scheme not reduced to practice," and *speculative* (sense 2) is "theoretical; notional; ideal; not practical."

2. "For now we see through a glass darkly; but then face to face; now I know in part; but then shall I know even as also I am known" (I Corinthi-

ans xiii.12). SJ was to provide a similar opening for *Idler* 89 (29 December 1759): "How evil came into the world; for what reason it is that life is overspread with such boundless varieties of misery; why the only thinking being of this globe is doomed to think merely to be wretched, and to pass his time from youth to age in fearing or in suffering calamities, is a question which philosophers have long asked, and which philosophy could never answer."

3. *Free:* "Licentious; unrestrained" (sense 5 in *Dictionary*).

4. *Freedom:* "Unrestraint" (sense 5 in *Dictionary*).

5. *Licentiousness:* "Boundless liberty; contempt of just restraint" (*Dictionary*).

6. For SJ's views on Bolingbroke, see p. 358 and n. 4 above.

evil."[7] Yet he begins this enquiry by this declaration. "That there is a supreme being, infinitely powerful, wise and benevolent, the great creator and preserver of all things, is a truth so clearly demonstrated, that it shall be here taken for granted."[8] What is this but to say, that we have already reason to grant the existence of those attributes of God, which the present enquiry is designed to prove? The present enquiry is then surely made to no purpose. The attributes to the demonstration of which the solution of this great question is necessary, have been demonstrated without any solution, or by means of the solution of some former writer.

He rejects the Manichean system,[9] but imputes to it an absurdity, from which, amidst all its absurdities[1] it seems to be free, and adopts the system of Mr. Pope.

> That pain is no evil, if asserted with regard to the individuals who suffer it, is downright nonsense; but if considered as it affects the universal system, is an undoubted truth, and means only that there is no more pain in it than what is necessary to the production of happiness. How many soever of these evils then force themselves into the creation, so long as the good preponderates, it is a work well worthy of infinite wisdom and benevolence; and, notwithstanding the imperfections of its parts; the whole is most undoubtedly perfect.[2]

---

7. This is not a direct quotation but a piecing together of materials drawn from Jenyns, pp. 3–5.

8. Jenyns, p. 18.

9. Manichaeism, the religion of Mani or Manes, arose in Babylonia about the middle of the third century A.D., and is based on the idea of the essential and eternal contrast between good and evil, light and darkness. Jenyns says of the system: "To clear up the difficulty, some ancient Philosophers have had recourse to the supposition of two first Causes, one Good, and the other Evil, perpetually counteracting each others designs. This system was afterwards adapted by the *Manichean* Heresy, and has since been defended by the ingenious *Mons. Bayle:* but as the supposition of two first Causes is even in itself a contradiction, and as the whole scheme has been demonstrated by the best metaphysical Writers to be as false as it is impious, all further argument to disprove it would be needless" (pp. 8–9).

1. *Absurdity:* "The quality of being absurd; want of judgment applied to men; want of propriety applied to things" (sense 1 in *Dictionary*).

2. Jenyns, p. 18.

And in the former part of the letter, he gives[a] the principle of his system in these words,

> Omnipotence cannot work contradictions, it can only effect all possible things. But so little are we acquainted with the whole system of nature, that we know not what are possible, and what are not: but if we may judge from that constant mixture of pain with pleasure, and inconveniency with advantage, which we must observe in every thing around us, we have reason to conclude, that to endue created beings with perfection, that is, to produce good exclusive of evil, is one of those impossibilities which even infinite power cannot accomplish.[3]

This is elegant and acute, but will by no means calm discontent or silence curiosity; for whether evil can be wholly separated from good or not, it is plain that they may be mixed in various degrees, and as far as human eyes can judge, the degree of evil might have been less without any impediment to good.

The second letter *on the evils of imperfection,* is little more than a paraphrase of Pope's epistles, or yet less than a paraphrase, a mere translation of poetry into prose. This is surely to attack difficulty with very disproportionate abilities, to cut the Gordian knot[4] with very blunt instruments. When we are told of the insufficiency of former solutions, why is one of the latest, which no man can have forgotten, given us again? I am told, that this pamphlet is not the effort of hunger; What can it be then but the product of vanity? and yet how can vanity be gratified by plagiarism, or transcription?[5] When this specula-

---

a. give

---

3. Jenyns, pp. 14–15.
4. Jenyns introduces the *"Gordian* knot": "The Divines and Moralists of later Ages seem perfectly satisfied, that they have loosed the Gordian knot, by imputing the source of all Evil to the abuse of Free-will in Created Beings" (p. 11).
5. *Transcription:* "The act of copying" (*Dictionary*).

tist finds himself prompted to another performance, let him consider whether he is about to disburthen his mind or employ his fingers; and if I might venture to offer him a subject, I should wish that he would solve this question, Why he that has nothing to write, should desire to be a writer?

Yet is not this letter without some sentiments,[6] which though not new, are of great importance, and may be read with pleasure in the thousandth repetition.

> Whatever we enjoy is purely a free gift from our Creator; but that we enjoy no more, can never sure be deemed an injury, or a just reason to question his infinite benevolence. All our happiness is owing to his goodness; but that it is no greater, is owing only to ourselves, that is, to our not having any inherent right to any happiness, or even to any existence at all. This is no more to be imputed to God, than the wants of a beggar to the person who has relieved him: that he had something was owing to his benefactor: but that he had no more, only to his own original poverty.[7]

Thus far he speaks what every man must approve, and what every wise man has said before him. He then gives us the system of subordination,[8] not invented, for it was known I think to the Arabian metaphysicians,[9] but adopted by Pope; and from him borrowed by the diligent researches of this great investigator.

> No system can possibly be formed, even in imagination, without a subordination of parts. Every animal body must have different members, subservient to each other;

---

6. *Sentiment:* "Thought; notion; opinion" (sense 1 in *Dictionary*).
7. Jenyns, pp. 27–28.
8. *Subordination:* "The state of being inferior to another" (sense 1) or "a series regularly descending" (sense 2 in *Dictionary*).
9. Plato and Aristotle must be credited with having introduced the concept of the scale of being into western philosophy rather than Arabian metaphysicians, although such Arabian philosophers as Avicenna had a similar theory. See Arthur O. Lovejoy, *The Great Chain of Being* (1936), pp. 58–59. Relevant here also is Milton's idea of plenitude in *Paradise Lost*.

every picture must be composed of various colours, and of light and shade; all harmony must be formed of trebles, tenors, and basses; every beautiful and useful edifice must consist of higher and lower, more and less magnificent apartments. This is in the very essence of all created things, and therefore cannot be prevented by any means whatever, unless by not creating them at all.[1]

These instances are used instead of Pope's *oak* and *weeds,* or *Jupiter* and his *satellites;* but neither Pope, nor this writer have much contributed to solve the difficulty. Perfection or imperfection of unconscious beings has no meaning as referred to themselves; the *bass* and the *treble* are equally perfect; the mean and magnificent apartments feel no pleasure or pain from the comparison. Pope might ask the *weed,* why it was less than the *oak,* but the *weed* would never ask the question for itself. The *bass* and *treble* differ only to the hearer, meanness and magnificence only to the inhabitant. There is no evil but must inhere in a conscious being, or be referred to it; that is, evil must be felt before it is evil. Yet even on this subject many questions might be offered which human understanding has not yet answered, and which the present haste of this extract will not suffer me to dilate.[2]

He proceeds to an humble detail of Pope's opinion:

> The universe is a system whose very essence consists in subordination; a scale of beings descending by insensible degrees from infinite perfection to absolute nothing: in which, tho' we may justly expect to find perfection in the whole, could we possibly comprehend it; yet would it be the highest absurdity to hope for it in all its parts, because the beauty and happiness of the whole depend altogether on the just inferiorty of its parts, that is, on the comparative imperfections of the several beings of which it is composed.

---

1. Jenyns, p. 26.
2. *Dilate:* "To speak largely and copiously" (sense 2 in *Dictionary*).

It would have been no more an instance of God's wisdom to have created no beings but of the highest and most perfect order, than it would be of a painter's art, to cover his whole piece with one single colour the most beautiful he could compose. Had he confined himself to such, nothing could have existed but demi-gods, or archangels, and then all inferior orders must have been void and uninhabited: but as it is surely more agreeable to infinite benevolence, that all these should be filled up with beings capable of enjoying happiness themselves, and contributing to that of others, they must necessarily be filled with inferior beings, that is, with such as are less perfect, but from whose existence, notwithstanding that less perfection, more felicity upon the whole accrues to the universe, than if no such had been created. It is moreover highly probable, that there is such a connection between all ranks and orders by subordinate degrees, that they mutually support each others existence, and every one in its place is absolutely necessary towards sustaining the whole vast and magnificent fabrick.[3]

Our pretences for complaint could be of this only, that we are not so high in the scale of existence as our ignorant ambition may desire: a pretence which must eternally subsist; because, were we ever so much higher, there would be still room for infinite power to exalt us; and since no link in the chain can be broke, the same reason for disquiet must remain to those who succeed to that chasm, which must be occasioned by our preferment. A man can have no reason to repine, that he is not an angel; nor a horse, that he is not a man; much less, that in their several stations they possess not the faculties of another; for this would be an insufferable misfortune.

---

3. Jenyns, pp. 28–30. SJ omits several pages in the Jenyns text, taking the following paragraph from pp. 36–37.

This doctrine of the regular subordination of beings, the scale[4] of existence, and the chain of nature, I have often considered, but always left the inquiry in doubt and uncertainty.

That every being not infinite, compared with infinity, must be imperfect, is evident to intuition; that whatever is imperfect must have a certain line which it cannot pass, is equally certain. But the reason which determined this limit, and for which such being was suffered to advance thus far and no further, we shall never be able to discern. Our discoverers tell us, the Creator has made beings of all orders, and that therefore one of them must be such as man. But this system seems to be established on a concession which if it be refused cannot be extorted.

Every reason which can be brought to prove, that there are beings of every possible sort, will prove that there is the greatest number possible of every sort of beings; but this with respect to man we know, if we know any thing, not to be true.

It does not appear even to the imagination,[5] that of three orders of being, the first and the third receive any advantage from the imperfection of the second, or that indeed they may not equally exist, though the second had never been, or should cease to be, and why should that be concluded necessary, which cannot be proved even to be useful?

The scale of existence from infinity to nothing, cannot possibly have being. The highest being not infinite must be, as has been often observed, at an infinite distance below infinity. Cheyne,[6] who, with the desire inherent in mathematicians

---

4. *Scale:* "Regular gradation; a regular series rising like a ladder" (sense 7). SJ defines *Chain* as "A series linked together" (sense 4 in *Dictionary*).

5. *Imagination:* "Fancy; the power of forming ideal pictures; the power of representing things absent to one's self or others" (sense 1 in *Dictionary*).

6. George Cheyne, *Philosophical Principles of Religion: Natural and Revealed. In Two Parts* (London, 1715). See the preface to part II (p. [iv]) and chap. II. Robert Eberwein observes that it is SJ, rather than Cheyne, "who suggests that between finite and infinite, and finite and nothing, there is room for an infinite series of existence" ("Samuel Johnson, George Cheyne, and the 'Cone of Being,'" *Journal of the History of Ideas*, XXXVI [1975], 155). The concept of infinitesimals is as old as the *Physics* of Simplicius and Zeno of Elea, although

to reduce every thing to mathematical images, considers all existence as a cone, allows that the basis is at an infinite distance from the body. And in this distance between finite and infinite, there will be room for ever for an infinite series of indefinable existence.

Between the lowest positive existence and nothing, wherever we suppose positive existence to cease, is another chasm infinitely deep; where there is room again for endless orders of subordinate nature, continued for ever and for ever, and yet infinitely superior to non-existence.

To these meditations humanity is unequal. But yet we may ask, not of our maker, but of each other, since on the one side creation, wherever it stops, must stop infinitely below infinity, and on the other infinitely above nothing, what necessity there is that it should proceed so far either way, that beings so high or so low should ever have existed. We may ask; but I believe no created wisdom can give an adequate answer.

Nor is this all. In the scale, wherever it begins or ends, are infinite vacuities. At whatever distance we suppose the next order of beings to be above man, there is room for an intermediate order of beings between them; and if for one order then for infinite orders; since every thing that admits of more or less, and consequently all the parts of that which admits them, may be infinitely divided. So that, as far as we can judge, there may be room in the vacuity between any two steps of the scale, or between any two points of the cone of being for infinite exertion of infinite power.

Thus it appears how little reason those who repose their reason upon the scale of being have to triumph over them who recur to any other expedient of solution, and what difficulties arise on every side to repress the rebellions[7] of presumptuous[8] decision. *Qui pauca considerat, facile pronunciat.*[9]

SJ's probable source, at least in part, is Cheyne's discussion of "Limits" in *Philosophical Principles* (part II, pp. 48–51; Eberwein, pp. 157–58).

7. *Rebellion:* "Insurrection against lawful authority" (*Dictionary*).

8. *Presumptuous:* "Arrogant; confident; insolent" (sense 1) and "irreverent with respect to holy things" (sense 2 in *Dictionary*).

9. He who considers few things, easily gives a decision. SJ repeats the clause

In our passage through the boundless ocean of disquisition[1] we often take fogs for land, and after having long toiled to approach them find, instead of repose and harbours, new storms of objection and fluctuations[2] of uncertainty.

We are next entertained with Pope's alleviations of those evils which we are doomed to suffer.

> Poverty, or the want of riches, is generally compensated by having more hopes and fewer fears, by a greater share of health, and a more exquisite relish of the smallest enjoyments, than those who possess them are usually bless'd with. The want of taste and genius, with all the pleasures that arise from them, are commonly recompenced by a more useful kind of common sense, together with a wonderful delight, as well as success, in the busy pursuits of a scrambling world. The sufferings of the sick are greatly relieved by many trifling gratifications imperceptible to others, and sometimes almost repaid by the inconceivable transports occasioned by the return of health and vigour. Folly cannot be very grievous, because imperceptible; and I doubt not but there is some truth in that rant of a mad poet, that there is a pleasure in being mad, which none but madmen know. Ignorance, or the want of knowledge and literature, the appointed lot of all born to poverty, and the drudgeries of life, is the only opiate capable of infusing that insensibility which can enable them to endure the miseries of the one, and the fatigues of the other. It is a cordial administered by the gracious hand of providence; of which they ought never to be deprived by an ill-judged and improper education. It is the basis of all subordination, the support of society, and the privilege of individuals: and I have ever thought it a most remarkable instance of the divine wisdom, that

---

in *A Course of Lectures on the English Law* (Vinerian Law Lectures), ed. Thomas M. Curley (1986), I.195.

1. *Disquisition:* "Examination; disputative enquiry" (*Dictionary*).

2. *Fluctuation:* "Uncertainty; indetermination" (sense 2 in *Dictionary*).

whereas in all animals, whose individuals rise little above the rest of their species, knowledge is instinctive; in man, whose individuals are so widely different, it is acquired by education; by which means the prince and the labourer, the philosopher and the peasant, are in some measure fitted for their respective situations.[3]

Much of these positions is perhaps true, and the whole paragraph might well pass without censure, were not objections necessary to the establishment of knowledge. *Poverty*[4] is very gently paraphrased by *want of riches*. In that sense almost every man may in his own opinion be poor. But there is another poverty which is *want of competence*,[5] of all that can soften the miseries of life, of all that diversify attention, or delight imagination. There is yet another poverty which is *want of necessaries*,[6] a species of poverty which no care of the publick, no charity of particulars, can preserve many from feeling openly, and many secretly.

That hope and fear are inseparably or very frequently con-

---

3. Jenyns, pp. 33–35.

4. *Poverty:* "Indigence; necessity; want of riches" (sense 1 in *Dictionary*). SJ quotes a passage from John Rogers: "There is such a state as absolute *poverty*, when a man is destitute not only of the conveniencies, but the simple necessaries of life, being disabled from acquiring them, and depending entirely on charity." The *Poor* [collectively]: "Those who are in the lowest rank of the community; those who cannot subsist but by the charity of others; but it is sometimes used with laxity for any not rich" (sense 10 in *Dictionary*). Cf. *Rambler* 49: "He that thinks himself poor, because his neighbour is richer" (par. 4; III.265) and SJ's observation in the life of Ascham: "Men are rich and poor, not only in proportion to what they have, but to what they want" (*Works of Samuel Johnson* [1825], VI.512).

5. *Competence* or *Competency:* "Such a quantity of any thing as is sufficient, without superfluity" (sense 1) and "Such a fortune as, without exuberance, is equal to the necessities of life" (sense 2 in *Dictionary*).

6. *Necessaries:* "Things not only convenient but needful; things not to be left out of daily use" (*Dictionary*). In the life of Sir Francis Drake (1740–41) SJ had considered the difference between necessities and needs generated by civilization: "Among Savage nations, imaginary wants find . . . no place; but their strength is exhausted by necessary toils, and their passions agitated not by contests of superiority, affluence, or precedence, but by perpetual care for the present day, and by fear of perishing for want of food" (*Works of Samuel Johnson* [1825], VI.356). See also his comments on the relative happiness of people in "civilized" and "savage" societies (pp. 366–67). Cf. *Rambler* 49 (par. 3; III.264).

nected with poverty, and riches, my surveys of life have not informed me. The milder degrees of poverty are sometimes supported by hope, but the more severe often sink down in motionless despondence. Life must be seen before it can be known. This author and Pope perhaps never saw the miseries which they imagine thus easy to be born. The poor indeed are insensible of many little vexations which sometimes imbitter the possessions and pollute[7] the enjoyments, of the rich. They are not pained by casual incivility, or mortified[8] by the mutilation[9] of a compliment; but this happiness is like that of a malefactor who ceases to feel the cords that bind him when the pincers are tearing his flesh.[1]

That want of taste for one enjoyment is supplied by the pleasures of some other, may be fairly allowed. But the compensations of sickness I have never found near to equivalence, and the transports of recovery only prove the intenseness of the pain.

With folly[2] no man is willing to confess himself very intimately acquainted, and therefore its pains and pleasures are kept secret. But what the author says of its happiness seems applicable only to fatuity,[3] or gross dulness, for that inferi-

---

7. *Pollute:* "To corrupt by mixtures of ill" (sense 3 in *Dictionary*).

8. *Mortify:* "To humble; to depress; to vex" (sense 5 in *Dictionary*). Among the quotations for this sense in the *Dictionary* are two from Addison: "He is controuled by a nod, *mortified* by a frown, and transported by a smile" (*Guardian* no. 113, par. 4) and "How often is the ambitious man *mortified* with the very praises he receives, if they do not rise so high as he thinks they ought" (*Spectator* no. 256, par. 8).

9. *Mutilation:* "Deprivation of a limb, or any essential part" (*Dictionary*).

1. Donald Greene has suggested that this is an allusion to the execution of Francois-Robert Damiens on 28 March 1757 for his attempted assassination of Louis XV of France on 5 January. A graphic description of the execution had been published in the April issue of *GM* (XXVII, 151). See "Pictures to the Mind: Johnson and Imagery," in *Johnson, Boswell and their Circle: Essays Presented to Lawrence Fitzroy Powell in Honour of his Eighty-Fourth Birthday,* ed. Mary M. Lascelles, et al. (1965), pp. 141–42. Cf. SJ's remark in *Rambler* 48: "those who do not feel pain, seldom think that it is felt" (par. 2; III.259).

2. *Folly:* "Want of understanding; weakness of intellect" (sense 1); "criminal weakness; depravity of mind" (sense 2); "act of negligence or passion unbecoming gravity or deep wisdom" (sense 3 in *Dictionary*).

3. *Fatuity:* "Foolishness; weakness of mind; some degree of frenzy" (*Dictionary*).

ority of understanding which makes one man without any other reason the slave, or tool, or property of another, which makes him sometimes useless, and sometimes ridiculous,[4] is often felt with very quick sensibility. On the happiness of madmen, as the case is not very frequent, it is not necessary to raise a disquisition, but I cannot forbear to observe, that I never yet knew disorders of mind encrease felicity: every madman is either arrogant and irascible, or gloomy and suspicious, or possessed by some passion[5] or notion[6] destructive to his quiet. He has always discontent in his look, and malignity in his bosom. And, if he[b] had the power of choice, he would soon repent who should resign his reason to secure his peace.

Concerning the portion of ignorance necessary to make the condition of the lower classes of mankind safe to the public and tolerable to themselves, both morals and policy[7] exact a nicer enquiry than[c] will be very soon or very easily made. There is undoubtedly a degree of knowledge which will direct a man to refer all to providence, and to acquiesce in the condition which omniscient goodness has determined to allot him; to consider this world as a phantom[8] that must soon glide from before his eyes, and the distresses and vexations that encompass him, as dust scattered in his path, as a blast that chills him for a moment, and passes off for ever.

b. we   c. that

---

4. *Ridiculous:* "Worthy of laughter; exciting contemptuous merriment" (*Dictionary*). SJ cites Milton's *Paradise Lost:* "Thus was the building left / Ridiculous; and the work confusion nam'd" (XII.62).

5. *Passion:* "Violent commotion of the mind" (sense 2 in *Dictionary*).

6. *Notion:* "Thought; representation of any thing formed by the mind; idea; image; conception" (sense 1) and "sentiment; opinion" (sense 2 in *Dictionary*).

7. *Policy:* "Art; prudence; management of affairs; stratagem" (sense 2 in *Dictionary*).

8. *Phantom:* "A spectre; an apparition" (sense 1) or "a fancied vision" (sense 2 in *Dictionary*). SJ illustrates the second sense with a passage from John Rogers's *Sermons:* "Restless and impatient to try every scheme and overture of present happiness, he hunts a *phantom* he can never overtake." SJ mentions reading Rogers's sermons on 27 August 1736 and 30 March 1771? (*Diaries,* pp. 35, 136) and he is cited frequently in the *Dictionary.* See Robert DeMaria, Jr., *Johnson's Dictionary and the Language of Learning* (1986).

Such wisdom, arising from the comparison of a part with the whole of our existence, those that want it most cannot possibly obtain from philosophy, nor unless the method of education and the general tenour of life are changed, will very easily receive it from religion. The bulk of mankind is not likely to be very wise or very good: and I know not whether there are not many states of life, in which all knowledge less than the highest wisdom, will produce discontent and danger. I believe it may be sometimes found, that a *little learning* is to a poor man a *dangerous thing*.[9] But such is the condition of humanity, that we easily see, or quickly feel the wrong, but cannot always distinguish the right. Whatever knowledge is superfluous, in irremediable poverty, is hurtful, but the difficulty is to determine when poverty is irremediable, and at what point superfluity[1] begins. Gross ignorance every man has found equally dangerous with perverted knowledge. Men left wholly to their appetites and their instincts, with little sense of moral or religious obligation, and with very faint distinctions of right and wrong, can never be safely employed or confidently trusted: they can be honest only by obstinacy,[2] and diligent only by compulsion[3] or caprice.[4] Some instruction, therefore, is necessary, and much perhaps may be dangerous.

Though it should be granted that those who are *born to poverty and drudgery* should not be *deprived* by an *improper education* of the *opiate* of *ignorance;* even this concession will not be of much use to direct our practice, unless it be determined who are those that are *born to poverty*. To entail irreversible poverty upon generation after generation only because the ancestor happened to be poor, is in itself cruel, if not unjust,

---

9. "A little learning is a dangerous thing," Pope, *Essay on Criticism* (215).

1. *Superfluity:* "More than enough; plenty beyond use or necessity" (*Dictionary*).

2. *Obstinacy:* "Stubbornness; contumacy; pertinacy; persistency" (*Dictionary*).

3. *Compulsion:* "The act of compelling to something; force; violence of the agents" and "the state of being compelled; violence suffered" (sense 2 in *Dictionary*). SJ defines the verb as "to force to some act; to oblige; to constrain; to necessitate; to urge irresistibly" (sense 1).

4. *Caprice:* "Freak; fancy; whim; sudden change of humour" (*Dictionary*).

and is wholly contrary to the maxims of a commercial nation, which always suppose and promote a rotation of property, and offer every individual a chance of mending his condition by his diligence. Those who communicate literature to the son of a poor man, consider him as one not born to poverty, but to the necessity of deriving a better fortune from himself. In this attempt, as in others, many fail, and many succeed. Those that fail will feel their misery more acutely; but since poverty is now confessed to be such a calamity as cannot be born without the opiate of insensibility, I hope the happiness of those whom education enables to escape from it, may turn the ballance against that exacerbation[5] which the others suffer.

I am always afraid of determining on the side of envy or cruelty. The privileges of education may sometimes be improperly bestowed, but I shall always fear to with-hold them, lest I should be yielding to the suggestions of pride, while I persuade myself that I am following the maxims of policy; and under the appearance of salutary restraints, should be indulging the lust of dominion, and that malevolence which delights in seeing others depressed.

Pope's doctrine is at last exhibited in a comparison, which, like other proofs of the same kind, is better adapted to delight the fancy than convince the reason.

> Thus the universe resembles a large and well-regulated family, in which all the officers and servants, and even the domestic animals, are subservient to each other in a proper subordination: each enjoys the privileges and perquisites peculiar to his place, and at the same time contributes by that just subordination to the magnificence and happiness of the whole.[6]

The magnificence of a house is of use or pleasure always to the master, and sometimes to the domestics. But the magnifi-

---

5. *Exacerbation:* "Encrease of malignity; augmented force or severity" (sense 1) and "height of a disease; paroxysm" (sense 2 in *Dictionary*). Cf. *Idler* 26 (14 October 1748) and 29 (4 November 1758) for SJ's view on educating the poor. Yale *Works,* II.80–83, 89–92.

6. Jenyns, p. 40.

cence of the universe adds nothing to the Supreme Being; for any part of its inhabitants with which human knowledge is acquainted, an universe much less spacious or spendid would have been sufficient; and of happiness it does not appear that any is communicated from the beings of a lower world to those of a higher.[7]

The enquiry after the cause of *natural evil* is continued in the third letter, in which, as in the former, there is mixture of borrowed truth, and native folly, of some notions just and trite, with others uncommon and ridiculous.

His opinion of the value and importance of happiness is certainly just, and I shall insert it, not that it will give any information to any reader, but it may serve to shew how the most common notion may be swelled in sound, and diffused in bulk, till it shall perhaps astonish the author himself.

> Happiness is the only thing of real value in existence; neither riches, nor power, nor wisdom, nor learning, nor strength, nor beauty, nor virtue, nor religion, nor even life itself, being of any importance but as they contribute to its[d] production. All these are in themselves neither good nor evil; happiness alone is their great end, and they desireable only as they tend to promote it.[8]

Success produces confidence. After this discovery of the value of happiness, he proceeds without any distrust of himself to tell us what has been hid from all former enquirers.

> The true solution of this important question, so long and so vainly searched for by the philosophers of all ages and all countries, I take to be at last no more than this, that these real evils proceed from the same sourse as those imaginary ones of imperfection before treated of, namely, from that subordination, without which no created system can subsist; all subordination implying im-

---

d. is

---

7. The 15 April to 15 May 1757 installment ends here.

8. Jenyns, p. 46.

perfection, all imperfection evil, and all evil some kind of inconveniency or suffering: so that there must be particular inconveniencies and sufferings annexed to every particular rank of created beings by the circumstances of things, and their modes of existence.

God indeed might have made us quite other creatures, and placed us in a world quite differently constituted; but then we had been no longer men, and whatever beings had occupied our stations in the universal system, they must have been liable to the same inconveniencies.[9]

In all this there is nothing that can silence the enquiries of curiosity, or calm the pertubations of doubt. Whether subordination implies imperfection[1] may be disputed. The means respecting themselves, may be as perfect as the end. The weed as a weed is no less perfect than the oak as an oak. That *imperfection implies evil, and evil suffering* is by no means evident. Imperfection may imply privative[2] evil, or the absence of some good, but this privation produces no suffering, but by the help of knowledge. An infant at the breast is yet an imperfect man, but there is no reason for belief that he is unhappy by his immaturity, unless some positive pain be superadded.

When this author presumes to speak of the universe, I would advise him a little to distrust his own faculties, however large and comprehensive.[3] Many words easily understood on common occasion, become uncertain and figurative when applied to the works of Omnipotence. Subordination in human affairs is well understood, but when it is attributed to the universal system, its meaning grows less certain, like the petty distinctions of locality, which are of good use upon our own

---

9. Jenyns, pp. 47–48. SJ omits three long sentences by Jenyns and then continues the quotation in the following paragraph (Jenyns, pp. 49–50).

1. *Imperfection:* "Defect; failure; fault, whether physical or moral; whether of persons or things" (*Dictionary*).

2. *Privative:* "Causing privation of any thing" (sense 1) and "Consisting in the absence of something; not positive. *Privative* is in things, what negative is in propositions" (sense 2 in *Dictionary*). SJ defines *Privation* as "removal or destruction of any thing or quality" (sense 1).

3. *Comprehensive:* "Having the power to comprehend or understand many things at once" (sense 1 in *Dictionary*).

globe, but have no meaning with regard to infinite space, in which nothing is *high* or *low*.

That if man, by exaltation to a higher nature were exempted from the evils which he now suffers, some other being must suffer them; that if man were not man, some other being must be man, is a position arising from his established notion of the scale of being. A notion to which Pope has given some importance by adopting it, and of which I have therefore endeavoured to shew the uncertainty and inconsistency. This scale of being I have demonstrated to be raised by presumptuous imagination, to rest on nothing at the bottom, to lean on nothing at the top, and to have vacuities from step to step through which any order of being may sink into nihility[4] without any inconvenience, so far as we can judge to the next rank above or below it. We are therefore little enlightned by a writer who tells us that any being in the state of man must suffer what man suffers, when the only question, that requires to be resolved is, Why any being is in this state?

Of poverty and labour[5] he gives just and elegant representations, which yet do not remove the difficulty of the first and fundamental question, though supposing the present state of man necessary, they may supply some motives to content.

> Poverty is what all could not possibly have been exempted from, not only by reason of the fluctuating nature of human possessions, but because the world could not subsist without it; for had all been rich, none could have submitted to the commands of another, or the necessary drudgeries of life; thence all governments must have been dissolved, arts neglected, and lands uncultivated, and so an universal penury have overwhelmed all, instead of now and then pinching a few. Hence, by the by, appears the great excellence of charity, by which men are enabled by a particular distribution of the blessings and enjoyments of life, on proper occasions, to prevent that

---

4. *Nihility:* "Nothingness; the state of being nothing" (*Dictionary*).

5. *Labour:* "The act of doing what requires a painful exertion of strength, or wearisome perseverance; pains; toil; travail; work" (sense 1 in *Dictionary*).

poverty which by a general one omnipotence itself could never have prevented: so that, by inforcing this duty, God as it were demands our assistance to promote universal happiness, and to shut out misery at every door, where it strives to intrude itself.

Labour, indeed, God might easily have excused us from, since at his command, the earth would readily have poured forth all her treasures without our inconsiderable assistance: but if the severest labour cannot sufficiently subdue the malignity of human nature, what plots and machinations, what wars, rapine and devastation, what profligacy and licentiousness must have been the consequences of universal idleness! so that labour ought only to be looked upon as a task kindly imposed upon us by our indulgent creator, necessary to preserve our health, our safety and our innocence.[6]

I am afraid that *the latter end of his commonwealth forgets the beginning.*[7] If God *could easily have excused us from labour,* I do not comprehend why *he could not possibly have exempted all from poverty.* For poverty, in its easier and more tolerable degree, is little more than necessity of labour, and, in its more severe and deplorable state, little more than inability for labour. To be poor is to work for others, or to want the succour[8] of others without work. And the same exuberant fertility which would make work unnecessary might make poverty impossible.

Surely a man who seems not completely master of his own opinion, should have spoken more cautiously of omnipotence, nor have presumed to say what it could perform, or what it could prevent. I am in doubt whether those who stand highest in *the scale of being* speak this confidently of the dispensations of their maker.

For fools rush in, where angels fear to tread.[9]

---

6. Jenyns, pp. 50–52.
7. *The Tempest,* II.i.153–54.
8. *Succour:* "Aid; assistance; relief of any kind; help in distress" (sense 1 in *Dictionary*).
9. Pope, *Essay on Criticism* (l. 625).

A FREE INQUIRY

Of our inquietudes of mind his account is still less reasonable. "Whilst men are injured, they must be inflamed with anger; and whilst they see cruelties, they must be melted with pity; whilst they perceive danger they must be sensible of fear."[1] This is to give a reason for all evil, by shewing that one evil produces another. If there is danger there ought to be fear; but if fear is an evil, why should there be danger? His vindication of pain is of the same kind; pain is useful to alarm us, that we may shun greater evils, but those greater evils must be presupposed that the fitness of pain may appear.

Treating on death,[2] he has expressed the known and true doctrine with spriteliness of fancy and neatness of diction. I shall therefore insert it. There are truths which, as they are always necessary, do not grow stale by repetition.

> Death, the last and most dreadful of all evils, is so far from being one, that it is the infallible cure for all others.
>
> *To die, is landing on some silent shore,*
> *Where billows never beat, nor tempests roar.*
> *Ere well we feel the friendly stroke, 'tis o'er.*
>   GARTH.[3]
>
> For, abstracted from the sickness and sufferings usually attending it, it is no more than the expiration of that term of life God was pleased to bestow on us, without any claim or merit on our part. But was it an evil ever so great, it could not be remedied but by one much greater, which is by living for ever; by which means our wickedness, unrestrained by the prospect of a future state, would grow so insupportable, our sufferings so intolerable by perseverance, and our pleasures so tiresome by repetition,

---

1. Jenyns, p. 52.
2. *Death:* "The extinction of life; the departure of the soul from the body" (sense 1); "mortality; destruction" (sense 2); and "[In theology.] Damnation; eternal torments" (sense 10 in *Dictionary*). To illustrate the last sense SJ cites the Church Catechism: "We pray that God will keep us from all sin and wickedness, from our ghostly enemy, and from everlasting *death*."

3. SJ perhaps emphasizes the lines (III. 225–28) from Samuel Garth's *The Dispensary* (1699) by placing them in italics.

that no being in the universe could be so compleatly miserable as a species of immortal men. We have no reason, therefore, to look upon death as an evil, or to fear it as a punishment, even without any supposition of a future life: but if we consider it as a passage to a more perfect state, or a remove only in an eternal succession of still improving states (for which we have the strongest reasons) it will then appear a new favour from the divine munificence; and a man must be as absurd to repine at dying, as a traveller would be, who proposed to himself a delightful tour through various unknown countries, to lament that he cannot take up his residence at the first dirty inn which he baits at on the road.[4]

The instability of human life, or the changes of its successive periods, of which we so frequently complain, are no more than the necessary progress of it to this necessary conclusion,[e] and are so far from being evils deserving these complaints, that they are the source of our greatest pleasures as they are the source of all novelty, from which our greatest pleasures are ever derived. The continual succession of seasons in the human life, by daily presenting to us new scenes, render it agreeable, and like those of the year, afford us delights by their change, which the choicest of them could not give us by their continuance. In the spring of life, the gilding of the sun-shine, the verdure of the fields, and the variegated paintings of the sky, are so exquisite in the eyes of infants at their first looking abroad into a new world, as nothing perhaps afterwards can equal. The heat and vigour of the succeeding summer of youth ripens for us new pleasures, the blooming maid, the nightly revel, and the jovial chace: the serene autumn of complete manhood feasts us with the golden harvests of our worldly

---

e. conclusion?

---

4. *Bait:* "To stop at any place for refreshment; perhaps this word is more properly bate; to abate speed" (*Dictionary*). The 15 May to 15 June installment ends here.

pursuits: nor is the hoary winter of old age destitute of its peculiar comforts and enjoyments, of which the recollection and relation of those past are perhaps none of the least; and at last death opens to us a new prospect, from whence we shall probably look back upon the diversions and occupations of this world with the same contempt we do now on our tops and hobby-horses, and with the same surprize, that they could ever so much entertain or engage us.[5]

I would not willingly detract from the beauty of this paragraph, and in gratitude to him who has so well inculcated such important truths, I will venture to admonish him, since the chief comfort of the old is the recollection of the past, so to employ his time and his thoughts, that when the imbecillity[6] of age shall come upon him, he may be able to recreate its languors by the remembrance of hours spent, not in presumptuous derisions,[7] but modest inquiries, not in dogmatical[8] limitations of omnipotence, but in humble acquiescence[9] and fervent adoration. Old age will shew him that much of the book now before us has no other use than to perplex the scrupulous,[1] and to shake the weak, to encourage impious presumption, or stimulate idle curiosity.

Having thus dispatched the consideration of particular evils, he comes at last to a general reason for which *evil* may be said to be *our good*.[2] He is of opinion that there is some inconceivable[3] benefit in pain abstractedly considered; that

---

5. Jenyns, pp. 54–58.
6. *Imbecility:* "Weakness; feebleness of mind or body" (*Dictionary*).
7. *Derision:* "The act of deriding or laughing at" (sense 1) and "contempt; scorn; a laughing-stock" (sense 2 in *Dictionary*). SJ defines the verb: "To laugh at; to mock; to turn to ridicule; to scorn" (sense 1).
8. *Dogmatical* or *Dogmatick* "Authoritative; magisterial; positive; in the manner of a philosopher laying down the first principles of a sect" (*Dictionary*).

9. *Acquiescence:* "Submission" (sense 3 in *Dictionary*).
1. *Scrupulous:* "Nicely doubtful; hard to satisfy in determinations of conscience" (sense 1 in *Dictionary*). SJ defines *Scruple* as "Doubt; difficulty of determination; perplexity: generally about minute things" (sense 1). See *Rasselas*, (Yale *Works*), XVI.163, n. 5.
2. "Evil be thou my Good," Milton, *Paradise Lost* IV.110.
3. *Inconceivable:* "Incomprehensible; not to be conceived by the mind"

pain however inflicted, or wherever felt, communicates some good to the general system of being, and that every animal is some way or other the better for the pain of every other animal. This opinion he carries so far as to suppose that there passes some principle of union through all animal life, as attraction is communicated to all corporeal nature, and that the evils suffered on this globe, may by some inconceivable means contribute to the felicity of the inhabitants of the remotest planet.

How the origin of evil is brought nearer to human conception by any *inconceivable* means, I am not able to discover. We believed that the present system of creation was right, though we could not explain the adaptation of one part to the other, or for the whole succession of causes and consequences. Where has this enquirer added to the little knowledge that we had before. He has told us of the benefits of evil, which no man feels, and relations between distant parts of the[f] universe, which he cannot himself conceive. There was enough in this question inconceivable before, and we have little advantage from a new inconceivable solution.

I do not mean to reproach this author for not knowing what is equally hidden from learning and from ignorance. The shame is to impose words for ideas upon ourselves or others. To imagine that we are going forward when we are only turning round. To think that there is any difference between him that gives no reason, and him that gives a reason, which by his own confession cannot be conceived.

But that he may not be thought to conceive nothing but things inconceivable, he has at last thought on a way by which human sufferings may produce good effects. He imagines

f. the *om.*

(*Dictionary*). Jenyns says of pain: "I am persuaded there is something in the abstract nature of pain conducive to pleasure; that the sufferings of individuals are absolutely necessary to universal happiness; and that, from connections to us inconceivable, it was impractical for Omnipotence to produce one, without at the same time producing the other.... A certain alloy of pain must be cast into the universal mass of created Happiness and inflicted somewhere for the benefit of the whole" (pp. 60–61).

that as we have not only animals for food, but choose some for our diversion, the same privilege may be allowed to some beings above us, *who may deceive, torment, or destroy us for the ends only of their own pleasure or utility.*[4] This he again finds impossible to be conceived, *but that impossibility lessens not the probability of the conjecture, which by analogy is so strongly confirmed.*[5]

I cannot resist the temptation of contemplating this analogy, which I think he might have carried further very much to the advantage of his argument. He might have shewn that these *hunters whose game is man* have many sports analogous[g] to our own. As we drown whelps and kittens, they amuse themselves now and then with sinking a ship, and stand round the fields of Blenheim or the walls of Prague,[6] as we encircle a cock-pit. As we shoot a bird flying, they take a man in the midst of his business or pleasure, and knock him down with an apoplexy.[7] Some of them, perhaps, are virtuosi,[8] and delight in the operations of an asthma, as a human philosopher in the effects of the air pump. To swell a man with a tympany[9] is as good sport as to blow a frog. Many a merry bout have these frolic beings at the vicissitudes of an ague,[1] and

g. analagous

---

4. Jenyns, p. 67.

5. Jenyns, pp. 67–68.

6. Blenheim, a village in Bavaria, was the scene of the defeat of the French and Bavarians under Marshals Tallard and Marsin on 13 August 1704 by the duke of Marlborough and Prince Eugene. In spring 1757, during the Seven Years' War (1756–63), Frederick "the Great" defeated the Austrians at Prague and then besieged the city. At Blenheim, for example, the allies had 4,500 killed and 7,500 wounded and at Prague the Prussians lost 14,000 men, including 400 officers.

7. *Apoplexy:* In the *Dictionary* SJ defines the term with two quotations, one from John Quincy and the other from John Arbuthnot, to the effect that it is a sudden deprivation of all the senses.

8. *Virtuoso:* "A man skilled in antique or natural curiosities; a man studious of painting, statuary, or architecture" (*Dictionary*). Donald T. Siebert, Jr. suggests that Jenyns twice drew on SJ's language in this passage on men and animals for his attacks on the use of animals for sport and on cruelty to animals. See "Soame Jenyns's Debt to Johnson," *Studies on Voltaire and the Eighteenth Century*, CXLIII (1975), 186.

9. *Tympany:* "A kind of obstructed flatulence that swells the body like a drum" (*Dictionary*).

1. *Ague:* "An intermitting fever, with cold fits succeeded by hot. The cold fit is, in popular language, more particularly called the *ague*, and the hot the fever" (*Dictionary*).

good sport it is to see a man tumble with an epilepsy,[2] and revive and tumble again, and all this he knows not why. As they are wiser and more powerful than we, they have more exquisite diversions, for we have no way of procuring any sport so brisk and so lasting as the paroxysms of the gout[3] and stone[4] which undoubtedly must make high mirth, especially if the play be a little diversified with the blunders and puzzles[5] of the blind and deaf. We know not how far their sphere of observation may extend. Perhaps now and then a merry being may place himself in such a situation as to enjoy at once all the varieties of an epidemical[6] disease, or amuse his leisure with the tossings and contortions of every possible pain exhibited together.

One sport the merry malice of these beings has found means of enjoying to which we have nothing equal or similar. They now and then catch a mortal proud of his parts,[7] and flattered either by the submission of those who court his kindness, or the notice of those who suffer him to court theirs. A head thus prepared for the reception of false opinions, and the projection[8] of vain designs, they easily fill with idle notions, till in time they make their plaything an author: their first diversion commonly begins with an ode or an epistle, then rises perhaps to a political irony, and is at last

---

2. *Epilepsy:* Defined by SJ on the authority of John Quincy as "an convulsion, or convulsive motion of the whole body, or of some of its parts, with a loss of sense" (*Dictionary*).

3. *Gout:* The arthritis; a periodical disease attended with great pain" (*Dictionary*).

4. *Stone:* "Calculous concretion in the kidneys or bladder; the disease arising from a calculus" (sense 5 in *Dictionary*). *Calculose, Calculous, Calculus:* SJ defines the adjective as "Stony; gritty" and the noun as "The stone in the bladder" (*Dictionary*). *Concretion:* "The mass formed by a coalition of separate particles" (sense 2 in *Dictionary*).

5. *Puzzle:* "Embarrassment; perplexity" (*Dictionary*). SJ defines the verb: "To be bewildered in one's own notions; to be aukward."

6. *Epidemical* or *Epidemick:* "That which falls at once upon great numbers of people, as a plague" (sense 1 in *Dictionary*).

7. *Parts:* "[In the plural] Qualities; powers; faculties; or accomplishments" (sense 13 in *Dictionary*).

8. *Projection:* "Scheme; plan of action" (sense 3 in *Dictionary*). SJ defines *projector* as "One who forms schemes or designs" (sense 1) and "One who forms wild impracticable schemes" (sense 2).

brought to its height, by a treatise of philosophy. Then begins the poor animal to entangle himself in sophisms,[9] and flounder in absurdity, to talk confidently of the scale of being, and to give solutions which himself confesses impossible to be understood. Sometimes, however, it happens that their pleasure is without much mischief. The author feels no pain, but while they are wondering at the extravagance of his opinion, and pointing him out to one another as a new example of human folly, he is enjoying his own applause, and that of his companions, and perhaps is elevated with the hope of standing at the head of a new sect.

Many of the books which now croud the world, may be justly suspected to be written for the sake of some invisible order of beings, for surely they are of no use to any of the corporeal inhabitants of the world. Of the productions of the last bounteous year, how many can be said to serve any purpose of use or pleasure. The only end of writing is to enable the readers better to enjoy life, or better to endure it:[1] and how will either of those be put more in our power by him who tells us, that we are puppets, of which some creature not much wiser than ourselves manages the wires. That a set of beings unseen and unheard, are hovering about us, trying experiments upon our sensibility, putting us in agonies to see our limbs quiver, torturing us to madness, that they may laugh at our vagaries, sometimes obstructing the bile, that they may see how a man looks when he is yellow; sometimes breaking a traveller's bones to try how he will get home; sometimes wasting a man to a skeleton, and sometimes killing him fat for the greater elegance of his hide.

This is an account of natural evil which though, like the rest, not quite new is very entertaining, though I know not

---

9. *Sophism:* "A fallacious argument; an unsound subtilty; a fallacy" (*Dictionary*).

1. "The task of an author," SJ says in *Rambler* 3 (par. 1; III.14–15), "is, either to teach what is not known, or to recommend known truths, by his manner of adorning them; either to let new light in upon the mind, and open new scenes to the prospect, or to vary the dress and situation of common objects, so as to give them fresh grace and more powerful attractions."

how much it may contribute to patience. The only reason why we should contemplate evil is, that we may bear it better, and I am afraid nothing is much more placidly endured, for the sake of making others sport.

The first pages of the fourth letter are such as incline me both to hope and wish that I shall find nothing to blame in the succeeding part. He offers a criterion of action, an account of virtue and vice, for which I have often contended, and which must be embraced by all who are willing to know why they act, or why they forbear, to give any reason of their conduct to themselves or others.

> In order to find out the true origin of moral evil, it will be necessary, in the first place, to enquire into its nature and essence; or what it is that constitutes one action evil, and another good. Various have been the opinions of various authors on this criterion of virtue; and this variety has rendered that doubtful, which must otherwise have been clear and manifest to the meanest capacity. Some indeed have denied that there is any such thing, because different ages and nations have entertained different sentiments concerning it: but this is just as reasonable as to assert, that there are neither sun, moon, nor stars, because astronomers have supported different systems of the motions and magnitudes of these celestial bodies. Some have placed it in conformity to truth, some to the fitness of things, and others to the will of God. But all this is merely superficial: they resolve us not why truth, or the fitness of things, are either eligible or obligatory, or why God should require us to act in one manner rather than another. The true reason of which can possibly be no other than this, because some actions produce happiness, and others misery: so that all moral good and evil are nothing more than the production of natural. This alone it is that makes truth preferable to falshood, this that determines the fitness of things, and this that induces God to command some

actions, and forbid others. They who extol the truth, beauty, and harmony of virtue, exclusive of its consequences, deal but in pompous nonsense; and they who would persuade us, that good and evil are things indifferent, depending wholly on the will of God, do but confound the nature of things, as well as all our notions of God himself, by representing him capable of willing contradictions; that is, that we should be, and be happy, and at the same time that we should torment and destroy each other; for injuries cannot be made benefits, pain cannot be made pleasure, and consequently vice cannot be made virtue by any power whatever. It is the consequences, therefore, of all human actions that must stamp their value. So far as the general practice of any action tends to produce good, and introduce happiness into the world, so far we may pronounce it virtuous; so much evil as it occasions, such is the degree of vice it contains. I say the general practice, because we must always remember in judging by this rule, to apply it only to the general species of actions, and not to particular actions; for the infinite wisdom of God, desirous to set bounds to the destructive consequences which must otherwise have followed from the universal depravity of mankind, has so wonderfully contrived the nature of things, that our most vitious actions may sometimes accidentally and collaterally produce good. Thus, for instance, robbery may disperse useless hoards to the benefit of the public; adultery may bring heirs and good humour too into many families, where they would otherwise have been wanting; and murder free the world from tyrants and oppressors. Luxury maintains its thousands, and vanity its ten thousands. Superstition and arbitrary power contribute to the grandeur of many nations, and the liberties of others are preserved by the perpetual contentions of avarice, knavery, selfishness, and ambition: and thus the worst of vices, and the worst of men are often compelled by providence to serve the most beneficial purposes, contrary to their own malevolent tendencies and inclinations; and thus private vices become public benefits by the force only of accidental circumstances. But this impeaches not the truth of the criterion of virtue before mentioned, the only solid foundation on which any true system of ethicks can be built, the only plain, simple, and uniform rule by which we can pass any judgment on our actions; but by this we may be enabled, not only to determine which are good, and which are evil, but almost mathematically to demonstrate the proportion of virtue, or vice which belongs to each, by comparing them with the degrees of happiness or misery which they occasion. But tho' the production of happiness is the essence of virtue, it is by no means the end: the great end is the probation of mankind, or the giving them an opportunity of exalting or degrading themselves in another state by their behaviour in the present. And thus indeed it answers two most important purposes; those are, the conservation of our happiness, and the test of our obedience; for had not such a test seemed necessary to God's infinite wisdom, and productive of universal good, he would never have permitted the happiness of men, even in this life, to have depended on so precarious a tenure, as their mutual good behaviour to each other. For it is observable, that he who best knows our formation, has trusted no one thing of importance to our reason or virtue: he trusts only to our appetites for the support of the individual, and the continuance of our species; to our vanity or compassion, for our bounty to others; and to our fears, for the preservation of ourselves; often to our vices for the support of government, and sometimes to our follies for the preservation of our religion. But since some test of our obedience was necessary, nothing sure could have been commanded for that end so fit and proper, and at the same time so useful, as the practice of virtue: nothing has[h] been so justly rewarded

h. have

with happiness, as the production of happiness in conformity to the will of God. It is this conformity alone which adds merit to virtue, and constitutes the essential difference between morality and religion. Morality obliges men to live honestly and soberly, because such behaviour is most conducive to publick happiness, and consequently to their own; religion, to pursue the same course, because conformable to the will of their creator. Morality induces them to embrace virtue from prudential considerations; religion from those of gratitude and obedience. Morality therefore, entirely abstracted from religion, can have nothing meritorious in it; it being but wisdom, prudence, or good oeconomy, which, like health, beauty, or riches, are rather obligations conferred upon us by God, than merits in us towards him; for tho' we may be justly punished for injuring ourselves, we can claim no reward for self-preservation; as suicide deserves punishment and infamy, but a man deserves no reward or honours for not being guilty of it. This I take to be the meaning of all those passages in our scriptures in which works are represented to have no merit without faith; that is, not without believing in historical facts, in creeds, and articles; but without being done in pursuance of our belief in God, and in obedience to his commands. And now, having mentioned scripture, I cannot omit observing, that the christian is the only religious or moral institution in the world, that ever set in a right light these two material points, the essence and the end of virtue; that ever founded the one in the production of happiness, that is, in universal benevolence, or, in their language, charity to all men; the other, in the probation of man, and his obedience to his creator. Sublime and magnificent as was the philosophy of the ancients, all their moral systems were deficient in these two important articles. They were all built on the sandy foundations of the innate beauty of virtue, or enthusiastick patriotism; and their great point in view was the contemptible reward of human glory; foundations which were by no means able to support the magnificent structures which they erected upon them; for the beauty of virtue independent of its effects, is unmeaning nonsense; patriotism which injures mankind in general for the sake of a particular country, is but a more extended selfishness, and really criminal; and all human glory but a mean and ridiculous delusion. The whole affair then of religion and morality, the subject of so many thousand volumes, is in short no more than this: The supreme being, infinitely good, as well as powerful, desirous to diffuse happiness by all possible means, has created innumerable ranks and orders of Beings, all subservient to each other by proper subordination. One of these is occupied by Man, a creature endued with such a certain degree of knowledge, reason, and free-will, as is suitable to his situation, and placed for a time on this globe as in a school of probation and education. Here he has an opportunity given him of improving or debasing his nature, in such a manner as to render himself fit for a rank of higher perfection and happiness, or to degrade himself to a state of greater imperfection and misery; necessary indeed towards carrying on the business of the universe, but very grievous and burthensome to those individuals, who, by their own misconduct, are obliged to submit to it. The test of this his behaviour, is doing good, that is, co-operating with his creator, as far as his narrow sphere of action will permit, in the production of happiness. And thus the happiness and misery of a future state will be the just reward or punishment of promoting or preventing happiness in this. So artificially by this means is the nature of all human virtue and vice contrived, that their rewards and punishments are woven as it were in their very essence; their immediate effects give us a foretaste of their future, and their fruits in the present life are the proper samples of what they must unavoidably produce in another. We have reason given us to distinguish these consequences, and regulate our conduct; and, lest that should neglect its post, Conscience also is appointed as an instinctive kind of monitor, perpetually to remind us both of our interest and our duty.[2]

Si sic omnia dixisset![3] To this account of the essence[4] of vice and virtue, it is only necessary to add, that the consequences of human actions being sometimes uncertain and sometimes remote, it is not possible in many cases for most men, nor in all cases for any man to determine what actions will ultimately produce happiness, and therefore it was proper that *Revelation*[5] should lay down a rule to be followed invariably in opposition to appearances, and in every change of circumstances, by which we may be certain to promote the general felicity, and be set free from the dangerous temptation of *doing evil that good may come.*

Because it may easily happen, and in effect will happen very frequently, that our own private happiness may be promoted by an act injurious to others, when yet no man can be obliged by nature to prefer ultimately the happiness of others to his own. Therefore, to the instructions of infinite wisdom it was necessary that infinite power should add penal sanctions. That every man to whom those instructions shall be imparted may know, that he can never ultimately injure himself by benefiting others, or ultimately by injuring others benefit himself; but that however the lot of the good and bad may be huddled together in the seeming confusion of our present state, the time shall undoubtedly come, when the most virtuous will be most happy.

I am sorry that the remaining part of this letter is not equal to the first. The author has indeed engaged in a disquisition in which we need not wonder if he fails, in the solution of questions on which philosophers have employed their abilities from the earliest times,

---

2. Jenyns, pp. 83–95.
3. If only he had spoken everything thus!
4. *Essence:* "Constituent substance" (sense 6 of *Dictionary*).

5. *Revelation:* "Discovery; communication; communication of sacred and mysterious truths by a teacher from heaven (*Dictionary*).

*And found no end in wand'ring mazes lost.*⁶

He denies that man was created *perfect,* because the system requires subordination, and because the power of losing his perfection of *rendering himself wicked and miserable is the highest imperfection imaginable.*⁷ Besides the regular gradations of the scale of being required somewhere *such a creature as man with all his infirmities about him, and the total removal of those would be altering his nature, and when he became perfect he must cease to be man.*⁸

I have already spent some considerations on the *scale of being,* of which yet I am obliged to renew the mention whenever a new argument is made to rest upon it, and I must therefore again remark, that consequences cannot have greater certainty than the postulate from which they are drawn, and that no system can be more hypothetical than this, and perhaps no hypothesis more absurd.

He again deceives himself with respect to the perfection with which *man* is held to be originally vested. *That man came perfect, that is indued with all possible perfection, out of the hands of his creator, is a false notion, derived from the philosophers. — The universal system required subordination, and consequently comparative imperfection.*⁹ That *man was ever indued with all possible perfection,* that is with all perfection of which the idea is not contradictory or destructive of itself, is undoubtedly *false.* But it can hardly be called *a false notion,* because no man ever thought it, nor can it be derived from the *philosophers;* for without pretending to guess what philosophers he may mean, it is very safe to affirm, that no philosopher ever said it. Of those who now maintain that *man* was once perfect, who may very easily be found, let the author enquire whether *man* was ever omniscient, whether he was ever omnipotent, whether he ever had even the lower power of Archangels or Angels. Their answers will soon inform him, that the supposed perfection of *man* was not absolute, but respective, that he was perfect in a sense

---

6. Milton, *Paradise Lost* II.561.
7. SJ paraphrases Jenyns, p. 99.
8. Jenyns, pp. 98–99.
9. SJ paraphrases Jenyns, p. 98.

consistent enough with subordination, perfect not as compared with different beings, but with himself in his present degeneracy,[1] not perfect as an angel, but perfect as man.

From this perfection, whatever it was, he thinks it necessary that man should be debarred, because pain is necessary to the good of the universe; and the pain of one order of beings extending its salutary influence to innumerable orders above and below, it was necessary that man should suffer; but because it is not suitable to justice that pain should be inflicted on innocence, it was necessary that man should be criminal.

This is given as a satisfactory account of the original of moral evil, which amounts only to this, that God created beings whose guilt he foreknew, in order that he might have proper objects of pain, because the pain of part is no man knows how or why, necessary to the felicity of the whole.

The perfection which man once had, may be so easily conceived, that without any unusual strain of imagination we can figure its revival. All the duties to God or man that we neglected we may fancy performed, all the crimes that are committed we may conceive forborn. Man will then be restored to his moral perfections, and into what head can it enter that by this change the universal system would be shaken, or the condition of any order of beings altered for the worse.

He comes in the fifth letter to political, and in the sixth to religious evils. Of political evil, if we suppose the origin of moral evil discovered the account is by no means difficult: polity being only the conduct of immoral men in public affairs. The evils of each particular kind of government are very clearly and elegantly displayed, and from their secondary causes very rationally deduced, but the first cause lies still in its antient obscurity. There is in this letter nothing new, nor any thing eminently instructive; one of his practical deductions, that *from government evils cannot be eradicated, and their excess only can be prevented*,[2] has been always allowed; the ques-

---

1. *Degeneracy:* "A departing from the virtues of our ancestors" (sense 1); "A forsaking of that which is good" (sense 2); and "Meanness" (sense 3 in *Dictionary*).

2. SJ paraphrases Jenyns, p. 145.

tion upon which all dissension arises; is when that excess begins, at what point men shall cease to bear, and attempt to remedy.

Another of his precepts, though not new, well deserves to be transcribed, because it cannot be too frequently impressed.

> What has here been said of their imperfections and abuses, is by no means intended as a defence of them: every wise man ought to redress them to the utmost of his power; which can be effected by one method only: that is, by a reformation of manners: for as all political evils derive their original from moral, these can never be remov'd, until those are first amended. He, therefore, who strictly adheres to virtue and sobriety in his conduct, and inforces them by his example, does more real service to a state, than he who displaces a minister, or dethrones a tyrant; this gives but a temporary relief, but that exterminates the cause of the disease. No immoral man then can possibly be a true patriot; and all those who profess outrageous zeal for the liberty and prosperity of their country, and at the same time infringe her laws, affront her religion, and debauch her people, are but despicable quacks, by fraud or ignorance increasing the disorders they pretend to remedy.[3]

Of religion he has said nothing but what he has learned, or might have learned from the divines, that it is not universal, because it must be received upon conviction,[4] and successively received by those whom conviction reached; that its evidences[5] and sanctions[6] are not irresistible, because it was intended to induce,[7] not to compel, and that it is obscure, be-

---

3. Jenyns, pp. 149–50.
4. *Conviction:* "The act of convincing; confutation; the act of forcing others, by argument, to allow a position" (sense 2 in *Dictionary*).
5. *Evidence:* "Testimony; proof" (sense 2 in *Dictionary*).
6. *Sanction:* "The act of confirmation which gives to any thing its obligatory power; ratification" (sense 1 in *Dictionary*).
7. *Induce:* "To persuade; to influence to any thing" (sense 1 in *Dictionary*).

cause we want faculties to comprehend it. What he means by his assertion that it wants policy I do not well understand, he does not mean to deny that a good christian will be a good governor or a good subject, and he has before justly observed, that the good man only is a patriot.[8]

Religion, has been, he says, corrupted by the wickedness of those to whom it was communicated, and has lost part of its efficacy[9] by its connection with temporal interest and human passion.

He justly observes, that from all this, no conclusion can be drawn against the divine original of christianity, since the objections arise not from the nature of the revelation, but of him to whom it is communicated.

All this is known, and all this is true, but why, we have not yet discovered. Our author, if I understand him right, pursues the argument thus: The religion of man produces evils, because the morality of man is imperfect; his morality is imperfect, that he may be justly a subject of punishment: he is made subject to punishment, because the pain of part is necessary to the happiness of the whole; pain is necessary to happiness no mortal can tell why or how.

Thus, after having clambered[1] with great labour from one step of argumentation to another, instead of rising into the light of knowledge, we are devolved[2] back into dark ignorance, and all our effort ends in belief that for the evils of life there is some good reason, and in confession, that the reason cannot be found. This is all that has been produced by

---

8. Jenyns observes: "It [Christianity] had many defects in its institution, and was attended with many and great Evils in its consequences; in its institution it wanted Universality, Authenticity, Perspicuity and Policy; and in its consequences it was soon corrupted, and from that corruption productive of the most mischievous effects. Its great Author designed it not to be exempted from any of these Imperfections" (p. 158). In the fourth edition (1761) Jenyns added footnotes to explain "Policy," as well as "Authenticity" and "Perspicuity" (pp. 199–201). See p. 408, n. 7 above. *Patriot:* "One whose ruling passion is the love of his country" (*Dictionary*).

9. *Efficacy:* "Power to produce effects; production of the consequence intended" (*Dictionary*).

1. *Clamber:* "To climb with difficulty; as with both hands and feet" (*Dictionary*).

2. *Devolve:* "To roll down" (sense 1 in *Dictionary*).

the revival of Chrysippus's untractableness of matter,[3] and the Arabian scale of existence. A system has been raised, which is so ready to fall to pieces of itself, that no great praise can be derived from its destruction. To object is always easy, and it has been well observed by a late writer, that* *the hand which cannot build a hovel, may demolish a temple.*

***New Practice of Physic*[4]

---

3. *Untractableness:* "Unwillingness, or unfitness to be regulated or managed; stubborness" (*Dictionary*). The natural philosophy of Chrysippus, third century B.C. Stoic philosopher, has two dominant motifs, monism and determinism. The "untractableness of matter" is quoted from Jenyns (p. 17), although he does not mention Chrysippus. Both Jenyns and SJ are drawing on Justus Lipsius's *Physiologia Stoicorum* (1604).

4. Several works with the title, *New Practice of Physic,* appear in ESTC but none of them contains this passage.

INDEX

An index to a translation differs from that to an original text. The focus is on SJ and no attempt has been made to supply a subject index to Crousaz's or Du Resnel's work; SJ's table of contents (pp. 3–17) provides a description of the subjects covered by each work.

Abbott, John Lawrence, xlvi, xlvi n.
Adams, Dr. William (*1706–89*), Master, Pembroke College, Oxford, 391
Addison, Joseph (*1672–1719*), essayist and critic, 359
Alexander the Great, 367
Algarotti, Francesco (*1712–64*), Italian writer, xxx n.
Aristotle, 26, 344, 355, 400 n.
Ascham, Roger (*1615–68*), author, SJ life of, 406 n.
Atterbury, Francis (*1662–1732*), bishop of Rochester, 375 n.
Audra, E., xxxix n.
Augustus (*63 B.C.–14 A.D.*), Roman emperor, 278, 366
Avicenna (*980–1037*), Arab philosopher and physician, 400 n.

Bailey, Nathan (d. *1743*), lexicographer, 89 n., 260 n.
Barker, A. D., xxiii n., xxx n.
Bathurst, Allen, first earl Bathurst (*1684–1775*), 199 n.
Bayle, Pierre (*1647–1706*), French philosopher, 97, 119 n., 179
Belsunce Castel-Moron, de (*1671–1755*), French Jesuit, bishop of Marseille, 269 n.
Berkeley, Dr. George (*1685–1753*), bishop of Cloyne, 118 n.
Bible: *I Corinthians*, 397 n., *James*, 32 n., *John*, 240 n., *Psalm*, 337 n., *Nehemiah*, 78 n.

Birch, Thomas (*1705–66*), biographer and historian: his copy of Elizabeth Carter translation of Algarotti, xxx; *General Dictionary*, directs, 119 n.; letter to Elizabeth Carter on publication of Crousaz *Examination*, xxiv, xxxiii
Blair, Dr. Hugh (*1718–1800*), divine and critic, 199 n.
Blenheim, 419
Boerhaave, Herman (*1668–1738*), Dutch physician: SJ life of, xx, 74 n.
Boileau-Despréaux, Nicolas (*1636–1711*), French critic and poet, 344
Bolingbroke. *See* St. John
Bossuet, Jacques Bénigne (*1627–1704*), French preacher, bishop of Meaux, 361 n.
Boswell, James (*1740–95*), friend and biographer of SJ: *Life:* 69 n.; Crousaz, SJ role in translating, xxiii–xxvii; George III, report of SJ visit with, 348; Jenyns "Epitaph" on SJ, 395; passion of love, reports SJ observation, 176 n.; Politan, sees proposals for subscription for edition of, xvii n.; SJ on Pope's indebtedness to Bolingbroke for *Essay on Man*, 199 n.; review, SJ's interest in undertaking one, 391; Sir William Temple, SJ forms style on, 359–60 n.; SJ on Warburton making Pope a Christian, 380 n.; *Journal of a Tour of the Hebrides:* xxii, 97 n.; Bossuet, SJ

Boswell, James (continued)
thinks no one reads, 361 n.; Boswell disagrees, 361 n.; Fénelon's *Télémaque*, SJ view of, 280 n.; *Laird of Auchinleck 1778–1782:* records SJ account of translating Crousaz, xxii
Bouhier, Jean (*1673–1746*), French jurist, 351 n.
Bouhours, Dominique (*1628–1702*), French Jesuit, grammarian, classicist, and critic, 364 n.
Boyer, Abel (*1667–1729*), miscellaneous writer and editor: his *Dictionnaire Royale Français and Anglais* (*1699*): xxxvii n., xliii, xlix, 36 n., 65 n., 71 n., 81 n., 83 n., 87 n., 89 n., 90 n., 138 n., 159 n., 160 n., 198 n., 199 n., 203 n., 295 n., 345 n., 360 n.
Brocklesby, Dr. Richard (*1722–97*), physician, xxvi n.
Buckingham. *See* Villiers
Burnet, Gilbert (*1643–1715*), bishop of Salisbury, historian, 280 n.
Burney, Dr. Charles (*1726–1814*), musician and author, 358 n.

Carache (Caracci), Lodovico (*1555–1619*) or Agostino (*1557–1602*) or Annibale (*1560–1609*), Italian painter, 371
Carter, Elizabeth (*1717–1806*), poet and author: Francesco Algarotti *Il Newtonianisimo pa le Dame*, translation of, xxx n.; Crousaz *Examen*, translation of, xxii, xxiv, xxv, xxix–xxx, xxxiii, xxxiv, xxv, 36, 36 n.; letter from Birch on, xxiv, xxxiii; letter from father on publication of, xxix–xxx
Carter, Dr. Nicholas (d. *1774*), divine, father of the preceding: letter to daughter on publication of Crousaz's *Examination*, xxix–xxx
Cary, Lucius, second viscount Falkland (*1610?–43*), 269 n.
Catiline (Lucius Sergius Catilina) (d. 62 B.C.), Roman patrician, 167
Cave, Edward (1691–1754), printer, founder of *Gentleman's Magazine*, xxxvii; bookseller for Crousaz's *Commentary* and *Examination*, xxii, xxix–xxxv, xxxviii; his dilatoriness, xxx, xxx n.; SJ life of, xxxviii n.; SJ letter to, on publication of *Commentary* and *Examination*, xxiii–xxiv, xxvi, xxvii, xxix, xxxi, xxxii, xxxv; SJ letter to, on editorial chores for *GM*, xviii–xix; SJ letter to, on publication of *London*, xvii
Cervantes Saavedra, Miguel de (*1547–1616*), Don Quixote, 340
Cheyne, Dr. George (*1671–1743*), physician, 403–4 n.
Chrysippus (ca. *280–207* B.C.), Greek Stoic philosopher, 432 n.
Churchill, John, first duke of Marlborough (1650–1722), 419 n.
Cicero, Marcus Tullius, 366, 367, 368 n.
Clifford, James L., xxiv n.
Colson, John (*1680–1760*), Lucasian Professor at Cambridge, xvii
Corneille, Pierre (*1606–84*), French dramatist, 358 n.
Courthope, John William, xxviii, xxviii n.
Cowley, Abraham (*1618–67*), poet: SJ life of, li, 356 n.
Critical Review: 389
Croker, John Wilson (*1780–1857*), politician and essayist, xxvii
Crousaz, Jean Pierre de (*1663–1750*), Swiss theologian: his abilities, SJ good opinion of, xx–xxi; *Commentaire*, attacks on Pope, weakness of, xxi, xxxviii–xli, l–lii, 36 n., 37 n., 38 n., 41 n., 51 n., 64 n., 65 n., 71 n., 74–75 n., 76 n., 78n., 97 n., 104 n., 124 n., 131–32 n., 143 n., 145–46 n., 160 n., 164 n., 166n., 178 n., 182 n., 188 n., 218 n., 229 n., 230 n.; attribution to SJ, xviii; Forman translation of the first epistle for Curll, xxiv n., xxx–xxxi, xxxiii–xxxiv, xxxviii–xli, xli n., 37 n., 57 n., 51 n., 67 n., 69 n., 72 n., 74 n., 87 n., 99 n., 102 n., 108 n.; SJ translation of *Commentaire*, xx–lii, 4–341; *Examen*, attributed

INDEX 435

to SJ, xxiv–xxvii, xxv n.; SJ contributions to, xxii, xxiv, xxxi, xxxviii; mentioned, 34, 295; Leibnitzian tendencies of Pope attacked in, xxi; translated by Elixabeth Carter, xxii, xxiv, xxv, xxix–xxx, xxxiii, xxxiv, xxv, 36, 36 n.; his *Examen du Pyrrhonisme,* 103, 118, 119 n.; his religious views, xx–xxi; theological tendencies of Pope's *Essay on Man,* suspicions of, xx–xxi; Warburton, defends Pope against his attacks, xxvii, 379, 380; his *Treatise on the Mind of Man,* 329

Curll, Edmund (*1675–1747*), bookseller, xxiv n.; his edition of Crousaz *A Commentary,* xxiv n., xxx–xxxi, xxxiii–xxxiv, xxxviii, xxxix, xxxix n., 74

Curtius, hero of Roman legend, 167

Dacier, Anne Lefèvre (*1654–1720*), classical scholar, 351

Damiens, Robert-François (*1715–57*), failed assassin of Louis XV of France, 407 n.

Decius Mus, Publius, Roman consul, 167

DeMaria, Jr., Robert, xvii n., 408 n.

Dennis, John (*1657–1734*), critic: attack on Pope's *Essay on Criticism,* 344 n.

De Reaumur. *See* Réaumur

Descartes, René (*1596–1650*), French philosopher, 26, 69, 100

Desfontaines, Pierre François Guyot (1685–1745), French critic, 371 n.

Digby, Robert (d. *1746*), 269 n.

Dillon, Wentworth, fourth earl of Roscommon (ca. *1637–85*), poet: SJ life of, 350 n.; text of *Essay on Translated Verse,* 352 n.; on translation, xlii, xlii n., xliii, li, 37, 37 n., 73, 73 n., 350 n., 351, 352, 352 n.

Dodd, Anne (fl. *1726–?43*), mercury, xxii, xxxiii

Dodsley, Robert (*1703–64*), bookseller, dramatist, and poet, 392

Dryden, John (*1631–1700*), poet: SJ life of, l, 176 n., 362 n.; his theory of translation, xlii, SJ takes books by him to Oxford, xlii n.

Du Halde, Jean Baptiste (*1674–1743*), French Jesuit writer: *Description géographique . . . de l'empire de la Chine:* xviii n., xxx n.

Duperron, Jacques Davy (*1556–1618*), French cardinal, 151

Du Pin, Louis Ellies (*1657–1719*), French theologian and historian, 266

Du Resnel, Abbé Jean-François du Bellay (*1692–1761*), French critic and translator of *Essay on Man,* xxi, xxi n.; French language, description of, 352 n.; Italian language, description of, 356 n.; his poetry, quality of, xxxix, xl, xli, 40 n., 41 n., 42 n., 44 n., 50 n., 51 n., 62 n., 68 n., 73–74 n., 74–75 n., 78 n., 87 n., 102 n., 104 n., 114 n. 124 n., 130 n., 131–32 n., 141–42 n., 164 n., 166 n., 175–76 n., 178 n., 182 n., 188 n., 203 n., 218–19 n., 229 n., 233 n.; Preface to his edition of the *Essay on Man,* translated by SJ, 343–75; his translation of the *Essay on Criticism,* 343–44

Duvergier de Hauranne, Jean du, known as Saint-Cyran (*1581–1643*), abbé of the Monastère de Port Royal, 151, 152 n.

Eberwein, Robert, 403–4 n.
Eddy, Donald D., 389, 393, 395
Edial, xvii
Elwin, Whitwell, xxv n., xxvii
Eugène, François de Savoie, Prince (*1663–1736*), 419 n.
European Magazine, xxv–xxvi

Faden, William (né Mackfaden) (*1711–83*), printer, 389
Fénelon, François de Salignac de la Mothe (*1651–1715*), archbishop of Cambrai, 280 n., 350
Fitzjames, James, duke of Berwick (*1670–1734*), Maréchal de France, 269 n.
Fleeman, J. D., xxxv n.

Fontanini, Justi (Giusto) (*1666–1736*), Italian critic and antiquarian, archbishop of Ancyra, 364 n.
Forman, Charles (d. *1739*), writer: translates Crousaz *A Commentary*, xxx, xxxiv, xxxviii–xli, xli n., 37 n., 57 n., 51 n., 67 n., 69 n., 72 n., 74 n., 87 n., 99 n., 102 n., 108 n.
Frederick the Great (*1712–86*), king of Prussia, 419 n.; SJ life of, 389

Garrick, David (*1717–79*), actor, xvii
Garth, Sir Samuel (*1661–1719*), physician and poet: SJ's life of, xxi n.; 415 n.
Gay, John (*1685–1732*), poet and dramatist, xix
Gentleman's Magazine (*GM*), xviii–xx, xxxv, 379–81, 383–86, 389, 394, 395
George I (*1660–1727*), king of England, 372 n.
George III (*1738–1820*), king of England, 348 n.
Gildon, Charles (*1665–1724*), author, 350 n.
Gold, Joel J., xlii, xlv
Gower. *See* Leveson-Gower
Gray, James, xliii, xliii n.
Gray, Thomas (*1716–71*), poet: SJ life of, lii n.
Green, John (fl. *1737*), translator with William Guthrie of Du Halde's *History of China*, xviii n.
Greene, Donald, 407 n.
Guthrie, William (*1708–70*), miscellaneous author: pariamentary debates, reports of, xviii; translator with John Green of Du Halde's *History of China*, xviii n.

Hanley, Brian J., 393
Hawkins, Sir John (*1719–89*), magistrate, musicologist, friend and biographer of SJ: *Life:* Crousaz, SJ translation of, xxiv, xxv, xxv n., xxvi, xxvii; *Dictionary*, meeting to settle accounts with SJ, 390; *Examination*, attributes to SJ, xxiv, xxvi, xxvii; humor, SJ talent for, 394; "Letter to the *GM* on the Controversy," attributed to SJ and published, 381; SJ moderator between Crousaz and Warburton, xxvii; opinion of SJ as translator, xliv, xliv n.; Politan, sees proposals for edition of, xvii n.; John Wilcox, story of SJ borrowing money from, xviii n.
Hazen, Allen T., xxviii
Hegesias of Magnesia (ca. *300* or *250* B.C.), Greek orator and historian, 366 n.
History of the Works of the Learned, 379
Homer, xlii, 214 n., 363
Horace, xlii, 318 n., 344, 366, 367, 373

Jenyns, Soame (*1704–87*), miscellaneous writer: account of, 392, 420–21; Bolingbroke, compared to, 397; concern for SJ health, 395; his "Epitaph" for SJ, 395; his "Essay on Virtue," 392; *A Free Inquiry into the Nature and Origin of Evil:* SJ review of, l, lii n., 389–432; his confidence, 411; on death, 415–17; on education, 409–10; on evil, 393, 397–99, 401, 411–13, 415, 417–18, 421, 429; his feeble defense of the work in 1761 edition, 394; on government, 429–30; on happiness, 402–8, 410, 411, 427; harshest review by SJ, why, 392–94; on ignorance, 408–9; on labor, 413; life, must be seen to be known, 407; limits of knowledge, failure to understand, 394, 397, 399, 403, 404, 408, 409–10, 412, 414, 418, 428, 431; madmen, 408; Manichaean system, rejects, 398; perfection in human beings, 402, 403, 412, 428–29; Pope, compared to, 398, 399, 400, 401, 405, 410, 413; poverty, views on, 406–10; religion, 431; a speculatist, 397, 400; on subordination, 400, 402–4, 412, 413, 419–20, 428; his vanity, 394, 399, 404, 420; why did he write book, SJ wonders, 399–400; wisdom, of God, 398, 402, 404

INDEX 437

JOHNSON, SAMUEL (*1709–84*)
LIFE AND CHARACTER: Appleby School, applies for mastership, xxxvii; Birmingham, resides there, xvii; Edial, his school, xvii; French, knowledge of, xliii–l; footnotes, writer of, xlvii–xlviii; *Gentleman's Magazine*, contributor and editor, xviii–xix; humor, 394; ideas shared with Crousaz and du Resnel, liii; knowledge, wish to have more than possible, 394; Lichfield, leaves for London, xvii; return to, xviii; London, arrival, xvii, xviii; leaves, xviii, xxxvii; Master of Arts degree, attempt to obtain one from Trinity College, Dublin, xxxviii n.; money, need for, xvii, xix, 390; Pemboke College, Oxford, attendance, xvii; pension, 390; printing-house practice and his writing, liii–liv; procrastination, awarding prizes in poetry contest, xix; Sarpi *History*, xix; review, monthly, undertaking one, 391; satirist, 394; scholar, wish to become one, xvii n.; Temple, Sir William, one of the writers on whom he formed his style, 359–60 n.; tragedy, wishes to become writer of, xvii, xviii; translator, xvii, xxxvii, xli–xlvii; payment for, xxxvii; translation of Crousaz, Forman used to assist in, xxxviii–xli; Lobo, *A Voyage*, xvii; Sarpi, *History*, xviii, xix; Schultens' eulogy for Boerhaave, xx. *See* Crousaz

OPINIONS AND ATTITUDES: accounting, 390; Artificer, Eternal, import of, 160 n.; author, task of, 421; body and soul, relationship, 143 n.; book reviewing, 389–90; Bolingbroke, 199 n., 397; Bossuet, 361 n.; competence, 406; death, 415–17; time and manner of, 64 n.; Dennis, attack on *Essay on Criticism*, 344n.; diligence, 410; education, 409–10; *end*, import of the word, 65 n.; epitaphs, xix; evil, li,–lii, 397–99, 401, 411–13, 415, 417–18, 421, 429; Fénelon's *Télémaque*, 280 n.; folly, 407; Fitzjames, James, duke of Berwick, SJ interest in, 269 n.; freeman, 37 n.; free-will, li–lii, 166 n.; French language, 352 n.; French people, called "airy," 175 n.; government, 429; happiness, 69 n., 402–8, 410, 411, 427; ignorance, 408–9; India, 97 n.; Italian language, 356 n.; *Journal des Savans*, 348 n.; labor, 413–14; life, must be known, 407; knowledge, limit of, 394, 397, 399, 403, 404, 408, 409–10, 412, 414, 417, 418, 428, 431; love, passion of, effects much exaggerated, 175–76 n.; marks of a Frenchman's genius, 175 n.; madmen, 408; David Mallet, 358 n., 359 n.; Manichaean system, 398; nation, commercial, 410; *nature*, import of the word, 71–72 n.; nations, barbarous and savage, 97 n.; civilized, 97 n.; necessaries, 406; novels, 175 n.; old age, 417; Original Sin, li; passions, indulgence of, 145 n.; pain, 407, 419; perfection in man, 402, 403, 412, 428–29; poetry, English: 37 n., 51 n., 76 n., 114 n., 128 n., 218–19 n.; poetry, French: 37 n., 51 n., 76 n., 114 n., 128 n., 175 n., 218–19 n.; poor, 407, 408–10; poverty, 406, 407, 409, 413, 414; present never a happy state, 69 n.; pride, 394, 397, 410, 420–21; religion, 97 n., 430–31; revelation, 427; rich, 407; romances, 175 n.; Roscommon, text of *Essay on Translated Verse*, 352 n.; on translation, 37 n., 73 n., 352 n.; ruling passion, xxviii, li–lii, 145–46 n., 166–67 n.; scale of being. *See* subordination; slave, 37 n.; speculatists, 397, 400; stage, representations on, 175–76 n.; subordination, 400, 402–4, 412, 413, 419–20, 428; tragedy, representation of human nature and real life, 175–76 n.; translation, theory and practice of, xli–l, 37 n., 230 n.; vanity, 399; vices, 178 n., essence of, 427; of the great, 38 n.; virtue, essence of, 427; Warburton, 380 n.;

JOHNSON, SAMUEL (continued)
  wisdom, of God, 398, 402, 404;
  writing, end of, 421
WORKS (*see* also Crousaz, Du Resnel,
  and Jenyns)
"Ad Urbanum," xviii
The Adventurer, lii n., no. 58, 368 n.; no.
  111, 94 n.
Advertisement for Crousaz's *Examination* in *Daily Advertiser*, possibly by SJ,
  xxxi–xxxii
Ascham, Roger, SJ life of, 406 n.
Bible, SJ quotes, I Corinthian xiii.12;
  Psalm xxxix.6; SJ translation of,
  James i.5–8, 32 n.; John vii.16–17,
  240 n.; Nehemiah i.11 and v.19, 78 n.
Birmingham Journal, essays for, xvii
Boerhaave, Herman, SJ life of, xx, 74 n.
Cave, Edward, SJ life of, xxxviii n.
Chinese and English manners, "Eubulus" on, xviii, xviii n.
Condolence, "Pamphilus" on, xix
A Course of Lectures on the English Law,
  404–5 n.
Diaries, Prayers and Annals, 394, 408 n.
Dictionary of the English Language, Preface, xlviii; publication, 390; the
  following words are defined or discussed: *absurdity*, 398 n.; *acquiescence*,
  417 n.; *ague*, 419 n.; *anger*, 309 n.;
  apoplexy, 419 n.; *artificer*, 160 n.; *calculose, calculous, calculus*, 420 n.; *caprice*,
  409 n.; *chain*, 403 n.; *clamber*, 431 n.;
  competence, competency, 406 n.; *comprehensive*, 412 n.; *compulsion*, 409 n.;
  concretion, 420 n.; *consoler*, 190 n.;
  conviction, 430 n.; *death*, 415 n.; *degeneracy*, 429 n.; *derision*, 417 n.; *devolve*,
  431 n.; *disquisition*, 405 n.; *dogmatical,
  dogmatick*, 417 n.; *ducat*, xxxvii n.;
  efficacy, 431 n.; *epidemical, epidemick*,
  420 n.; *epilepsy*, 420 n.; *essence*, 427
  n.; *elogy, eulogy*, 294–95 n.; *evidence*,
  430 n.; *exacerbation*, 410 n.; *fatuity*,
  407 n.; *fluctuation*, 405 n.; *folly*,
  407 n.; *frank*, xxxvii n.; *free, freedom*,
  397 n.; *generous*, 360 n.; *gout*, 420 n.;
  imagination, 403 n.; *imbecility*, 417 n.;
  imperfection, 412 n.; *impression*, 211 n.;
  inconceivable, 417 n.; *induce*, 430 n.;
  labour, 413 n.; *leaf*, 276 n.; *licentiousness*, 397 n.; *madrigal*, 89 n.; *mortify*,
  407 n.; *mutilation*, 407 n.; *necessaries*,
  406 n.; *nihility*, 413 n.; *notion*, 408 n.;
  obstinacy, 409 n.; *parts*, 420 n.; *passion*, 408 n.; *patriot*, 431 n.; *period*,
  138 n.; *phantom*, 408 n.; *plagiarism*,
  399 n.; *policy*, 408 n.; *pollute*, 407 n.;
  poor, 406 n.; *poverty*, 406 n.; *presumptuous*, 404 n.; *privative, privation*,
  412 n.; *projection, projector*, 420 n.; *pry*,
  xlix; *puzzle*, 420 n.; *rebellion*, 404 n.;
  revelation, 427 n.; *ridiculous*, 408 n.;
  sanction, 430 n.; *satire*, 83 n.; *scale*,
  403 n.; *scrupulous, scruple*, 417 n.;
  sentiment, 400 n.; *sophism*, 421 n.;
  speculatist, speculator, speculation,
  397 n.; *stone*, 420 n.; *stamina*, 199 n.;
  strive, 225 n.; *subordination*, 400 n.;
  succour, 414 n.; *superfluity*, 409 n.;
  sure, 152 n.; *temper*, xlix n.; *throng*,
  220 n.; *transcription*, 399 n.; *tympany*, 419 n.; *untractableness*, 432 n.;
  virtuoso, 419 n.
Drake, Sir Francis, SJ life of, 406 n.
Du Halde. *See* Chinese and English
  manners
Firbrace, Lady, verses to, xviii
Gay's monument, "Pamphilus" on, xix
Gentleman's Magazine, occasional contributions, xviii, xix, xxvii, xxxv,
  379–86, 394
The Idler, lii n.; no. 26, 410 n.; no. 29,
  410 n.; no. 68, xlii; no. 69, xlii; no.
  89, 397 n.
Irene, xviii, xxxvii
"Letter to the *GM* on the Controversy
  between Warburton and Crousaz on
  Pope's *Essay on Man*," xxv, 377–86
Letters, "bred a bookseller," xxiii n.;
  to Cave, negotiating publication of
  London, xviii; to Cave, describing
  state of editorial tasks, xviii–xix; to
  Cave, on publication of *Commentary*
  and *Examination*, xxiii–xxiv, xxvi,
  xxvii, xxix, xxxi, xxxii, xxxv; to *Daily
  Advertiser* on publication of Sarpi's
  History of the Council of Trent, xxxii;

INDEX

to Hester Maria Thrale, quoting the *Commentary*, 36 n.
Literary Magazine, 389–432
Lives of the Poets, xlii. *See* Cowley, Dryden, Garth, Gray, Mallet, Milton, Pope, Roscommon
London, negotiates with Cave to publish it, xviii
"Memoirs of the King of Prussia," 389
Messiah, Pope's, translation into Latin, xlii
Parliamentary debates, reports of, xviii
Politan, proposal for *Angeli Politiani Poemeta Latina*, xvii
The Preceptor, Preface to, xxi n.
The Rambler, lii n.; no. 3, 421 n.; no. 14, 397 n.; no. 48, 407 n.; no. 49, 406 n.; no. 63, 94 n.; no. 93, 393–94
Rasselas, lii n.
Sarpi, Paolo, *Istoria del concilio Tridentino*, proposed translation by SJ, xviii, xix, xxxvii; *Daily Advertiser*, SJ letter to, on his translation, xxxii; SJ life of, xix, 74 n.
Sermons, no. 5, lii n.
Shakespeare, 380 n.; Preface to *Works*, l, 176 n., 390 n.
Sydenham, Dr. Thomas, SJ life of, xxxv n.
The Vanity of Human Wishes, 292 n.
Voyage to Abyssinia, xvii, xix, xlii, xliii, xliv, xliv n.

Journal des Savans, 348 n.
Journal or *Mémoires de Trévoux*, 346 n., 373

Kaminski, Thomas, xvii n., xix, xxx, xxxvii, xlvi, 381

La Bruyère, Jean de (*1645–96*), French essayist, 361
Lactantius Firmianus (fourth century), Christian writer, 21
Le Courayer, Pierre François (*1681–1776*), French divine, xviii
Le Grand, Abbé Joachim (*1653–1733*), French divine, xvii
Leibnitz, Gottfried Wilhelm (*1646–1716*), German philosopher, xxi, 21, 27, 34, 328 n., 331, 335 n., 336
Leveson-Gower, John, first earl Gower (*1694–1754*), Lord Privy Seal, xxxviii n.
Lichfield, xvii, xviii
Livy (Titus Livius) (59 B.C.–A.D. *17*), Roman historian, 367
Lobo, Father Jerome (*1595–1678*), Portuguese Jesuit missionary, xvii, xix
London: xvii, xviii, xxxvii
Louis XV (*1710–74*), king of France, 407 n.

McAdam, Jr., E. L., xxviii
Mack, Maynard, xx n.
Mallet, David (*1705?–65*), poet and miscellaneous writer, 358 n.; SJ life of, 359 n.
Malone, Edmond (*1741–1812*), critic and editor, xxiv
Mandeville, Bernard (*1670–1733*), author of *The Fable of the Bees*, 224 n.
Manichaeism, 398, 398 n.
Manilius, Marcus (fl. first century A.D.), author of *Astronomica*, 255–56, 256 n.
Marchin (Marsin) de, Ferdinand, count (*1656–1706*), French general, 419 n.
Milton, John (*1608–74*), poet: *Paradise Lost*, 367 n., 408 n., 417, 428; SJ life of, lii n.
Montaigne, Michel de (*1533–92*), French philosopher, 361
Monthly Review, 389
Motte, de la, Antoine Houdart- (*1672–1731*), French critic and dramatist, 369 n.

Nero (A.D. *37–68*), Roman emperor, 166 n.
New Practice of Physic, 432 n.
Newbery, John (*1713–67*), bookseller, 389
Newton, Isaac (*1642–1727*), natural philosopher, 44, 130, 131, 132, 132 n.

Ovid, 90
Oxford, Pembroke College, xvii

Palmer, Dr. Richard (ca. *1714–1805*) prebendary of Canterbury and rector of St. Swithin, London, xxiv

Paul, St., 78

Percy, Dr. Thomas (*1729–1811*), bishop of Dromore, 391

Petronius Arbiter (d. A.D. *65*), Latin satirical writer, 351 n., 359 n.

Plato, 400 n.

Plautus, Titus Maccius (ca. *250–184* B.C.), Roman writer of comedies, 366

Plutarch (ca. A.D. *46–ca.120*), Greek biographer, historian, and moral philosopher: "Life of Alexander," 366 n., 367 n.

Poliziano, Angelo (Angelus Politan) (*1454–94*), Italian scholar: SJ proposals for an edition of, xvii

Pope, Alexander (*1688–1744*), poet: SJ life of, xx–xxi, xxv, xxvi, xlii, l, li–lii, lii n., 39 n., 119 n., 344 n., 356 n., 359 n., 372 n., 379, 380, 380 n., 392; *Essay on Criticism,* 409, 414, Dennis attack on, 344 n.; translation of, by Du Resnel, 343–44; *Essay on Man,* approbation of, xx; history of reception, xx n.; Indian, objections to his portrait of, 97 n.; theological tendencies of, xx–xxi; *Messiah,* SJ Latin translation of, xlii; his Roman Catholicism, xxi. *See* Crousaz, Du Resnel

Powell, L. F., xxii n., xxvii, xxviii, xliv

Prague, 419

Quintilian (Marcus Fabius Quintilianus) (b. ca. A.D. *35*): *Institutio Oratoria,* 368 n.

Réaumur, René Antoine Ferchault de (*1683–1757*), French man of science, 111

Reed, Isaac (1742–1807), editor of Shakespeare, xxvi

Richardson, J. (fl. *1753–63*), bookseller, 389

Richelieu, Armand Jean du Plessis, duc de (*1585–1642*), French cardinal and statesman, 152 n.

Robethon, John (Jean de) (d. *1722*), secretary to George I, 372 n.

Rochefoucauld, François, duc de la (1613–80), French author, 374–75

Rogers, John (*1679–1729*), divine, 408 n.

Romkey, Ronald, 392 n.

Roscommon. *See* Dillon

St. Cyran. *See* Duvergier de Hauranne

St. John, Henry, first viscount Bolingbroke (*1678–1751*), stateman: SJ antipathy toward, 358–59 n., 369 n., 397

Sallust (Gaius Sallustius Crispus) (*86–35* B.C.), Roman historian, 367

Sarpi, Paolo (*1552–1623*), Italian theologian: *Istoria del concilio Tridentino,* proposed translation by SJ, xviii, xix, xxxvii; *Daily Advertiser,* SJ letter to, on his translation, xxxii; SJ life of, xix, 74 n.

Scarron, Paul (*1610–60*), French author, 90

Schultens, Albert (*1686–1750*), Dutch Orientalist and theologian, xx

Schwartz, Richard B., li n., 393, 395

Scot's Magazine, xxxv

Ségur, Jean-Charles de (ca. *1695–1748*), bishop of St. Papoul (*1724–35*); 30 n.

Shakespeare, William: *The Tempest,* 414

Shenstone, William (*1714–63*), poet, 391

Sidney, Sir Philip (*1554–86*), soldier, statesman, and poet, 269 n.

Siebert, Jr., Donald T., 419 n.

Silhouette, Etienne de (*1709–67*), French controller general: his prose translation of *Essay on Man,* xx, xxi, xxi n., 36 n., 75 n.

Simplicius (ca. *529*), Neo-Platonic philosopher and commentator on Aristotle, 403 n.

Smith, John (fl. *1755*), printer and author, lv

INDEX

Socrates, 240
Spinoza, Baruch or Benedict (*1632–77*), Dutch philosopher, 110, 124, 348
Steevens, George (*1736–1800*), editor of Shakespeare, xxvi, xxvi n.
Strahan, Rev. George (*1744–1824*), vicar of Islington, 380 n.
Sydenham, Dr. Thomas (*1624–89*), physician, SJ life of, xxxv n.

Tacitus, Publius (or Gaius) Cornelius (b. *56 or 57*-d. after *117*), Roman historian, 367
Tallard or Tallert, de, Camille d'Hostun- (*1652–1728*), French general, 419 n.
Tasso, Torquato (*1544–95*), Italian poet, 367
Temple, Sir William (*1628–99*), statesman and author, 359–60 n.
Thrale, Hester Maria (*1764–1857*), "Queeney," eldest daughter of Henry and Hester Lynch Thrale, 36 n.
Titian (Tiziano Vecellio) (*1477–1576*), Italian painter, 371
Titus (Titus Flavius Vespasianus) (ca. *40–81*), Roman emperor, 167, 278, 279
Tonson, Jacob (d. *1767*), bookseller, 390 n.
Turenne, Henri de la Tour d'Auvergne, vicomte de (d. *1675*), 269 n.

Vander Meulen, David L., xxiii n.
Vergier. *See* Duvergier de Hauranne
Villiers, George, second duke of Buckingham (*1628–87*), 359 n.
Virgil, xlii, 367
Voltaire (*1694–1778*), French philosopher, historian, and critic, 370 n.

Waller, Edmund (*1606–87*), poet, 358 n.
Walmsley, Gilbert (*1680–1751*), Registrar of the Ecclesiastical Court, Lichfield, xvii
Warburton, Dr. William (*1698–1779*), bishop of Gloucester, 358 n., 379, 380 n.; defense of Pope in *Vindication:* xxvii, 379, 380; edition of Shakespeare, 380 n.
Warren, Thomas (d. *1767*), Birmingham printer and bookseller, xvii, xliii
Warton, Rev. Thomas (*1728–90*), historian of English poetry, 391
Wilcox, John (fl. *1721–62*), bookseller, xxvii, xviii n.
Wilkie, John (fl. *1756–78*), bookseller, 389
William III (*1650–1702*), king of England, 372 n.

Zeno of Elea (ca. *490* B.C.), Greek philosopher, 403 n.

Sorbonne, 250
Spinoza, Baruch de (Benedict) (1632–77), Dutch philosopher, 110, 145, 328
Steevens, George (1736–1800), editor of Shakespeare, xxxi, xxxii n.
Stephen, Rev. George (1794–1874), vicar of Islington, 380 n.
Stothadine, Dr. Thomas (1675–1697), physician, St Ive, 71, xxx n.

Taurus, Publius (or Calvus) Cornelius (b. 55 to AD, d. after 117), Roman historian, 307
Talfard or Talfer, the Famille d'Horace (1671–1700), French general, 231 n.
Tasso, Torquato (1544–95), Italian poet, 287
Temple, Sir William (1628–99), statesman and author, 355–56 n.
Theale, Traves them (1589–1667), Queen's chief Justice; or of Henry and Theale Lands Banks, 300
Tobias, Pasetro (1670–1679?), Italian painter, 277
Torrento, Palma (1550–1600?), Italian Kamma emperor, 285–93 n.
Tomson, John H. (1682), bookseller, 100 n.
Thomas, Mauritius la Baou d'Amerique almanah. 36 ff., 40 fl., 67 n.

Sanders, Mordaz, David L., xxxii n.
Vergiler, Sir Theodgin de Hanover Villers, George, second duke of Buckingham (1628–87), 300 n.
Virgil, xlii, 397
Voltaire (1694–1778), French philosopher, historian, and critic, 150 n.

Walker, Edmund (1606–87), poet, 138 n.
Wallace, Gilbert (1679–1751), Register of the Exchequer of Ireland, xxviii
Warburton, Dr Willam (1698–1779), bishop of Gloucester, 298 n., 374, 391 n.; critique of Pope, 353 n.; quotes xxxii, 391, 399; editor of Shakespeare, 392 n.
Weston, Thomas of, 1727, learning free writer and bookseller, xxiii
Weston, Rev. Thomas (1732–96), historian of English poetry, xxi
Wilkie, John G., 1721–62, bookseller, xxxi, xxiii n.
Wilson, John (d. 1738–77), bookseller, 223
William III (1650–1702), king of England, 325 n.

Xenophon (c. 435 BC–354 BC), Greek philosopher, 304 n.